"Rhody Redlegs

"Rhody Redlegs"

*A History of the Providence Marine
Corps of Artillery and the 103d
Field Artillery, Rhode Island Army
National Guard, 1801–2010*

ROBERT GRANDCHAMP,
JANE LANCASTER
and CYNTHIA FERGUSON

Foreword by Col. Howard F. Brown

McFarland & Company, Inc., Publishers
Jefferson, North Carolina, and London

Robert Grandchamp has also written *The Boys of Adams' Battery G: The Civil War Through the Eyes of a Union Light Artillery Unit* (McFarland, 2009) and *The Seventh Rhode Island Infantry in the Civil War* (McFarland, 2008).

LIBRARY OF CONGRESS CATALOGUING-IN-PUBLICATION DATA

Grandchamp, Robert.
"Rhody Redlegs" : a history of the Providence Marine
Corps of Artillery and the 103d Field Artillery, Rhode Island Army
National Guard, 1801–2010 / Robert Grandchamp, Jane Lancaster
and Cynthia Ferguson ; foreword by Howard F. Brown.
p.   cm.
Includes bibliographical references and index.

ISBN 978-0-7864-6375-6
softcover : 50# alkaline paper ∞

1. Providence Marine Corps of Artillery.
2. Rhode Island. National Guard. Field Artillery, 103rd.
3. Rhode Island — History, Military.
I. Lancaster, Jane, 1945–
II. Ferguson, Cynthia.
III. Title.
UA436.5.P76G73   2012   358'.12309745 — dc23   2011029506

BRITISH LIBRARY CATALOGUING DATA ARE AVAILABLE

On the cover: *top* button worn on uniforms of Providence Marine Corps of Artillery members (courtesy PMCA); *photos clockwise from left* the colors of the 103d on parade at Fort Sill (courtesy PMCA); the 103d with Iraqi Police trainees (courtesy PMCA); group shot of the PMCA in their dress uniforms, 1877 (Robert Grandchamp); a three-inch ordnance rifled cannon of the Civil War (Robert Grandchamp)

Manufactured in the United States of America

*McFarland & Company, Inc., Publishers
Box 611, Jefferson, North Carolina 28640
www.mcfarlandpub.com*

To those who fell following the Red Guidon
"Play the Game"

CONTENTS

There's a breathless hush in the Close to-night —
Ten to make and the match to win —
A bumping pitch and a blinding light,
An hour to play, and the last man in.
And it's not for the sake of a ribboned coat.
Or the selfish hope of a season's fame,
But his captain's hand on his shoulder smote —
"Play up! Play up! And play the game!"

The sand of the desert is sodden red —
Red with the wreck of a square that broke; —
The Gatling's jammed and the colonel dead,
And the regiment blind with dust and smoke.
The river of death has brimmed its banks,
And England's far, and Honour a name,
But the voice of a schoolboy rallies the ranks —
"Play up! Play up! And play the game!"

This is the word that year by year,
While in her place the school is set,
Every one of her sons must hear,
And none that hears it dare forget.
This they all with a joyful mind
Bear through life like a torch in flame,
And falling fling to the host behind —
"Play up! Play up! And play the game!"

> —Sir Henry Newbolt
> *Vitaï Lampada*
> "They Pass on the Torch of Life"

ACKNOWLEDGMENTS

It is not every day that a historian is asked by an elite group of soldiers to edit a history of their unit. As the editor in chief of this volume, I have felt the honor of the challenge to "Play the Game," through editing and writing part of the proud 200-year legacy of the Providence Marine Corps of Artillery (PMCA) and, through its extension, the 103d Field Artillery Regiment. Through it all, I have had several key people who have assisted me greatly in the task.

First and foremost are Brigadier General Richard J. Valente and Command Sergeant Major Thomas Caruolo, two remarkable veterans of the 103d who gave all they had to ensure this book was completed. They provided an unbelievable wealth of material, while Gen. Valente kindly wrote the chapter on the Cold War era, which was part of his amazing thirty-five year career. Then there is the book committee of the PMCA: Colonel Richard Kanaczet, Sergeant Major Paul G. Lambert, Command Sergeant Major William B.J. O'Mara, Colonel James F. Ryan, Brigadier General Joseph N. Waller, and Colonel Dennis J. Zifcak. These retired veterans have opened up their archives, memories, and arsenals to me. The guidance and attention to detail offered throughout the process has been most rewarding and I hope that this tome meets their expectations.

I was very fortunate in my researching of the World War II chapter to meet and interview Colonel Howard F. Brown and Sergeant Bill Fusco, two exceptional veterans who fought under General Barker in the 103d Field Artillery. Although recalling events that happened six decades ago, their sharp memories and wits provided the best view of the combat of the 43rd Division Artillery in World War II. It was here that I learned of the glory gained at Munda and Luzon and the great effectiveness of the artillery. These men were among those who sacrificed all to save the world and one of the highlights of my life has been meeting these two distinguished soldiers.

Cynthia Ferguson and Jane Lancaster of the Rhode Island Historical Society were originally contracted by the PMCA back in 2001 to write the history of the regiment. They dug into the archives and began the work that finally resulted in much of this manuscript. My deepest appreciation to both of them.

Several members of the Rhode Island Army National Guard and the 103d Field Artillery provided welcome input. Major Christian Neary and Captain Mark Bourgery, two current veterans of the 103d Field Artillery who served in Iraq, graciously reviewed and updated the text, while providing firsthand accounts and images. First Sergeant Patrick Curran greatly updated and expanded the sections on Battery B. Master Sergeant James Loffler, command historian, provided the necessary lineages to link the PMCA to the 103d and answered many important questions. It was an honor to work with these men who have risked their lives to defend our freedom.

Phil DiMaria of the re-created Battery B, First Rhode Island Light Artillery, has always been there to answer my questions over the many years I have been honored to call him a friend. He helped immensely in uncovering that vital twenty-year period between 1845 and 1865 when the PMCA came onto the world stage. Phil's assistance has made this work not just possible but better. The accomplished historian Glenn Laxton, himself a veteran, greatly assisted with understanding the violence of the strikes in Central Falls. Fellow National Park Ranger and Rhode Islander Tom Frezza provided an interesting anecdote about his ancestor who served in the 103d in World War I. My grandmother, Joyce Knight Townsend, kindly filled the role of secretary during my four-month sabbatical to Harpers Ferry and kept everything organized. Timothy Pray of Tap Printing and Terace Greene have provided invaluable assistance in scanning and cleaning up archived images that were frequently in poor condition.

Although he is no longer with us, General Harold Barker deserves a special mention of thanks. His two volumes on the 43rd Division Artillery and the Rhode Island batteries in the Civil War and World War II are the basic building block for anyone researching Rhode Island in these two time periods. A half century after their publication they remain the best books in the field. In addition, the many members of the PMCA who donated their papers to repositories or took the time to record their remembrances are to be congratulated for helping to remember this complicated story.

For my own research, I am again indebted to my usual assortment of friends and fellow historians who have generously shared their research material. At the Rhode Island Historical Society, Elizabeth Demars was again extremely helpful in guiding me to those vital clues to the past. Ken Carlson's careful indexing of the Adjutant General Papers has definitely been worthwhile to draw material from. Ken is a remarkable historian and his guidance over the last decade has been most helpful. Kris VanDenBossche again provided guidance, while his previous work is always there to provide the foundation needed for any project involving Rhode Island in the Civil War era. At my usual hunting grounds for historical material — the Library of Congress, the National Archives, the Hay Library, Carlisle Barracks, and the Providence Public Library — the staffs all assisted greatly in finding material related to the PMCA and the First Rhode Island Light Artillery Regiment.

Above all, however, this work could not have been possible without the bravery, fortitude, and sacrifice of the men and women of the Providence Marine Corps of Artillery and the 103d Field Artillery Regiment. In the 200 years since their founding, the unit has left an indelible mark in the history of their state and nation. From the battlefields of Chepachet, Gettysburg, the Mexican border, Meuse-Argonne, Munda, and Baghdad, these soldiers have left a tradition of excellence second to none.

Play the Game.

Robert Grandchamp

FOREWORD BY
COL. HOWARD F. BROWN

Many units of the United States Army have histories dating back a good number of years, including some which predate the Revolution. The Providence Marine Corps of Artillery does not go back quite that far. The PMCA was founded in 1801 by a group of sea captains to arm their ships as a means of protecting them from depredations of the British navy and the Barbary Pirates. Fortunately, throughout the many years of service, some members had the ambition to keep accurate records of the events of the corps. The members of the PMCA have been involved in every conflict engaged in by the United States from the War of 1812 through the war on terror today. Because of the efforts of several present members, we are able to present a comprehensive history of the corps' actions from the beginning in 1801 right through Operation Iraqi Freedom. This book was made possible by the determined efforts of General Harold Read, and, upon his demise, the continued efforts of General Richard Valente, Robert Grandchamp, and the PMCA Book Committee.

Col. Howard F. Brown joined the 103d Field Artillery in Providence in 1937. He was mobilized for federal service on 1 February 1941 for a year's training but this changed on 7 December 1941 and he fought with the 169th Field Artillery through the entire Pacific campaign. In 1950 he was mobilized for the Korean War. After a distinguished career spanning 30 years, he retired. Col. Brown is the senior member of the 103d Regimental Association (the PMCA) and serves as adjutant.

1

PREFACE

The field artillery of the United States Army has been given the peculiar nom de guerre "King of Battle." Indeed this is an accurate description. Time and again the American cannoneers have saved the day. At Yorktown they helped end the Revolution, provided hard-hitting mobile firepower on the plains of Mexico, stopped Lee's attacking legions at Gettysburg, cleared the San Juan Heights in the Spanish-American War, fired relentlessly during the Meuse-Argonne Offensive in the Great War, drove fanatical Japanese defenders from their hideouts in the South Pacific, repulsed the NVA during the Battle of Khe Sahn in Vietnam, and today drive fanatical terrorists from their caves in the war on terror. The men who wear the red are the elite of the United States Army, and the Rhode Islanders have always been known as the best in what they do.

This book came to me as if one of those shells had burst in midair. I was working as a National Park Ranger in West Virginia and one night received a call from Brigadier General Richard J. Valente, a retired member of the Rhode Island National Guard's 103d Field Artillery and a former commander of the 103d Field Artillery Brigade. Ironically, the dispatch came as I was standing on one of the historical battlefields in the Shenandoah Valley where the Rhode Islanders once fought. In retrospect, it seemed to be an eerie place to receive such a dispatch — to write about the history that took place exactly where I was standing. Knowing the previous work I had done in the field of Rhode Island military history, the general asked if I would be interested in editing a history of the Providence Marine Corps of Artillery (PMCA). Without hesitation I answered in the affirmative, that it would be an honor to perform the task.

Anyone even remotely interested in Rhode Island's rich military past knows the story of this elite unit. Formed by a group of wealthy shipowners in response to fears of piracy, the unit evolved into a battery of field artillery, pioneering many important developments along the way. During the Civil War, the soldiers trained by this unit fought in nearly every major engagement of the conflict. Later, in different forms, the PMCA assumed the identity of Battery A and the 103d Field Artillery Regiment of the Rhode Island National Guard. This unit has fought on the Western Front in World War I, in the South Pacific in World War II, and in Iraq during the war on terror. Whenever their country has called, the men of Rhode Island have been quick and eager to serve.

This present work was begun nearly a decade ago by the PMCA in commemoration of their bicentennial. Today the unit does not serve a combat role, but rather strives to support the Rhode Island National Guard as an active and vibrant veteran's association. The first draft was laboriously researched and written, but no action came of it for several years due to the unfortunate illness and final muster of Major General Harold Read, the longtime PMCA commander. With the assistance of the PMCA Book Committee, World War II veterans, and recently returned war on terror veterans who collaborated with me, the project finally got downrange. The results have been impressive. Traveling far and wide, I have unearthed every stone trying to find those tidbits of the past to put into context this rich and interesting story. From old and faded regimental histories and important letters from the front, to yellowed newspaper clippings, tattered images, the tangible artifacts left behind, and the crisp and sharp memories of World War II heroes, all have interjected themselves into this writing. The results are this book.

This tome was a true collaborative effort, with portions being written by 103d Field Artillery veterans and professional historians Jane Lancaster, Cynthia Ferguson and myself. In this somewhat unique arrangement, Jane Lancaster wrote chapters 1 through 5, and Cynthia Ferguson wrote chapters 7 through 13. Cynthia also prepared a brief draft of chapter 14, which was expanded to cover the Cold War by General Valente. In addition to editing the entire work and locating all images used in the narrative I wrote chapter 6 and Appendix V. In conjunction with unit after-action reports and the assistance of 103d OIF Veterans I completed chapter 15.

In my role, I have carefully reviewed each page, adding and annotating as needed. All words quoted are the actual words of the veterans themselves and have been left unaltered for historical accuracy. Some must be taken in context with the difficult times that the soldiers went through.

In the past two hundred years, there have been several histories of the Providence Marine Corps of Artillery and the 103d Field Artillery Regiment, but this is the first one ever to tell the complete, comprehensive story of the unit. After the Civil War, nearly every battery of the First Rhode Island Light Artillery Regiment published a history, while the same process was repeated in World War I. In 1964, General Harold Barker wrote a massive tome covering the experiences of the Rhode Island Artillerymen in World War II. Unfortunately, today these books are rare and unavailable to most readers. This present work is designed to tell the full history and the traditions of these illustrious Rhode Islanders.

From the War of 1812, when they garrisoned a fort in Providence, to a violent insurrection in their home state in 1842, to the glory gained on the fields of Bull Run, Antietam, and Gettysburg, the disappointment of the Spanish-American War, the carnage of the Western Front, the terrible conditions of the mosquito-infested islands and fanatical enemy of the Pacific Theatre, and the deserts of the war on terror, this is the narrative of those brave soldiers of the Providence Marine Corps of Artillery and the 103d Field Artillery Regiment, who have decided to "Play the Game."

Robert Grandchamp

INTRODUCTION: CITIZEN-SOLDIERS

The Second Amendment to the United States Constitution firmly states "a well regulated Militia, being necessary to the security of a free state, the right of the people to keep and bear Arms, shall not be infringed." These words have been carried true in the heart by an elite group of soldiers from the smallest state on many bloody fields around the world as they have stood up time after time to defend American freedom. The soldiers of the Rhode Island National Guard are the living embodiment of the Founding Fathers' concept of the citizen-soldier.

Fearful of a strong centralized government and a powerful standing army, the Founding Fathers saw the citizen-soldier and local militia organizations as the greatest deterrent to tyrannical rule. This belief was so widely held by most Americans of the time that protection of the militia system was guaranteed in the Second Amendment of the Constitution. The American militia system was initially a form of military training, with all men of a certain age required to serve in units operated by the states or locales within them. As the compulsory system waned in the late eighteenth century, independent volunteer groups grew in both number and military value.

In 1801, Governor Arthur Fenner of Rhode Island granted the Providence Marine Corps of Artillery its independent charter. As in most volunteer organizations, its members were prominent residents of the community. They elected their own officers and provided their own, often gaudy, uniforms. Parades and banquets filled many hours, but the elite volunteer militia also produced the state's finest troops and military officers.

In the chapters that follow, the more than 200-year history of the Providence Marine Corps of Artillery (PMCA) will be traced and we will examine the ways in which it served its members and the nation in times of peace and in times of war. The PMCA has changed its name and its organization over the years, but it still exists to support the artillerymen of the Rhode Island National Guard. In its various incarnations, the PMCA has served the nation well. During the Civil War, PMCA provided the basis and the training for the eight batteries of the First Rhode Island Light Artillery Regiment, widely considered the best in the Union Army. In addition, they composed two independent units, while members served in every Rhode Island Regiment. Later, as Battery A it trained in preparedness for the Spanish-American War and in 1916 deployed to the Mexican border. During World War I in France, Battery A provided the nucleus for expansion to the 103d Field Artillery Regiment. In World War II, the 103d Field Artillery provided the command structure and two battalions to the 43rd Infantry Division Artillery in the Pacific. This same role was duplicated during the Korean War, when the 43rd Division served in Europe. Most recently during the war on terror, the First Battalion of the 103d Field Artillery Regiment was activated to federal service and its batteries served in Operation Noble Eagle at Quonset Point, Rhode Island, and Operation Iraqi Freedom in Iraq during the period 2003–2008.

This is necessarily a military history. The PMCA's wartime service and its metamorphosis from a group of shipowners and mariners determined to protect their shipping to an integral part of today's National Guard is a fascinating story. It is also a social history, placing the PMCA firmly within its local context and examining the lives of some of the colorful and influential men who have belonged to the PMCA over the last two hundred years.

The story of the Providence Marine Corps of Artillery and the 103d Field Artillery Regiment is one of a proud tradition. It is a history of constantly looking into the past to remember the history made in order to carry on that proud tradition on battlefields all over the world. The numerous battle honors on their artillery red regimental flag are silent reminders of glory and sacrifice. Even today long gone soldiers by the names of Wheaton, Sprague, Tompkins, Monroe, Peck, Glassford, Chaffee, Barker, Files, and Read are still spoken of with reverence and awe by the members of the command.

This is a history of that tradition of excellence. It is the story of an illustrious band of Rhode Islanders who in the two hundred years since the founding of their unit have answered their country's call time and again. These brave men and women have turned their backs on home and gone "over there" to defend the United States of America against all enemies, foreign and domestic, simply because it was the right thing to do.

IN MEMORIAM: MAJOR GENERAL HAROLD NEWTON READ

Major General Read was born on May 5, 1923, in Pawtucket, Rhode Island. His parents were Harold N. Read, Jr., and Edith Beatrice Jarvis Read. Siblings included brothers, Robert and Donald, and a sister, Dorothy. Read was educated in Pawtucket and graduated from Pawtucket East Senior High School on June 21, 1941. Although very much involved in music, he eventually went to work for the Industrial Trust Bank.

General Read enlisted in the Rhode Island State Guard and was inducted into the army in February 1943 at Fort Devens, Massachusetts. After basic training, he went to Oklahoma A&M for aircraft engineering and operations training. From there he was sent to Baer Field, Fort Wayne, Indiana, and assigned to the 436th Troop Carrier Group, 81st Troop Carrier Squadron, at Alliance, Nebraska. Gen. Read flew in C-47's and served with the 436th until January 1945.

The 436th flew the 101st Airborne Division into Normandy on D-Day, June 6, 1944. The 436th also flew the First British Air Borne Division from Italy to southern France in August 1944. The next month, September 1944, the 436th flew the 101st Airborne to Holland as part of Operation Market-Garden. In December 1944, the 436th took part in the aerial resupply of the 101st, by then besieged in the Belgian city of Bastogne. Due to severe infantry losses during the Battle of the Bulge, selected senior Army Air Corps noncommissioned officers such

as Sgt. Read were asked to accept assignments as second lieutenants in the infantry. After a short introductory course, General Read was sent to the 9th Infantry Division, where he became a member of the security force for the headquarters of General George S. Patton. He trained at Munich and then reported to Third Army Headquarters (Lucky Forward) at Bad Tolz, where he remained until December 1946.

In the fall of 1945, then Lt. Read was assigned as adjutant of the 503rd Military Police Battalion. Lt. Read, as the "paper work guru" of the 503rd, wrote his own orders for a thirty-day leave at home in Rhode Island. He arrived in Pawtucket on New Year's Eve 1946 and proposed to Winifred that very night. They were married on January 12, 1946. Gen. Read was released from active duty to the U.S. Army Reserve in May of 1946.

As a true citizen-soldier, he then went to work

for Liberty Mutual Insurance Company in Providence as a claims adjuster. Militarily, he transferred from the reserve to the 43rd Division Artillery (DIVARTY) of the Rhode Island National Guard in the fall of 1947. Their son Reginald was born in January 1948 and daughter Elaine in Sept. 1949. In 1950, the Reads moved to Holden, Massachusetts, where Gen. Read lived for all of two weeks before being called to active duty with the mobilized 43rd Division. The division moved to Fort Pickett, Virginia, and shortly thereafter Gen. Read, with his dependents, moved from Blackstone, Virginia, to Fort Sill, Oklahoma. When he received orders for overseas movement, the 43rd was in Germany; Winifred and family moved back to Pawtucket. A second daughter, Nancy, was born at the United States Naval Hospital at Quonset Point. A German telephone operator called him with the news. Following service during the Korean War, Capt. Read was promoted to major and assigned to the 103d Field Artillery, where he served as operations officer for eleven years.

In 1968, Col. Read assumed command of the 103d Field Artillery Group, followed by promotion to brigadier general and command of the new 43rd Military Police Brigade. Gen. Read culminated his military career by transferring to the United States Army Reserve and assumed command of the 94th Army Reserve Command where he was promoted to major general. After returning from active duty in 1954, Gen. Read served in several parish and diocese capacities—superintendent of the church school, chair of the stewardship committee, vestryman, warden and senior warden. He also served as chairman of Boy Scout Troop 10 Riverside.

Then the sea beckoned, and the Reads moved through a succession of boats, culminating in a thirty-three foot Pacemaker that they enjoyed for 25 years. He joined the Narragansett Terrace Yacht Club, eventually becoming commodore. He also joined the Narragansett Bay U.S. Power Squadron, where he was elected commander. He served for four years and earned an advanced piloting rating.

In 1960, he was moved to Liberty's home office in Boston as administrative assistant to the Vice President and general claims manager. He designed and prepared training programs for claims countrywide, a first in the insurance industry. In time, his unit prepared customized safety programs for several nationwide policyholders and received national recognition awards for their work.

In 1980, he was named manager of personnel development for Liberty. To accomplish this mission Gen. Read built several training centers in major U.S. cities and Canada. He retired from Liberty in 1988.

He served in numerous other capacities, including manager of volunteers for New Year's First Night celebration in Providence; cochair of the New England Army Chief of Staff Retirees Council for eighteen years; director and president of the Armed Forces Civilian Council at Quonsett Point; director of the 100 club for five years; chairman of the American Heritage subcommittee of the Rhode Island Heritage Commission; member of the board and president of the Squantum Association; and executive secretary of the 436th Troop Carrier Group Veterans Association.

His first love was the Providence Marine Corps of Artillery, where he served from 1973 to 2006, becoming the longest serving lieutenant colonel commanding. He spent untold hours researching PMCA archives and always had a new tale of PMCA history for the various gatherings of the PMCA. The PMCA is officially recognized by Department of the Army as the regimental founder of today's 103d Field Artillery Brigade.

Gen. Read was officially inducted into the Rhode Island Heritage Hall of Fame in 2005. Maj. Gen. Harold N. Read passed away on January 2006 and is interred in St. John's Episcopal Church Cemetery in Barrington, Rhode Island.

1

EARLY BEGINNINGS, 1801–1829

We are desirous to form a corps of artillery in the town of Providence for the purpose of improving in the use of cannon, and in the tactics employed in the attack and defense of ships and batteries.

— Providence Marine Corps of Artillery Charter, 1801

The history of the Providence Marine Corps of Artillery (PMCA), which would go on to fight in some of the nation's greatest battles, began with one man's vision on Saturday, July 4, 1801. On that day, Seth Wheaton, an officer during the Revolutionary War and a member of the Providence Marine Society (PMS), took part in the celebrations of the young nation's independence. Nearly all of Providence's 7,000 residents were present to celebrate the occasion. Only a quarter of a century earlier the war had come to their very doorsteps when the British controlled access to Narragansett Bay. The Revolution had been costly to Rhode Island in terms of lives lost and was a severe blow to the state economy. All of that was in the past, however, and now the roaring of militia cannons and the pealing of the church bells echoed through the streets of the city as these Rhode Islanders gave thanks for their freedom with a parade, followed by a good dinner and a generous helping of rum. Wheaton was joined by his friend Amos Maine Atwell, who had retired from the sea and now made a living as a merchant. Atwell was an importer who sold such items as "real Bordeaux Brandy," gunpowder, and decanters by the dozen.[1]

As well-respected members of the Providence community Wheaton and Atwell were active in the town. Besides being a member of the Providence Marine Society, Wheaton was also a member of the newly formed Providence School Committee. In addition, he was an active Freemason, and in 1799 he became the first master of the newly founded Mount Vernon Lodge. During the parade, Seth Wheaton saw his old friend, another retired captain, Samuel Aborn, whose house had been struck by lightning the previous week. Aborn told Wheaton and Atwell, to their amazement, that the lightning had damaged the frame of a portrait of Benjamin Franklin which hung over a fireplace in his house, while his lightning rod, one of Franklin's inventions, was untouched.[2]

On this July 4, Wheaton, Atwell and Aborn were waiting to march with the Providence Marine Society contingent in the annual Independence Day procession. It was a holiday, and the streets were lined with people, including those from outlying towns who came in to town to view the spectacle. Promptly at eleven, the procession set off, the Providence Light Dragoons leading the way, resplendent in their bright uniforms and with their swords shining in the sun. All the volunteer militia groups such as the Young Masters, United Train of Artillery and the National Cadets were present. Indeed, they represented much of the Rhode Island Militia at the time. As vice president of the PMS, Seth Wheaton marched behind its bright silk banner, accompanied by Capt. John Updike, the president of the PMS. Other officers of the society, including Jonathan Treadwell and Edward Carrington, marched behind. Drums beat and fifes played as the long procession wound its way up Westminster Street and down Weybosset and then back across the bridge to the First Baptist Meeting House.[3]

Once everyone was settled, a group of patriotic young women in white muslin frocks and with red, white, and blue ribbons in their bonnets presented the colors to their favorite militia groups. Then Tristam Burges, an up-and-coming young lawyer, strode to the pulpit and started to speak. Those present knew it was going to be a long speech; still, they gave their attention to the gifted speaker in the hot building. Burges spoke at length about the Declaration of Independence, claiming, "Once more the annual sun of our political year has risen on the world; our national independence is still our own, and again we hail the morning hallowed to freedom."[4]

Although the Americans had won their freedom in the Revolution, the young nation did not know when strife might return. In 1776, it had been clear who the enemy was. Wheaton, along with many of his countrymen, had assumed that life could return to something resembling normal after the Revolutionary War ended in 1783. But the British saw no reason to give their upstart former colony colonial preference in trade with the West Indies. The Dutch, Spanish and French also restricted American access to their Caribbean colonies. Some Rhode Island merchants, like Wheaton's former employer John Brown, responded by switching a portion of their trade to the Baltic and the Far East; but in both cases the Barbary States of North Africa had interfered with free passage across the Atlantic. Wheaton knew of several sailors who had been captured, enslaved by the pirates, and eventually returned home broken men.

1801 PMCA Charter (PMCA).

Seth Wheaton had spent the last dozen and a half years avoiding the Barbary pirates, negotiating with Chinese merchants in Canton, and outwitting Dutch customs officials in Surinam. Wheaton was forty-one years old, had spent over half his life at sea, and had prospered by it. He was ready to stay on land now. Life as a ship's captain had never been easy; but the last two or three years had been the most difficult, and he blamed the politicians in Philadelphia for that. In 1798, America almost went to war with France, despite President John Adams' desperate attempts to remain neutral in the escalating conflict between Britain and France. Jay's Treaty, signed in 1794, had not helped. In return for evacuating the forts on the Western frontier, and allowing the Americans limited trading rights in the Caribbean, the British expected that French privateers be ordered to leave American harbors and that the Americans stop trading with France. The French were furious and unleashed their own privateers on American merchant ships. Adams still tried to avoid war, in spite of the insulting behavior of the French foreign minister, Prince Talleyrand, who demanded a ten million dollar "loan" before he would start peace negotiations. Adams published the correspondence and "Millions for Defense, but not One Cent for Tribute" became the toast of the day. Amos Atwell's advertisements in the *Providence Gazette* jokingly reflected this sentiment. After listing his stock he declared, "The above Articles will be sold for Cash. '*Il faut de l'Argent — il faut beaucoup de l'Argent*— that is, in plain English, MONEY! MONEY! He wants Money as much as a Frenchman."[5]

Because of unsettled international affairs, the United States Army was increased in size, and to the delight of New England, the Navy Department was created. Coastal fortifications were rehabilitated, six frigates were built, including the *United States* and the *Constitution,* each with forty-four guns, and Congress appropriated a million dollars towards building six seventy-four-gun warships. It appeared as though the United States was ready for war once more, this time against a former ally.[6] All of these events had happened in the 1790s. Now the situation appeared calm for the time being, but the threat was always present.

In his 1801 oration Burges sounded a familiar Federalist note: the French were not to be trusted, nor were seditious foreigners, and Thomas Jefferson's new Republican government in Washington was little better. Wheaton, and almost everyone else in Rhode Island, profoundly mistrusted the new administration. The recent election had taken months to resolve, as Jefferson and Burr had tied for first place in the electoral college. After thirty-five tied votes in the House there was talk of civil war and the election was finally determined by the abstention of some Federalist, representatives. This result was not favorable to the Federalists who were concentrated in New England. Jefferson, a southerner with western support, wanted to reduce expenditure, and one of his first areas of reduction was the

The original banner of the Providence Marine Society (PMCA).

navy. The seventy-fours were cancelled and replaced by a fleet of shallow-draft gunboats, each with one, or at most two, cannon which would be manned by a naval militia. Their purpose would be purely defensive, as they would be deployed to safeguard American harbors against invasion.[7]

In May 1798, when the Quasi-War with France was at its height, a group of shipmasters had met at Uriel Rea's new coffee house on the corner of Market Square. John Updike, a neighbor of Wheaton's on Benefit Street, was in the chair. They decided that they needed to look after their own interests and those of their families, and accordingly they drafted a charter for a Marine society and presented it to the Rhode Island General Assembly the following month. The Providence Marine Society had two principal purposes. One was to act as an insurance society to look after the widows and orphans of its members, and the second was to share Marine intelligence, which was printed daily in the Providence papers. Article 15 of the bylaws instructed every member "on his arrival from sea" to "communicate his observations respecting the variation of the Needle, the soundings, courses, and distances of capes, headlands, or rocks and shoals, from each other, currents, tides, and other things remarkable about this or other coasts, as well as any other observation promotive of Nautical information, in writing, to be examined and digested by a committee appointed for that purpose." The Providence papers would report these finding throughout the nineteenth century in a column called "Marine Intelligence."[8]

It was clear that by 1801 these aims, laudable as they were, needed revision and the Providence Marine Society needed more than pensions and shipping reports to protect its members. Wheaton was thinking about Jefferson, the French, the navy, and the problems of neutral shipping as Tristam Burges reached the climax of his speech, a clarion call to neutrality overseas and extreme partisanship at home. Pointedly failing to mention the newly inaugurated President Jefferson, Burges declaimed:

> Let the nation, satisfied with the enjoyment of her own liberties, rise in all the magnanimity of impartial attitude, and stand superior alike to acrimonious enmity, and fond prepossession. Then shall the arrows of political deception fall pointless by our side, and our freedom and independence flourish, unwounded and immortal; then shall ADAMS, the younger brother in the cause of liberty, forget American ingratitude, and the memory of WASHINGTON be eternal in the spirit of his country.[9]

The speech finally being over, the procession re-formed, marched around the town again and then dispersed around two o'clock.

Wheaton, along with Atwell, Updike and other "first citizens" then went to the Society of The Cincinnati dinner. Like all members of the society, he had served as an officer in the Continental Line during the Revolution. Course followed course, then toast followed toast. The first, naturally, was "Our Country." The second was "the memory of the mighty dead — who does not mourn for Washington?" Number six was "the Militia of the United States — May they be ever renowned for discipline and subordination, as well as for bravery and patriotism," and so it went on. The ninth toast, however — "the Navy of the United States!" — set Seth Wheaton thinking. If the regular military of the United States could not protect the vessels sailing from Providence, the sailors themselves should take matters into their own hands.[10]

Accordingly, when Wheaton went to the Providence Marine Society meeting at Rea's Coffee House early that evening, he arrived with a proposal to protect the vessels sailing out of Providence, and out of that meeting came the Providence Marine Corps of Artillery. The members of the Providence Marine Society were more than ready to create a volunteer naval militia if Jefferson's administration was unwilling to help them. Insurance societies existed for the protection of the vessels, but they did not provide physical protection. Many members of the PMS were shareholders in the newly founded Providence Insurance Society; Amos Atwell was its secretary. Others members were part of the Washington Insurance Society. The problems they faced would, they felt, be better avoided by self-defense than solved by claiming insurance for a lost cargo or ship. There was never any way of knowing when the British, the French, or the Barbary pirates would attack the American vessels. These Providence masters wanted to protect themselves and their crews from capture.[11]

Wheaton spent the summer and early fall discussing the need for armed merchant ships with friends and colleagues. When the PMS met again in early October, its members voted unanimously to petition the Rhode Island General Assembly for a charter for a Marine artillery company. Fifty-nine PMS members signed the petition, which made their purpose crystal clear: they were "desirous to form a corps of artillery in the town of Providence for the purpose of improving in the use of cannon, and in the tactics employed in the attack and defense of ships and batteries."

The Providence Marine Corps of Artillery, with a membership "not exceeding two hundred men, exclusive of officers," wished to be a "body politic for the purpose of improving themselves in the art military." They were to meet at least four times a year, and had the power to make their own rules governing fines for absence or punishment for "any riotous, mutinous, or disorderly behavior on parade. All those who shall be duly voted or enlisted into said company, shall, so long as they continue therein, be exempted from bearing arms or doing military duty in the militia, watching and warding excepted." These laws would govern the organization for years to come.[12]

The PMCA was to be an independent, volunteer militia, very different in tone and spirit from the state militias which were by this time were falling into disrepute. Militia service was, at least in theory, universal and obligatory, though many men found ways of avoiding it; volunteer companies were, by definition, made up of those who wanted to serve. The oldest such group, Boston's Ancient and Honorable Artillery Company, had been founded in 1638 on the lines of London's Honourable Artillery Company, formed a century earlier, in 1537.[13]

The men of Providence were not beginning a new trend by forming an artillery company in the state. The tradition of artillery in Rhode Island began in 1741 with the founding of the Artillery Company of Newport. First engaged in the French and Indian War, the unit remains the oldest continuously chartered militia unit in the United States. This company was joined in 1774 by the United Train of Artillery. Headquartered in Providence, the unit was chartered by the Rhode Island General Assembly to provide supporting fire for the militia companies then in the state. Called to service in May of 1775, the Rhode Islanders joined the Grand American Army besieging the British in Boston. Even from a distance, there was no mistaking these men were Rhode Islanders. They wore a distinct wave-shaped helmet with the motto of their state upon it: *In Te Domine Speramus* (In God We Hope). Moving to New York in 1776, the battery was one of only eight in the Continental Army. The legendary status of the Rhode Island artilleryman began in the summer of 1776, during the Battle of Long Island. The Rhode Islanders became part of the rearguard as the Americans retreated off the island. They lost half of their strength, while significantly contributing to the successful American withdrawal by sacrificing themselves to hold off the British. By wars' end, the United Train of Artillery remained in service, fighting in every major engagement with Washington's main army. It served as a learning platform for the senior officers of the Continental Artillery; two of its officers rose to senior positions of leadership in the artillery ranks.[14]

Volunteer companies were often formed in response to a perceived emergency and were elite in their composition. The PMCA was no exception. Many of the volunteers were men of property, anxious to preserve their livelihood and their possessions and unwilling to submit to much political control. They were self-governing, electing their own officers, though this

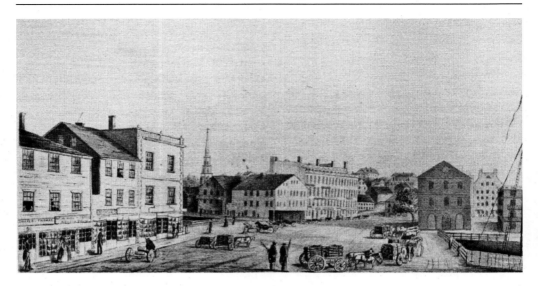

Rea's Coffee House (center) was an important social and meeting location for the PMCA in the early years (PMCA).

was subject to approval by the governor of the state. They were also elite in their position in the army; they usually served as light artillery or cavalry, rarely as line infantrymen. They provided their own uniforms, which were often dazzlingly expensive, and paid for elaborate dinners, armories and equipment out of their own pockets, another factor in guaranteeing that only the wealthy would be able to join.

The PMCA charter was approved in late October 1801, and the following March Seth Wheaton, who had been named in the charter as the lieutenant colonel commanding, called another meeting at Rea's Coffee House, this time to draw up a set of bylaws. Notable among the bylaws were a series of fines for nonattendance at drills, usually fifty cents, though officers had to pay more. Members were required to display a "soldier-like manner and accoutrements on parade." There were no uniforms yet, though endless debates on the matter were not far the future.[15]

On April 10, 1802, one hundred and twenty members of the Providence Marine Society crowded into Uriel Rea's long room and signed their names to a document that read: "We the subscribers hereby associate ourselves in a Company of Marine Artillery under the charter granted to John Updike, Seth Wheaton, Amos M. Atwell and others." The names of the six officers named in the charter headed the list of signatories. An election was planned for April 26, the last Monday in the month, and these men would be confirmed in office then. The bylaws stated that all officers of the PMCA had to be members of the Providence Marine Society, and thus shipmasters. This rule was in effect until May 1842, when the charter was amended.

Not all the members of the PMS joined the PMCA, but many of them did. The membership rolls show nine men joining on April 10, 1802, a further seven in September of that year, sixty-five in March and April 1803, four in 1804, and a further thirty-five in 1808. Most were aged between twenty-four and thirty-seven when they joined, though there was a sprinkling of men in their forties. Most of these early members belonged to old Rhode Island families; men joining in the first twelve months included a Tillinghast, a Fenner, a Lippitt, a Dexter, a Farnum, a Coggeshall, a Jenckes, a Mathewson and an Olney. Not everyone who joined stayed in the PMCA and by 1808 at least nine members had died or resigned. Most were lost at sea, though the unfortunate James Bird was dismissed at his own request in 1807, "he being lame." He died the following year.[16]

Most of the men who joined the PMCA from 1801 through 1803 were mariners in their thirties and forties. There were occasional exceptions: Pearce Coggeshall was a farmer on Poppasquash Neck in Bristol and a Freemason; John F. Greene went to sea as a young man without success and then became a shopkeeper, but despite his "fair character," he failed to prosper. Many members were related, fathers and sons, brothers or brothers-in-law. A prime example was Scott Jenckes, who married the daughter of John Updike, the founding president of the Providence Marine Society and a founding member of the PMCA.

Many other captains from Providence joined what was destined to become a prestigious group. They included men who had traveled the rough seas around the Cape to trade in China, others who made their fortune in the slave trade, and others who were coastal merchant seamen. All had their particular reasons for joining the Marine Society. Scott Jenkes tired of the shipping life and became a plantation owner in Cuba. William F. Magee spent twenty years in China as a contract agent for the Providence firm of Brown and Ives, while Daniel Olney was killed in the Pacific during a battle with natives. Death at younger ages was common in the nineteenth century, especially at sea. Among the members of the PMCA who died of illness while on their voyages abroad were Preston Daggett, Gideon Young, and Frederick Bowler. During times of crisis, some of these captains served in the newly expanded United States Navy. Moses Andrew and John Donovan are two of the men from the PMCA who gave their lives for their country during the War of 1812. They would be the first of many to make the ultimate sacrifice.[17]

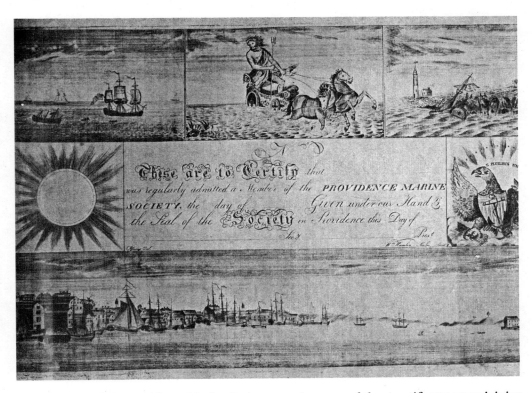

Each member of the Providence Marine Society was given one of these certificates upon joining (PMCA).

The Mauran brothers Carlo, Joshua, and Oorondates were three of the ten children of Guiseppe (Joseph) Mauran, who arrived in Rhode Island from Sardinia by way of a British man-of-war, which kidnapped him and his cousin in the Mediterranean in 1760. After serving two years as a cabin boy, young Joseph, by then 14, jumped ship in New London, Connecticut, and ran towards a group of men working in a field. When British officers came to retrieve the boy, farmers with pitchforks and hoes drove them away. After working in Westerly, probably as an indentured servant, Mauran moved to Barrington, where he soon married Olive Bicknell, his employer's daughter, and went back to sea. Eventually he commanded the gunboat *Spitfire* and the schooner *Washington* and later the privateer *Weazle*. Several of his sons went to sea as young men. Carlo and Joshua later became merchants and partners in the firm of C & J Mauran. Joshua was elected second lieutenant of the PMCA in 1814, and for the rest of the decade he served in numerous offices. Oorandates moved to New York, where he owned the Staten Island Ferry, in partnership with Commodore Vanderbilt; he also owned the first Italian opera house erected in New York City. One of their descendents, Edward Mauran, would be named Rhode Island's adjutant general sixty years later during the most critical period in the Rhode Island Militia's history.[18]

As one of his first acts as commander, Lt. Col. Seth Wheaton procured some artillery pieces for the use of his company. There was little point in practicing the military arts unless there was something to practice with. In 1802 six iron guns and gun carriages were ordered at a cost of $384.53. In a receipt for the initial purchases, the clerk's spelling left a little to be desired:

Coast Gun Cariges H. Stoddard	$200.16
Thompson and Simans Carpenters	66.27
Elios Bastor, Timber	1.50
George L. Pilcher, Painting	4.—
Francis Bailey-Ditto	10.77
Valentine Martin for wheels	60.—
Nat'l Cook for sundries to Bill	22.62
Do Do for Commissions	19.21
	$384.53[19]

Seth Wheaton stepped down in 1804 as the commander of the PMCA; he had become president of the new Roger Williams Bank, which took up a great deal of his time. During his brief command, America was starting to change. The territory of the United States expanded dramatically with the purchase of Louisiana, and Lewis and Clark's exploration of the Northwest promised further expansion. Political problems continued: some New England Federalists, heartily sick of Jefferson's administration, had started to discuss secession from the Union, a discussion that came to nothing. At the annual meeting held in April 1804 Amos Maine Atwell was elected lieutenant colonel, a post he was to fill for nine years.[20]

Wheaton, Atwell, and other prominent Rhode Islanders had started a tradition in 1801. They formed the PMCA to protect their own interests, both domestically and abroad. Little could they have imagined where the unit they formed would go in the centuries to follow.

2

The PMCA and the Napoleonic Era

It is highly proper said Corps should be in uniform.
— Lt. Col. Amos M. Atwell, PMCA

With the great task of forming the PMCA completed, the volunteers could finally settle into a routine. Lt. Col. Atwell's command coincided with some interesting years in American politics and in world affairs. In 1804, Vice President Aaron Burr killed former treasury secretary Alexander Hamilton in a duel. Later, in 1806, Burr conspired to "liberate" Mexico from Spain. The war between the British and the French resumed, with both sides trying to starve the other by naval blockades. The Royal Navy, plagued by desertion, claimed the right to impress British subjects, even if they were serving on American ships. In 1807 matters came to a head when the British ship *Leopard* fired three broadsides at the United States frigate *Chesapeake* and impressed four of its crew, three Americans and Jenkin Ratford, an organizer of British naval deserters. Even the New England Federalists were outraged and supported war against the British, but Jefferson, to their dismay, preferred economic sanctions. As a result, in December 1807 Congress passed the Embargo Act.[1]

American vessels were forbidden to sail to foreign ports and all exports to foreign countries were prohibited. The Embargo Act was a disaster for ports like Providence, and for the next fourteen months every ship that was not already abroad was either tied up or restricted to the coastal trade. Twenty-two-year-old Warren Lippitt is perhaps typical of those afflicted. He joined the PMCA in 1808, having spent most of the previous five years at sea. Lippitt had been to Australia, China, the West Indies, Africa, where he did some slave trading in 1805, and Argentina. The embargo forced him to stay closer to home, he joined the PMCA to pass the idle time.[2]

Warren Lippitt was born in 1786, left school at sixteen and went to sea in 1803; during Jefferson's Embargo he carried on a coastal trade. He rose rapidly and was named captain of the brig *Swift* at the age of twenty-two. He married Eliza Seamans in 1811 and they had ten children. One of them, Henry, an active member of the PMCA, served as governor of Rhode Island (1875–1877). After sitting out the War of 1812 as a partner in his father-in-law's grocery business, Warren Lippitt went back to sea for a while but soon returned to trade. In 1816, he became a cotton merchant in Savannah, where he spent nine months of each year. After the death of his father in 1845, he became treasurer of the Lippitt Manufacturing Company in Coventry. He died in 1850.[3]

Jefferson's last action on leaving office in 1809 was to repeal the Embargo Act, but New England's problems were far from over. The incoming president, James Madison, replaced it with the Non-Intercourse Act, promising to resume trade with whichever country first repealed its decrees against the United States. A year later, in May 1810, this was reversed in Macon's Bill No. 2, which permitted Americans to trade with both Britain and France. However, neither one of those countries recognized America's neutral rights—to stop trading with the other. For many, the fears of the quasi-war period were resumed.[4]

Few of these political problems are reflected in the PMCA's records, though bills for the annual meetings suggest a certain amount of conviviality, reflecting, perhaps, extra leisure time. At the annual meeting in 1808 the group consumed six gallons of punch, four quarts of brandy, two bottles of wine, and three pints of gin, as well as a rather small amount of crackers and cheese, which came to a total of fifteen dollars and seventeen cents; the following year they added hams and subtracted the gin, but managed to consume seven quarts of brandy and five pitchers of punch. From these lists, it is clear that in the early years the PMCA was more a social organization than a military unit.[5]

In 1808, however, the issue of the PMCA's uniform became urgent, and a special committee was formed to recommend to the membership what they should wear on parade. Amos Atwell, Benjamin Gorton and Cornelius Bowling suggested an elegant outfit: a vision in red, white and blue, with gold lace and gilded buttons. A clerk recorded it as follows:

> Round black hat—black Cockade ornamented with the figure of a foul Anchor—mettle gilt— Blue broad Cloth out side Jacket without skirts with lapels ornamented with Gold Lace & appropriate Buttons—Red broad Cloth Waistcoat single Breasted ornamented with gold Lace & 3 Rows Buttons—Blue broad Cloth Pantaloons welted with Red ornaments as before—White Stockings & black shoes—White Shirt ruffled at the Bosom only—Black Collars
> Equipments: 1 Brace of hansome Pistols 12 inches long to be worn in a red Morocco Belt round the Waist with Cartridge Box attached in the Center—Broad Sword, with hilt completely guarded for actual Service worn in a red morroco Belt over the Shoulder.[6]

An anonymous member later "humbly submitted" minor amendments to the committee's suggestions, though his final remarks suggest he was concerned that preoccupation with uniform might have been taking precedence over military drill. He wrote, "NB when Equiped, some suitable person to be employed by the Company to *teach the whole* the art of using the Broadswords— which together with the exercise of the Pistol and Pikes will form a handsome and warlike appearance if properly apply'd." He added cautiously, "In maneuvering it will be necessary that a sufficient distance be allowed in the Ranks so that in forming & closeing each man may have Room to wield his Sword & Pikes." The PMCA was still thought of as a naval organization and these weapons were highly effective in boarding operations.[7]

Members of the PMCA wore these buttons on their uniforms for nearly a century (PMCA).

Macon's Act allowed trade to resume in 1810, though the American government was more than a little naïve in dealing with Napoleon, who announced "his majesty loves the Americans" and declared that his decrees against neutral shipping would

A punch bowl used in the early years of the PMCA's history (PMCA).

be rescinded in November of that year. Madison fell into the trap, renewed sanctions against Britain, and seized trade. The British government finally gave in. The news, however, did not arrive in Washington in time to prevent war, which was declared on June 18, 1812.[8]

In May 1812, the Rhode Island General Assembly had announced that the independent companies would be required to help fill the state's militia quota. The conversation over the PMCA's uniform was clearly not yet resolved, so Amos Atwell's committee revisited the question, concluding, a little irritably:

> It is highly proper said Corps should be in uniform in point of *Dress* as well as equipment in order to secure themselves from Ridicule and Contempt; your committee are also of Opinion that these measures ought to be adopted as a Duty the said Corps owe themselves as an independent military Body; and more especially as an Obligation recently enforced by an Act of the Gen. Assembly of this State.[9]

With a uniform or not, every able-bodied man was now needed to join the ranks of the Rhode Island Militia. As a state whose trade depended on the ocean, Rhode Island could not afford to have Narragansett Bay shut off by the British as it had been during the Revolution.

Amos Atwell's words, combined with the excitement of the War of 1812, finally moved the PMCA members to action, and on September 1, 1812, forty-two members agreed to pay "our proportion of the expense that might arise in purchasing Broad swords and uniforms." Over the next few weeks, orders for broadcloth, gilt buttons, and sword belts were placed. Miss Abby Mumford made twenty-seven cockades and received payment of $10.12½. The total bill came for the uniforms came to $731, each member paying seventeen dollars, a not inconsiderable sum. The Marines were ready to fight, and fight elegantly, but there are no records that the PMCA did anything in the War of 1812 of military value. Despite this, many members took to the seas in the newly formed United States Navy or as privateers out of Providence; at least two men, Moses Andrew and John Donovan, died fighting on American naval warships.[10]

Warren Lippitt, meanwhile, had given up trying to make a living at sea, at least temporarily. Accordingly, he went into the grocery business in partnership with his wife's father,
Young Seamans. The same was true of other members of the PMCA; they had to find a way
to make a living while the war went on. Unfortunately, they received no chance to show what
they had been learning as naval artillerymen, for all the naval battles were fought on the
frontier on Lakes Erie and Ontario by Rhode Islander Oliver Hazard Perry, or in the South
at places like Chesapeake Bay. Their only duty was to help man fortifications, near Providence
at Field's Point, against the British; indeed the unit was responsible for organizing the entire
defense of Providence. One member wrote, "Until the close of the war of 1812, the company
was in a very efficient state of drill and discipline; the forts and preparations for the defense
of the harbor were constructed under their direction. Despite the constant preparedness for
war and the building of the fortifications, the British never arrived to test them and the PMCA
was not engaged as a unit.[11]

Despite their non-deployment in the War of 1812, the men of the PMCA did not let their
guard down and entered into a continual state of preparing for war. In 1814 Amos Atwell's
last act as commander was to upgrade the PMCA's equipment. Accordingly, he started a fund
to pay for a pair of new gun carriages, raising money from members and prominent merchant
houses. He managed to collect $169.75, with contributions ranging from twenty dollars from

*An honor guard of 103d Field Artillery soldiers pose in two uniforms of the PMCA. The soldiers with
swords wear the 1808 style uniform, while those in the center wear that of 1859. From left to right, the
soldiers are SGT Glen Hazard, SFC Raymond R. Petrin, SGT Scott Sheridan, SPC Fred Rohrer, and
SSG Jamie Melo (PMCA).*

This fort at Field's Point was manned by the PMCA during the War of 1812 (RG).

the firm of Brown and Ives, the wealthiest partnership in the city, to numerous smaller dona-
tions of three to five dollars. Long before all the money was in, he ordered work to begin on
the gun carriages. The detailed account, preserved in the PMCA records, gives a fascinating
insight into the costs, and perks, of labor in 1813 as well as the clerk's difficulty with spelling
the word "carriage":

April 26	To chaise to Rehoboth with Carpenter to look at the Timber	$2.
	Toll going & returning	.25
29	To paid Labour for getting guns out of the store and trucking them to the Blacksmiths	2.25
	To Paid men for going after timber to put it on the Cart & toll over the Bridge	1.62½
30	To paid getting timber on the Saw pit	.50
May 18	To pd Mssrs Thompson & Simmons on acct	6.
	To paid for Rum	.50
	To paid for Going after paint & priming guns	.75
June 4	To paid Mssrs Thompson & Simmons on acct of Carriages	16.
10	To paid Harding Stoddard for Receipt	50.00
	To paid Labour dragging carigges to the blacksmiths & for mounting one of the guns	.50
12	To pd for Boxes for the wheels of the other Cariage	4.\
14	To pd for mounting the other gun	.50
	To pd for Priming the Carridges	1.50
16	To paid Valentine Martin on acct wheels for Rict	50.
	To pd for Rum for People to draw the guns under the Shead	.25
July 3d	To pd Geo Pitcher for Bill for Painting Gun Carridge	4.12
		$140.75[12]

Amos Atwell left office in April 1814 and died a year later. Cornelius Bowler, who had
worked his way up through the officer corps, was now the PMCA's lieutenant colonel. He
tightened up discipline in the corps, adding a new bylaw requiring roll to be called at least
twice, once at the beginning of a meeting and again at an unspecified later time, to avoid the
crafty slipping away. New members had to pay six dollars on joining the PMCA and five dollars, plus any outstanding fines for nonattendance, if they wished to leave. A rather poignant
letter in the company's records suggests that Lt. Col. Bowler was strict in enforcing attendance.

Large and unwieldy naval cannons like this were used by the PMCA in the early days (RG).

Nov. 25th 1814

Col. Bowler,

Sir, I have to make known in conformity with the bylaws of the PM Artillery, that when the compy met at the Court House about the Third instant, my Notice was left at my house, but I did not know it until the morning after the Meeting of the compy.

When the Comp-y met on the Bridge to go on fatigue duty I informed you that in consequence of a Child lying at the point of death in my family, I could not attend. The Child died about Noon the same day — therefore if you think the above a sufficient excuse for non-attendance please order the remission of both fines.

I oblige yours respectfully

Solomon Tyler[13]

By 1815, the PMCA had been formed and in existence for fourteen years, serving its social and military functions within the town of Providence. The ocean trade that the corps had been created to defend was declining as Rhode Island shifted to an industrial-based economy. The members of the Providence Marine Corps of Artillery would change in time as well, becoming a land-based organization. None of the members could see into the future, however, or suspect that the corps would soon be called out to fight in their own state.

3

THE DORR REBELLION

I will leave my bones on Acote's Hill.
— Governor Thomas Wilson Dorr

The years from 1814 to 1843 saw many changes in Providence. One of the most spectacular events was the Great Gale, which flooded much of the city in September 1815. Some fifty ships were torn from their moorings, almost all the riverside warehouses were damaged, and two bridges were washed away. The most dramatic sight that day was a sixty-ton sloop which swept across Weybosset Street and came to rest outside a house on Pleasant Street. Fortunately, for the PMCA, Rea's Coffee House was saved.[1]

Perhaps of more relevance to the seafaring members of the Marine Artillery, the China trade flourished for a while and then started to decline as the economic base of the state shifted toward manufacturing. The population of Rhode Island started to change. As mills dotted the valleys of Rhode Island and the Blackstone Canal linked Providence and Worcester, large numbers of Irish and French-Canadian Catholics arrived to build the canal or work in the mills. The small state was a changing place and the PMCA changed with the times, bringing in new members, constantly upgrading their equipment, and practicing their drill. Despite these new Rhode Islanders, the PMCA remained a repository for the elite of Providence.[2]

If the Providence Marine Corps of Artillery did anything important or interesting in the years between 1814 and 1829 historians will never know of it, for in spite of the careful record keeping of many of the corps' clerks, in spite of the piles of leather-bound scrapbooks, account books and minute books, the records for those years are missing. The year 1829 saw a new low in the organization, as there is no record of an election and no returns were made to the general assembly. In 1830, the PMCA's charter was amended to allow nonmembers of the Providence Marine Society to become officers of the PMCA. Despite opening up its membership, the PMCA did not thrive in the 1830s. Interest in militia, whether state or voluntary, was minimal. There was no direct foreign threat and some even went so far as to reckon the Regular Army be disbanded, as the United States would never fight another war. Despite the low numbers who turned out for drill, a few dedicated members kept the Providence Marine Corps of Artillery alive during these difficult times.

During that period, however, there were a number of civil disturbances, including two incidents which could justifiably be called race riots. The Hard Scrabble riot of 1824 was an attempt to rid the north end of Providence of its black population. The instigators were brought to trial but were let off because they had cleared a "nuisance" away. Many whites were resentful of the black population, some of whom were better off than they. The blacks were resentful because of their limited freedom, including the vote, which had been taken away in the 1820s. The more serious disturbance took place seven years later in Snow Town, the name given to the black district at the end of Olney's Lane. In several days of tensions between Providence's minority black population and out-of-work white sailors, five were killed and dozens were injured. Although other Providence militia groups, including the First Light Infantry, the Light Dragoons and the Cadets, were used to quell the 1831 riot, the PMCA was not called upon, and their round of drills and dinners continued undisturbed. Nevertheless, Rhode Island was on the brink of disaster.[3]

In the early 1840s the situation came to a head. While states such as New Hampshire and Vermont all but disbanded their remaining militia companies, Rhode Island's thrived, with new units such as the Westerly Rifles, Mechanics Rifles, Pawtucket Light Guard, and the Woonsocket Guard being added to the rolls each year. The general assembly passed an act "to Regulate the Militia" in 1840. It was aimed mainly at those who avoided duty in the state militia, but the PMCA was still in disarray; numbers were low, morale was lower and they had mislaid most of their equipment. A committee formed to retrieve it reported that they had not been as successful as they hoped, but

> [w]e have been able to find the Bass Drum, but not in good order, as it is broken in several places. The Standard or Ensign we fear is lost; as we cannot obtain any trace of it; and of all the knapsacks, we have found *three* & left them with Mr. Robins. We have also examined the Field Pieces & find that they want repairing & cleaning. We recommend that they be repaired & removed from the present place. The Cart is so much decayed that it would be inexpedient to repair or remove it. The shafts & wheels are entirely gone. It will be necessary to remove the Pieces ere long, as the Brick building belonging to the City is to be taken down.[4]

The search for the drum and the effort to repair the field pieces was a sign that things were about to change. In 1841, a twenty-nine-year-old banker, merchant, and insurance company president, George C. Nightingale, took command of the corps, and he was followed by several able and energetic men who revitalized the company. Nightingale took charge just in time, for in 1842 the PMCA was to actually see action for the first time.

George Corliss Nightingale was born in 1812 and raised in Warwick; he began work as a clerk to a commission merchant at the age of thirteen and later became a prosperous manufacturer and bank director. He commanded the PMCA during the Dorr Rebellion, after which some of the women of Providence who were "ever appreciative of true gallantry" presented him with an elegant sword, a memorial of "the days that tried men's souls." He was commander from 1841 to 1844, an eventful period in the PMCA's history. During his watch the Benefit Street Arsenal was built, an "elegant" uniform was adopted and he financed the famous excursion to Stonington.[5]

Another prominent member of the PMCA at this time was Henry Lippitt. Born in Providence in 1818, he started work at fifteen in a whaling products store in Warren, Rhode Island. At seventeen, he became a bookkeeper for a cotton dealer, and by the age of twenty he was a partner in his own firm and later owned several very profitable textile mills throughout the state. He was also a banker, a railroad promoter and the man behind the building of the Narragansett Hotel and the Providence Opera House. He joined the PMCA in 1840, rose rapidly through the ranks, and was elected lieutenant colonel in 1846. First Lt. Lippitt led a section of the PMCA during the Dorr Rebellion. During the Civil War, he was enrollment commissioner for Rhode Island and was, like several PMCA members, elected governor in 1875 and 1876.[6]

The development of cotton manufacturing and the growth of Providence, which became a city in 1832, meant a major shift of population away from the southern part of the state to the mill towns in the north. The growth of an industrial economy also signaled a decline in maritime trade. A new PMCA charter, granted in May 1842, reflected this fact. Henceforward any formal links with the Providence Marine Society were severed and members and officers could come from any background, though they still tended to be of relatively prosperous Yankee stock; very few Irish surnames appear in the list of members and African Americans had to wait until the Dorr Rebellion to form their own units.[7]

Unlike most states, Rhode Island did not rewrite its constitution after the War for Independence and it was still governed by the colonial charter secured by John Clarke in 1663 from King Charles II. The franchise to vote was based on the ownership of freehold property, which meant only about 40 percent of the white male population could vote in Rhode Island. It goes without saying that women could not vote and black men had lost their voting rights in the 1820s. There was no mechanism to change the Charter without the consent of the general assembly, which was deaf to calls for reform.

Thomas Wilson Dorr, a member of a prominent Rhode Island family, decided that action had to be taken. A lawyer, he had been interested in broadening the suffrage since he was elected to the general assembly in 1834. In 1841, he became leader of the People's Party, which called a convention, wrote a new constitution and held elections. On May 3, 1842, Dorr was installed as governor. There was one major problem, as Rhode Island already had a governor, Samuel Ward King, who was reelected by a "Law and Order" coalition of Whigs and rural Democrats. Knowing he had the backing of the people, and considering him to be the rightfully elected governor, Dorr's followers took up arms to install their candidate into office. Rhode Island was on the brink of civil war.[8]

Very quickly Rhode Islanders had to decide if they were for the People's forces or the Charter Government. For the Marines, there was no choice in the matter. Members of the PMCA were wholeheartedly on the side of Law and Order. Their first opportunity to prove their loyalty to the status quo came on May 18 when Dorr, accompanied by several hundred supporters—accounts of their numbers vary considerably—tried to seize the state arsenal on Cranston Road. Dorr's forces arrived there at about two in the morning. It was a foggy, moonless night and a certain amount of confusion ensued. The Marine Artillery had already been in position on the upper floor of the arsenal for four hours; and according to the report in the *Providence Journal*, a virulently anti–Dorr newspaper, they were well aware of the rebels' movements. Not only had scouts penetrated the Dorr ranks, but also the order to march "was announced by signal guns, with a few scattering musket shots," which was, as the newspaper commented, "a singular preparation for a night attack."[9]

The arsenal was full of Thomas Dorr's relations, many of whom went outside to try to dissuade him, without success. His father was there; his brother-in-law Samuel Ames, who, as Rhode Island quartermaster general was in charge of the five cannon; and his younger brother Sullivan Dorr Jr., who was a member of the PMCA. One of the other defenders said to the younger Dorr, "It can't be possible that your brother intends to fire on this building when he knows that you, his father and his uncles are

Thomas Wilson Dorr led an armed rebellion to change the election process in Rhode Island (RG).

all in it." Sullivan replied calmly, "I guess you are not acquainted with the breed." Since he considered himself the rightfully elected governor of the State of Rhode Island and Providence Plantations, Dorr, along with his followers, prepared to engage his fellow statesmen in battle.[10]

Prior to launching the assault, the insurgents had stolen two Revolutionary War cannon, imported from France, from the armory of the United Train of Artillery. The guns had been given the mythic names of "Tantae" and "Pallas" and had first seen service in 1778 at the Battle of Rhode Island. Ironically for the PMCA now in their path, these two pieces had been among the cannon they had operated at Field's Point during the War of 1812. Because they were in such a hurry, the Dorrites had forgotten ammunition and loaded the guns with nails and crushed glass. When all was in position, Governor Thomas Wilson Dorr gave the order to fire at the arsenal with the Marines inside. The attack quite literally fizzled out when the two cannon failed to fire; the damp night air had rendered the powder wet. It was a fortunate mistake: "If a gun had been fired, the cannons in the arsenal might have plowed down the attacking force." Although little did he know it, the rebel governor had prevented a bloodbath on the streets of Providence. Dorr managed to escape as his men abandoned the cannon and fled towards Connecticut. The PMCA had an exciting few hours' marching to Dorr's headquarters on Atwells Avenue, in company with five other militia groups and numerous volunteers. According to the *Journal*, "the whole force numbered about seven hundred muskets, with six field pieces, two French eights and four four-pounders." The PMCA was dispatched to guard their own guns and then returned to face the insurgents' cannon on Atwells Avenue. At this point, there were only a few Dorrites left, and they were not pursued by Law and Order forces.[11]

It had been a long night but eventually the PMCA returned to their headquarters and were dismissed. There were several immediate results. Two officers, Maj. Ellery and Lt. C.G. Bradford, resigned their commissions, saying that the "exigencies of the time" demanded that more experienced men take their place; Henry Lippitt and Augustus M. Tower took their places. Military enthusiasm ran high in June 1842. Rumors were circulating about Dorr's whereabouts, while his supporters gathered in the village of Chepachet in western Rhode Island. The Law and Order Party had been trying to undercut Dorr's support since the abortive attack on the arsenal; it had conceded some reforms, as well as cementing an alliance with Providence's black community, by promising them the vote in return for their support. Nevertheless, the people who supported Governor King were preparing for a showdown.[12]

Two of the major players in the history of the PMCA during the Dorr Rebellion were Augustus M. Tower and William Rodman. Tower was born in Newport and after serving as colonel of the PMCA in 1845 and 1846, he served in the Civil War. In 1864, at the time of his death from consumption, he was working as an army paymaster. Rodman also was born in Newport in 1814. He became mayor of Providence from 1857 to 1858. In 1863, he was president of the Franklin Mutual Insurance Company and remained there until his death in 1868.[13]

Efforts by the PMCA to find a lot and build their own armory were renewed, and training was intensified. In June, they took their new brass pieces to the Red Bridge over the Seekonk River and practiced shooting, whereby, "much to the satisfaction of all, the target [was] handsomely perforated with six balls out of twenty shots." The PMCA's clerk, William F.M. Rodman, who clearly enjoyed his role as company scribe, described the scene when they returned from the Red Bridge:

> [T]he merry strains of martial music came throbbing through the bland atmosphere. It proved to be the Fourth Ward Volunteers in their return march after the performance of company drills—whereupon the Marine Artillery formed company, took arms—left the Armory in order and formed a line upon Benefit St for the purpose of presenting the soldiers salutations to their

The attempt on the Arsenal on the night of May 17th

The first military action of the Dorr Rebellion was an aborted attempt to take the state armory. The PMCA manned the upper floors of the armory (PMCA).

brethren in arms which was accordingly done in a soldier like manner as this valiant band of gray hairs and youthful patriots marched in their martial order, on to their headquarters, they returning the salutations in the fullness of a soldiers heart!![14]

Plans were being made for a major display of force on the Fourth of July. The PMCA decided to parade with their brass pieces and Frank Mauran was instructed to procure two horses for each gun. They also planned to have seven pieces of music. These arrangements were rudely interrupted by Governor King's declaration of martial law on June 26, 1842. W.M. Rodman's description of the PMCA's activities during the "Battle of Chepachet" constitutes a vivid eyewitness account of the practicalities and the confusion of military activity. With their plans for a parade temporarily sidelined, the soldiers of the PMCA prepared for a real soldiers' mission.[15]

On Monday morning June 27, 1842, the PMCA assembled at the Cadet Armory on Benefit Street for a dress parade, but they were immediately dismissed and told to reassemble in thirty minutes ready to march to Chepachet. They supplied eighty-nine muskets and two field pieces and joined about 3,000 militiamen who came from all over the state. Governor King planned a three-pronged attack against Dorr's forces. One brigade of men from Washington County marched up through Foster to block Dorr's escape route into Connecticut; another was to travel through Scituate and assault from the south. The main force would comprise the companies from Providence, Newport, and Bristol counties and march in from the east. Furthermore, parties were dispatched north into the Blackstone Valley, the main area of Dorr's support, to search for members who had not marched to Chepachet. For the Providence column, it was a leisurely march. They stopped for lunch at Fruit Hill, less than three miles from Providence. In addition to the meal, the women of the city supplied the militiamen with alcohol, which added to their sense of bravery for a time. Indeed, some men became tipsy and made fools of themselves as they marched along, looking disheveled. A Providence resident at the time remembered the Marines as "tall and stout." The division then marched another seven miles to Greenville, where the PMCA was quartered in the Waterman Tavern for the night.[16]

This was not as comfortable a billet as it sounds, as the whole company was on guard duty and it was pouring rain. About midnight they were ordered to march "immediately" to Chepachet. They set off at 3:30 on the morning of June 28 and marched "through mud and mire, through rain and mist" towards Dorr's fortifications. In Scituate the brigade from Providence met another brigade that had come up through Scituate, including the Artillery Company of Newport, and the two forces rendezvoused as they marched steadily towards Chepachet. All the while, in the distance the rumble of artillery fire could be heard, signifying a battle ahead. The Putnam Pike on which the Rhode Island Militia marched was a quagmire of mud. The Marines and the rest of the force were on constant alert, scanning the woods and fields that lined the road to insure they were not ambushed. They halted about a quarter of a mile from Acote's Hill, and while scouts reconnoitered the only military fatality of the Dorr Rebellion occurred.

A militiaman from Portsmouth shot his brother-in-law. In Rodman's words, "During this pause, for some trivial affront a private in the Company of Rhode Island volunteers from Portsmouth deliberately shot his brother-in-law, a Mr. Gould, through the head, who expired almost immediately. (The individual's name was Barker, and he was evidently

William Rodman was the longtime clerk of the PMCA, in addition to serving as mayor of Providence. He was an eyewitness to one of the most pivotal events in Rhode Island history (PMCA).

deranged. He was badly wounded by those immediately around him; but he will doubtless recover, though wildly insane.)" The body of Lieutenant Robert Gould would be returned to Middletown for burial. Let it be remembered that a member of the Rhode Island Militia did lay down his life in the suppression of the Dorr Rebellion; it was not a bloodless affair.[17]

The "People's Governor," Thomas Wilson Dorr, anxiously waited in Chepachet; indeed he had been there since the twenty-fifth of June. He had returned from New York for a renewed effort to assert his power in Rhode Island. Dorr issued proclamations and expected militia forces loyal to his cause to come to his aid as he and his most loyal supporters took over the Sprague Tavern. Dorr was amazed that so many men had voted for the People's Constitution but now in the moment of need only 200 men, mostly poor workers, stood ready in Chepachet to defend their rights. This placed Dorr in quite a predicament. He received word that an entire division of the Rhode Island Militia was marching towards Chepachet, his escape routes were about to be severed, and he only had enough ammunition for a fifteen-minute stand. As a lawyer, Governor Dorr possessed enough common sense to realize there was no possible way he could make a stand on Acote's Hill. Faced with these options, he ordered the few supporters who had shown up to return to their homes as he and the most loyal of his followers fled towards Connecticut and thence to New Hampshire on the night before the battle. The Battle of Chepachet would never happen.

Leaving the "deranged" Barker behind, the troops marched up to Dorr's fort only to discover that Dorr had fled, and that apart from some drunk rebels in the Sprague Tavern there was no one to be seen. Several cows were captured in the abandoned fortifications. The artillery noises had come from several boys who were playing with the abandoned cannons on the hill. The insurgents were captured and placed with others who had been apprehended on the road, then the PMCA fired their cannon for the first time in a victory salute. According to the poetic Rodman, it "made the hills and valleys echo with the glad notes of joy — joy for the triumph of law over misrule and monocracy — joy for the victory of truth over error — joy for the safety of our institutions, our laws, our privileges, our kindred and our homes." The brigade from Washington County remained encamped at Foster for several days, blocking the road to Connecticut, before returning home. By July 1, all of the militia had been dismissed and returned home.[18]

The PMCA spent the rest of the day searching for rebel weapons and ammunition. They found "Swords, Pikes, Dirks, Guns & Powder" in the most extraordinary places, including

The Rhode Island Militia stormed Acote's Hill on June 27, 1842 (RG).

"under beds, wrapped up in women's underclothes yet all ready for immediate use." After finding the military items, the entire force of Rhode Island Militia that invaded Chepachet went wild, looting shops, breaking windows and arresting anyone in sight who even looked like they supported Dorr. The most important discoveries came at the Sprague Tavern, which had served as Dorr's headquarters. His personal papers were found, but of more importance, several gallons and bottles of rum, which fueled the efforts of the militia; an innocent bystander was shot in the thigh while sitting in the Sprague Tavern's taproom.

It took a great amount of energy and time for the officers to gain control of their men. The spoils of victory included eight tents, and the members of the PMCA slept in them that night in a Mr. Hunt's yard on Main Street in the village. The officers settled into Hunt's home for the evening. During the searches at least one other militiaman and several cows were shot. Rodman's account of the PMCA in the engagement is a very valuable and important historical resource, as it has often been understood that the Dorr Rebellion was a bloodless, almost comical affair, but in reality, at least two people died in connection with the brief period of the insurrection and a dozen were injured. Noted Rhode Island historian Dr. Patrick Conley called the Dorr Rebellion "no tempest in a teapot." It was an event that had national reper- cussions, and the families of those who died would never forget.[19]

The return of the PMCA to Providence the next day was not without incident. Taking about 140 captured rebels with them they stopped for lunch in Greenville, where the prisoners, according to Rodman, were also served lunch, *exactly alike.* Soon after they resumed their march, however, a pistol fell from the belt of an unnamed member of the PMCA, hit a stone and discharged into what seemed to be "the vitals" of one of their members, Pvt. Lemuel H. Arnold Jr. He fell bleeding into the quartermaster's arms. Arnold was the son of former Whig governor Lemuel H. Arnold, who was one of Governor King's advisors. Leaving Lemuel Jr. with the surgeons in a neighboring house the corps moved on "with saddened and depressed hearts." The shot almost created a massacre. When it went off, the Marines were positive that it had come from one of the prisoners who had smuggled a weapon from Chepachet and had been bound until now. They instantly cocked their muskets and prepared to fire at the pris- oners, until an elderly woman came to them and told them what actually had occurred, thus saving many lives. The well-trained members of the PMCA instantly shouldered their weapons and resumed the march.[20]

It was a weary band of Marine Artillery that marched into Providence that afternoon, but their spirits were revived by the crowds who welcomed them on Westminster Street, where young women "literally smothered" the militiamen with flowers and wreaths. Invigorated by this appreciation, the PMCA marched to Smith Hill where they fired a twenty-six gun salute in honor of "the triumph of law over wild and mad ambition, over the plans and schemes of one whose only attribute of greatness is an indomitable will."[21]

A week later, the PMCA marched in full dress uniform in Providence's Independence Day parade. They made a glorious picture in red, white, and blue. The uniform in 1842 con- sisted of scarlet caps trimmed with brass and topped with a flowing scarlet-tipped black plume; the coats were blue, trimmed with scarlet, and had scarlet epaulets the pantaloons were white. Their belts and cartridge boxes were black leather. It was still the age of fancy uniforms and trappings; only twenty years later, some of the PMCA soldiers would be reduced to literally wearing rags during the Civil War.[22]

Dr. Francis Wayland, president of Brown University, a great center of Law and Order Party support, offered a prayer "full of noble and patriotic thought and humble thankfulness." Whig attorney John Whipple, who had been at the heart of unsuccessful efforts to obtain Fed- eral troops to put down the rebellion, made a speech which even Master Clerk Rodman thought was going a little too far when he "burst upon us with a full tide of fulsome flattery and

The Benefit Street Arsenal forms the backdrop to a political cartoon about the Dorr Rebellion (PMCA).

promiscuous praise, telling us that as soldiers of the Rhode Island line 'you have covered yourselves all over with glory.' Tis true," conceded Rodman, "the soldiers have all performed their duty manfully — nobly — in rescuing their state from the hands of ruthless demagoguery, and deserved, among the most deserving stood our band of brave Marines. Still we could not but feel that Mr. Whipple stepped over the mark of true discretion." On their way back from Smith's Hill the PMCA stopped at Governor Arnold's house on Benefit Street, where they found to their great joy that Lemuel Arnold was "rapidly recovering." After "three loud cheers" they proceeded to the Cadets' Armory and were dismissed.[23]

One of the most enduring images of the Dorr Rebellion is a cartoon widely circulated in 1843 in which the new arsenal on Benefit Street played an important role. Dorr's supporters and enemies all appear against the backdrop of the PMCA building. A caption printed in the *Providence Journal* in 1902 mentioned the organization and its role in putting down the rebellion:

> It has been said that no man or organization can be termed famous until he or it has appeared in caricature. If this is the test, the PMCA attained fame at that time. In one of the Dorr War Pictures, "the Old Arsenal" on Benefit Street figures as well as the members and name of the organization. Party feeling ran high in the Dorr War times. Hence the picture reproduced above, in which Gov. Fenner is represented with horns; Gov. King in armor supporting the standard of Law & Order; Gov. Dorr joisted & exclaiming "Leave my bones on Acote's Hill;" Followers include a Spartan Band Member; Toughs Arsenal in the background carrying the Tammany mug slung ala growler on the hip. The old PMCA and all: the Armory of the PMCA, Prov., RI, Law & Order is the Foundation of Democracy. In those days, as today, training and Esprit de Corps of the battery made it a prominent figure in support of the state.[24]

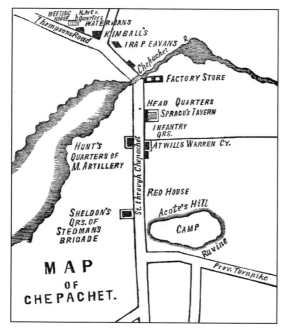

After the Battle of Chepachet, the PMCA camped at the Hunt House (RG).

It was those first actions in the Dorr Rebellion that set the standard of excellence in the PMCA.

Although Dorr's Rebellion had been militarily unsuccessful, the men who had formed up in Chepachet to fight the best of Rhode Island did indeed change the political system of the state. Dorr himself escaped to New Hampshire. He later returned to Providence, was arrested and sentenced to life in prison. Even with Dorr's imprisonment, the PMCA was still not finished with the former governor. A popular liberation movement erupted and the protestors would occasionally march on the prison where Dorr was being held. In one march, "1,268 ladies" formed up to protest the harsh treatment of their leader. In these tense moments the Marines responded by placing the cannon around the prison entrance to keep back the protesters. Only once did they become violent, when a PMCA corporal thrust his pistol into the chest of a New York newspaper editor who was reporting on the case and told him to leave at once or die; the New Yorker obeyed the command of the Rhode Islander. (Dorr was freed within eighteen months. He died in 1854.) In September 1842, a constitutional convention was held in East Greenwich that passed the People's Constitution. The new document allowed nearly every Rhode Island male to vote. The Dorr Rebellion had been a success after all.[25]

In June of 1842, the PMCA had answered their state's call to arms. It was the first time that the unit had seen active field service, and it would not be the last. Although on active duty for only one week, the soldiers had demonstrated their ability to act when the government they swore to defend was under siege. The Dorr Rebellion also showed the weakness of the unit; the muskets and old fieldpieces were of no further use except on the parade ground and would have to be replaced. The next time the Rhode Islanders were called into action they would be equipped with the best that money could buy.

4

THE GOLDEN AGE OF THE PMCA

The Company went through the drill of flying artillery, and the guns were fired with great precision.

—Corp. Robert G. Lippitt, PMCA

By the 1840s the PMCA had been in existence for almost half a century without a proper home of its own. The corps had used space in various other militia headquarters and by 1842 they were meeting in the Arcade on Westminster Street. Occasional discussions about a new armory had come to nothing, but the excitement of the Dorr Rebellion and the renewal of military spirit in the 1840s inspired them to build the armory on Benefit Street which was to become their permanent base. The lot cost one thousand six hundred dollars. Funds were scarce and they did not have enough money to pay for both the land and the building so they entered into discussions with the State of Rhode Island. Officers of the state, alarmed by Dorr's attack on the state arsenal out of the Cranston Road, wanted to keep their cannon in a more central place.[1]

The PMCA was told that if they allowed the state to use part of the arsenal they would be relieved of ground rent "for the present" and furthermore the state would recommend to the General Assembly that the ground "be secured" to the company. Negotiations dragged on for nearly ten years; in 1849, six years after the armory opened, a committee of the PMCA officers was instructed to talk to the state. Three years later an exasperated resolution in the minutes released that committee from its duties and passed the responsibility to Col. Joseph P. Balch to finalize the deal.[2]

The eventual arrangement was that the PMCA bought the property and deeded it to the state, which in turn leased it back to them for a thousand years at the huge sum of six and a quarter cents a year. One of the PMCA's favorite documents is a receipt dated February 18, 1947, from the State of Rhode Island, Military Staff Division, for six dollars and twenty-five cents, being the ground rent for a hundred years.[3]

In January 1843 Maj. W.G. Dorrance loaned the PMCA six hundred dollars towards the building of the armory, and by the following year it was ready for its grand opening. After members had voted that smoking and spitting be prohibited, "as it is very desirable that our new Armory be kept in that order and beauty which now characterizes it," everything was ready for the first meeting, which took place on March 14, 1843. The chandeliers were lit, the Marine Artillery band played and the corps admired their new building, which they were confident equaled or even surpassed any other armory in New England.[4]

The following week there was a grand ball to celebrate the dedication of the armory. As the irrepressible William Rodman described it, all were as "merry as a marriage bell." Men and women, young and old, officer and privates gathered at 8:30 P.M. and danced the PMCA Quickstep to the strains of the Providence City Brass Band until "Aurora unlocked the gates of morn." The tune was composed for the PMCA by B.P. Robinson and arranged by S. Knaebel of Boston in 1843. The PMCA dined at one in the morning in the upstairs room, which was as yet unfinished; but it was decorated with so much greenery it had, again according to Rodman, "the aspect of a beautiful and wildly luxuriant grove." The decorations downstairs were more militaristic; among more greenery and artificial flowers was an arrangement of twenty-six burnished horse pistols radiating from a gilded center and surrounded by a double circle of dirk hangers, which formed a "dazzling display."[5]

The PMCA had to wait fourteen years until the upstairs rooms were finished. By 1856, the Rhode Island General Assembly had authorized the building work, but funds were delayed. A major economic downturn in 1857 meant many PMCA members were unemployed, so William Sprague, then colonel of the PMCA, paid for the work out of his own pocket, partly as a way to keep his men in work. Two years later the general assembly repaid him the sum of $683.40.[6]

The PMCA's revival of interest in things military was marked by a number of excursions, which involved contact with other volunteer militia groups. The PMCA's "networking" served several functions: sociability, a display of their grand uniforms and equipment, and the exchange of military knowledge. A typical example occurred in August 1843 when the PMCA went on an excursion to Stonington, Connecticut, by way of Newport. It was a mixture of camaraderie and comedy. At their first stop, they were received by the Newport Artillery but

The Benefit Street Arsenal has been the home of the PMCA for many years (PMCA).

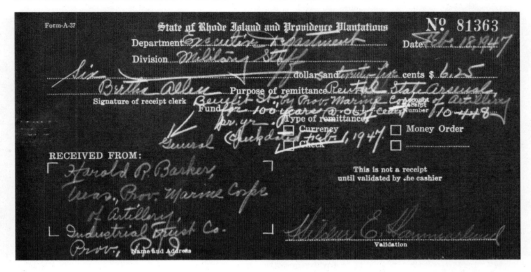

In 1947, Gen. Harold Barker, then commander of the PMCA, paid the State of Rhode Island for the next 100-year lease period on the Benefit Street Arsenal (PMCA).

declined their offer to stay in their armory as it was a beautiful summer day. Instead, the PMCA decided to pitch their tents, newly confiscated from Dorr's followers at Chepachet, near the Old Stone Mill. Company Clerk William Rodman was poetically inspired. He wrote the following:

> The tents, all pitched, and Banner reared,
> The band struck up a glee
> When the sergeant said, "Mariners fall in
> And downward march to tea.

The rejection of the indoor quarters was a poor choice, as the torrential rain caused severe flooding and the next morning's parade had to be cancelled. The storm dampened the PMCA's uniforms and their tents but not, however, their enthusiasm for lunch.

In the afternoon, the PMCA set off for Connecticut by boat. The storm had not abated, and the water off Beavertail on Conanicut Island was very rough. As Rodman put it, "a sicker soldier set, [was] not oft in ocean met." After a while the weather changed and the fog came down. Now they were becalmed: the PMCA spent its first night at sea, and finally arrived in Stonington in time for lunch the next day. The "Excursion to Stonington" was the subject of a witty poem composed by a member of the PMCA in 1842. It was set to music and sung at banquets thereafter, and several verses were recited by Everett S. Hartwell in 1952 on the occasion of the PMCA's 150th anniversary. The poem follows:

> At 3 o'clock we one and all
> For Stonington set sail
> Aboard the good *Rhode Island*
> With Colonel Nightingale.

> The wind was east and thick the fog
> And heavy was the sea
> And the way these Mariners turned pale
> Was wonderful to see.

> And soon along the steamer's side
> In line they were arrayed

And loudly rang the merry laugh
While Bicknell did cascade.

But soon the lines were thickly formed
With many a new recruit
And Bicknell only had to grunt
For Grant to follow suit.

And sick, as death was Cushman Ives
And pale as spectre's shroud
And heaving like the singing sea
Beside him stood Ike Proud.

And many more to see the fun
Up to the sick line ran
And loudest 'mong the jolly band
Were Lippitt and Mauran.

But soon was hush'd their merry shout
As Lippitt's cheeks turned pale
And Ned Mauran; he soon began
To vomit by detail!

Balch stood there, chock full of fun,
Loud laughing in his glee
And oft would Ned his chowder throw
As oft Joe counted three.

And though the quartermaster tried
To brave the frolic through
He had to join the spouting band
As did Bill Chandler too.

And far along toward the bow
As still as he was able
The Colonel sat avomiting
Behind the box of cable.

Then Major Leonard marched around
The spouters to review
And Major Earle was on the ground
To look upon us too.

Captain Larcher too was there
And to sit still was able
Yet everyone who saw him knew
He felt abominable.

And like a Tower, upon the dock,
Our bold lieutenant stood
And laughing said "spout on my boys"
T'will do you all much good.

As thick and thicker grew the fog
And darker grew the night
And we shut our anchor overboard
Beside the Watch Hill light.

The meeting in Stonington was a festive affair, with representatives of the Maryland Cadets from Baltimore, and from Providence the Light Infantry, the Sea Fencibles and the Cadets. Lunch was enlivened by "wit, song and sentiment" and, perhaps more important, "mutual interchange" of information about their various activities. But soon it was time to board the train and return to their Providence headquarters, where they drank a toast to their benefactors—especially to Col. Nightingale, who had paid the bill—and then went home.[7]

The PMCA's "golden age" was the period between 1843 and 1861. The immediate cause was paradoxical, as the general decline in state militias contributed to the rise in importance and professionalism of the volunteer militias. In Rhode Island, the general assembly decided in June 1843 to organize a uniform state militia. It was a mixture of centralization and local control. The state provided a skeleton regiment while the individual militias ran themselves, though they were required to drill together twice a year, in May and October. After "protracted debate," the PMCA voted twenty-nine to twenty-three to join the state militia. They were to be under the control of a state major general, in return for which the state would provide modest funding. In 1847, the PMCA's share amounted to $69.12, though there were several years when the state's payment was slow in coming.[8]

More important was the provision by the state of new guns to replace the heavy equipment the men had hauled to Chepachet and back. The Militia Act stipulated that each artillery company should have "two good brass field pieces with carriages and apparatus complete; with an ammunition cart, forty round shot, forty rounds of canister shot, tumbrels, harness, implements and a quantity of powder, annually, not exceeding one hundred pounds, to be expended on days of inspection and review, and in experimental Compy."[9] The PMCA nevertheless petitioned the general assembly in September 1847 for four guns and reorganized itself as a battery of light artillery. The new clerk, Robert G. Lippitt, recorded with some satisfaction that on October 16, 1847, "the Company went through the drill of flying artillery, and the guns were fired with great precision."[10]

The first time the PMCA marched as a light artillery battery was during the funeral of Maj. John Rogers Vinton, a career soldier born in Providence in 1801. He had served in the Seminole War and the Mexican War and was killed at Vera Cruz on March 22, 1847. His body, along with the cannonball that felled him, was returned to Rhode Island, where he was given a state funeral on May 11, 1848. The PMCA was one of eleven militia groups which led the parade through the streets of Providence to the newly opened Swan Point Cemetery. Today Vinton lies in a stately sandstone tomb, adorned with the symbol of his trade: the cannonball that killed him.[11]

In 1848, the PMCA became a part of the Militia of the State of Rhode Island and acquired no small fame from pioneering in the development of horse-drawn artillery. First used to great effect by the Americans during the Mexican War, these tactics combined the concept of mobile firepower by instantly being able to change positions under fire, as well as using smaller weapons, a concept ideally suited for the field. The PMCA became the first militia unit in the country to form a unit of light horse-drawn artillery, which was at that time called "flying artillery." Now they could provide the hard-hitting, mobile firepower needed to provide support to the Rhode Island Militia. The citizen-soldiers drilled constantly in the art of using the new weapons of war, often attracting a crowd from the citizens of Providence. The pioneering tactics that they developed in these drills included the ability to instantly bring effective fire on targets farther away than ever before seen on the battlefield, as well as maneuvering effectively on the field of battle, bringing the guns to bear on any target that could be seen. Most important, the soldiers of the PMCA began a tradition still carried on today of passing on the knowledge gained by a previous generation to the next. At this time, Col. Joseph P. Balch was in command.[12]

A year later the PMCA was ready to take their new equipment on the road. Accordingly, in late September 1848 they set off for New Bedford, which was at that time, as a result of the whaling industry, one of the wealthiest towns in Massachusetts. They took with them their four new guns and four new caissons, each pulled by four horses. Sixteen drivers controlled the thirty-two horses, while the thirty members of the PMCA sat on the gun carriages or on top of the caissons. Recording Clerk Lippitt reflected that "we made a handsome appearance." When they arrived in New Bedford, the streets were lined with people curious to see the new flying artillery. After the PMCA pitched their tents, which had been sent ahead by train, they partook of an "elegant collation" in a local hotel, listened to many speeches and did "ample justice to the viands and wine on the board." Next day they had a full dress parade through the center of the town before returning to Providence.[13] The following month their new status was made official in time for the state militia exercises. Lippitt recorded with great satisfaction in October 1848 that the company, "after marching upon the hill were placed on the extreme right of the line, for the first time, taking the rank of 'flying artillery.'" This performance before the rest of the state started a tradition that continues to this day, with the artillery being the star of the Rhode Island Militia.[14]

For the next four years, the PMCA drilled conscientiously and adopted a new uniform based on that of the United States Light Artillery, though they decided to have light blue rather than dark blue pants, with a red stripe down each leg, hence the name of artillerymen being called "redlegs." In addition, the uniform consisted of a tight-fitting blue and red trimmed shell jacket, and a large shako with red plume and cord. At the annual drill day in 1851, both their new uniform and their "unusual drill of light artillery" were admired by "a large concourse of spectators."[15]

PMCA member William H. Reynolds had a colorful and very prosperous career. Born

In 1852, the PMCA made an excursion to Boston, drilling on Boston Common and gaining national recognition (PMCA).

"Flying artillery" changed the face of combat in the mid–nineteenth century (RG).

in Richmond, Rhode Island, in 1827, his parents were too poor to permit him to attend college so he started work as a clerk and became known as one of the best cotton buyers in Rhode Island by the time he was twenty-one. He joined the PMCA in 1847 and became third sergeant two years later. Then he left suddenly, being "seized with the California fever," made a fortune as a partner in an import-export firm in San Francisco and returned to Providence in 1853. He was a strong supporter of William Sprague and was active in the Civil War. Reynolds led the first three-year battery that left Rhode Island, and they were attached to Gen. Burnside's Brigade at Bull Run. Later the Treasury Department used his skills and contacts as a cotton buyer to secure Southern cotton. He resigned in the summer of 1862 to pursue his own business affairs. After the war, he went into business, owning cotton mills and ironworks in Rhode Island, immense tracts of land in the West, mines in Colorado and Mexico, and navigation rights in South America, he introduced the Bell telephone system in England. He was also active in the PMCA. As his obituary noted, with commendable understatement, "he has carried on the business of a promoter on a very large scale."[16]

In September 1852, the PMCA spent a week camped on Boston Common. Under the command of Joseph P. Balch, they paraded and drilled and showed their speed in firing, despite the torrential rain. They galloped around the common and fired one hundred shots in just over six minutes. A local newspaperman was there and was amazed by the Rhode Islanders' performance. Although he had seen a similar drill performed by the men of Thomas West Sherman's Battery of the Third United States Artillery at Fort Adams in Newport, the reporter was more impressed by the volunteer militia from Rhode Island: "The Providence Corps, fired *one hundred* guns (notwithstanding a rain storm), in a second over six minutes with four pieces, while Sherman's Battery took seven minutes. The drill and discipline of the Marine Artillery was most excellent."[17] The expedition was commemorated in verse ("Poem on the Excursion to Boston") by Thomas Campbell, a member of the PMCA:

> (The Flying Artillery: A Parody on Hohenlinden)
> In Boston at the sun's retreat,
> All mudless was the trodden street
> And fierce and glowing was the heat
> Of Sol declining rapidly.
> But Boston saw another sight:

A letter from the Boston Artillery thanking the PMCA for their training services (PMCA).

When the rain beat at dead of night;
With not a star of Heaven to light
   The darkness of her scenery.
All drenched and drabbled by the storm
Each horseman urged his steed along
And every dripping soldier's song
   Was, "Oh for a bed's sweet luxury."
Then shook the sky with thunder riven,
Then rushed the steed by fury driven,
And wetter than the rain of heaven

Came the Flying Artillery.
And wetter shall those soldiers grow,
On Boston Common's surface low,
And faster still shall be the flow
　　Of floods descending rapidly.
Tis morn yet scarce one soldier brave
Can look upon the clouds that lave
In that dark and thundering grave
　　That forms a threatening canopy.
The thunder deepens. On ye fools,
Who rush to Boston through the pools!
Enjoy thy ardor e'er it cools
　　And charge with thy Artillery.
Ah! few there be that shall return
Without some headache or ill turn.
And brighter shall the fires burn
　　To dry each soldier's drapery.
　　　　　　　Tydides[18]

Local citizens were so impressed with the PMCA that in a matter of weeks a light artillery battery was formed in Massachusetts, and its officers traveled to Providence to learn the secrets of the PMCA's efficiency. They were drilled by Col. Balch at the armory on Benefit Street. Thus the Providence Marine Corps of Artillery can claim with some justification to be the progenitor of the flying artillery in Massachusetts as well as in Rhode Island, and by extension in many other states of the United States.[19]

5

COLONEL WILLIAM SPRAGUE
AND THE PMCA

You have made your drill a science as well as of use, a study and a progress, so unlike your former parade of show.

— Col. William Sprague, PMCA

Over the centuries, many men would have a lasting impact on the PMCA, but perhaps none more than William Sprague, who joined the corps in his late teens. He was elected first lieutenant when he was twenty and treasurer two years later. Although he resigned in 1853 after a stint as second lieutenant colonel he returned as colonel in 1856, his election being due in equal parts to his enthusiasm for things military, his political connections, and his deep purse. In his later political life, some would attribute his leadership and professional skills to those he learned in the PMCA.[1]

William Sprague, the "Boy Governor," was one of the most colorful and controversial figures in Rhode Island history. Born to great wealth in 1830, he dramatically increased the holdings of his family firm, A. & W. Sprague, so that by 1873 the Spragues' net worth was said to be nineteen million dollars. Along the way, he offended many of the most powerful people in the state, notably "Boss" Henry B. Anthony, a Republican senator and owner of the *Providence Journal*. Sprague ran as a Democrat for governor in 1860, spending $125,000 of his own money amid accusations of large-scale bribery. His enthusiasm, plus his money, enabled Rhode Island troops to reach Washington within days of the outbreak of the Civil War, and his brother Amasa Sprague supplied many of the horses from family firms. Sprague served as an aide to Col. Ambrose Burnside at the Battle of Bull Run, though he declined the offer of a brigadier generalship, insisting he should be a major general instead. Sprague served as governor of Rhode Island until 1863 when he took his seat in the United States Senate, serving as a Republican from 1863 to 1875. In the late 1860s his industrial empire started to falter, and the local banks, heavily influenced by the Browns and the Goddards, refused to extend his credit. He responded with a series of speeches in the Senate criticizing the grip of capital on government, which further outraged his political opponents.

In 1873, in the middle of a countrywide financial crisis, the Sprague industrial empire declared bankruptcy. Zechariah Chafee was appointed trustee but somehow managed to emerge wealthy and unscathed while few creditors were paid and Sprague lost almost everything. Meanwhile, Sprague's private life was in shambles. He had married Kate Chase in 1863. She was the beautiful and ambitious daughter of Lincoln's secretary of the treasury Salmon P. Chase and wanted to use Sprague's wealth to further her father's political career. The marriage was turbulent and each accused the other of infidelity. In 1879 Sprague tried to shoot Senator Roscoe Conkling, whom he believed was having an affair with his wife. After widely publicized and scandalous proceedings, Kate Chase was granted a divorce in 1882. Sprague remarried the following year and retired to Canonchet, his large and ornate house at Narragansett Pier. He died in Paris in 1915 at age eighty-five.[2]

William Sprague was a very active commander, taking part in drills and parades as well as dinners and celebrations. Under his watch the PMCA acquired two brass twelve-pounder howitzers, together with all the necessary ancillary equipment such as a traveling forge, five battery wagons, and " a sett complete of Drag Ropes, Bricoles, Prolongues, Picket Ropes," as well as entrenching tools "sufficient for six pieces."[3] In addition, they bought a complete set of overcoats, plus an entire new uniform, consisting of dark coat, black pants with a red stripe, fatigue cap and white gloves, for each member. Furthermore, they obtained a complete set of horse equipment for the sergeants and noncommissioned officers and pistols for the officers and a complete stand of rifles. Everything but the clothing was supplied and paid for by the state.[4]

The PMCA had a fundraiser in 1856 to pay for the new greatcoats. The "Overcoat Collation" featured stewed oysters, eight kinds of meat, and five sorts of dessert, plus ice cream and nuts, all liberally washed down with champagne, brandy and sherry. There were speeches by nine officers, and, according to the program card, "during the interval of picking teeth, Messrs George Peabody, Alex. Duncan, John C. Fremont and others will amuse the company by relating numerous 'Nanecdotes' of their childhood sports." The money was well spent and paid for this vital piece of clothing to keep the men warm; now no weather could stop the PMCA from drilling.[5]

Sprague encouraged his men to drill, offering prizes for the detachment recruiting the most new members or exhibiting the best drill. This emphasis on competition was not, however, without its down side, as the men were encouraged to fire their fieldpieces as fast as possible. On July 4, 1856, for example, a proud clerk recorded that using four pieces they had fired a salute of one hundred guns in four minutes twenty-six seconds "in honor of the day."[6] Less than a year later this pride in speed led to an unpleasant incident when Corp. Charles Lincoln, "in the act of withdrawing his rammer," was burnt "very severely in the face and eyes." Corp. Nathaniel Searle, who was standing about eight feet away, described the confusion, recalling "there were several boys back of me hallooing 'Load' 'Fire' and other orders and at the fifteenth discharge he could not recall who gave the word 'Fire' as there were so many orders given." After listening to a dozen or more eyewitness accounts, Col. Sprague attributed the accident to "carelessness," and so the matter rested, at least for a while.[7]

(Corp. Searle was not to rest, however. A few weeks later he turned up for a corps meeting presumably the worse for drink; he was charged with "insubordination and improper conduct." After interviewing Searle, Sprague reported that he "appeared

Col. William Sprague brought the PMCA into the modern era and later served as governor and U.S. senator from Rhode Island (RG).

Col. Sprague often had the PMCA parade through Providence (RG).

to feel very sorry for his conduct" and he was reinstated on September 28 in "good standing" with the corps. His good standing did not last long, however, as four days later he drowned in Narragansett Bay. At first efforts to find the body were fruitless, so Sprague ordered a piece to be fired in order to bring the body to the surface. Although the minutes do not record whether this effort was successful there was a body by October 12 when PMCA members attended his funeral and his fellow corporals acted as bearers.[8])

There was a strange postscript to the injury of Corp. Lincoln accident. In November of the same year the Seventh New York Militia Regiment, in whose honor the salute had been fired, sent a thousand dollars for the support of Corp. Lincoln's wife and children. This was an enormous amount of money. The PMCA appointed Col. Sprague and Capt. William Parkhurst trustees "to use the same for the sole use and benefit of himself [Lincoln] and family as they may in their discretion see fit paying to him the income from the same and such part of the principal from time to time as they may deem necessary for his support and for the best interests of the wife and children of the said Lincoln."[9]

Lincoln continued to be a member of the PMCA, and soon became armorer. At a banquet to celebrate William Sprague's return from Europe in 1859, he reappeared dressed in the uniform of a Zouave that Sprague presented to the corps.[10] The saga of Lincoln was not yet over, however, as by 1864, matters were seriously awry and he was accused of misappropriating PMCA funds. His response was that he used the money "for support of his family, to keep them from starving and himself from jail — and that the company owed him money with which he intended repaying it." The PMCA set up a committee to investigate: a week later Lincoln resigned and the matter was dropped.[11]

Liquor was clearly a problem in the 1850s; as militias were part social club, alcohol in most militia units flowed freely all the time. In 1858, the company clerk recorded with some satisfaction that the recent exercises had gone exceptionally well, noting, "No liquor was furnished the Corps during the day, a circumstance which deserves notice, and this absence added much to the efficiency displayed by the Corps."[12]

A more unusual disciplinary problem was noted at great length in the PMCA minutes; this was the case of Pvt. William Barker's dog. It seems that Barker left the ranks without permission and then conducted himself in "a disorderly fashion" in "attempting to fight with Armorer Hammond." It seems that Barker's dog had followed him to the armory and was running around "obstructing the movements of the line." Hammond put it outside but it came back in through a side door. At this point Lt. Col. Charles Tompkins insisted that the dog be put out, upon which instruction Barker announced that if the dog went, he went too, took off his coat and lunged at Hammond. When questioned later, Hammond testified that Barker "did not appear under the influence of liquor, and seemed about as usual." The corps made at least two attempts to try Barker, who in time-honored barrack-room lawyer fashion argued that the prosecution, conducted under the State Militia law, was illegal. Barker was voted, after vigorous debate, guilty by a vote of twenty to fifteen.[13]

Barker was not the only PMCA member in trouble. At the next meeting four men — Corp. Charles Addison, Corp. Robert White, Corp. Willis J. Thornton and Pvt. William T. Lawton — were charged with disorderly conduct. They seemed to have had quite a party: according to the charges recorded in the minutes they "did by theft possess themselves of liquors belonging to the officers," then they "did partake" of these liquors "to

In 1856, as shown by this expansive menu, the PMCA hosted a fine supper to pay for a new set of overcoats (PMCA).

excess, in the armory" and then were "parties to the destruction of [a] certain looking-glass, three spittoons and other articles, the property of the corps."[14] The men apologized, begged for lenience, and the charges were withdrawn. Drilling, meanwhile, continued unabated.

These events, trivial as they may seem, were symptomatic of Sprague's efforts to tighten up discipline, and under his watch the PMCA's equipment was updated, the Benefit Street Arsenal was finished and drilling improved, in particular to the art and science of gunnery. His successful efforts to upgrade their efficiency meant that by 1859 he could tell the corps, "You have made your drill a science as well as of use, a study and a progress, so unlike your former parade of show."[15]

Some of Rhode Island's most prominent citizens served in the ranks during the antebellum period. Among the distinguished members of the PMCA in the nineteenth century, with the date of their highest rank in the corps were the following:

CAPT. WILLIAM R. STAPLES (1825): later chief justice of the Rhode Island Supreme Court.

QUARTERMASTER SAMUEL AMES (1836): later a state supreme court judge.

1ST LT. SETH PADELFORD (1837): Governor of Rhode Island from 1869 to 1873.

LT. JABEZ C. KNIGHT (1838): Mayor of Providence and paymaster general of the state during the Civil War.

LT. JOHN RUSSELL BARTLETT (1840): Rhode Island secretary of state from 1855 to 1872. In the antebellum period, he explored the West and mapped the boundary with Mexico. He was a noted bibliophile in addition to editing the epitome *Memoirs of Rhode Island Officers*.

2ND LT. HENRY LIPPITT (1842): Governor of Rhode Island from 1875 to 1877.

QUARTERMASTER WILLIAM RODMAN (1842): Mayor of Providence from 1857 to 1858.

SURGEON USHER PARSONS (1844): Served on Oliver Hazard Perry's flagship at the Battle of Lake Erie in 1813.

John Russell Bartlett served in the PMCA, later becoming Rhode Island's secretary of state. He was also a noted bibliophile and western explorer (Library of Congress).

QUARTERMASTER EDWARD MAURAN (1845): Became adjutant general of Rhode Island during the Civil War.

LT. COL. CHARLES T. ROBBINS (1850): Afterwards he was major general of the State Militia, and in 1862 he was briefly the colonel of the Ninth Regiment of Rhode Island Volunteers.

COL. JOSEPH P. BALCH (1849–1852): Major commanding the First Rhode Island Regiment at Bull Run and a brevet brigadier general of volunteers.

CAPT. HENRY HOWARD (1850): Governor of Rhode Island from 1873 to 1875.

COL. GEORGE M. ANDREW (1853–1856): Joined the Regular Army as a major and after the Civil War was commander of the 25th United States Infantry.

PVT. GEORGE W. ADAMS (1854): Served bravely as a lieutenant in Battery B and was later made captain of Battery G, where he was brevetted three times for gallantry. Led the mission that earned his battery seven Medals of Honor on April 2, 1865.

LT. LYMAN B. FRIEZE (1857): Became quartermaster general of the state during the 1860s.

CAPT. WILLIAM PARKHURST (1857): Served in the Civil War as a staff officer

An unidentified member of the PMCA wearing the 1859 uniform (RG).

and later joined the Third Rhode Island Cavalry as lieutenant colonel.

PVT. THOMAS DOYLE (1856): Mayor of Providence 1864–1869, 1870–1871, and 1884–1886. He married William Sprague's sister Almira.

COL. WILLIAM SPRAGUE (1856–1860): Governor of Rhode Island 1861–1863; United States Senator 1863–1875.

QUARTERMASTER JOHN G. HAZARD (1856): Fought in the Civil War as captain of Battery B. He later became chief of artillery in the Second Army Corps. He replaced Charles Tompkins as the regimental colonel and became a brevet brigadier general.

MAJ. HENRY T. SISSON (1858): Became colonel of the Fifth Rhode Island Heavy Artillery, then lieutenant governor of the state 1875–1877.

LT. COL. WILLIAM H. REYNOLDS (1860): Became lieutenant colonel of the First Regiment of Rhode Island Light Artillery.

COL. CHARLES A. TOMPKINS (1860): Became colonel of the First Regiment Light Artillery and chief of artillery of the Sixth Army Corps. He was promoted to brevet brigadier general.

PMCA member Edward C. Mauran was Rhode Island's adjutant general during the Civil War (USAMHI).

SGT. GEORGE E. RANDOLPH (1860): Served in Battery A as a sergeant and was promoted to captain of Battery E. He was commander of the Third Corps Artillery Brigade and was severely wounded at Gettysburg. He was eventually promoted to colonel by brevet.

LT. WILLIAM B. WEEDEN (1860): Served as the captain of Battery C. Later became a well-regarded Rhode Island historian.

SGT. CHARLES D. OWEN (1861): At the age of nineteen he became the youngest battery commander in the Union Army, leading Battery G. Resigned in 1862 to take up millwork.

PVT. T. FRED BROWN (1861): Quit Brown University to join Battery A. As a lieutenant and captain he became the well-respected commander of Battery B and was severely wounded at Gettysburg.

LT. COL. EDWIN C. GALLUP (1863): Captain of the Tenth Rhode Island Battery in 1862 and 1863.

LT. COL. JOHN A. MONROE (1868): Captain

George Randolph was a PMCA member who served as captain of Battery E (USAMHI).

Left: *Thomas Doyle served in the PMCA and was a longtime mayor of Providence (RG)*. Right: *Col. Charles Tompkins of the PMCA created the finest regiment of light artillery to serve in the Union Army (USAMHI)*.

of Battery D, First Regiment Light Artillery, and rose to the position of chief of artillery of the Ninth Army Corps as lieutenant colonel.[16]

In the war to come, these men would bring fame and honor to their state on many bloody fields at the head of one of the finest combat forces the world has ever seen.

When he was elected governor in 1860, Sprague left the PMCA in more than capable hands. This was in the form of Col. Charles H. Tompkins. A twenty-seven-year-old merchant with piercing blue eyes and wearing a flowing beard to cover up his boyish looks, he had been active in the PMCA since 1853. Among Tompkins' first duties as commander was to lead a contingent of the PMCA to Ohio, the longest and last of the unit's antebellum outings. On September 10, 1860, a statue to Rhode Islander Oliver Hazard Perry was erected in Cleveland. Governor Sprague was invited to represent Perry's home state of Rhode Island and brought Secretary of State John Russell Bartlett, a former PMCA member, and the First Light Infantry, together with the PMCA. As usual, the PMCA contingent made a fine appearance, receiving praise for their piety by attending a Sunday church service. After dedicating the monument to one of the state's most famous sons, the PMCA again performed well at a ball given in Rhode Island's honor. At the concluding dinner, Governor William Dennison of Ohio praised Col. Tompkins for the fine showing and offered a toast in his behalf, stating, "To the citizen-soldiery of Rhode Island — Energetic, prosperous, and patriotic in their pursuits of peace; capable, successful, and honored in the issues of war." The colonel was honored by the recognition and replied to the governor that he "felt proud in his command" and looked forward to continuing the training regimen. Before parting, Governor Sprague invited Dennison to Providence to watch the PMCA drill in the tactics of flying artillery.[17]

With the Ohio expedition behind them, Col. Tompkins and his men again carried on with their weekly meetings and training. As the new colonel of the PMCA, Tompkins would continue what Sprague had already begun. He was more than sure that his Rhode Island boys would be ready for anything to come their way. War clouds were rolling in, and the time would soon arrive when the PMCA would put their scientific drill to good use. Soon farmers' fields and city streets would become killing grounds and the men from Rhode Island would be in the thick of it all.[18]

6

Artillery Primer

No arm of the service calls for greater intelligence, capacity, and judgment than the light artillery.

— Lt. Col. J. Albert Monroe, First Rhode Island Light Artillery

These words were written by Lt. Col. J. Albert Monroe in 1886. The leader of a battalion of artillery during the bloodiest single-day battle in the nation's history, Monroe was a member of the PMCA who knew how to handle his guns in combat. During the Civil War, field artillery was unique among the three main branches of both Federal and Confederate armies: infantry, cavalry, and artillery. The officers who commanded and the men who carried out their orders each had a specific function as they performed their deadly duties. At their hands were the most modern killing machines of the time, capable of dealing out death and mayhem at ranges never before seen on the battlefield. They were also equipped and organized along different lines than their counterparts in the infantry and cavalry. The tactics, weapons, and drill of the mid nineteenth century deserve to be told in full, in order to better understand their function on the battlefield.[1]

The basic building block of the artillery was the battery. A battery was the equivalent of a company in the infantry or cavalry. It was composed of either four or six artillery pieces, referred to as guns. The unit contained 150 men at full strength and was commanded by a captain. During the Civil War, Rhode Island raised ten batteries, eight of which served as part of the First Rhode Island Light Artillery Regiment. Although a regimental structure was in place, the units served independently of their regiment, reporting directly back to the adjutant general's office in Providence. In the Union army, the batteries were formed into commands of four to eight units called artillery brigades, from which they were attached to the much larger corps, which formed the Union army in the field.

An individual battery rarely mustered its full strength, often only numbering one hundred men when in combat. As casualties mounted, they were allowed to draft men from the infantry regiments who would serve a given period as an attached man, working for and assigned to the battery. Once the command left the state, recruits were sometimes hard to obtain, even though they wanted to join the light artillery. Politicians sent them to the infantry regiments where more commissioned officers would bring more political favor. A soldier was normally always at home acting as a recruiter, trying to draw additional men to the battery, which sometimes worked and oftentimes failed. The Rhode Island batteries would always be short of men in the field. The field artillery was considered the safest branch of the service to join, but would often see the most hazardous service on the battlefield. Although relatively small, a battery provided as much firepower as an infantry regiment and at a greater distance.[2]

A battery organization was broken down into two to three smaller commands called

A typical Union artillery battery in combat with all men at their posts (Library of Congress).

sections, each containing two guns. They were designated as the, right, center, and left sections. The sections were commanded by a lieutenant. The next level of organization was called a detachment under a sergeant and contained not only the actual artillery piece but a caisson as well. The cannon and caisson had a corporal in command of each piece of equipment.[3]

A captain commanded the battery. His was a position of great responsibility, honor, and scrutiny. A guidebook for officers offered the following: "A battery commander should possess not only executive ability, but he should be mentally qualified, as well as naturally inclined, to acquire a familiarity with every detail of the material under his charge." The captain was positioned in the middle of the battery so he could keep an eye on the action around him. Always near him was a musician and the guidon bearer, a soldier who carried a small American flag and served as the captain's orderly. In the initial assignment to the Rhode Island batteries, all of the first captains were members of the Providence Marine Corps of Artillery.

By the end of the war, with one exception, all of the battery commanders who began the conflict as enlisted men were promoted through the ranks to receive the double bars of a captain, the insignia of his rank. This position required the officer to perform many duties, such as maintaining order and inspecting the men daily. The captaincy brought with it a certain sense of pride because a battery was a reflection of its commander; it was only as good as he was. When assigned to the larger artillery brigades, field officers were often in short supply. At such times, the senior captain would command the brigade. The Regulars were often hampered by the fact that the artillery captains left their batteries to become generals in the infantry. During the Civil War, a captaincy was often the highest an artillery officer could aspire to. Most states did not have a full regiment of artillery as Rhode Island did; few of the artillerists made it to these higher ranks.[4]

In a six-gun battery, two first and two second lieutenants were assigned to the unit. The two first lieutenants commanded the right and left sections, while the most junior officer commanded the center section so the senior officers could watch him and cover his flanks. The lieutenants identified the target, called out the range, and ordered what type of ammunition was to be used upon it. Thus, an artillery lieutenant had a far greater responsibility than an infantry platoon commander. He not only had this duty but also had to act as an ordnance officer, engineer, topographer, and adjutant, all during battle. The senior second lieutenant commanded the caissons, baggage train, artificers, and other spare men. In addition, the senior first lieutenant served as the second in command and took care of the long trails of paperwork the battery produced. When the captain was absent, the senior first lieutenant commanded the unit. Because the larger artillery brigades often did not contain the staffs necessary to properly operate them, one subaltern was normally always permanently detached on staff duties ranging from being a judge advocate to an aide-de-camp. When this occurred, the first sergeant or a duty sergeant commanded his section. If too few officers were present with the battery, the officer in command would divide it in half and give each lieutenant three guns to command.[5]

One of the most crucial positions in the battery was that of the first, or orderly, sergeant. Designated by three stripes surmounted by a diamond, this man insured that the day-to-day operations of the battery as ordered by the captain were carried out. Wherever the captain went, the first sergeant was close by and answered only to him. He also maintained the books and accounts of the battery. This sergeant could hold the noncommissioned officers and privates to discipline on his own accord and was required to report it to the captain only after the fact. In addition, he always knew where the privates were; those failing to report were bound to be assigned to extra fatigue duty. The first sergeantcy, as with all noncommissioned positions, was directly appointed by the captain, and this honor was given to only the most qualified, sober, and respected of the sergeants.[6]

William S. Perrin was one of the many young lieutenants who performed a multitude of tasks in battle, until he lost a leg at Ream's Station (RG).

Unique to the light artillery was a quartermaster sergeant. Because the units were separated from their parent regiments, this noncommissioned officer collected and distributed food for the men and forage for the horses. In addition he maintained a supply of clothing, which he was responsible for. The position was often filled by a clerk or merchant from civilian life, for they had the experience necessary to maintain the many required accounts for each army department. A recruiting poster for a Rhode Island battery announced, "Every company is allowed a Quarter Master Sergeant, thereby dispensing with red tape circumlocution in this department." The quartermaster sergeant did not have to go into combat and remained in the rear watching the baggage wagon and other equipment left behind.[7]

Every battery had six duty sergeants called the "chief of the piece." These men were the true leaders in any battery, commanding a detachment of sixteen men. "He should have all the dash and impetuosity of a cavalry and, all the coolness of an infantry commander, for at times he must throw his piece forward like a whirlwind to the very front line and fling his iron hail into the very ranks of the enemy," wrote one Rhode Island battery commander. Under the command of this man were the artillery piece and the men who performed the work. He required a cool head and calm demeanor, but he had to be stern and insure all was moving smoothly on his gun. The position also required the sergeant to have the same knowledge as a lieutenant; oftentimes the officers would allow the sergeant to work his own gun in combat, as he knew the piece best. When not engaged in battle, the sergeant lived with and supervised the daily fatigue details of his men. An artillery sergeant had the same responsibility as an infantry first sergeant. He called the roll of his men and issued them their rations.[8]

At nineteen, PMCA member Charles D. Owen became the youngest battery commander in the Army of the Potomac (RG).

The corporal was the living embodiment of the soldier, clean, disciplined, and well drilled. In a battery there were twelve corporals, two assigned to each detachment. The first corporal was called the gunner and supervised the cannon. After the sergeant identified the target, the gunner sighted the piece using a pendulum sight and an elevation screw near the breech of the gun. Since there was no indirect fire capability, as such, the corporal had to see the target and have a clear line of sight for the round to find its mark. When the gun was loaded and ready, he gave the order and the cannon was fired. The second corporal was referred to as the chief of the caisson. He was positioned near the second vehicle in the detachment. This corporal supervised the ammunition being supplied and maintained a listing of what type of rounds were being fired. When the ammunition was gone in a limber chest, the chief of the caisson supervised the changing of the chests containing the rounds to insure the gunner always had a constant supply. When a sergeant was disabled, a corporal would move up to command the detachment; likewise when there was no corporal present, a private became a lance, or acting, corporal. In camp, the corporal directly supervised the men and led fatigue duties, guard mount, and other mundane camp tasks. Because of the small size of a battery, and a larger amount of noncommissioned officers, privates in the artillery had a far better chance of sewing on the coveted two stripes of a corporal than in an infantry company.[9]

Each battery was assigned two musicians who played the bugle. In order to insure they were proficient with the task, professional musicians were ideal for the position. In the smoke of the battlefield, oftentimes the sounds of the bugle were all that could be heard to command the men. The bugler had to memorize thirty calls. So vital was this task that musicians were

Top: *One of the most important leaders in the battery was the first sergeant. First Sgt. William Child commanded Battery B after the debacle at Ream's Station (RG).* Bottom: *Sgt. Albert Straight of Exeter was typical of the gruff, no-nonsense sergeants who led the men and guns into combat. Sgt. Straight died of disease in 1863 (RG).*

paid an additional dollar per month. In order that they would be seen on the battlefield, the buglers were mounted on white horses and wore distinct red herringbone trimmed jackets.[10]

Due to the mobile nature of the battery, equipment was bound to wear out and break down. Consequently each battery was assigned two blacksmiths who operated a small forge from which they could make and shod the over 100 horses assigned to a battery, in addition to fixing the metal on the vehicles. Two harness makers maintained the yards of leather harnesses needed to hook the horses to the carriages and the other leather implements. In addition, two wheelwrights did as their name implies; they replaced the broken wood on the carriages, and performed other duties given to them. Furthermore, several wagoners drove the necessary wagons containing the vital supplies. These soldiers remained in the rear during battle, often completing repairs while the carnage raged around them so the guns could quickly return to the front. All of these men were referred to as artificers.[11]

The most important men in the battery and the ones that it could not function without were the 122 privates who composed the bulk of the unit. In the light artillery, privates were divided into two categories: cannoneers and drivers. During the forming of the command, the privates had a choice as to what position they wanted to take. Many considered the drivers to have a safer position in combat but serving on the gun to be a higher honor.

The drivers were responsible for the horses that pulled the guns and caissons. Each vehicle was assigned six horses, which were harnessed together in three sets of two. The drivers rode on the left side and had to control both horses; their equipment was carried on the right horse so that if they had to switch them, the other horse was used to the weight of the driver. From the front, the pairs were named the lead, swing, and wheel horses. The drivers

Above: *Musicians served an important task in any battery. Bugler John F. Leach of Battery A was cited for bravery under fire four times (RG).* Right: *Corp. Henry E. Nye of Battery F was one of many young Rhode Island gunners who accurately sighted their cannons (RG).*

had to be watchful for the horses colliding together while the battery galloped into action, so they wore a metal brace on their right leg to protect it. During combat, the drivers remained mounted on their horses in the event the battery had to quickly limber up and change position. The horses assigned to the command were often sick and unused to the rigorous service of the artillery. They were often leftovers, after the cavalry and medical corps had received the best mounts. However, the drivers were proud of their horses, spending many idle hours grooming and tending to the animals. Veterinarian care was unknown and many horses died along the road during the long marches. One of the few ways to stop a battery in combat was to shoot at the horses. In their after action reports, battery commanders always gave two counts of their losses: men and horses.[12]

The cannoneers were part of a brotherhood; they depended upon each other for their very survival. Each man was assigned a position, which had a specific task. They had to work as one on the battlefield; if they did not chaos would occur. Not every man was suited for the light artillery. Sergeant John H. Rhodes of Providence wrote of the ideal qualities of an artilleryman:

> A first class cannoneer had to be cool, intelligent, keen, and quick to understand, also being able to perform the duties of two or more posts at the gun, as was often necessary when in action. A slow, awkward person should hold no place in a gun detachment. A detachment of artillery was

like a machine, no one worked individually but all in unison and with the precision of clock-work, every man on time and in time; one mistake or awkward movement would cause confu-sion and tend to dire results. If one or two men were suddenly disabled it would cause confusion and retard its working; but such was not the case, provision was made for casualties but none for mistakes or blunders.

Each soldier learned the details of the job above him, and indeed those below him. As such the field artillery became the crack branch of the Union army.[13]

Every member of the gun crew was assigned a number and was known by that number in action. The Number One man stood to the right muzzle of the cannon. He was equipped with a large staff called a sponge rammer. On one end was a wool swab that was dipped in a bucket of water attached to the front of the gun that was then inserted into the cannon to extinguish any embers remaining from the last shot. This was one of the most significant actions in the battery. If there were any sparks remaining in the barrel, the next round would explode when it was inserted. In the heat of combat to ensure a faster firing of the gun, Number One would sometimes forgo sponging, often resulting in an explosion. On the opposite end was a flat rammer used to push the round down the muzzle and seat it at the breech of the gun. Across from him was Number Two. His task was simple; he inserted the round into the piece.[14]

Of all the men in the detachment, Number Three held the lives of the others by his thumb, and was the most important man on the entire team. He stood near the breach of the cannon, in back of Number One. On his left thumb was a small glove called a thumbstall that

Left: *Pvt. Albert Whipple served as a driver and was wounded at Gettysburg (RG).* Above: *Thomas Aldrich of Providence served as a driver (RG).*

Top: *The cannoneers were part of a brotherhood who had to work together to fire the cannon (RG).*
Bottom: *Civil War drivers often had to face the elements to deliver the guns into action. Here Battery G confronts a swamp at the Battle of Fair Oaks (RG).*

was placed over the vent at the rear of the piece as the tube was sponged. The vent was the small opening into the powder chamber that permitted the fire from a primer to ignite the powder charge and the firing of the gun. If Number Three did not properly seal the vent, air would enter the hole and fuel the glowing embers in the tube. When the round was inserted the entire gun crew was at risk. Even in combat and fast firing, the vent was covered. The devotion of Number Three to his comrades was so much that if his thumbstall was burned away, he would stick his bare thumb over the vent, allowing it to burn down to the bone rather than give up the vital task. He also carried a small brass pick. The implement was inserted into the vent to open the powder bag below so it would ignite. Standing across from Number Three was the Number Four man, who actually fired the gun. He was equipped with a small box called a fuse pouch, which held friction primers, a copper tube containing fulminate of mercury and gunpowder. Four also carried a yard-long lanyard, which was hooked to the primer. When the gun was sighted, Number Four stepped to position and inserted a primer into the vent. With a steady pull, the fulminate of mercury exploded, sending a flame into the powder bag and the round out the cannon.[15]

The remaining cannoneers were stationed at the limber, which was the key to the American light artillery system. A two wheeled vehicle, it was used to pull the cannon and caisson. Upon it was an ammunition chest. Each cannon was assigned a caisson. This vehicle carried two additional chests of ammunition, a shovel and ax, spare limber pole and wheel; in addition it served as a place for the cannoneers to place their personal equipment. In the light artillery the cannoneers walked; only the officers, sergeants, and staff rode. If the battery needed to get into action quickly, there was room for the men to ride three abreast on the limber chests. As there were no shocks, they were in for the army version of a "Nantucket sleigh ride." The caisson was required to always follow the cannon it was attached to, as a gunner could go through a large amount of ammunition in a short time. The drivers were told they should follow the piece, "even if it went to hell." The caissons were so often bristling with the enlisted men's personal gear so that orders had to be given to reduce the equipment so the vehicle would not resemble a baggage wagon.[16]

Joseph D. Corey of Battery D served as a cannoneer (USAMHI).

Number Five stood to the left of the limber and moved the ammunition up to Number Two in a large leather bag. Instead of the standard black leather worn by the infantry and cavalry, all of the artillery equipment was made of russet colored leather. Number Six retrieved the ammunition from the chest and had a vast array of tools to cut fuses for the explosive types of ammunition. Number Seven handed the ammunition to Five and also alternated in running rounds forward. Number Eight was also the chief of the caisson and tendered to that vehicle.[17]

The caisson and limber provided the cannon with ammunition (RG).

Upon arrival into position during battle, the cannon would instantly be detached from the limber and swung into action. The lieutenant or sergeant would identify the range to the target as they relayed the information to the gun crews. Number Three stepped forward and stopped the vent, as One sponged the tube. Number Six selected the round, inserted the fuse if called for and passed the round to Seven, who gave it to Five to run forward and hand to Number Two. Two took the round and inserted it into the gun, as One quickly rammed it home. The gunner sighted the piece, as Three pricked the cartridge and Four inserted the primer, as he attached the lanyard. Once all was clear, the piece was ready to fire. When the command was given, Number Four pull his hand to the left and the cannon was fired. A battery could unlimber and begin firing in under a minute, while a good crew could fire two aimed shots in a minute.[18]

An artillery battery in combat was no place for those without a stout heart and an iron will. As soon as the gun was fired, mountains of smoke bellowed out of the muzzle, obscuring the battlefield. The recoil and noise were immense; after each shot the piece had to be rolled back into position. The first few rounds were critical for a commander to see where the shells were landing. Through the smoke, the musicians would be heard echoing their shrill bugle calls as the officers and sergeants screamed commands to the men loading and firing as fast as they could. As fire was exchanged, enemy shells screamed into the position. It was here that both officers and men showed their mettle: "Amid the noise of the guns, the tearing and bursting of the enemy's shot, the blinding smoke and general uproar, he can preserve all his facilities unimpaired." Men and horses would be shot down, and the privates instantly stepped into position to relieve their dead or wounded comrades. All of this chaos led to it being called an "artillery hell."[19]

The tactics used by the artillerists in the Civil War were updates of those used by the American artillery in Mexico. The standard manual was titled *Instructions for Field Artillery*. It was 404 pages long and written by three experienced Regular Army artillery officers, all of whom rose to the highest ranks during the war. One of the authors was Henry Jackson Hunt, who would go on to command the artillery in the Army of the Potomac. The manual combined tactical thoughts with the duties of each man, including how to maneuver by section and battery. In addition, it contained information on ordnance, vehicles, and other pertinent information of the battery's operations. Handsomely wrapped in red Moroccan leather, the tome was commonly referred to as "the red book" by the officers. A battery officer would not be found without a copy; it was sold at several locations in Providence for three dollars.[20]

Due to the three-section complement, the battery could engage separate targets at the same time. Principal dictated two main types of firing practices: counter-battery fire was used to suppress enemy artillery and antipersonne fire to stop advancing infantry or cavalry. A commander's goal was to place his battery in a position to enfilade an enemy's flank with fire, thus causing it to collapse. Standard principle in the early stages of the war directed that guns be used mainly on the defensive, while remaining stationary; it seemed as though what had brought success on the fields of Mexico had been forgotten. Beginning at Chancellorsville, some brash young commanders would revive the old system by using the guns as an offensive weapon. This included moving while under fire, shooting over the heads of friendly troops at extreme long range, and using the right type of ammunition on target. The artillery remained vulnerable to an assault, so an infantry regiment was usually stationed near it to protect the guns. Frequently the rigorous gun drill was laid aside so the men could get the pieces into action and firing in the shortest amount of time, but also assuring that every round hit its target.[21]

The field artillery was divided into two main types: rifled and smoothbore pieces. In the Union army, a battery contained the same caliber guns; this was so that the same ammunition was present, making it easier to supply from the quartermaster. Furthermore, the pieces were named after the size of the ammunition they fired, such as a twelve-pounder Napoleon, which shot a twelve-pound iron ball and had a 4.62-inch bore. An artillery brigade would have pieces of different types and calibers to insure a corps could provide its own firepower at different ranges. Confederate artillery was hampered by having several different caliber pieces in one battery, often placing one section out of combat when the guns could not hit at that range.[22]

The rifles, as their name implies, had a series of lands and grooves giving a spin to the round, which allowed it to hit targets at a maximum distance of two miles. Some gunners could accurately place a round through a window at one mile. Two main types of rifles were the mainstay of the Federal light artillery; both fired a three-inch diameter round, which weighed ten pounds. The three-inch ordnance rifle was the preferred rifle of the Union field artillery. It was also the lightest of the field guns, weighing slightly over 800 pounds. The ordnance rifle was made out of welded iron bands, which strengthened the piece so it would not burst. The gun never failed in combat and was favored by all who used it — Federals who were issued the cannon and Confederates who could capture it. On the opposite side, cannoneers hated to be on the receiving end of its fire, as the rounds were bound to hit their target at long range.

The counterpart of the ordnance rifle was the ten-pounder Parrott, identifiable by a large metal jacket welded around the breach to strengthen the weapon. Two types of Parrotts were issued, one with a 2.9-inch diameter barrel, the other three inches, creating logistical nightmares for the overworked ordnance officers. These cannon were made of cast iron, which often resulted in air bubbles forming in the metal. The poor construction often resulted in the gun exploding on the battlefield. The Parrott earned the sobering title of "the cannoneer killer." A larger version of the Parrott firing twenty-pound projectiles was sometimes utilized by both sides.[23]

The first Rhode Island units were armed with the James Rifle, the first piece of rifled artillery used by the United States Army. They were designed by Charles Tillinghast James of East Greenwich, who developed a unique way to transform old, worn-out smoothbores into new, highly effective rifled pieces. Because they were bronze tubes, firing an iron projectile, the rifling in the barrels quickly wore down. In addition the shells did not always explode properly upon impact. Furthermore, in their three engagements — Bull Run, Bolivar Heights, and Balls Bluff — the weapons had proven to be very inaccurate, so much so that at Bull Run the rounds were later found three miles from their intended targets. As a result, the Rhode

Top: *The ten pounder Parrott was a favored gun among Rhode Island cannoneers and was effectively used by Battery A at Antietam (RG).* Bottom: *The James rifle was first used by Rhode Island soldiers (RG).*

C-Battery cannoneers (DiMaria).

Islanders turned the guns into the Ordnance Department and were reequipped with standard field pieces. (James would be killed by his own invention in 1862.[24])

In the Mexican War, all American artillery pieces were brass smoothbores, most of which fired a six-pound projectile. As the Civil War began, the six-pounders were relegated to training duty, and in its place came the twelve-pounder Napoleon. Based on a French design, the smoothbore Napoleon could fire a projectile up to 1,300 yards. This gun was made of bronze instead of iron; like the ordnance rifle, it never failed in combat. This cannon was also the heaviest in the Federal field arsenal, weighing over 1,200 pounds. The Napoleon was referred to as a gun-howitzer in that it replaced the older howitzers, guns that fired explosive shells at a high degree of elevation. This cannon was the preferred smoothbore weapon of the Civil War.[25]

A battery or section commander had four different types of ammunition to fulfill his mission, each designed for a specific purpose. Solid shot was a ball of iron used to punch a hole in the target or engage in counter-battery fire. The old Regular Army officers put much faith into this round and often scolded their young subordinates for relying upon explosive rounds. Shell was similar to solid shot, but it was hollow in the center, the cavity packed with gunpowder. Shell was used to engage enemy troop formations and could go into a target before exploding.

Case shot and canister were the two most lethal types of ammunition. Case consisted of a hollow cavity, which was packed with lead balls and powder. It could be used in any capacity

and wreaked havoc on enemy infantry columns and disabled artillerymen in counter-battery fire. It required Number Six on the gun crew to cut a fuse for it to work properly. Canister turned the cannon into a giant shotgun, the shot was a tin can containing large iron balls. Canister was an antipersonell weapon used at distances of under 400 yards. The iron balls left the container and scattered upon being fired. This round was most effective fired from a smoothbore, as it had a greater scattering effect. Canister was particularly harsh on a rifled gun, as it damaged the rifling; in addition, it was not as effective because of the smaller bore of the barrel, which negated the scatter effect. If a battery was facing the enemy at extremely close range, double and even triple rounds could be fired to keep the foe at bay. If a commander ran out of canister, he

Above: *The three-inch ordnance rifle was the preferred rifled cannon of the Civil War (RG).* **Right:** *Maj. Gen. Henry Jackson Hunt commanded the Army of the Potomac's field artillery and was one of many Regulars who respected the Rhode Island Light Artillery (RG).*

could switch to shell or case shot without a fuse, as it would explode upon leaving the muzzle.[26]

Smoothbores used the same type of ammunition, manufactured in government arsenals. Made into a single round with the powder bag attached, the whole projectile was inserted into the cannon. The United States government issued many contracts to private contractors for the rifle ammunition, named after the company it was made by. This ammunition had to be the caliber of the cannon, but it varied in quality. Rifle ammunition would pose a problem throughout the entire war as rounds blew up in the gun or did not take to the rifling. In addition, the rifle required two actions to be loaded. Number Five first had to bring a linen powder bag to Two, which had to be rammed home before Seven brought the round up.[27]

Between the brutal years of 1861 and 1865, these tactics, weapons, and skills would be used by many artillerymen wearing both blue and gray, on battlefields throughout the United States. Many of the tactics, weapons and skills were pioneered in a small gray armory on Benefit Street in Providence, Rhode Island. It was from this building that one of the finest groupings of men to ever wear the blue and red of the United States Army would hail. In the storm to come, the PMCA would become legendary and earn the title "Mother of the Batteries."

7

THE CIVIL WAR

The conduct of officers and men was gallant in the extreme and merits the hearty commendation of all who witnessed it. Rhode Island has just cause to be proud of such men.
— Col. Charles H. Tompkins, First Rhode Island Light Artillery

Years of sectional conflict over the debate of slavery and states' rights had caused militias on both sides to drill and equip constantly. After the John Brown Raid of 1859, both sides knew what was coming: a terrible conflict. Col. Charles Tompkins, the new commander of the PMCA, made sure to drill his men frequently, for he was sure they would be in the center of the storm. Much of the South had cheered when William Sprague, a Democrat, was elected governor of Rhode Island in early 1860. Southerners pointed to the Democratic victory in a northern Republican state as further evidence that the North was divided on the issue of secession. They were wrong.

Although the abolition movement was indeed weak in Rhode Island and Sprague's win was due in large part to his conservative views on the issue, the former commander of the PMCA was firmly committed to maintaining the integrity of the Union. Rhode Islanders shared this commitment and later that year voted overwhelmingly for the Republican presidential candidate, Abraham Lincoln. They then watched in disbelief as one state after another seceded and as nearly half of the United States Army, including dozens of high-ranking officers, pledged loyalty to the South.

With the Providence Marine Corps of Artillery refitted and readied, the unit became the crack instrument of the Rhode Island Militia. With the election of Abraham Lincoln to the presidency of the United States in 1860, there was little doubt that a war would be coming soon. In late 1860, Governor Sprague sent Maj. Joseph Balch of the corps to visit Maj. Gen. Winfield Scott to offer the Rhode Island Militia for service. Scott rebuffed Balch. Knowing that a war was not yet occurring and not wishing to strain tensions between North and South, he did not accept the offer. Remembering his War of 1812 service, Scott told Balch, "I know the stuff they are made of. The Rhode Island men were the best troops I commanded." Scott's compliment would soon be put to the ultimate test.[1]

Lincoln believed that until his inauguration on March 4, four months after his election, he could do or say little to stem the secession movement. In the meantime, incumbent President James Buchanan insisted he lacked the legal authority to coerce the seceding states into remaining within the Union. "A feeling of alarm that well-nigh grew into terror was developed throughout the North among the loyal citizens, and was fully experienced in Providence," wrote Welcome Arnold Greene in his 1886 history of the city.[2]

In December and again in January, Governor Sprague offered Buchanan the services of his state militia, but the president, like Gen. Scott, flatly rejected both offers, not wanting to push the South into the war. He would let Lincoln handle it. "It was a time that tried men's

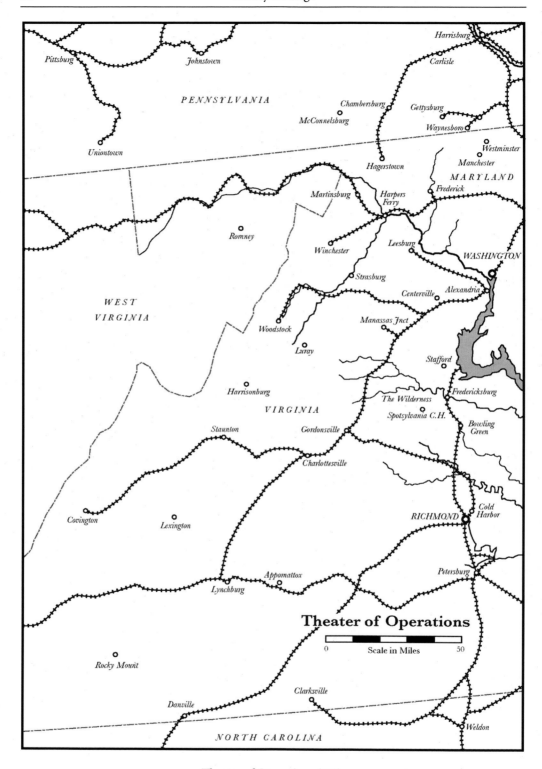

Theater of Operations

Scale in Miles 0 — 50

Theater of Operations (RG).

***The smoothbore Napoleon was the predominate fieldpiece of the Civil War and was both feared and
respected by friend and foe alike (RG).***

souls," Greene noted. "We of the North were lying supinely on our backs, held by reverence
to the forms of the law, while the executive, whose duty it was to enforce the laws and protect
the country, was allowing the vulture of secession unobstructively to tear out its vitals."[3]

Despite the rejected offers of help, Sprague ordered sixty-four new overcoats for the
PMCA and urged his former battery to intensify training for what he feared lay ahead. Like
others, the governor remained convinced that a military conflict was inevitable. On February
22, 1861, the First Light Infantry and the PMCA held a special service at the Benefit Street
Arsenal in memory of Washington's birthday. The main speaker was Episcopal Bishop Thomas
M. Clark, who told the following to the more than 100 PMCA officers and men who participated in a parade and ceremony:

> I am glad to see the officers and members of the Marine Artillery present with us today. The
> sight of this company with its formidable equipments, its ponderous cannon manned by such
> sturdy and courageous men, always impress me with a sort of peculiar majesty. It comes with it
> the thought of invincible power, of terrible facility, and range of execution in the hours of bat-
> tle. The thunder of your guns breaks upon the stillness of the air like a voice of superhuman
> warning, forefending assaults of any foreign foe, and silencing the murmurs of domestic rebel-
> lion. Days of terrible contests and nights of weary watching may await you. The turf may be
> your dying bed and the drum your requiem. The two great virtues of a soldier are courage and
> obedience. I do not believe that you will be wanting in either.[4]

Although a religious man by training, Bishop Clark was a member of Rhode Island society
and knew that the PMCA would be needed in the war that even the staunchest supporter of

peace could not doubt was coming. The thunder from Providence would soon be heard nation-wide.

In February, Maj. Balch was again dispatched south to visit Lincoln's private secretary to ask if the guns would be of any service during the inaugural in March. There was a perceived fear that Lincoln would be assassinated as he entered the city. The president-elect did not accept the offer of the escort. Eager for his small state to show their ardor, Sprague wrote another letter to Lincoln on April 11, just hours before the storm broke. In the letter, the boy governor promised the president that Rhode Islanders "would do their utmost to maintain the Union." Sprague then reported on the military conditions in the state: "We have a Battery of Light Artillery, 6 pdrs, horses + men complete—Unsurpassed or at any rate not surpassed by a similar number in any country—who would respond at short notice to the call of the government for the defence of the capital. The artillery especially, I imagine would be very serviceable." The time had come for the Rhode Island cannoneers to show their mettle.[5]

It was almost with relief that the PMCA and other Rhode Islanders learned of the April 12 attack on Fort Sumter, a Federal outpost in Charleston Harbor, South Carolina. Even before Lincoln issued a call to arms three days later, Sprague offered the services of an artillery battery from the PMCA and a regiment of 1,000 volunteer foot soldiers, under the command of Col. Ambrose E. Burnside, to defend the capital. Sprague himself would accompany the Rhode Island regiment as Burnside's volunteer aide.[6]

In his April 15 proclamation, Lincoln called for 75,000 men for a period of ninety days, the maximum term of service a militia could be sent outside its own state. Just hours later, at an emergency meeting held that night at the Benefit Street arsenal, seventy-five PMCA members eagerly signed a pledge to serve, while hundreds of jubilant city residents milled about outside. "The greatest excitement was manifested, not only inside but outside," noted the PMCA clerk in his reports. "People crowded in and around in every direction as far as they could hear or see, manifesting great intent in the proceeding and occasionally cheering for the country, the flag and the battery. Never was there so much confusion in and about the arsenal as there was during the whole time until the [battery] left for the seat of war."[7]

Within days, many more would sign the pledge, far more than the 145 needed for the battery of light artillery that would depart on April 18 under the command of Capt. Charles H. Tompkins. That morning, as the officers and men were busily moving around the arsenal preparing for war, moving horses and gun, Lieutenant Governor Samuel Arnold, himself a member of the PMCA, appeared and addressed the men regarding the duty before them:

> It is no holiday sport for which you have volunteered. A firm resolve on your part to submit cheerfully to the most rigid discipline without regard to personal comfort can alone bring to that state of efficiency, which the crisis commands. Anyone who hesitates to endure every hardship, to obey without question every order, to think of himself merely as part of the corps, or to merge his individuality in the organization should leave at once. A glorious cause demands that life itself should be given up if need be, a willing sacrifice upon the altar of our country.

Little did the Rhode Islanders know, but many of their number would be required to give the supreme sacrifice in the years ahead.[8]

In full dress, Tompkins' Battery filed through the massive doors of the armory and, with hundreds of cheering spectators in tow, marched down Benefit Street to Fox Point. There the men boarded the *Empire State*, the steamer that would take them, along with their 100 horses and six smoothbore cannon, to Jersey City, the first stop on their journey to the nation's capital. They were the first troops of any state to leave for the war and the first volunteer battery mustered into the United States Army during the Civil War.[9]

As their vessel pulled out of the harbor and headed down Narragansett Bay, the men

The PMCA was the first unit of northern militia to respond to Lincoln's call. Here they leave Providence on April 18, 1861 (RG).

heard a parting cannon salute fired off Fields Point by their comrades in the PMCA who had stayed behind for an important task, to train future Rhode Island artillerymen. "Almost every vessel in the vicinity was covered with spectators and every available standing place had its occupant," reported the *Providence Journal* the following day. "[It] presented a spectacle such as has not been witnessed in the lifetime of a majority of those who beheld it."[10]

From Jersey City, the battery marched to Easton, Pennsylvania, where it exchanged its smoothbore guns for James rifled cannon; the old six-pounders were returned to the Benefit Street Arsenal to be used as training implements for future Rhode Island artillerymen passing through its massive doors. The unit became the first battery of light artillery in the United States Army to be equipped with rifled cannon. "They fire with great exactness," a private noted in a letter to the PMCA. "They were made for Alabama but were never delivered because the state seceded."[11]

The men remained in Easton for a week of drilling, impressing Regular Army officers with their skill and dexterity, and then moved on to Washington. Marching gallantly down Pennsylvania Avenue on May 2, the battery halted in front of the White House to parade before President Lincoln. A Washington correspondent watching recorded the event: "The magnificent Providence Marine corps artillery passed in review before President Lincoln, who expressed himself as much pleased with the completeness of the battery, and with the patriotism of the noble little State which has come out so nobly in defence of the Union." The PMCA was the first artillery battery to reach the nation's capital.[12]

With a Regular Army of fewer than 17,000 men, most of them stationed on the western frontier, Lincoln soon saw the need for additional volunteers. In his second call on May 3, the president asked for a pledge of three years or the duration of the war, whichever was shortest. The three-month militia terms of the past would hardly provide the experienced soldiers required for what many now feared was to be a lengthy conflict. Many of the men who enlisted in the early regiments, including the First Rhode Island, would provide the necessary trained cadre of officers needed to train the new volunteers.[13]

Anticipating the need for more men, Rhode Island began recruiting immediately after the departure of the First Regiment and First Battery in April. Four days after Lincoln's second call, Sprague authorized a second artillery battery, drawn from the ranks of the PMCA, to be known as the Second Rhode Island Battery under the command of Capt. William H. Reynolds[14] and the Second Regiment of Rhode Island Volunteers, commanded by Col. John S. Slocum, a highly decorated Mexican War veteran. Like the First Battery had been before them, the Second Rhode Island Battery was the first three-year volunteer battery mustered into the service.[15]

On June 22, after several weeks of training at Providence's Dexter Training Ground, the Second Battery and the Second Regiment joined their fellow Rhode Islanders at Camp Sprague just a mile north of Washington. After a brief ceremony there, "the lines were soon dismissed and there was great intermingling, hunting up old acquaintances, shaking hands and getting news from home," reported a private in the First Battery.[16] The men in the First Battery were particularly delighted to see Capt. Reynolds, a much loved and admired officer who had left their battery a month earlier in order to command the new unit.

On July 9, during a routine drill, a tragic accident occurred that shook Reynolds to the core. Improperly packed ammunition in the limber box of one of the cannons had exploded, killing two men, Pvt. William E. Bourn and Corp. Nathan T. Morse, and injuring three others. "For the first time since leaving Providence I was not present at the drill," wrote Reynolds to the PMCA commander, Benjamin F. Remington. "You may have some conception of my feelings as I rode forward to the hospital and there found the mangled bodies of my dead and dying men who had but an hour before left their quarters in good health and spirits. Col. Burnside, Governor Sprague and Col. Slocum told me that there was no blame or fault with me or my officers, but I feel heart sick. I should not feel as badly if twenty men had been killed in battle as I do about this." There was a lesson to be learned from the tragedy; field artillery was a dangerous enterprise and great care had to be taken with the ammunition.[17]

While the men of the Second Battery dealt with tragedy at Camp Sprague, the men of Capt. Tompkins' First Rhode Island Battery had been sent into the Shenandoah Valley and continued to drill high on the plateaus around Harpers Ferry, Virginia. Maj. Gen. Robert Patterson, an aged War of 1812 veteran, attempted to launch a campaign to retake the old armory town, held by Gen. Joseph E. Johnston and made famous by the radical abolitionist John Brown. While the First Rhode Island Regiment had returned to Camp Sprague, the Rhode Island Battery remained, as it was the only artillery in the area. The steep terrain and peaceful setting provided ample opportunities to practice the art of gunnery. As Patterson and his troops marched endlessly about in the area of Charles Town, Virginia, Johnston slipped away to report to Gen. Pierre G.T. Beauregard at Manassas Junction. He did, however, leave a rear guard of cavalry near the small crossroads town of Bunker Hill.

On July 15, the Providence Marine Corps of Artillery, in the guise of the First Rhode Island Battery, had its baptism by fire. Gen. Patterson saw the Rebels in a woodlot and instantly called on Capt. Tompkins to engage. Augustus Woodbury recalled what happened next: "The battery fired a number of rounds, shelling the woods, freeing them from any lingering party of the enemy, mortally wounding one officer, and two privates, and slightly injuring a sergeant. The battery took possession of the vacated rebel camp, the fires of which were still burning." Not one Rhode Islander was injured in the engagement.

Although forgotten in history today, the July 15, 1861, engagement at Bunker Hill would have serious ramifications for the PMCA. It was their first real engagement, barring the 1842 action at Acote's Hill, and would set a precedent in the Union army: to always call on the Rhode Island Light Artillery. The battle would play an important role in the history of the PMCA, in setting their tradition on the fields of the South. Only two weeks later the enlistments of Capt. Tompkins' Battery ran out and the men returned to Providence to a hero's welcome; nearly all would see service again, while their captain would see stars in his future. Unfortunately, their service in the Shenandoah Valley was not successful and Patterson's inability to detain Johnston would have serious consequences.[18]

Among the men of Tompkins' Battery who had been sent back to Washington was Pvt. James Allen of the PMCA. Allen had experimented with the new art of ballooning before the war and brought this knowledge to war with him. He recruited Pvt. William H. Helme of the First Rhode Island Regiment and the two set about building two balloons for use in reconnaissance operations. Gen. Irvin McDowell became impressed and was looking forward to gaining the information used in the flights. Unfortunately, the two balloons were destroyed before being used in combat. In the battle to follow, McDowell was saddened not to have the Rhode Islanders and their balloons. Augustus Woodbury wrote: "The commanding general was deprived of information which would have been of great advantage on the day of battle." Allen later joined Thaddeus Lowe's United States Balloon Corps and fought in the Peninsula Campaign of 1862, finally getting to use the device to observe Confederate troop movements.[19]

The mood at the Union camp on July 20, the eve of the First Battle of Bull Run, was almost jubilant. The recruits would finally meet their enemy and, they thought, quickly crush them. "We soon had fires burning and coffee cooking in our cups," wrote Pvt. Elisha Rhodes of the Second Rhode Island Regiment, which would be supported the following day by the Second Battery. "I enjoyed the evening by the fire and speculating on what might happen on the morrow." Others, however, were more apprehensive, including Rhodes' commanding officer, Col. Slocum, who told Col. Burnside, "Today victory and a star or a soldier's grave."[20]

Burnside's Brigade, which included the Second Battery, the First and Second Rhode Island Regiments,[21] the Second New Hampshire and 71st New York, was attached to Gen. David Hunter's Column. The Second Rhode Island, followed closely by the Second Battery, led the advance and were the first two units to engage in battle. The Second Rhode Island had entered the fray and begun a desperate engagement when but five minutes later Col. Burnside ordered, "Forward Your Artillery." The unit was going in to support their brothers and provided critical point-blank fire support against the enemy infantry and artillery. Among the earliest of the day's casualties

Battery C's William S. Perrin wears the unique Rhode Island uniform of 1861. He ended the war as a brevet captain, a testament to the training given by the PMCA to promote worthy soldiers from the ranks (RG).

The Rhode Island Brigade fought hard at Bull Run (Library of Congress).

was Col. Slocum, who went down yelling, "Now show them what Rhode Island can do!" The words would become a rallying cry among Rhode Islanders throughout the rest of the war. The brave colonel would die two days later of his wounds, a true Rhode Island hero.[22]

The battle raged most of the morning. For an hour, alone and unsupported, the two Rhode Island regiments and their battery held Matthew's Hill against two brigades, waiting in vain for reinforcements to come up. When it was over, over 200 Rhode Islanders lay dead or wounded on the slopes of the hill — a heavy toll for the smallest state thus far in the conflict, and the second bloodiest day in Rhode Island history. Of the men in the Second Battery, three were dead and fourteen were wounded. By early afternoon there was a lull in the fighting as both sides backed down for the death blows to come in the afternoon. Union soldiers smelled victory; civilians, many of them with picnic lunches, cheered them on. Yet as the battle resumed, with the arrival of fresh Confederate troops, some of them Johnston's men, the tide began to turn. Strong Union artillery held the enemy back for a while, but was decimated when the 33rd Virginia, dressed in blue uniforms and mistaken as battery support, were allowed to come within seventy yards of the Union guns.[23] The fatal mistake occurred just as the Rhode Islanders had positioned its guns between two other batteries. "We withdrew with a loss in material of only a caisson, the pole of which was broken in the endeavor to turn to the side hill," wrote Lt. John Albert Monroe.[24]

As the Union retreat began in earnest, Monroe described the scene as "one of indescribable confusion, although there appeared to be no fright or terror in the minds of the men leaving the field. Officers seemed to have lost all identity with their commands; subalterns and even colonels moved along in the scattered crowd as if their work was over and they were wearily seeking the repose of their domiciles." During the withdrawal, as the Rhode Islanders were being pushed down the Warrenton Turnpike by a furious Confederate bombardment and approaching the Cub Run Bridge, a major problem occurred. The bridge was jammed with traffic and retreating Federal soldiers. Faced with no other option, Reynolds gave the command for the men to abandon the guns and make their way back to Washington as best as possible.[25]

The men of the Second Battery were given quarters that night in a privately owned house in nearby Centreville. Exhausted from the day's grueling battle, the men fell quickly to sleep, most of them on floors, porches and stoops. But they were awakened by the late-night return of Pvt. Charles V. Scott, who in the confusion of the retreat had lost contact with his battery. To the delight and glee of the battery, Scott had not only survived the battle but had also retrieved a precious souvenir. Hitched to the horses he was driving was one of the battery's cannons, a James rifle that had been sent off the field for lack of ammunition.

From July 21, 1861, to the present, this has been the greatest controversy in the history of the PMCA: who actually saved the "Bull Run Gun," as it became known, and which cannon it actually was. There is no doubt that the Second Rhode Island Battery used the James rifle at Bull Run. Shells, fired from this type of weapon only, have been recovered from the site, while all of the veterans are unanimous that the Second Battery was using the same type of James rifled pieces as the First Battery. Indeed, Batteries B, C, and D would all go to war armed with this weapon. There is another cannon in the possession of the Squantum Association in East Providence, Rhode Island, that is also claimed to be the cannon saved from Bull Run. Unfortunately this gun, a six-pound bronze smoothbore cast in 1847, cannot be the Bull Run cannon. This is because of what it is: a smoothbore. The Rhode Islanders were using rifled pieces. The PMCA, however, was using the six-pound smoothbores in the antebellum period, and they continued to be used at the Benefit Street Arsenal for a time as a training aid. This smoothbore cannon was presented to the Squantum Association by Ambrose Burnside and Senator Henry B. Anthony. Clearly the true Bull Run Gun is a James rifle.[26]

The second major disagreement is who actually saved the cannon. There are four names of Rhode Island soldiers, all present at the battle, to whom credit for saving the piece was given. The first appeared in 1864 in Edwin M. Stone's *Rhode Island in the Rebellion*. Stone wrote that the cannon was saved by Lt. John A. Tompkins, Col. Tompkins brother and a PMCA member. This would look like a dramatic gesture by a brave officer, but it could not be, as Tompkins was not in a position to rescue the cannon. Next in line was Theodore Reichardt, who in 1865 transcribed his field diary to publish *Diary of Battery A*. In his small tome, Reichardt that, after the battle, "our battery consisted of one gun, and the six horse team, drove by Samuel Warden." In the years ahead, as the veterans fought each other with pen and paper, neither Stone nor Reichardt would receive much attention.[27]

The most believable account, in 1878, was by PMCA member J. Albert Monroe, who commanded the section to which the cannon had been attached. During the engagement the cannon had run out of ammunition and Monroe sent it off the field. During the retreat it had been abandoned far ahead of the other cannon at the Cub Run Bridge. This is where Charles V. Scott found it. While walking through the woods, Scott explained, he had stumbled across the cannon, still hitched to its horses. With the help of some infantrymen who were also astray, the determined Scott brought the piece back to camp. When it arrived back in camp, Monroe instantly recognized it as his cannon. The sight of their lost gun greatly restored the spirits of the disheartened men and the private was greeted with hearty cheers. Pvt. Scott was recommended for, and would receive, a commission as lieutenant for his actions in saving the gun. Two other members of the battery, including Charles D. Owen, a PMCA member, attested this is what occurred, as Lt. Scott could not speak for himself because he died in the war. Unfortunately, Monroe's account would not be the last.[28]

The last account is that of Thomas Aldrich, who in his 1904 history of Battery A wrote

This James rifle at the Rhode Island State House was the only cannon from the Second Rhode Island Battery to escape capture at Bull Run (State of Rhode Island).

much of the same account of Scott's discovery of the cannon, except Aldrich himself had found the piece in the woods. Furthermore, he adds Governor Sprague into the picture and writes that Sprague ordered the private to drive the cannon back to camp. Aldrich had nearly a half century after the events to craft his own story of what happened, and indeed he would be accused by many veterans of lying. Written so long after the engagement, none of the veterans were left to tell the story of what truly happened in July of 1861.[29]

The Bull Run Gun remained a thorn in the side of the PMCA for decades to come. After the battle the cannon was brought back to Rhode Island and displayed as a war trophy. The Rhode Island General Assembly voted to turn the gun over to Sprague, who displayed it on the lawn of his mansion in Narragansett. In 1863, when he was elected to the United States Senate, Sprague turned the gun over the PMCA, who saw fit to have the following inscription carved on its chase: "The only gun of the 2d R. Island Battery to be saved from the Battle of Bull Run and presented by the General Assembly of Rhode Island to Governor Sprague and by him placed in trust with the Providence Marine Corps of Artillery with the motto Don't Give up Your Guns." Sprague never officially relinquished control of the gun and it was displayed in the Benefit Street Arsenal. In 1869 when serving in the Senate, Sprague lost the support of many veterans when he openly attacked Ambrose Burnside's performance at Bull Run and called his Rhode Island soldiers "a craven band of misfits." This cooled Sprague's once powerful relationship with the PMCA, who refused to turn the cannon over to the senator when Sprague was voted out of office because of his comments in 1874.[30]

For years the cannon occupied a corner of the Benefit Street Arsenal, occasionally being forgotten and neglected by the membership in more turbulent times, until the state erected a small granite pedestal next door at the Old State House, where it was displayed outside. All the while, Sprague tried to get his property back. Finally in the 1890s he told the PMCA, "Are you tired of keeping that gun? If you are let me have it. I'd sink it in the deepest part of Narragansett Bay before I give it up to the state." Finally, in 1903, a new state house was built on Smith Hill and all of the Rhode Island battle flags were moved out of Benefit Street and placed in the new facility with other war relics. Many in the state, including the militia, wanted Sprague's cannon; indeed, they had been trying to have him turn over his deed to it for a decade. Finally, on July 27, 1907, the ex-governor relented and authorized Maj. James Abbott of the Rhode Island Militia to go to the PMCA and collect his property.

When Maj. Abbott appeared at the Benefit Street Arsenal, Col. Charles H. Weaver, the commander, refused to release the gun, telling Abbott that he would have to hold a special meeting before the PMCA would turn it over; it had been in their possession since 1863. The members convened, remembering Sprague's threat to toss the cannon into Narragansett Bay.

Pvt. Charles V. Scott was responsible for saving the Bull Run Gun and was killed at Cedar Creek while trying to save another gun from Confederate capture (RG).

They relented and agreed to turn the James rifle over to Maj. Abbott. On July 21, 1909, the forty-seventh anniversary of the Battle of Bull Run, the veterans of the Second Rhode Island Battery finally escorted their cannon to the new state house, where it was placed in a special hall dedicated to Rhode Island's Civil War relics.[31]

After the engagement, Battery A was sent to Harpers Ferry, where they were met by the men of the First Rhode Island Battery. Before going home, the men of Tompkins' command gave the three-years men their guns to carry on the struggle. The cannon, forever known as the "Bull Run Gun," now resides in the Rhode Island State House with another famous war relic from Gettysburg. With the loss of five of their cannon, the motto of the PMCA throughout the Civil War became "Don't Give up Your Guns."

The first engagement of the Civil War did indeed shake the confidence of the North, but most historians agree that the battle highlighted what would become a Federal hallmark, good artillery. John Rhodes of Battery B wrote, "In this mass of power Rhode Island was fairly represented." Indeed, their performance at the first major engagement of the war had been spectacular. In the next four years, the artillery would emerge as the most efficient arm in the Union armies, and the eight batteries sent from the arsenal on Benefit Street were among the finest in the grand army that went south to fight in the "War of the Rebellion."[32]

During the rest of his term of governor, William Sprague would leave an excellent mark on his state. He spurred recruitment, offering funds and other incentives for men to enlist in the regiments and batteries forming. In addition, he moved the economy of Rhode Island into action to fuel the war effort as the many small mills in western and southern Rhode Island produced cloth for the war effort, and the financial center of Providence funded it. Most important, Governor Sprague was constantly in the field, visiting his Rhode Island soldiers, often acting in his capacity of captain-general of the state militia. During one incident

An August 1861 image after the First Rhode Island Detached Militia returned home. Among the PMCA members present are, far left, Capt. Henry Sisson, who became colonel of the Fifth Rhode Island. Seated to his right are Maj. Joseph Balch and Col. Ambrose Burnside, an honorary PMCA member. Also present are Sgt. Maj. John Shaw, who died at Spotsylvania, and Isaac Peace Rodman (sash across shoulder), who would die as a brigadier general at Antietam. Seated next to Burnside is noted Civil War historian Augustus Woodbury (Library of Congress).

on the Peninsula, Sprague assisted Rhode Island's Battery G in operating its cannon by accurately sighting them at the Confederate works during the Battle of Yorktown. As he had been to the PMCA, Sprague was an inspiration to the Rhode Island soldiery.[33]

Following the departure of the Second Battery in June 1861, at intervals of less than a month, seven additional batteries, Batteries B through H, would leave the arsenal and complete the First Regiment of Rhode Island Light Artillery. The Second Battery was renamed Battery A, as the units became lettered. Capt. Charles Tompkins was promoted to colonel and placed in command of the regiment and the entire complement of field and staff officers of the regiment was composed of PMCA members. Under Tompkins' strict rule of discipline, the men would become professionals. Indeed, it is impossible to separate the identities of the individual batteries of the First Rhode Island Light Artillery without identifying them closely with the PMCA, and the histories of all reach back to the gothic-looking building on Benefit Street. Thirty years after the war, Lt. Samuel Pearce of the Tenth Rhode Island Battery wrote, "The Providence Marine Corps of Artillery was the mother of the ten batteries of light artillery. By sending recruits to fill the depleted ranks they performed an important duty."[34]

On May 24, 1862, the PMCA again responded with vigor to a plea from the president with a "Tenth Battery," recruited for a three-month term to defend the nation's capital.

The First Rhode Island Battery drilled thoroughly at Harpers Ferry (RG).

Stonewall Jackson had broken through the defenses in the Shenandoah Valley and was marching north, for what was feared to be an attack against the weakened capital. Like they had a year earlier, the corps again responded with vigor and within three days a full battery was mustered in and heading south to defend the capital. With so many PMCA members in the field on active duty, the battery was commanded by Capt. Edwin Gallup.

The men were eager for action, but unfortunately the would-be soldiers were sorely disappointed. While the men of the other nine units gained glory and fame on the battlefields, the soldiers of the Tenth Battery simply drilled in Washington, waiting for the call to arms that never came. Because it was a PMCA battery however, the enlisted men were drilled ruthlessly. Their only task was to guard the southern approaches to the capital; one corporal was killed by a runaway limber in a training accident.[35]

The First and Tenth batteries, and most of Battery A, were manned with members of the PMCA, but enlistment for all ten batteries took place at the organization's arsenal. The soldiers of Batteries A, B, C, D, E, F, and G actually joined the PMCA as members of the Rhode Island Militia, subject to the orders of PMCA officers. They remained in the pay of the state, drilling at the arsenal until the batteries were mustered into Federal service and left the state. Thus nearly every Rhode Island cannoneer served in the legendary organization, benefiting from the rigorous training that was provided. By 1862, the process was curtailed, as the recruits were sent directly to the batteries in the field; here the new recruits quickly came to grasp the demanding tactics of the light artillery. Ledgers with the signatures and occupations of the recruits, many of them still teenagers and some unable to write their own names, remain in the arsenal's archives. The PMCA provided a valuable cadre of trained officers to all the Rhode Island batteries. Indeed, those members who stayed behind helped just as much by training the eager but uneducated volunteers at the Benefit Street Arsenal. "By 1863 there had been enlisted for the Light Artillery Regiment, principally at the armory, 1,552 men who left the city under the command of 36 officers," noted the PMCA clerk.[36]

Throughout the war, the Benefit Street Arsenal was full of activity as men prepared to leave for war, while the PMCA continued to meet as an organization. The results of what happened in the small gray building on the hill were quite amazing. In the tight confines of the arsenal, the men of the PMCA were ruthless in their training. One small mistake on a gun

Left: *A prewar PMCA member, Harry Cushing enlisted in Battery A, gained a commission in the Regular Army and retired after twenty years of service as major of the 17th Infantry (RG).* Right: *Lt. Henry Pendleton was a member of the battalion of heavy artillery trained by the PMCA (RG).*

could result in the deaths of ten men; each step, each minute skill was practiced repeatedly, hour after hour. These discharged soldiers had seen the results of fighting when undisciplined armed mobs went at it; the results were disastrous. Any error found was bound to get a swift reprimand by a member of the corps. Perfection was at the heart of the PMCA, and nothing short of perfection would be found in the soldiers they trained. "Four hundred and thirty-five men commanded by 15 officers went forth from our armory to fill the Third Regiment R.I. Heavy Artillery. Moreover, twice did the Marine Artillery take the field in defense of the government, with 11 officers and 275 men. Surely our organization may justly lay claim to the title 'Mother of Rhode Island Batteries,'" proudly recalled one PMCA veteran.[37]

Surely it was, for the arsenal housed not only the recruiting activities but also the drilling and training of these illustrious batteries. In nearly every major engagement to come, the men trained by the PMCA would be heard amid the thunder of war. A January 1862 entry in the PMCA's records, detailing the training of one of the batteries, illustrates the arsenal's busy and productive life throughout the early years of the war:

> The 155 men quartered at the Marine Artillery Armory, drilling, eating and sleeping there. Everything is kept in perfect order and the strictest discipline prevails. The kitchen is in the basement and the men pass down there to receive their rations, eating them in the hall above. Meat is served out three times a day and coffee in the morning and tea at night. In the forenoon, squads drill with the pieces, and in the afternoon, the entire corps drills together in marching.[38]

The recruits came from all lifestyles and while most were in their twenties, some were in their forties and others were just out of school. The first batteries drew primarily from Providence and nearby cities, but recruitment later expanded into the state's more rural areas.

Left: *Albert D. Cordner served in Battery G (RG)*. Right: *David B. King was one of many Rhode Islanders who went to the Benefit Street Arsenal to join the artillery. He was killed at Gettysburg (RG).*

Young men hailing from towns like Foster and Exeter, many having never traveled more than twenty miles from their family farms, eagerly signed on for a journey that would shape their lives. Indeed some men would travel from as far as Massachusetts, New Hampshire, New York, and Pennsylvania for the privilege of joining the Rhode Island batteries. "[They] are tough and muscular, most excellent material to make a serviceable and efficient corps," noted the PMCA clerk in his records.[39]

At every decisive battle throughout the war, from First Bull Run to Appomattox, the Rhode Island batteries would win the respect of all who fought beside them. Emblazoned on their ragged guidons were the names of battlefields, towns and rivers that bore witness to some of the most horrific engagements in the nation's history. Today resting behind glass at the Rhode Island State House, the blood-stained, battle-torn flags will soon disintegrate forever because proper conservation steps were never taken. But the men who fought beneath these flags would never forget the carnage and fury they witnessed.

Among the fiercest battles was Antietam,

John G. Hazard enlisted as a private, was quickly promoted through the ranks to the command of Battery B, and ended the war as a brigadier general. He was also active in the PMCA (RG).

fought on the seventeenth day of September 1862. It was a battle remembered as "artillery hell" by Col. Stephen D. Lee, who commanded some of the Rebel guns. In a single day, Union casualties were more than double those of D-Day eighty-two years later. Batteries A, B, C, D and G were all there, representing five of the fifty-seven Union batteries engaged in the campaign. In an army with hundreds of batteries, the ones from Rhode Island were considered the best, and there were never enough of them to go around.

J. Albert Monroe's Battery D of the First Corps and John Tompkins' Battery A of the Second Corps went into position on the western bank of Antietam Creek on the night of September 16. At dawn the next day, the men of the First Corps advanced into the West Woods and Miller's Cornfield along the Hagerstown Pike to attack southern troop positions near the Dunker Church. Attack and counterattack left the field and woods littered with scores of dead

Lt. Phillip S. Chase of Battery F was one of many officers to rise through the ranks because of the training he received from PMCA members (RG).

and wounded from both sides by the incessant rattle of musketry and artillery fire. To aid the badly handled First Corps, the Twelfth Corps went into position into the East Woods; but their commanding general, Joseph Mansfield, was killed before the men deployed, causing panic in the ranks. The soldiers from the Twelfth, including a division led by Warwick's own Brigadier General George Sears Greene, entered the woods and found the Confederates waiting.

Joseph Hooker, in command of one wing of the Army of the Potomac, moved Battery D and the First New Hampshire Battery in to support the faltering infantry. Monroe placed his battery about 125 yards northeast of the Dunker Church and instantly began engaging the Confederate forces to his front. The Confederates shifted four brigades to counter the blow as Monroe ordered his guns loaded with canister and as a brigade of New Yorkers broke for the rear. Mounted on a horse, Monroe coolly directed the fear-driven mass of troops— with his sword — around the guns and directly in back of them. As soon as the Federal infantry was clear, the Rhode Islanders opened fire and quite literally liquidated the Confederates with the deadly blasts at close range. The Confederates engaged as well, hitting Rhode Island cannoneers with deadly accuracy. At one piece, all but two men were hit. Seven cannoneers lost their lives in the deadly fight. Running low on ammunition, and with hardly any Federal infantry left to the front, Monroe and his men had only a few brief moments to wait before the soldiers of Battery A arrived on the field to lend their aid.

Left: *PMCA Lt. Col. William Reynolds was the first captain of Battery A and later served the Union as a cotton broker (RG).* Right: *Edward H. Sears wanted to join the First Rhode Island Light Artillery so much that he resigned a captain's commission in the infantry to become a lieutenant (RG).*

"I have never in my soldier's life seen such a sight," wrote infantryman Elisha Rhodes in his description of the battlefield once the fighting had stopped. "The dead and wounded covered the ground. In one spot a rebel officer and 20 men lay near a wreck of a battery. It is said Battery A, First Rhode Island Artillery, did this work." Engaged for nearly four hours straight, the Rhode Islanders fired a remarkable 1,050 rounds and rendered their guns unfit for further use. Four of their men were killed and fifteen were wounded. The men of Battery A contributed materially to the Federal outcome of the battle, keeping the Confederates at bay near the Dunker Church and later engaging them at Bloody Lane. One historian later wrote that their performance outweighed that of any other Federal battery on the field.[40] In recognition of Battery A's bravery and skill at Antietam's "Bloody Lane," the uniform of its commanding officer, Capt. John A. Tompkins, is now prominently displayed in the National Park Service visitor center there. Meanwhile a line of Parrott rifles marks the position where Battery A fought.[41]

The performance of the Rhode Island artillery in the battle was praised by all those who saw it. Batteries A, D, and G were all heavily engaged. Battery G fought near Bloody Lane, engaging in long-range counter-battery fire and losing five wounded. Battery B was not engaged, and Battery C was held in reserve. After the battle, the *Providence Journal* ran a small statement from the *New York Commercial*: "Of light artillery there is a plentiful supply, and many of the volunteer batteries are equally famed to the famed Magruder's, Bragg's and Sherman's batteries of former days. Rhode Island furnishes the best light artillerymen."[42]

Even more of a compliment to the Rhode Island artillerymen was an editorial printed

Battery A, First Rhode Island Light Artillery, was responsible for inflicting this damage on the Confederates at Antietam (Library of Congress).

in the *Boston Traveler.* From the time Roger Williams had been banished from Massachusetts in 1636 and founded Rhode Island there had always been a sort of animosity between the two states, especially when it came to which was the best. The Bay State newspaper wrote this:

> The different batteries from Maine, Massachusetts, and Rhode Island are the occasion of many favorable comments among military and naval men in Washington. It is due to Rhode Island to say that her artillerists appear the bearer of the palm. The reason for this may be found in the fact that her batteries were among the first of the volunteer force in the field, and consequently, they have had the most practice. As far as the truth of the statement is established, it is credible to your little neighbor.[43]

These statements were but two of the many praising the Rhode Island Light Artillery for their actions on the battlefield. At Antietam, they more than proved to friend and foe alike their capabilities in combat operations.

Just three months later, Batteries A, B, C, D, E and G would meet at Fredericksburg, with Battery B playing a conspicuous role. Rhode Island's own Maj. Gen. Ambrose Burnside, who succeeded Gen. George McClellan as commander of the Army of the Potomac, ordered his men south to Richmond; but the fortified city of Fredericksburg stood in his way. After waiting for pontoon bridges to arrive from Washington, President Lincoln, anxious for victory, ordered an attack. As a soldier, Burnside obliged. The Confederates had built an impenetrable line in the rear of the city. The main focal point of the engagement was to be the capture of Marye's Heights, a fortified hill ranked with artillery and infantry. This action was set in motion despite warnings from Union generals that to do so would be "murder, not warfare."[44]

The battle began on the morning of December 13, 1862, with Rhode Islanders taking a prominent role in the engagement. In one bloody assault, 220 men of the Seventh Rhode Island went down in a gallant charge that almost brought them to the Confederate line. This was the bloodiest single-day loss by a Rhode Island regiment in any battle of any war. During one critical point in the battle, the Federal high command realized that they needed to relieve

Left: *Pvt. John Lawrence of Providence was killed at Antietam serving in Battery A (RG)*. Right: *Lt. John Knight Bucklyn earned the Medal of Honor for heroism at Chancellorsville (RG)*.

pressure on the assaulting infantry columns. The best way to do this was to send a battery onto the field, right into the midst of the hurricane of lead, to try to defeat the Confederates' own batteries, which were destroying the attacking Federals. The unit selected was Capt. John G. Hazard's Battery B, First Rhode Island Light. "There goes Battery B to hell," yelled men from Battery A as they watched their fellow Rhode Islanders make their way, under murderous fire, to within 150 yards of Marye's Heights. Upon being told by a staff officer that "a battery cannot live there," Maj. Gen. Darius Couch barked, "Yes, but it can die there."[45]

"The battery's position was a perfect hornets' nest," wrote Capt. Hazard, a PMCA member. "Minie balls were flying about with a zip and w-w-w, or a thud as they struck; though they flew thick and fast, the men were too busy to dodge. It was remarkable, considering the close action with the enemy, that none of the battery men was killed." Battery B held its ground for nearly a half hour before being replaced by another unit. Unfortunately Hazard was wrong in his judgment; of the seventeen men wounded, four later died because of their injuries. This deed inspired many of the infantrymen to hold on, despite the long odds against them. Battery B by sacrificing itself had performed the main duty of an artillery unit: to support the infantry with sheer firepower.[46] "Men never fought more gallantly," wrote Gen. Couch, who had ordered the charge. This one-day battle was the deadliest day in Rhode Island history. Eighty men died and over 300 more were wounded in the desperate charges up Marye's Heights.[47]

While seven of the eight batteries of the First Rhode Island Light Artillery Regiment fought through the "perils and glories of the Army of the Potomac," one of them did not. Perhaps Battery F is the forgotten battery of the regiment. It was raised in the early fall of 1861, primarily of men from Bristol and Newport counties. Unlike the other batteries, the first captain of Battery F was not a member of the PMCA. Capt. James Belger had served ten years in the Regular Army, including a tour at Fort Adams. As a first sergeant, he had fought with

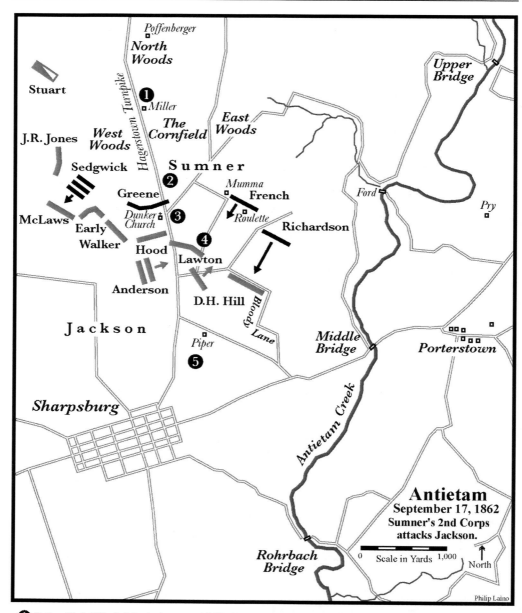

❶ Battery D, 1st Rhode Island advances with Hooker's 1st Corps. This first Federal assault fails.

❷ Battery A, 1st Rhode Island advances with Sedgwick. The 2nd Division of the 2nd Corps is mauled by McLaws.

❸ Battery G, 1st Rhode Island unlimbers near the Mumma farm and then is told to support Sedgwick. They deploy where Battery D had fought but as Sedgwick is routed, they withdraw back to the Mumma farm.

❹ Battery A, 1st Rhode Island has been withdrawn to a ridge north of Bloody Lane but runs out of ordinance. They are replaced with Battery G. After dueling with Confederate artillery, they then fire on Bloody Lane.

❺ Confederate artillery masses near the Piper house. Battery G starts a counterbattery duel with rebel guns.

The Battle of Antietam (RG).

Battery I of the First United States Artillery when they were overrun at Bull Run. Rather than marching to the Peninsula in the spring of 1862, Battery F joined Ambrose Burnside's Coast Division, which captured much of the North Carolina coast in March and April of 1862. Because of problems landing the horses from the vessels carrying the battery, the command was unable to fight at the Battle of New Berne. They were the only group of Rhode Island cannoneers until World War II to make an amphibious assault, thus carrying on the original function of the Providence Marine Corps of Artillery.

For the next four months however, the Rhode Islanders, because of the availability of their horses, served temporarily as cavalry. With no regular mounted forces in North Carolina, Burnside used Belger's men as pickets to scout the roads leading to New Berne. This was a very perilous operation, as the countryside was crawling with Confederates and the soldiers were armed only with their sabers. In late June the Third New York Cavalry relieved the Rhode Islanders, who soon took up garrison duty at New Berne. Because there was little enemy action, the men were supplied with full Regular Army dress uniforms, including dress helmets, and shoulder scales. They performed parade and escort duties, and fired the occasional salute for visiting dignitaries.

In December of 1862, the men of Battery F joined the Fifth Rhode Island and other Union regiments in a raid towards Goldsboro to ascertain if additional missions into the interior of the state were possible. The battery engaged the enemy at Goldsboro, Kinston, and Whitehall. At the latter battle on December 16, they successfully covered the withdrawal of a Union brigade as the Confederates pushed the Federals back towards New Berne. The Rhode Islanders held firm and lost two killed and four wounded. Much of 1863 was spent in New Berne.

In the spring of 1864, Battery F was

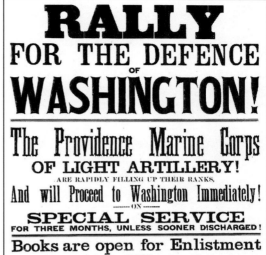

Top: *Recruiting posters were effective for gaining men for the Rhode Island batteries. This one is for Battery F (RG).* Above: *Pvt. Henry Hicks of Battery A lost both his feet at Fredericksburg (RG).*

*Left: **Pvt. John S. Babcock had a very unfortunate Civil War. He was wounded at both Marye's Heights
and Cedar Creek, and was captured after the Battle of Gettysburg (RG).** Right: **William J. Kenyon of
Battery B rose from private to first sergeant in one week (RG).***

transferred to the 18th Corps of the Army of the James as they pushed up through southern
Virginia near Petersburg to capture Richmond. At Drewry's Bluff and Proctor's Creek, Battery
F held firm; but at the latter battle it was overrun and suffered severe loss, including Capt.
Belger, who was captured. He eventually escaped that fall and was mustered out. Arriving at
Petersburg, the soldiers of the regiment finally met the men of the other Rhode Island batteries,
as Battery F had never been seen by these men. Although often engaged in parade and garrison
duty, the soldiers of Battery F proved to their comrades in the summer of 1864 at Petersburg
that they were not bandbox soldiers, but rather Rhode Island artillerymen, of that same mettle,
trained by the PMCA.[48]

After surviving a terrible winter, where dozens of Rhode Island cannoneers died of disease, the Federals were looking for retribution. It came five months later at Chancellorsville.
The Rhode Islanders again fought with distinction in one of the Confederates' greatest victories. At a small clearing near Fair View, Battery E remained in position, when all others had
run away, and tried in vain to stop Stonewall Jackson's flank attack. They remained until all
of their ammunition was expended and the Rebels were within twenty-five yards of the guns.
In addition Batteries A and C fought the enemy to a standstill near Chancellorsville itself. At
a separate engagement near Fredericksburg on May 3 called Marye's Heights, Batteries B and
G fought with great gallantry. Battery G, under command of Capt. George W. Adams of the
PMCA, who had held the captaincy for only eight hours, was sacrificed by Maj. Gen. John
Sedgwick to buy time for his Sixth Corps to form up and assault the hill. The Rhode Islanders
lost heavily, including Lt. Benjamin E. Kelley, who as a high school student had studied tactics

Battery B fought under hot conditions at the Battle of Fredericksburg (RG).

with the PMCA. Capt. Adams and his Rhode Islanders purchased the time with their blood, which allowed Sedgwick to successfully take the hill. After the disaster at Chancellorsville, the batteries of the First Rhode Island Light Artillery joined the Army of the Potomac in a march north to destiny.[49]

At Gettysburg, the bloodiest battle of the war, Rhode Island Batteries A, B, C, E and G once again brought honor to their small state, as well as to those units. Three of the Army of the Potomac's artillery brigades were commanded by Rhode Islanders. It was the bloodiest battle in the regiment's history; at the end of the three days, twenty Rhode Islanders were dead and another eighty were wounded. During the brutal fighting on July 2, Batteries B and

Battery E attempted to hold back Stonewall Jackson's assault at Chancellorsville (RG).

E were overrun and shattered, but the enemy paid dearly for their act. Again, the Rhode Islanders sacrificed themselves so that others could live. Among the wounded was the PMCA's captain, George Randolph. Many credited John G. Hazard's skilled handling of the Second Corps Artillery Brigade with holding the center of the Union line and winning the day. Battery B stalled the Confederates long enough for Union reinforcements to come up and plug the gap; a quarter of the battery went down, including PMCA member and battery commander 1st Lt. T. Fred Brown. While Batteries A, B, and E fought with gallantry, Batteries C and G of the Sixth Corps had an equally hard time in getting to the battlefield, marching nearly forty miles in one day.[50]

On July 3, 1863, in fighting described as the "most terrible ever witnessed on this continent," the Confederates began a massive bombardment on the center of the Union line on Cemetery Ridge in preparation for the infantry attack known as Pickett's Charge. Batteries A and B from Rhode Island were in the center of the storm. During the cannonade, a Rebel shell struck Battery B's fourth gun, killing Privates Alfred G. Gardner and William Jones, who were in the process of loading the piece. Jones was instantly killed, as his head was blown off, and Gardner lost his left arm. Gardner's tent mate, Sgt. Albert Straight, rushed to his side as the private gave the sergeant his Bible and yelled, "Give this to my wife. Tell her I died happy. Glory to God Hallelujah. Amen!" Another sergeant, watching, was sickened by the results and yelled, "There go two of our men."

Yet the other men had to forget about the loss and continue working the guns. Sgt Straight and two remaining cannoneers tried loading the piece, but it was dented beyond repair. They managed to place a powder bag in the tube, but when the round was inserted, it became stuck in the muzzle as the hot cannon cooled and became permanently fixed there. Deemed unserviceable, the cannon, which was later known as the "Gettysburg Gun," was taken off the field. It was displayed in Washington until 1874 when Rhode Island asked that it be returned to Providence; there it was placed outside the old state house on North Main Street. In 1903, the gun was moved to the north portico of the new state house on Smith Street.[51]

In July of 1962, it was pointed out by a knowledgeable black powder shooter that muzzle loaders had the powder charge inserted into the barrel first and then the projectile. Since the cannonball had been stuck in the muzzle since the battle of Gettysburg, it was concluded that the powder charge had probably been in the cannon barrel all those years. The gun was carefully moved to a Rhode Island National Guard maintenance shop, grounded and immersed in a water bath, and the touchhole carefully drilled out. A black residue was flushed out, and upon drying, it fizzled and burned when it was touched by a lighted match.[52]

Captain John Tompkins was the brother of Col. Tompkins and effectively handled Battery A at Antietam (RG).

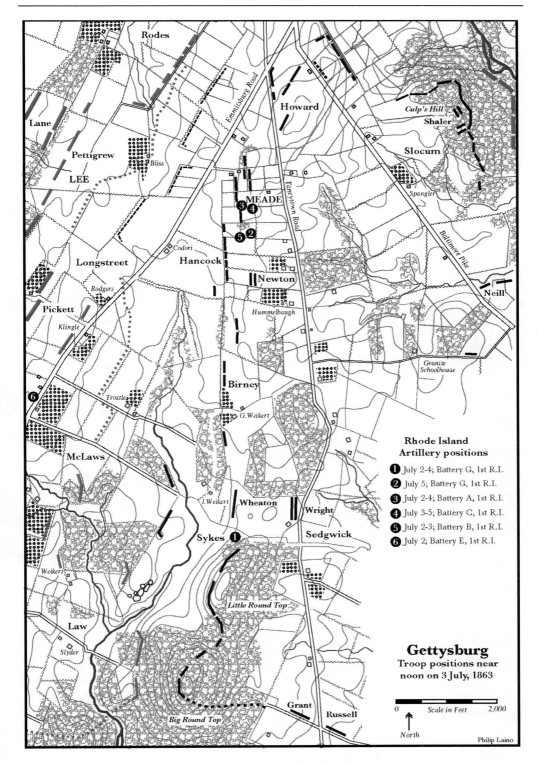

Rodes

Howard

Culp's Hill
Shaler

Slocum

Spangler

Lane

Pettigrew

LEE

Bliss

MEADE

❸❹

❺❷

Codori

Longstreet

Hancock

Rodgers

Newton

Neill

Pickett

Klingle

Hummelbaugh

Granite
Schoolhouse

Trostle

Birney

G. Weikert

**Rhode Island
Artillery positions**

❶ July 2-4; Battery G, 1st R.I.
❷ July 5; Battery G, 1st R.I.
❸ July 2-4; Battery A, 1st R.I.
❹ July 3-5; Battery C, 1st R.I.
❺ July 2-3; Battery B, 1st R.I.
❻ July 2; Battery E, 1st R.I.

McLaws

J. Weikert   Wheaton

Wright

Sedgwick

Sykes ❶

Weikert

Little Round Top

Law

Slyder

Gettysburg
Troop positions near
noon on 3 July, 1863

0   Scale in Feet   2,000

Grant

Russell

Big Round Top

North

Philip Laino

The Battle of Gettysburg (RG).

Back at home in Providence, the PMCA did not remain inactive during the conflict. They followed the campaigns and achievements of the Rhode Island batteries and regiments with enormous pride. News of a victory or the return of soldiers always triggered an enthusiastic salute. On very special occasions, the Bull Run Gun was used to fire salutes. Throughout the war, the doors of the Benefit Street Arsenal remained open for those needing training before going south to fight. Members also took part in soldiers' relief work to take care of the families left behind and to support those of deceased members of the PMCA.

In the spring of 1863, the Tenth Battery reorganized, again commanded by Lt. Col. Edwin C. Gallup, for the protection of Narragansett Bay's West Passage against "rebel pirates." The unit was stationed at the "Bonnet," now Bonnet Shores, about two miles below Narragansett Village, where the men mounted two thirty-two pound siege guns directed at passing ships. There was a perceived fear along the eastern seaboard that the Confederate raider *Alabama* would attack the United States' vital merchant shipping industry, the same reason why the PMCA had been formed a half century earlier.

"[They] blazed away blank cartridges at vessels which did not show a flag or whistle a salute to the battery flag on the bluff," noted the *Providence Journal* in a short history of the PMCA. "A solid shot was fired at a suspicious looking craft which did not show any bunting on one occasion. It turned out to be a revenue cutter and the battery got a return fire of a cannon ball that went whizzing over their heads. Another vessel, a freight steamer, had a copperhead captain who did not feel disposed to show all the courtesies of war in his daily trips up and down the bay. The battery got exasperated with him and fired a 32-pound shot across his bow. The copperhead saluted at once and never failed to do so afterwards; but the sequel came in a reprimand from Governor Smith, [who noted] that the battery had not been placed in position to fire at peaceable merchantmen."[53]

In his reports from the Bonnet, Gallup discusses a less serious problem: "All water used by the camp was brought from Providence in whisky barrels, giving the water such a flavor as to provoke both temperance and anti-temperance men. There was too much of the stuff for one class—not enough for the other." The duty on Narragansett Bay was similar to that performed by the PMCA during the War of 1812. They never knew when the enemy would appear, but the duty provided realistic training in their home state, keeping the vital bay open to commercial traffic.[54]

After the war, the veterans of the First Rhode Island Light Artillery were proud of their service. This monument to Battery E was erected at Gettysburg (RG).

While the members of the PMCA enjoyed the light duty at home, the men

The Gettysburg Gun was a relic from Battery B and was stored at the Benefit Street Arsenal until 1903 (RG).

of the First Rhode Island Light Artillery continued to show their mettle on the battlefield. During the nonstop, brutal Overland Campaign of 1864, the Rhode Island batteries were heard in earnest. For the first time all eight batteries were on the field in the same place. Losses in horses and men were unequaled, as Gen. Grant pushed southward, losing tens of thousands of men as he tried to end the rebellion. The worst of these battles was the brutal struggle at Spotsylvania on May 12, 1864, fought for twenty hours nonstop in the rain with clubs, swords, and bayonets. During one part of the struggle Battery B actually charged the Confederate works with their Napoleons, wheeling them into the enemy fortifications to blow out the Confederates with canister.

In another part of the engagement, Colonel Tompkins saw some of the Sixth Corps infantry break and run; he galloped along the line to get his batteries into action. Within thirty seconds Batteries C, E, and G were firing at the Confederate works.

Lt. Joseph S. Milne of Battery B was mortally wounded during Pickett's Charge. His last words were "Comfort my Mother and tell her I died doing my duty" (RG).

The PMCA took the field in 1862 as the Tenth Rhode Island Battery (RG).

Indeed, Battery G fired so many rounds that they shot away everything in the limber chests and had to find enemy ordnance to fire when their supply ran out. Day after day there were battles at places with names like Wilderness, Po River, Totopotomy, North Anna, Cold Harbor, Mechanicsville, Swift's Creek, Bermuda Hundred, Drewry's Bluff, and Petersburg. When it was all over, no Rhode Island home was left untouched. The batteries were in some cases reduced to seventy men, while the Second and Seventh Rhode Island regiments mustered fewer than 100 men each at the end of the six-week ordeal.

Throughout the summer of 1864, the men of the batteries engaged in the dangers of siege duty around Richmond. Battalion commander J. Albert Monroe was given the task of organizing the Union siege artillery. The men were engaged day and night, and slept in "bombproofs," or underground shelters, to escape the murderous fire above. Throughout the summer, Gen. Grant tried to push ever westward in an attempt to cut off Lee's supply and communication lines. At Ream's Station on August 25, Battery B was overrun, losing four guns and sixty men to the enemy. Like a phoenix rising from the ashes, however, the Rhode Island battery was quickly rebuilt and within a month was back in the field.[55]

In the late summer of 1864, the combat shifted to the Shenandoah Valley where Batteries C, D, and G played a prominent role at the battles of Snicker's Gap, Opequon, Fisher's Hill, and Cedar Creek. On

First Lt. Peter Hunt was awarded the brevet of captain for gallantry in the Overland Campaign and met his death at Swift's Creek (RG).

July 18, 1864, at Snicker's Gap on the Shenandoah River, Batteries C and G effectively shelled the Confederate positions and prevented an overwhelming enemy force from pushing the Federals into the river; many considered the firepower of the two batteries the only reason the Union forces were able to withdraw to fight another day.

At Cedar Creek on October 19, Col. Charles Tompkins was forced to buy time for the retreating Union army and had to sacrifice Battery C and Battery G to the enemy to stall them as the Federals attempted to rally to launch a counterattack to the Rebel assault. The Rhode Islanders fought heroically but lost a third of their strength and four guns. Among those killed was Lt. Charles V. Scott, who had saved the Bull Run Gun; he was hit trying to save another gun. The men bought the critical time needed to rally the Union forces that re-formed for a counterattack in the afternoon; again, the batteries came onto line and shelled the Confederates with vigor until they had retreated. After the battle, General Horatio Wright, the Sixth Corps commander, personally thanked Capt. George W. Adams and his men from Battery G for their sacrifice during the fighting retreat, claiming they saved hundreds of lives.[56]

Among the Rhode Islanders wounded in the battle was Col. Tompkins, who received a debilitating arm wound as he tried to save a piece belonging to Battery G. He was withdrawn from field service for the rest of the war but was promoted to brevet brigadier general for his services. Shortly after the end of the war, he received a letter from Maj. Gen. Henry Jackson Hunt, the chief of artillery for the Army of the Potomac. This letter is the final, fitting epitaph for the services rendered by Col. Tompkins and the officers and men of his First Rhode Island Light Artillery Regiment:

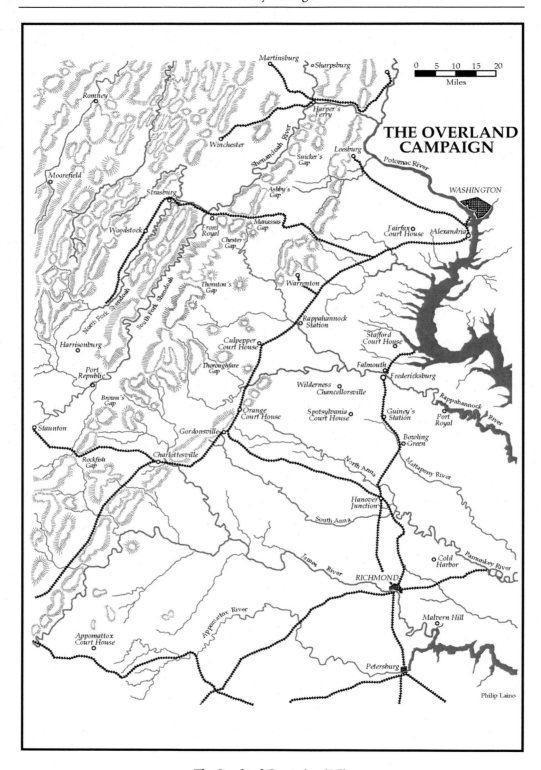

The Overland Campaign (RG).

Artillery Head-Quarters, Army of the Potomac, Washington, May 10, 1865

My Dear General: — The suppression of the rebellion, in the work of which you have borne so conspicuous and efficient a part, having terminated our official relations, I cannot part with you without expressing my sense of your long and gallant services in the artillery of this army, from its organization to the present time. Your services in the Peninsula campaign of 1862 and in the subsequent campaigns in which you commanded the artillery of the sixth corps d'armee; your gallantry and skill at all times, and especially in the great battles of Malvern, Fredericksburg, Salem's Church, Gettysburg, Spotsylvania Court House, in the Wilderness, in the Shenandoah Valley, and elsewhere are of official record, and have, from time to time been acknowledged by your corps commanders and myself. It now remains for me to return to you my hearty thanks, not only for these services in battle, but for laborious and important duties which you have performed in the organization and administration of your various commands, under the most adverse circumstances, and without the field and staff considered indispensible even in old and instructed armies. On the faithful performance of those duties, success in battle depended, and all that could be done by many was thoroughly done by you. For what ever of success I have had in the performance of my duties, I am indebted mainly to the commanders of the artillery of the army corps, and to none more than to yourself. My best wishes follow you in your retirement from the service, and I shall always remember with pleasure the relations, personal and official, that existed between us.

Believe me to be, as ever, very truly and sincerely yours,

Henry J. Hunt, Major-General, Chief of Artillery, Army Potomac

Although Brig. Gen. Tompkins would not see the last six months of the war, his Rhode Island batteries would be in it to the end, under the able leadership of Col. John Gideon Hazard, another PMCA member who had ascended the ladder of rank from Battery B. By April of 1865, Hazard, as well as Tompkins, was wearing a star.[57]

In 1864, isolated celebrations took place in Providence as soldiers, having completed their three years of service, began returning home. However, not until April of 1865, nearly four years after this sad chapter in the nation's history began, did the city truly rejoice. "The glorious news of the surrender of Gen. Robert E. Lee and his army to Gen. U.S. Grant was received this evening about 10 o'clock," noted the PMCA clerk in an entry dated April 9. "Major Smith, being in the [Providence] Journal office when the news came, immediately sent to his Honor Thomas A. Doyle a suggestion to have the bells rung, which was promptly heeded. [Smith] then proceeded to the residence of Governor James Y. Smith, who ordered a salute of two hundred guns at 12 P.M. [midnight]. The Marines were rallied and reported [to Smith's Hill] with their usual promptness."[58]

Sadly, the city's celebrations were only just beginning when, on April 15, the PMCA was called upon once again to fire its cannons, this time with none of the joy that had accompanied the previous week's salute. For the twenty-four hours following the announcement of Lincoln's death, the PMCA fired a gun every half hour. On April 19, four years plus one day since the PMCA had been the first to answer President Lincoln's call, and the official day of mourning in the city, it was with the Bull Run Gun that the organization honored its slain chief.[59]

In addition to performing the important duty of being the "Mother of the Batteries," the other members of the PMCA had also served in the war. Of the 146 men Capt. Charles Tompkins had left Providence with in April of 1861, nearly all reenlisted in another unit during the war. Members of the PMCA were represented in all of Rhode Island's eight infantry and three heavy artillery regiments, three regiments and one battalion of cavalry, in addition to the Rhode Island Hospital Guards, the Regular Army and Navy, plus the ten Rhode Island batteries. Some of these men, such as Sgt. Charles Mayo, who perished at Antietam, and Sgt. Jeremiah Fitzgerald, who died in a suicide charge at Kelley's Ford, all gave "the last full measure of devotion." The members of the PMCA served with distinction in nearly every battle of the war, and those who remained in civilian life ran the state while over 50 percent of the male population was at war. By providing a backbone of trained officers and serving their country in the critical moment of crisis, the men of the PMCA had stoically done their duty, carrying on the tradition of excellence. The pioneering use of field artillery as an offensive weapon of war had truly been forged by the Rhode Islanders.[60]

In the months that followed April 1865, soldiers still in the field returned home, many of them stopping in the nation's capital to march in the Grand Review. Soon most of them would slip quietly back into civilian life. The horrors they had witnessed, the cold and hunger they had endured, would fade in memory; but their membership in a particular battery or regiment would remain a source of pride throughout their lives. Many of the veterans from the First Rhode Island Light Artillery would return to the Benefit Street Arsenal throughout the rest of their lives to take part in veteran's activities.

The Rhode Island cannoneers fought in every battle with the Army of the Potomac. In addition, some batteries fought in obscure places such as North Carolina and Tennessee. Indeed, the regiment was so spread out in 1863, with batteries serving in Pennsylvania, Kentucky, Virginia, and North Carolina, that one veteran called it a "Geography Class." Battery A fired the first light artillery shots of the war at Bull Run and Battery H fired some of the last at Sailor's Creek. Of the 2,000 men who served in the regiment, over 250 made the supreme sacrifice to restore the Union and free the slave. After the war, the veterans would be proud to quip that the generals would not begin a fight unless there was a Rhode Island battery on the field.[61]

Of all the soldiers who served in the First Rhode Island Light Artillery Regiment, nine were rewarded by the United States government with the nation's highest award for military bravery: the Medal of Honor. This is the most awarded to any other Rhode Island regiment during the war. At Antietam, Corp. Benjamin Child of Battery A was severely wounded but refused to leave his cannon and stood by it in the midst of a terrible bombardment, sighting it with accuracy. Child would end the war as a lieutenant and later became chief of police in Providence. During a pivotal moment at the Battle of Chancellorsville, 1st Lt. John Knight Bucklyn of Battery E fought his guns with great gallantry, withdrawing only when the enemy was twenty-five yards away and his ammunition was expended. He would eventually become a professor and write extensively of his wartime service. During the pivotal Assault of Petersburg on April 2, 1865, seven men from Battery G made history by charging a Confederate fort, capturing two howitzers and using them on the retreating enemy. For heroism in the charge, seventeen men were nominated, but only seven received the Medal of Honor: Sgt. Archibald Malbourne, Sgt. John Havron, Corp. James A. Barber, Corp. Samuel E. Lewis, Pvt. George W. Potter, Pvt. Charles D. Ennis, and Pvt. John Corcoran. This is the most awarded to any battery in the history of the United States Army. For the complete story of their amazing feat, please refer to Appendix V. These nine men represented just a few of the scores of brave men who served in the Rhode Island batteries during the war.[62]

The artillerists from Rhode Island who fought in the Civil War continued the long-held tradition of artillery from the smallest state. At each battle they fought in, they were always mentioned favorably in both official and unofficial dispatches from the front. Lt. Col. William F. Fox in his *Regimental Losses in the Civil War* wrote one of them:

> The Rhode Island troops were prominent by reason of the fine regiment of light artillery furnished by that State. The light batteries of the command were remarkable for their efficiency, and the conspicuous part assigned them in all the battles of the Army of the Potomac. As a whole, they were unsurpassed, and they made a record, which reflected credit on their State. A comparison of their losses in action with those of other batteries tells plainly the dangers which they braved.[63]

In 1878, the State of Rhode Island published its official history, covering the first one hundred years as a member of the United States. In this tome, the soldiers who had saved the Union were featured prominently. The smallest state could not help but be proud of the men it had sent to war:

> This branch of the military service formed no unimportant feature in the history of the war, as it rendered valuable service in the suppression of the rebellion, as is attested by the record that it made in that severe struggle for the preservation of the American Union. This arm of the service required great promptness, endurance, and courage those qualities made a true soldier. This regiment, composed of its several batteries, did valiant service all through that long and terrible contest, and returning shared the praise it had thoroughly won.[64]

Despite being severely wounded, Corp. Benjamin Child remained by his cannon at Antietam and earned the nation's highest honor (RG).

The officers and men who had gone to war from the small, medieval structure on Benefit Street had been the flower of Rhode Island. Their blood had flowed freely to restore their country and their state was proud of what they had done.

As late as 1920, the Rhode Islanders were still eliciting praise, except now there were only a few score of the once plentiful number of men who had gone south wearing the blue and red to put down the "Great Rebellion." In his authorative *The History of the State of Rhode Island and Providence Plantations,* Thomas Williams Bicknell wrote of the actions of the Rhode Island artillery and placed the effectiveness of the regiment solely on the esprit de corps and training of the PMCA. Bicknell wrote, "It is not too much to say that Rhode Island men in the artillery were standards of military efficiency in the Union army. These branches of service attracted the choicest of our yeomantry. Many of the officers and men had been members of militia companies where discipline and a fair knowledge of the manual of arms and military tactics were the personal qualifications of all the men in the ranks."[65]

The Civil War was a trying experience for the PMCA, taking many of its best to an early grave. Besides those men trained by the PMCA who served in the batteries of the First Rhode Island Light Artillery, the following members of the PMCA gave their lives in the Civil War: Maj. Augustus M. Tower, Capt. Charles H. Tillinghast, 1st Lt. Walter B. Manton, 2nd Lt. Benjamin E. Kelley, 2nd Lt. Francis A. Smith, Sgt. William Brophy, Sgt. Jeremiah Fitzgerald, Sgt. Charles Mayo Read, Corp. James Flate, Corp. Benjamin Martindale, Corp. Nathan T. Moss, Pvt. Joseph T. Bosworth, Pvt. William E. Bourn, Pvt. James Horton.

Even the men of the PMCA were proud of the regiment they had forged; it was hard to remain humble when the Marines knew they were the best at what they did. Lt. Samuel Pearce wrote, "These batteries were distributed in the armies of Virginia and the West, and made a proud record for themselves and in the great battles of the war. Well may the old 'Mother of

Batteries' be proud of her children." The men from all corners of New England who served in the First Rhode Island Light Artillery had been trained well.[66]

Several factors made the Rhode Island Light Artillery such an effective combat force. According to one prominent historian, they "maintained a good standing in regimental cohesion." Because most of the batteries served together in the Army of the Potomac, qualified officers could be promoted from the ranks and sent to other batteries to increase knowledge of artillery theory. In addition, Rhode Island's excellent prewar education system had given the men the important math skills needed to operate the guns.[67]

Although their weapons had limitations, the cannoneers from the smallest state overcame the obstacles and proved what well-placed artillery fire could accomplish, transforming it into an offensive weapon of war. The most important factor, however, was Col. Charles H. Tompkins and the Providence Marine Corps of Artillery. It was in these roots that one of the finest regiments of artillery ever to serve in the United States Army was created.[68]

8

A PUSH FOR PROFESSIONALISM

When all obnoxious persons had been thus gotten rid of, a recruiting office was opened and soon the battery was sufficiently supplied with desirable men.

— Veteran's Advocate, 1891

On returning home and resuming their membership in the PMCA, many of the Civil War veterans were dismayed by what they found. With so many of the organization's members at the front during the four-year conflict, the PMCA had been forced to fill its ranks with what one member called "an undesirable element of the population." "[They were] very good food for powder but too destitute of 'sand' to perform the best acts possible," noted George B. Peck, who joined the PMCA in 1863 while still a student at Brown University.[1]

George Bacheler Peck was one of the most influential men to take a leading role in the PMCA after the Civil War. Born in 1843, he came from a long New England line and graduated from Brown in 1864. The same year, he was commissioned as a second lieutenant in the Union army and assigned to the Second Rhode Island. In his first and only engagement, at Sailor's Creek, Lt. Peck received a severe wound. After the war he tried his hand at clerking but soon took up the study of medicine and spent the rest of his life in that field. Peck also was an amateur historian and took an active role in the Grand Army of the Republic and the Rhode Island Soldiers and Sailors Historical Society. The historian of today owes Peck a huge debt for his meticulous record keeping and writing skills in remembering the story of the men in the state. He would help bring the PMCA back into shape and would rise to the rank of major. When Peck died in 1934 he was the last surviving Rhode Island officer from the Civil War.[2]

In 1866, several of these "undesirable" men were given commissions, according to Peck, and at the 1867 annual election "this gang loudly boasted they would capture the entire organization."[3] Although no mention of this unpleasantness appears in the PMCA's minutes, the drama of the election is highlighted in an article that appeared a dozen years later in the *Veteran's Advocate*. The reporter, who suggested that the outcome could have had devastating consequences to the state's artillery interests, offered this vivid description of the episode:

> In 1867 the personnel of the [PMCA] had so deteriorated that a large majority of the active members contemplated running for commanding officer a certain man who was utterly unfit for a sergeant's warrant although he had worked his way to a commission.[4]
> This angered Lt. Col. George H. Smith who went at once to work and rallied to the rescue the entire available force of fined, past and honorary members. On election night a double rank of men sternly faced each other from opposite sides of the Benefit Street Arsenal. Many of the active line glared furiously at their antagonists for they saw in them the potential of their own destruction. Still, as the other line was the shorter they doggedly held their ground until they found themselves whipped by a small but unchanging majority.[5]

"The friends of the battery rallied," explained Peck, "and after a determined contest elected Gen. Joseph P. Balch to the command for the ensuing year."[6] Perhaps what was even more significant, the "friends of the battery" elected Peck to serve as first sergeant. In turn Peck asked five of the highest ranking men in the organization, Gen. John G. Hazard and Colonels John Albert Monroe, Frank G. Allen and Edwin C. Gallup, past commanders of the PMCA, and Lt. Frank A. Rhodes to be his line sergeants. All of the men were Civil War combat veterans. Their mission was clear: to rid the PMCA of all disreputable members. "I owed my position to the simple fact that I was acquainted with the men and knew whom we should free ourselves from," Peck noted. "My subordinates took hold with a will and performed faithfully all duties required of them in the [arsenal], dropping out only as the process of reorganization progressed."[7]

On July 4, the newly rebuilt unit again took the field to lead the annual Independence Day Parade through Providence. Due to manpower shortages and grudges of many of the members, only two guns could be taken out. Still, however, the Marines made a fine appearance. Sgt. Peck commanded one gun, while Sgt. J. Albert Monroe commanded the other. As first sergeant, Peck found it odd and could not bring himself to com-

George B. Peck served in the Civil War and later helped to reestablish the reputation of the PMCA (RG).

mand Monroe, who had traded the silver leafs as lieutenant colonel of the First Rhode Island Light Artillery for "an old coat that had been handed down from Sprague's adminstration, with plain service chevrons on his sleeves, a forage cap on his head, and a regulation cavalry sabre by his side."

Even though the problems had been occurring in their unit, both Peck, Monroe, and the others that marched that day considered it their duty to lay down their differences and march in their country's honor. Sgt. Peck thought it strange that Monroe had gone from commanding thousands of men during the war when he commanded an artillery training camp to now commanding one gun. The following year Monroe was elected lieutenant colonel and continued until he resigned to pursue more work in his engineering firm. Eventually the colonel was made an honorary member of the PMCA when he could not keep up an active membership. J. Albert Monroe, one of the PMCA's most talented members, would be remembered for his "modesty, fidelity, and loyalty." When the colonel died in 1891 it would be the PMCA who would lay him to rest.[8]

By the end of 1867, nearly 125 men had been expelled, discharged or simply "dropped" from the corps, most of them within two months of that fateful April election. The plan of the men who had actually gone to fight in the war had worked against the shirkers who had stayed home. Given the option of a court-martial or an honorable discharge, most chose to leave the organization quietly.[9]

With the purge almost over, it was time for the PMCA to go back to its long tradition of providing ceremonial services for the State of Rhode Island. In 1869 they participated in a statewide memorial service for all those from the state who died in the Civil War. Of the 24,000 Rhode Islanders who went south, 2,500 gave "the last full measure of devotion." Now, four years after the end of the conflict, the state finally honored the fallen brave by erecting a forty-five-foot tall monument. Capped by a lifesize figure of Columbia and adorned with statues representing soldiers of all four branches of the service, it listed the names of all those who had died, including the hundreds from the First Rhode Island Light Artillery Regiment. The mounted battery led the procession, and then fired salutes as the memorial was unveiled. It was a solemn sight as the veterans—some of whom were missing limbs, a mute testament to the dangers of the artillery service—stood next to the fancifully dressed members of the PMCA as the entire state momentarily paused to honor the fallen brave.[10]

J. Albert Monroe learned the art of gunnery in the PMCA and became a lieutenant colonel in the Union army (RG).

"When all obnoxious persons had been thus gotten rid of, a recruiting office was opened and soon the battery was sufficiently supplied with desirable men," explained the *Veteran's Advocate.* In the early 1870s, life in the PMCA once again assumed a comfortable rhythm: drills every Monday evening; regularly scheduled banquets and target competitions with nearby artillery organizations; week-long camps by the sea every summer; festive Christmas dances with elaborate dinners; and, of course, parades, marking every possible holiday and occasion. The elegant and heavily debated dress uniforms now included Prussian style helmets. Despite these social activities, the PMCA remained on constant alert, never knowing when they would be called upon again. These would be the final days of volunteer militias as they had been known. Increasingly, states sought to bring their assorted militia into a regimental organization that more closely resembled that of the United States Army. Such organization, state officials argued, would reduce costs, increase efficiency and heighten professionalism.[11]

A new militia bill was drafted requiring the state militia to conform to the proposed regimental organization, but the state's six independent chartered companies—the Newport Artillery, the Kentish Guards, the Providence Marine Corps of Artillery, the Bristol Train of Artillery, the United Train of Artillery, and the First Light Infantry Regiment—had the right to refuse and remain independent. Doing so, however, meant forfeiting all state pay and allowances. These units were all considered the "ancient corps" of the Rhode Island Militia; most dated their charters to the Revolutionary period. They bore the titles of regimental companies in that there was always a full regimental staff present. But the number of enlisted men in each unit amounted to only 100, which presented an interesting and motley sight during parade days. Something had to be done to fix this problem.[12]

Adjutant General Hebert LeFavour believed that winning the acceptance of the independents was critical to the regimental organization he was trying to achieve. "Although there

Members of the PMCA in their dress uniforms in 1877. Col. Robert Grosvenor is on the far left (RG).

are but five of these commands," LeFavour explained in his 1874 annual report, "they number 816 men and if there should be a reduction of the militia to 1,800 men, which the adjutant general was recommending, and these companies still remain unattached to the line, it would leave the balance in a very unsatisfactory shape, especially as these commands are undeniably the best troops in the state. By their adopting the regimental organization similar to that of the U.S. Army, in common with the rest of the militia, the standard of the whole would be very much elevated."[13]

The issue of whether to accept the new militia bill, passed by the general assembly in 1875, created a bitter division within the PMCA, as it did within all of the independent companies. Just a year short of celebrating their seventy-fifth anniversary, many PMCA members felt the state was asking them to relinquish not only their autonomy but also a proud identity. By accepting the provisions of the new law, the organization could no longer perform its military functions under the banner of the PMCA, but only as "Battery A of the First Battalion of Light Artillery."[14]

This separation began the present function of the unit. The Providence Marine Corps of Artillery would serve primarily as a supportive social organization, composed of active members of Battery A. On April 19, 1875, the PMCA agreed, by just one vote, to accept the provisions of the new law, and on December 20 of that year, the members voted, "after a great amount of argument," to meet from then on as Battery A.[15] Governor Henry Lippitt, a former member of the PMCA, warned the artillerymen that if they did not accept the provisions of the militia law, he would not call them out in times of trouble or even for the traditional salute.[16]

Still, the debate and hard feelings continued to surface well into the following year. Lt.

Col. Frank G. Allen bitterly opposed relinquishing the battery's independence and resigned from the commander's position just weeks after being reelected in April 1876. He often boasted he was the last commissioned officer of the Providence Marine Corps of Artillery.[17]

Of the six independent chartered companies given the option to accept the new law, only the PMCA and the First Light Infantry Regiment accepted. That four of the organizations declined was a huge disappointment to the adjutant general, who believed Rhode Island would have had one of the most effective militia systems in the country if all six independents had joined the line. The PMCA was applauded for "being willing to sacrifice many of its own interests for the general good of all." The reorganization of the PMCA changed its focus from that day forward.[18]

For several years after leaving the PMCA as an active member, George H. Smith sought to organize a veteran's association so that as a result he and other former members could "revive old and pleasant memories" and, when needed, give the corps the "benefit of their interest and influence." This would begin another tradition in the state by not only making history, but remembering it as well.[19]

Smith, who had served as the PMCA's quartermaster for many years and as its commander for two, called a meeting of veterans in 1873, but few responded. A year later, however, thanks to the ambitious letter campaign of George R. Drowne, Elisha Dyer Jr. and John Albert Monroe, 162 former members arrived at the arsenal on January 21 to discuss the proposed organization. At that first meeting in 1874, the members elected a colonel, George C. Nightingale, a lieutenant colonel in the person of veteran officer John Albert Monroe, a major, a captain, two lieutenants and several other officers. They also set up committees, including one charged with the selection of uniforms, and drew up a constitution. Just as Smith had hoped, bringing the veterans together did indeed trigger fond memories. With the official business of the evening completed, the arsenal was soon filled with laughter and applause as one man after another recalled stories surrounding the PMCA's famous march to Chepachet in 1842 and its celebrated excursion to Boston a decade later.

The Veteran Association of the PMCA often sent representatives to local military functions and it participated in many of the PMCA's outings, sometimes marching with the active corps. Most important, however, the VA saw itself as the caretakers of the PMCA's proud history. In 1901, for example, it organized the festivities surrounding the organization's centennial, and in 1917, it arranged for a tablet honoring the many batteries that had left the PMCA arsenal to serve the country in war. The Veterans Association's ledgers include in-depth biographical sketches of the organization's members, most of the sketches written by Dr. George B. Peck, who served as the Veteran Association's historian for four decades. These often fascinating and highly informative biographies were written within a year of a member's death.[20]

Initially, membership to the Veteran Association's was limited to those who had served with the PMCA for at least five years. To boost recruitment in 1897, the Veteran Association reduced that requirement to three years and opened its membership to members of all batteries that left for war from the Benefit Street Arsenal. The Veteran Association, as an organization separate from the PMCA, appears to have ceased meeting shortly after World War I, in 1921. At this time, the unit became what it is today.[21]

On July 4, 1876, in a parade celebrating the centennial anniversary of American Independence, the PMCA marched, for the first time, as Battery A. Prior to the event, Lt. Col. John D. Lewis warned his men, in no uncertain terms, that a refusal to participate would result in a court-martial. It was no idle threat. Three who left the city just before the parade were tried and expelled the following month.

Rhode Island's new militia law required that the state militia be divided into two brigades. The first was to include three battalions of infantry and one of cavalry, and the second comprising three battalions of infantry and one of artillery. Battery A, which was the PMCA, and Battery B, which was formerly the Tower Light Battery of Pawtucket, were the two four-gun batteries making up the "First Battalion of Light Artillery, Field and Staff" in the Second Brigade. Within a year of the reorganization, LeFavour recommended a consolidation of the two brigades, and by 1880 the state had organized its militia into one brigade with five battalions of infantry, one battalion of cavalry and one battery of light artillery, Battery A, formerly known as the Providence Marine Corps of Artillery. Later in the decade, a second battery, Battery B, but not PMCA raised, was equipped with Gatling guns, and became a machine gun battery.[22]

Concern over civil unrest and violent labor disputes was, in fact, at the root of the country's renewed interest in its militia. In the summer of 1877, when the railroad riots swept across much of the nation, calls for strengthening the state militia systems grew louder. "A citizen soldiery with all its defects is our only defense against internal disorders and we should use every effort to increase its efficiency," argued the *Providence Journal*, a newspaper that typically represented the interests of big business in the nineteenth century.[23]

Like Rhode Island, other states had started organizing their militia into regiments and were demanding more professionalism. A depressed economy in Rhode Island in the 1870s kept the state from moving forward as quickly as LeFavour had hoped, but by 1881 Adjutant General C. Henry Barney proudly reported that "the uniform and equipment of [Rhode Island's] brigade of militia is superior to that of the troops of any other state in the union and equal to that of the regular army of the United States."[24]

Heading the Brigade of Rhode Island Militia at this time was none other than Brig. Gen. Elisha Hunt Rhodes, that young enlisted man who had served so proudly with the Second Rhode Island Regiment throughout the Civil War and who had spoken so highly of the state's artillery batteries. All of the troops within the Rhode Island brigade were now wearing a standard, publicly owned uniform, a move that improved both discipline and morale, according to the adjutant general. "There is a feeling that a handsome uniform gives a degree of superiority to the organization possessing it and a mistaken idea that good clothes can be relied upon to take the place of proficiency in military acquirements," wrote Barney in 1878 when he first argued for a standard uniform.[25]

Two years later, when the regulation United States Army uniforms were issued, Barney noted that the new attire "weeded out men who simply liked to parade in fancy uniforms and [attracted] men with more interest in militia."[26] Through the 1880s, training and annual inspections acquired a far more professional tone. Those "summer encampments" of the past, often viewed as pleasurable holidays by the sea, evolved into rigorous training sessions on land the state leased at Oakland Beach in Warwick. When the area developed into a popular summer resort and was sold off as house lots, the state set up a permanent training camp at Quonset Point in 1893.[27]

Typical of these encampments was one held from July 8 to July 13, 1894, at Quonset, in conjunction with the rest of the Rhode Island Militia. Battery A as usual made a splendid appearance — the pride of the state. The unit arrived in camp with four officers and sixty-nine enlisted men. This training in 1895, however, would be the last of the traditional and the first of the new. Adjutant General Frederic M. Sackett, himself a former lieutenant in Battery C during the Civil War, proposed several sweeping changes for Battery A. Sackett proposed the old muzzle-loading artillery pieces that the corps had used nearly one hundred years be replaced by the newer breechloaders. In addition, the general had to find a suitable site closer to Providence for Battery A to practice firing. The annual training at Quonset was the only time the battery could actually live fire its cannon.

Most important, Sackett proposed that Battery A disband its mounted services. The horses would be sold off, while the drivers would be relegated to the position of cannoneers. When the unit had to take to the field as mounted artillery, horses and drivers would be contracted out for service. In addition, the 1894 encampment was one of the first where members of the Rhode Island Militia competed against each other in rifle marksmanship, trying to attain the position and badge of "marksman" or "sharpshooter." Only six members of Battery A were able to score high enough to earn a medal, showing that they were artillerymen, not foot soldiers. Despite these new activities to improve themselves militarily, Battery A had seen enlistments lagging throughout the 1890s. According to accounts from the period, it was the battery's demoralizing experiences during the period that would be to blame for its recruitment problems at the turn of the century, including not having modern equipment and not being sent to Cuba.[28]

While the National Guard emerged as its own potent force in the late 1890s to form the nation's first line of defense and also a force ready to be called up at any moment, the War Department tried to cut costs, as usual. Unfortunately for the smallest state, one of the units targeted for inactivation was Rhode Island's Battery A. For years, as a cost cutting measure, the federal government had been reluctant to spend the money to equip the battery with the new breech-loading cannon. Finally, in 1898 Governor Elisha Dyer Jr., himself a former PMCA member and Civil War veteran, wrote a letter to the secretary of war pleading for the new guns:

> The state of Rhode Island is proud to have as a part of its militia one of the best drilled and best manned light batteries in the national guard of the country. This battery is, so to speak, a lineal descendent of the famous Providence Marine Corps of Artillery, which from the very beginning of the late Civil War furnished to the United States government so many superb batteries of distinguished and gallant officers and men. Rhode Island cannot afford to have the cost of the battery taken out of its annual appropriation of supplies & from the war department, but it makes bold to ask that it be furnished with such modern armament for its light battery as will enable to offer to the government, in case of need, the services of one of the best drilled artillery organizations in the national guard of the country.[29]

As many had done in the past and would in the future, Dyer turned his letter's attention to the important tradition of excellence in the artillery service begun by the PMCA. However, an emergency would soon arise that would again require Battery A's attention, and it would be nearly a decade before Dyer's request was placed through.

While the politicians and soldiers were arguing over the proper cannon for the command, events across the Atlantic would soon have a profound impact upon the PMCA and Battery A. A young English author named Henry Newbolt wrote a poem about a battle in the Sudan in the 1870s where a British square had been broken by Sudanese fighters. The poem recalled a British officer who attempted to rally the shattered formation by repeating the same words that his coach had urged upon him as a boy growing up playing cricket. The poem was called *Vitaï Lampada* ("They Pass on the Torch of Life") and went as follows:

> There's a breathless hush in the Close to-night —
> Ten to make and the match to win —
> A bumping pitch and a blinding light,
> An hour to play, and the last man in.
> And it's not for the sake of a ribboned coat.
> Or the selfish hope of a season's fame,
> But his captain's hand on his shoulder smote —
> "Play up! Play up! And play the game!"
>
> The sand of the desert is sodden red —
> Red with the wreck of a square that broke; —

The gatling's jammed and the colonel dead,
And the regiment blind with dust and smoke.
The river of death has brimmed its banks,
And England's far, and Honour a name,
But the voice of a schoolboy rallies the ranks—
"Play up! Play up! And play the game!"

This is the word that year by year,
While in her place the school is set,
Every one of her sons must hear,
And none that hears it dare forget.
This they all with a joyful mind
Bear through life like a torch in flame,
And falling fling to the host behind —
"Play up! Play up! And play the game!"

The poem instantly became popular with military forces throughout the Western world as a means of representing the glory of nineteenth century combat. Translated from the Latin, *Vitaï Lampada* means "they pass on the torch of life." These few stanzas best represent what the Providence Marine Corps of Artillery has done since the beginning. They have always passed on the torch of life from one generation to the next. The central theme in that tradition has been one of excellence in field artillery. By 1900, the motto of both Battery A and the PMCA had become "Play the Game," which is still used on the crest of the 103d Field Artillery Regiment of the Rhode Island Army National Guard.[30]

Wounded at the start of the Civil War, Elisha Dyer, Jr., rose to become the commander of the PMCA and as governor activated Battery A in 1898 (RG).

On April 23, 1898, President William McKinley called for 125,000 volunteers for two years of service to oust Spanish forces from Cuba and Cuban waters. In anticipation of this call, Governor Dyer had ordered a thorough investigation of the state militia and its equipment. For the weeks leading up to the president's call, "the different military offices of the State was of a more stirring and eventful character than at any time since 1865," according to a book chronicling the history of Battery A.[31]

Thanks largely to Dyer's foresight, no state was better prepared to respond to the call than Rhode Island. Washington authorized the state to enlist a regiment of infantry, and on April 25 the PMCA voted unanimously to offer its services for foreign duty as Battery A. The corps would wait more than a month before its offer was formally accepted, but on June 8, under the command of Capt. Edgar R. Barker, the battery left the arsenal for Quonset Point and was mustered into service twenty days later. For the two weeks prior to leaving the arsenal, the 162 officers and men "exerted themselves to the limit" preparing for service, "drilling in relays day and night."[32]

When told in Quonset that only 110 of them,

four officers and 106 enlisted men, would be mustered into service, most of the remaining fifty-two men signed up with the Regular Army. Not since the Civil War had patriotic fervor reached such heights. For four months, Battery A trained and drilled in Quonset, eagerly awaiting orders that would take them to the front. Although the men had experienced camp life during the summers at Quonset, this present time was more important as hours of constant drill and the monotony of camp life. With home only twenty miles away, many were homesick; yet they wanted the orders to deploy, to finally put all they had learned

A member of the PMCA had this small pin privately made and wore it on his uniform (RG).

into practice. It was not to be. On October 26, 1898, the battery was mustered out, never having left camp, when President McKinley declared hostilities in the Caribbean over. "I am sure you can appreciate the disappointment of those men that the efforts of their commanding officer were to no avail in obtaining orders which would assign the command to an active theatre of the war," wrote Everett S. Hartwell in his historical sketch of the PMCA.[33]

The celebration of the PMCA's centennial on October 30, 1901, was undoubtedly the PMCA's most ambitious event in the years after the Spanish-American War. The ten-hour program was under way at 2:00 P.M. with a 100-gun salute, fired by members of the active corps in front of the state house. The crowd of veterans, members of Battery A, state officials — many of them former members of the PMCA — and other friends of the organization then moved to the arsenal for entertainment and speeches. At 5:30, a line was formed in front of the arsenal — headed by the American Band — and the group of several hundred past and present artillerymen marched with dozens of dignitaries down Waterman Street to the Trocadero, a banquet hall on Mathewson Street. There the group feasted on a lavish menu of oysters, soup, halibut, turkey and champagne. Many of those joining in the festivities had served with one of the legendary batteries that had left the arsenal during the Civil War.[34]

For the occasion of their centennial anniversary, a special pin was struck for the PMCA members: crossed cannons, superimposed on the symbol of Rhode Island, an anchor, further having the initials PMCA superimposed thereon. This pin was reproduced and again issued to all members on the bicentennial anniversary of the PMCA in 2001. In appearance, the crossed cannons and the anchor are very similar to the 103d Field Artillery Brigade patch formerly in use. This badge of honor, which was approved by the United States Army Institute of Heraldry, was worn from 1985 until September 6, 2008.[35]

After the disappointment attendant on the failure of Battery A to see active service in the Spanish-American War, there was "little incentive to lure prospective soldiers into the militia," according to Hartwell. "Subsequent to Capt. Edgar R. Barker's resignation in 1899, the proficiency of the battery declined." In many ways, Battery A's experience in the Spanish-American War reflected a growing lack of respect some Army Regulars held for state troops. "The Army's effort to bypass the National Guard in 1898 represented the culmination of efforts by a minority of regular officers to alter fundamentally the way in which the United States waged war," wrote Jerry Cooper in his history on state militia and the National Guard. "The war presented the opportunity to eliminate the cumbersome, decentralized mobilization practice centered on the state military systems."[36]

While disappointment reigned in 1898, by 1902 things had changed for the better. To the

Battery A at Quonset in the summer of 1898 preparing for action in the Spanish-American War, action that never came. Captain Edgar R. Barker is front and center with moustache and sword (RG).

delight of both the Rhode Island Militia and the adjutant general, work had finally commenced on a $500,000 state armory at Cranston and Dexter streets in Providence. Finally, for the first time, the entire brigade could be quartered in the same structure, providing ample opportunities for training, drill, office space, and recreational purposes.[37]

Perhaps the most important feature to come out of the Spanish-American War was the Federal Militia Act of 1903, often known as the Dick Act for the part Representative Charles

This commemorative pin was issued to members of the PMCA on the centennial and bicentennial of the unit's founding (PMCA).

Dick had in initiating it. Dick himself was an Ohio National Guard general and had seen the results of the force during the crisis of 1898. This act of Congress officially established the National Guard, further standardizing its organization, structure, armaments and discipline. One of the most striking policies was the stopping of the election of commissioned officers by the men. This had been a cherished right in the American militia since the beginning. Now the officers would have to go through the same branch training as regular officers and would be commissioned by both the president and the governor of their state. Although conflicts between the state military forces and the Regular Army would continue to surface periodically, the new law gave the civilian soldiers the recognition, and funds, they often had lacked in the past. In return, however, there would be new obligations imposed by the federal government, including yearly War Department inspections, mandatory drill attendance, and compliance with army regulations. The increased military demands of the Guard brought pride and respect, but they also made recruitment more difficult. The elite social nature of most nineteenth-century volunteer military organizations had now fully disappeared.[38]

Heavy lobbying by National Guard officers effectively resulted in the state soldiery becoming the nation's first line reserve. The independent companies, such as the Artillery Company of Newport and the Kentish Guards, that did not join continued as social clubs, often accused by the real soldiers as playing the part; when the professionals went off to fight, the militia stayed home and paraded. "The Guard at last acquired a legal claim to the volunteer role," wrote Cooper.[39]

After Battery A's experience in the Spanish-American War, many members of Battery A felt that something great had been lost; it was the first conflict since the PMCA's founding in which the unit had not played an active part. The main reason was that the war was too short to actively initiate a full militia call out. Despite this, Rhode Island's Battery A had lost something in 1898 — the razor sharp edge that had once made it such a potent combat force. Something had to be done to bring back the tradition.

9

RESTORING THE LEGACY

The privates seemed to have but little idea of promptness in obeying any except the mess calls.

— Maj. Charles W. Abbott, U.S. Army

With recruitment and morale declining steadily in the early 1900s, the Rhode Island National Guard pinned its hope for the future on the new state armory. Although construction had commenced in 1902, the massive building on Cranston Street was still a year from completion when Adjutant General Frederic M. Sackett noted in 1906 that the Guard was "sadly handicapped" by the lack of suitable armories in the state. Many of the arsenals built more than half a century earlier were deteriorating and most were too small to conduct contemporary drills and exercises. And while many of the state's militia organizations contended with leaking roofs and inadequate space, Battery A was quite literally without a home at all. The Benefit Street Arsenal, which stood at the corner of Benefit Street and Arsenal Lane, was built of chipped stone covered with stucco. The building measures seventy-four feet deep and forty-four feet wide, with two square towers on the east wall.[1]

In 1906, the New York-New Haven and Hartford Railroad Company was planning to build a tunnel through College Hill to the Seekonk River. The bore of this tunnel would be so close to the surface of the arsenal that the building was condemned. Cherishing the history of its sixty-six-year-old building, the PMCA agreed to allow the railroad company to move the three-story building to a location two hundred yards north of the original site. So, in 1906, the local firm of Maguire and Penniman was hired to move the arsenal to the corner of Benefit and Meeting streets. Before the move could even begin, however, the new site as well as the path to the site had to be cleared of the small wooden structures in the way. In addition, the new footings and foundations of concrete had to be poured and allowed to cure for the better part of a month before receiving the tremendous weight of the three-story stone building.

It was with great difficulty and even greater expense that the building was prepared for the move. First, the building was shored up with heavy timber cribbing. Then, the walls were braced by erecting a series of exterior columns of vertical timbers tied horizontally across the interior of the building with heavy iron rods and turnbuckles. It was critical that the arsenal be kept square and stabilized during the actual move. The move to the new foundation was accomplished by the use of new horizontal hydraulic jacks. The building was so unstable that the move took several days. Before the process was finished the local newspapers commented: "One thing is certain, if the old building doesn't fall to pieces in moving, it will be better than ever before when the contractors have completed it and it is finally turned over to the State to be occupied by the Providence Marine Corps of Artillery on a continuation of the famous 1,000-year lease."[2]

For more than a year during this arduous move, Battery A met in a room rented on North Main Street and stored its heavy equipment in a nearby warehouse. In the midst of these chaotic conditions, in the summer of 1906, Battery A was issued the newer three-inch guns in exchange for its 3.2-inch rifles. Sackett described the three-inch rifled gun as "being the latest adoption by the government and the one in use by field artillery of the regular army."[3]

The battery received four guns with limbers, caissons, battery forge and carriages; army officials arrived in Providence to train the battery officers. That year's report from the adjutant general spoke highly of the battery's early progress with the new equipment; it would be some years before such kind words would be given again. In 1907, Maj. Charles W. Abbot Jr. complained in the adjutant general's report that the men in Battery A were not progressing as hoped, despite a week-long camp at Fort Greble, Rhode Island, where they had received intensive instruction from Regular Army officers. It appeared that even a decade after the Spanish-American War, the demoralizing effects were still being felt. Maj. Abbot blamed the slow progress on a lack of interest and discipline. "The privates seemed to have but little idea of promptness in obeying any except the mess calls," Abbot wrote in his scathing report. He continued:

> The non-commissioned officers were not behind to push them, and officers failed to keep the non-commissioned up to their duty. The battery has a prestige from its past history second to no other organization in the state. It's only a question of planning employment for work hours, which shall keep every minute profitably occupied, and impressing upon both officers and men the fact that all bugle calls mean that something is to be done with a will the instant they are sounded.

It was critical to keep Battery A in Rhode Island; it was the state's only field artillery battery. In addition, if the unit went away, it would destroy a tradition dating to 1801, drastic measures had to be taken.[4]

In the spring of 1908 the long-awaited new armory on Cranston Street opened its doors, much to the delight of the adjutant general. "We now feel our troops have quarters that are a credit to the state," Gen. Sackett noted. Not only was the new facility large enough to house

The 3-inch gun used by Battery A on the Mexican border (Library of Congress).

Constructed at the turn of the century, the Cranston Street Armory was home to the Rhode Island National Guard for ninety years (PMCA).

all local National Guard units, including Battery A, but it also provided ample space for athletics and other amusements, which Sackett believed would encourage recruitment. Providing various forms of recreation, the adjutant general insisted, would attract "a more desirable class of men." After nearly seventy years, Battery A had finally moved from its home on Benefit Street.[5]

Battery A certainly hoped that the new quarters would provide a more centralized location to drill and recruit from the working class of Providence into the once heavily elitist battery, now desperate for men. By 1910, this once legendary organization was in such decline that Charles Abbot, who was now the state's adjutant general, noted in his report that the battery was in imminent danger of losing its equipment and funding. "The battery, since it received the new 3-inch material, has never seemed to appreciate the necessity for very hard work to obtain even a fair knowledge of how to handle it," Abbot wrote. "The attendance [at summer camp] was very small and the discipline was very unsatisfactory. The report of Lt. Pelham D. Glassford to the War Department was such that this office was officially notified that the present condition of the command could no longer continue and that if great improvement was not evident prior to Feb. 1, 1911, the battery material would be withdrawn from the state and placed elsewhere."[6]

Indeed, the situation was so grave that the governor stepped in. After accepting the resignations of most existing officers, Governor Aram J. Pothier asked Ralph S. Hamilton Jr., a former adjutant of the First Regiment of Infantry, to serve as the battery's captain and to oversee its reorganization. Hamilton knew that work on the battery's overhaul was already under way, and that there was at least one officer within the organization who cared deeply about its future. Before accepting the position of captain, Hamilton had spoken at some length

Left: *Ralph Hamilton was one of several officers who restored Battery A to its former greatness (RG).* Right: *Pelham D. Glassford was a Regular Army officer who also assisted in restoring Battery A. He was the first commander of the 103d in World War I and later became a brigade commander (RG).*

with a young man named Rush Sturges. After serving as a noncommissioned officer, Sturges had received his commission as a second lieutenant in 1908 and as a junior first lieutenant in 1911. "For three years he observed as an enlisted man the pitiful state of inefficiency to which this once proud organization had fallen," wrote Everett S. Hartwell in his history of the PMCA. "Enlistments were lagging, discipline was at an all-time low, and the battery was soon to be threatened with the loss of its guns and its National Guard status. In the fall of 1909 the dynamic Sturges took it upon himself to see what he could do to remedy this situation. Night after night he invited promising candidates to his house and with the enthusiasm of a reformer sold them the idea of enlisting in Battery A."[7]

Rush Sturges was a product of St. Paul's School in Concord, New Hampshire, Yale University and Harvard Law School. He had joined the PMCA and Battery A as a private in 1906. For three years he watched the legendary organization decline into what one historian called "a pitiful state of inefficiency."[8] Sturges recruited friends and colleagues, including Everitte St. John Chaffee and Ralph S. Hamilton, to rescue the once proud battery. By 1916, Battery A was recognized as the best artillery battery in the country, thanks in large part to the triumvirate of Sturges, Chaffee and Hamilton. After becoming a member of the Rhode Island Bar Association in 1907, Sturges joined — and later became a partner in — the law firm of Green, Hinckley & Allen, founded by Theodore Francis Green, Frank L. Hinckley and Arthur M. Allen. In 1928, Sturges and Chaffee were founding members of the investment firm Sturges, Chaffee and Hazard in Providence. Like his father, grandfather and brother, Sturges, an outspoken Republican, served for many years on the Providence City Council, eventually rising to minority leader when Democrats became the majority party in the 1930s. Sturges never saw combat in World War I. Because of a hearing problem that resulted from a childhood bout of scarlet fever, he was assigned a desk job in Washington, D.C., and Angers, France, for most of the war. In 1925, Sturges was elected lieutenant colonel of the PMCA, a position he held for two decades. He died March 19, 1967, at the age of eighty-seven.[9]

The governor and adjutant general charged Hamilton and Sturges with fully reorganizing the Guard's only battery of light artillery. "The national and state government have a right to expect and require that there shall be a better return for the money spent in the upkeep and training of the organization," wrote the exasperated adjutant general in 1910. The following year Hamilton and Sturges were joined by Everitte St. John Chaffee, a first lieutenant, in their mission to return Battery A to its former glory.

The governor named the three men who made up this triumvirate "commissioners," and in June he sent them along with Lt. Donald C. Barnes to a special training camp for officers at Fort Riley in Kansas. Here the officers learned the art of gunnery in the following classes: Material, Range Tables, Ammunition, Calculations, Accuracy of Fire, Shrapnel, Ranging, Application of Rules, and Explosives. Each officer had to take two weeks off from their business matters, but all agreed it was invaluable. Lt. Chaffee remarked, "The course was most instructive and valuable to me as an officer of Field Artillery." As a bonus, each day the officers received practice by firing sixty rounds at the range. At the battery's encampment that summer, the group demonstrated remarkable progress. "Lt. Glassford was present for the third consecutive year," wrote Abbot in his annual report. "He has nothing but praise for the splendid showing of this year, giving officers and men credit for much hard study and work in the short time between reorganization and the camp." Glassford was taking his time in training the officers and men in the battery. Indeed he was assigned to duty in Rhode Island to insure that Battery A became a razor sharp instrument of war. The work would pay dividends, and on the horizon the lieutenant would soon trade bars for stars.[10]

Of the four subalterns in Battery A, none learned more or carried a greater sense of duty than Everitte St. John Chaffee. A graduate of Yale University and Harvard Law School, he devoted nearly his entire life to military and public service. Born in Amenia, New York, Chaffee moved to Providence in 1904. Two years later he enlisted in Company C, First Infantry, and in 1908 he was made a captain in the Coast Artillery Corps. He joined Battery A in 1911 as a first lieutenant, playing an instrumental role in its reorganization. In 1916, Chaffee commanded the battery at the Mexican border. Known as a strict but fair disciplinarian, Chaffee shaped the men into a unit that earned the highest rating of any National Guard artillery battery sent to the border by the War Department.

Many of the men he trained later distinguished themselves in the two world wars that followed. Chaffee entered World War I as battalion adjutant in the 103d Field Artillery Regiment, but a few months later was promoted to major and given command of the regiment's Second Battalion, which he took to France in December 1917. In June 1918, Chaffee was promoted to lieutenant colonel and served as regimental executive under Pelham D. Glassford. The two men were widely celebrated for their bravery and resourcefulness at the front. After being promoted to colonel, Chaffee was ordered back to the United States to train new troops for combat overseas. When the armistice was signed, Chaffee was in command of the 55th Field Artillery at the School of Artillery Fire, Fort Sill, Oklahoma.[11]

Chaffee returned to civilian life after the war but remained active in the National Guard and the 103d Field Artillery. From 1919 to 1924 he served as commander of the PMCA. In 1925, Chaffee was appointed the first superintendent of the Rhode Island State Police, which initially had its headquarters in the Benefit Street Arsenal. "His nine years as head of the new department," noted the *Providence Journal* in Chaffee's obituary, "were marked by firm discipline and control, a reputation that earned him an additional duty of helping to reorganize the Providence police and fire departments." In 1934, amid a storm of protest from Chaffee's friends and admirers, Governor Theodore Francis Green replaced the colonel with Edward J. Kelly.

Still wearing their World War I–inspired uniforms, and with the military discipline ingrained in the state police persisting long after Chaffee's departure, the department was often referred to as a "soldiery police force." Chaffee, with long-time friend Rush Sturges, founded the investment firm of Sturges, Chaffee and Hazard in 1928. In 1945, the aged colonel was summoned out of retirement once again by the United States government. Col. Chaffee was sent to Berlin in the midst of the rebuilding efforts of the war-torn country. Here he established, along the lines of the Rhode Island State Police, the Berlin Constabulary to keep peace in the occupied capital. He died August 9, 1971, at the age of ninety-one. Comrades remembered him as "one of Rhode Island's finest soldiers."[12]

Col. Everitte St. John Chaffee helped to reorganize Battery A and later became the first chief of the Rhode Island State Police. He remains a hero of the corps (RG).

In 1913, Battery A began traveling to Tobyhanna, Pennsylvania, for its summer encampment, considered preferable to Rhode Island locations because the area was sparsely populated and more suited to target practice. One Rhode Islander wrote, "The land is a sucession of hills and valleys affording ideal places for targets and firing points, under conditions closely approximated with actual service, inasmuch as there is no danger in firing in any direction up to five or six thousand yards." The ten day encampments in Tobyhanna also gave the battery an opportunity to train with artillery batteries from the Regular Army. The battery's turnaround did not go unnoticed. In his report in 1914, the once highly critical Abbot wrote of it: "The personnel and esprit of the command are highly praised, two qualities which make everything possible after experience. The new armory, the ten day tours at Tobyhanna each year will soon put the battery in a condition of efficiency as high as can be expected of any command not composed of regular soldiers."[13]

In addition to the constant training, Battery A continued to perform ceremonial duties in Providence and performed a somber task on November 5, 1915. This was for former governor William Sprague, a former colonel of the PMCA. Sprague had moved to France and died there, still attending to the needs of wounded soldiers. The man who had done so much to prepare the PMCA and had mustered his small state to be the first to answer Lincoln's call was dead at age eighty-five. Although he had insulted the men of the PMCA, that was in the past and now they looked to honor their former leader. After services in Narragansett and Providence, Sprague's casket, draped with the American and Rhode Island flags, was placed onto one of Battery A's caissons for conveyance to Swan Point Cemetery. Thousands lined the

Battery A conducted its annual training at Tobyhanna, Pennsylvania, during its restoration years (USAMHI).

streets to watch the procession, which was under the command of Capt. Chaffee. At the cemetery, the entire command was present and fired a nineteen-gun salute in honor of their fallen chief. The new, younger men in olive drab stood beside old, grizzled veterans who had once worn the blue, and all remembered a Rhode Island hero who had made the Rhode Island artillery what is was.[14]

As the last shot from Sprague's funeral salute echoed off the Providence River, the men returned to the old Benefit Street Arsenal to again train and prepare. As it had done a half century earlier, this constant training would soon pay off. The reorganization was complete and now it was time for the Rhode Islanders to show their mettle and again prove they were the best at what they did, this time on the fields of France.

10

The Mexican Border

In 1915 Mexican revolutionary Francisco (Pancho) Villa, angered by American support for his political adversaries, initiated a series of raids on towns along the Mexican border. The most daring of these assaults took place the following year in March 1916 when Villa and 1,500 followers stormed into the town of Columbus, New Mexico, killing seventeen Americans and wounding many more. Villa and his men looted the town for several hours before galloping back into Mexico. Stunned and outraged by the boldness of the raid, Americans called for action. Within a day, President Woodrow Wilson and his cabinet authorized a "Punitive Expedition," under the command of Brig. Gen. John J. Pershing, to cross into Mexico and capture the outlaw. Pershing and about 12,000 soldiers engaged in several skirmishes with Villa but the popular desperado invariably managed to escape. Making matters worse, Mexican leader Venustiano Carranza, a former American ally, grew increasingly hostile to the presence of U.S. soldiers in his country and offered them little support. With raids on border towns continuing, Wilson issued a proclamation on June 18, 1916, ordering the entire National Guard to mobilize as quickly as possible. The president's order came without warning and found most National Guard organizations woefully unprepared.[1]

"[Most of the units] were far below war strength in numbers and poorly equipped with the necessaries of campaigning," wrote Pvt. Henry R.W. Stiness in his book chronicling Battery A's experience at the Mexican border. "Battery A of Rhode Island stood out in sharp contrast to this type of National Guard command," stressed Stiness, a member of the "Border Battery." "Not only was this single representative of Rhode Island field artillery practically at war strength but its equipment was also far above the average militia standard."[2]

In fact, Battery A could not have been better prepared to mobilize. The day before Wilson's order was issued, the battery had set out on a two-week march, fully supplied with rations and equipment. It was now the perfect opportunity to see if Glassford, Sturges, and Chaffee had performed their full duty in preparing the battery again for combat. The tradition was revived once more as they prepared for the Punitive Expedition to punish Pancho Villa for the atrocities he had committed.[3]

"Each (man) was equipped with the essentials of camp and field life; the caisson and limber chests were filled with service shrapnel," recalled Stiness. "Upon the arrival of the news that President Wilson had ordered the National Guard to mobilize, Battery A merely turned toward Quonset, the state mobilization site, and was in camp under canvas waiting developments before the country had fully awakened to the significance of the President's decision."

The battery, under the command of Capt. Everitte St. John Chaffee, received news of the mobilization order while marching in Scituate. As the long line worked its way south to

Quonset, Rhode Islanders along the route abandoned their kitchens and factories to cheer and salute their citizen-soldiers. "I think we sat more erect on our horses and on the gun carriages," wrote Pvt Stiness. "An old man, with bent body and white hair, brought himself to an erect posture and came to a stiff and rigid salute as we passed. We knew an apparition of sixty years ago stood before him in our place. An elderly lady, with a set and determined expression on her wrinkled face, waved an American flag steadily from the time we hove in sight until our last wagon passed beyond her sight. Through the mill towns, the usual occupations ceased and we were cheered. But it was a serious cheer."[4]

With no idea what the future would bring, the men arrived at Quonset excited and energized. Additional recruits, many of them former members of the battery, quickly brought the group up to "war strength," a military term just gaining currency. By the end of the month, after two weeks of intensive drilling, the battery strength stood at 175 men and five officers. Capt. Chaffee was in command of the battery, while one of his new second lieutenants was a young man named Harold R. Barker. His father was Edgar Barker, who had commanded the battery in the Spanish-American War. Young Harold was destined to make a name for himself in the years ahead.

In addition to the soldiers, tons of supplies, equipment, ammunition, carriages and eighty-two horses boarded the first of several trains to Fort Bliss in El Paso, Texas. Now this cactus-covered plot of land would be the battery's home for the next three months. "A less inviting piece of land than that which was allotted to our battery is unimaginable," wrote Pvt. Stiness. "Human beings had trod the ground, we could tell that from the debris of broken glass and tin cans which were strewn through the dense growth of cactus. Our first night was spent out under the stars. We were terribly tired. It seems now, in looking back, we were always tired. It is in this way lack of training makes itself most apparent. To develop a body of men able to withstand the essential physical labor and keep going under the strain of fatigue is the biggest duty of army officers."[5]

Recalling his experiences as a private in charge of the mules, Brown graduate and later Brigadier General Chester Files wrote the following "Tale of an Ancient Soldier." Files recited this from memory for many years at the General Files luncheon, an event that is still held annually on his birthday St Patrick's Day, March 17:

> Guess I never told you soldier 'bout them mules o' Battery A. That used to draw the wagons to haul manure away. That was 'fore the day o' tractors and the horses pulled the guns. When the B'try went on marches in the torrid Texas sun.

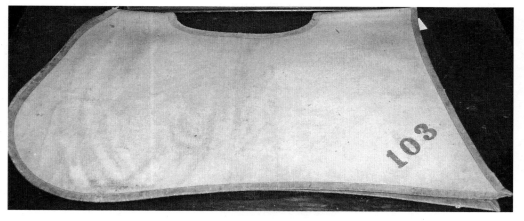

One of the most revered relics of the PMCA is Capt. Chaffee's saddle blanket, used on the Mexican border and in France (PMCA).

Had a captain name o' Chaffee, sort o' tough guy out o' Yale. Gammell, Hanley were first Louies, Babcock, Barker were Shavetails. Post Commander's name was Boley—very strict and maybe fair. Somehow got the name o' Holey but we thought he was a Square.

Every mornin' we had stables. Horse manure was raked in clumps. Then they'd toss it in the cart and I'd haul it to the dump. Used to sit up on the wagon with a pocket full o' rocks. Toss a pebble at the leaders, chaw tobacca, let 'em trot.

T'was a sultry day in August. Had to dig a new latrine. But the work was done by noon mess and the skipper seemed serene. Detail was for drawin' rations— Stiness said 'twaint very far. So we drove the mules 'long street side and went in the Mesa Bar.

Everybody had a grandy, maybe some of us had more. Then we thought we should get started and moved out toward the door. What we saw was quite surprisin' and it gave us quite a fright. Cause when we looked out on the street, there weren't no mules in sight.

Asked a feller had he seen 'em. Said they went off to'ard post. So we started walkin' over, Olney Arnold goin' first. Arnold must o' come from Injuns cause he tracked 'em right along. Up the road behind the barracks, guess the scent was

Harold Barker served on the border as a second lieutenant. Two years later, he was a battalion commander in World War I and would later gain a star (RG).

pretty strong. On behind the Captain's quarters and the Major's house we got. Till we came to Col. Boley's house, the biggest of the lot.

On the clothesline hung the washin' and we almost died because there them mules was with the leaders munchin Mama Boley's drawers. Seemed to think t'was tasty fodder and the way it went was shockin.' As I came up to that Jenny mule just reachin' for a stockin.' What to do was sure a question. Stiness said, "I got to go." Didn't think his friend the Colonel would care to see him so. In the front there was a picnic.

All the kids was havin' fun. Adams said, "I'll try divertin," and went off on the run. All the other boys skidaddled, left me standin' with the mules. So I got up on the wagon, took the reins, pulled back the fools, eased 'em out on to the back road, didn't see a soul around. Drove up to the commissary and arrivin' there I found all the boys awaitin' for me. Asked me where the heck I'd been, You'd a tho't they'd never known 'bout the pickle I'd been in. On the next day was an order read to all the troops at nine. Said there'll be no more stealin' ladies garments off clothes lines.

Gen. Files often laughed at an entry in a book chronicling the adventures of the "Border Battery": "Files gained neither fame nor shame. He worked with the mules."[6]

The physical rigors of the next three months, in heat that routinely climbed well above 100 degrees, did much to increase the stamina of the men and hone their skills. Still, it was clear to many observers that the National Guard, as a whole, had much room for improvement. The Guard's spirit and the speed of its response to the president's call were widely admired, but critics such as Army Chief of Staff Hugh L. Scott complained that most of the units needed months more of training before being ready for combat.[7]

Battery A's famous mules on the Mexican border, 1916 (PMCA).

Battery A of Rhode Island was perhaps the exception. In rating all of the eighty-five National Guard field artillery batteries stationed at the Mexican border, the War Department ranked Battery A number one, giving it a score of 23,983 credits. Battery A, First Massachusetts was the descendent unit of the original Boston Battery trained by the PMCA in the 1850s. The two batteries had always been rivals and now placed a relatively close second place, with 20,223 credits, but all other batteries trailed well behind. With such a high rating, Rhode Island's Battery A was one of only two National Guard batteries to be brigaded with Regular Army units.

As the battery settled in at Fort Bliss and assumed its daily routine of drills and house-keeping details, a remarkable bond or esprit de corps developed among the men. Indeed, Henry Stiness' book on the battery's experience at the border reads more like a high school yearbook than a military history, full of fond anecdotes about his comrades and their hijinks. Though the men represented different walks of life, they were fully united in their desire to bring honor to their battery and state. The War Department briefly threatened this camaraderie with two announcements, one in late July offering discharges to men with dependents, and a second several weeks later giving college men the option to return to their studies. "In all cases, it would have left bad gaps, which it would have been well nigh impossible to fill," Stiness wrote. "The difficulty of getting war strength enlistment was conspicuous in every state in the union."[8]

Within days of announcing the discharges for men with dependents, Congress appropriated one million dollars to be paid to families of national guardsmen at the rate of fifty dollars a week, if they had no other support.[9] "This ended talk on the subject, and all hands buckled down, back on the guns again," noted Pvt. Stiness. The issue of college deferments proved thornier as it divided the men largely by class. For several weeks after the War Department's announcement, the college men gathered nightly to discuss the merits of accepting the discharge while their comrades met elsewhere voicing bitterness over the offer. "The

Left: *Sgt. Chester Files returns from the Mexican border as the mule skinner of Battery A (PMCA).* Right: *Gerald T. Hanley was a Brown graduate who served in Battery A on the Mexican border. As a captain he commanded Battery B on the Western Front (RG).*

battery was pretty well divided in individual sentiment," reported Stiness. "A thorough thrashing out of the question finally ended up in a decision by all college men that once out with the battery meant always with her, or at least until the particular purpose of the mobilization had been fulfilled."[10]

For the remaining two months, the fair-skinned Rhode Islanders worked tirelessly under the relentless Texan sun. Despite the tediousness of daily drills and marches, morale remained high. By the end of September, however, as the men began to suspect they would not be sent into Mexico, many became eager to return home. "No one thought seriously that we should be ordered home until we had been given at least a taste of real firing with the service ammunition," wrote Stiness. "The news late in September that service firing was to begin soon was taken eagerly as an indication of an early departure from El Paso." It was also an event the men had been working toward since early July. The week-long service firing, with the cannoneers performing and responding as they would in an actual battle, was, according to Stiness, the highlight of Battery A's three-month stint in Texas:

> There is no smell of hostile powder nor rain of shrapnel bullets to guard against. The opposing cavalry against which the assault has been directed is imaginary; the hidden batteries are mythical. Only preparation and practice firing, but as supremely vivid and as thrilling as any approach to the real thing can well be. Like children pleased with a new toy, we craved for more and more. In camp, washed up and with a good supper put away, the events of the day were reacted over pipes and between songs. We were all terribly new at this firing business; and we all tried our best to talk and act as if we had always fired 3-inch guns.

As with all soldiers, the men of Battery A could drill till they could stand no more, but

First Platoon Battery A field practice.

only the practical experience of actual firing on a range could test if all the training would pay off.[11]

Two days after the service firing, the men dismantled their tents, packed up their equipment and boarded the train that would carry them home, as recalled by Henry Stiness: "On into the night we sped, around the foothills of the lordly Mount Franklin and up the valley of the Rio Grande, all of us obsessed with but one idea — we were at last going home. Home!" The mobilization call by President Wilson had come just two weeks after Congress passed the National Defense Act of 1916, a law that gave the National Guard drill pay, much larger federal appropriations, and a dual state-federal oath that made the Guard available for overseas duty.[12]

But with many units found to be ill-equipped, undermanned and poorly trained, and with nearly 25 percent of the men declared physically unfit for service, the border mobilization highlighted some of the Guard's limitations. The twentieth century had ushered in a new era. Warfare had become more complex and the United States was rapidly assuming a dominant role in international affairs. Proponents of a professional standing army argued that these new challenges demanded centralized planning and control and "left little room for the improvisational approach to war which had dominated American military history from its inception."[13]

Still, most Americans continued to cherish the country's long tradition of the volunteer civilian soldier, and the National Guard secured enough champions in Washington to ensure its role within the military system.[14] Wilson's mobilization call in 1916 affirmed the National Guard's position as the nation's first line of reserve, but it also gave professionals in the army a chance to correct what they perceived as the Guard's deficiencies. "The Army saw the mobilization as an opportunity to subject the Guard to intense training and reshape state forces

Top: *Battery A soldiers examining their new guns in San Antonio (PMCA).* Bottom: *A detachment of Battery A on the Mexican border, 1916. Lt. Harold R. Barker is at right (PMCA).*

so they conformed to authorized tables of organizations," wrote Jerry Cooper in his history on the state soldier.[15]

The state forces were clearly in better shape after their experience on the border. For Battery A the experience had been very important to finally put all the hard work and training by Sturgess, Glassford, and Chaffee into use. The field training in gunnery and experiences in camp life were the most realistic training possible, far more than could be had at the Cranston Street Armory. "However reluctantly, [the Guardsmen] gained a great deal of valuable experience," wrote John Mahon in his history of the Guard. "The Mexican rehearsal was especially worthwhile for officers and for state staff who had to direct mobilization."[16]

Men from all walks of life served in Battery A. These four comrades in civilian life worked for the Providence Journal. *From left to right they are Corp. Percy J. Cartwell, Pvt. John E. Hethermann, Pvt. Bernard J. McLaughlin, and Pvt. John Rigney (PMCA).*

For Battery A, there were several accomplishments that came out of the Punitive Expedition. The soldiers participated in a campaign that tested themselves and their weapons under warlike circumstances. A fresh crop of leaders arose from the battery who would make names for themselves for the next three decades. In addition, the men all received severe sunburns and laughed at the rollicking adventures of their mules. The service on the border, the only operation of a large military formation in the United States since the Civil War, was recognized with a special campaign medal issued to each member. In addition, the soldiers of Battery A formed the "El Paso Club" in Providence. Meeting at the Benefit Street Arsenal, the organization sought to honor those who served in 1916. The El Paso Club met until 1987, when its last member, Chester Files passed away.[17]

Pleased with recognition by the War Department as the National Guard's most efficient battery, Battery A returned home in mid–October to a cheering crowd. Although rated best in the nation, the men knew they were far better soldiers now than they had been just three months earlier. What they didn't know, at least not fully, was just how soon their newly acquired skills would be put to use — this time not on the battlefields of Virginia or Mexico, but on another continent, an ocean away.

11

WORLD WAR I

Men, we're off for another fight.
— Col. Pelham D. Glassford, 103d Field Artillery

In the summer of 1914 war on a grand scale broke out in Europe as Germany battled its way into France, which resulted in hundreds of thousands of casualties on both sides in places such as Flanders and the Somme. Despite American outrage over the sinking of the *Lusitania* in May 1915, President Woodrow Wilson held firmly to his policy of neutrality. In 1916, as Battery A rumbled across the prairie dog-ridden plains of Texas, only a few members believed they would be sent over to fight in the European war. As late as January 1917, Wilson still hoped to help the Europeans negotiate a peaceful settlement; but those dreams were dashed just weeks later when Germany declared an unlimited submarine campaign.

On April 2, after the deliberate sinking of American ships and an attempt by the Germans to instigate Mexico into action against the United States, with the infamous Zimmerman Note, Wilson could hesitate no longer. The president knew that a new world would come out of this war and he wanted the United States to have a seat in the peace negotiations; thus American soldiers would be committed in their first major overseas action. Arguing that the world must be made safe for democracy, the president asked Congress for a declaration of war against Germany, which the legislators gave by joint resolution on April 6.[1]

A call for volunteers followed almost immediately, although a draft bill was also in the works. Unlike the uproar national conscription created when it was first introduced in the Civil War, its use in 1917 was generally acceptable to most Americans, including guardsmen who believed it would stimulate volunteerism and help increase their ranks. On May 4, seventy-four men under the command of Capt. Chaffee, who was about to put on the gold oaks leave of a major, led a parade through Providence in celebration of Rhode Island Independence Day.[2]

With the declaration of war, Rhode Island began recruiting heavily. Battery A put on displays of drill on the parade ground of the Cranston Street Arsenal, hoping the reaction to the quick, responsive tactics of the field artillery would inspire men to join. Meanwhile, the PMCA did all it could do by hosting a rally on May 8 at the Benefit Street Arsenal. Among the speakers was Capt. Edgar Barker, who had led Battery A during the Spanish-American War. Now his son Harold was the commander of the famed unit. The recent recognition of Battery A's performance at the Mexican border brought dozens of enthusiastic young men to the enlistment station, at Providence's central fire house, seeking a spot with the legendary artillery battery. "Then we were ordered to report at the Marine Corps Armory for drill," recalled one of the enlistees. "Soon, enough men had raised their right hands, thus becoming members of Battery A, to make possible the division of that organization into three batteries."[3]

Battery A became the nucleus of three field artillery batteries, "A," "B" and "C" of the 103d Field Artillery of the 26th Division, American Expeditionary Force. Recruits were lured by the mysteries of army life and posters with a picture of an empty saddle and the words "Rhode Island's Finest has a place for you." Officers from Battery A with border experience "and other 'old men' from the original battery" provided the backbone of the three batteries. As had been the case in the First Rhode Island Light Artillery in the Civil War, the raising of the new units provided the older men an ample opportunity for promotion, in addition to providing a trained cadre of professionals to train the eager volunteers. Among the many names on the rolls were some familiar-sounding ones from a half century earlier, including Sgt. Raymer B. Weeden, whose grandfather had led Battery C, First Rhode Island Light Artillery, to war in 1861. The new recruits were anxious to have the old soldiers in their new units as they themselves were green and needed to be trained by the soldiers they so admired.[4]

Joining Rhode Island's three batteries in the 103d were Battery D from New Hampshire, itself a descendent of the legendary First New Hampshire Battery from the Civil War, and Batteries E and F from Connecticut. Troop M, Rhode Island Cavalry, became the Headquarters Company. Some 230 men from Maine and 246 Rhode Island National Guard coast artillerymen helped bring the batteries up to war strength by being transferred to the 103d. While these men went to war, the soldiers of the Coast Artillery Corps would remain behind to guard Narragansett Bay against feared U-boat attacks.[5]

Not every soldier from the Coast Artillery Regiments could go, however. Pvt. Almase A. Forgue of North Providence had been stationed at Fort Weatherill on coast watching duties when his unit was called to Fort Getty in Jamestown for mobilization. Forgue's grandson remembered how Forgue was one of the fortunate few to join the elite ranks of the 103d:

> When the U.S. entered the war, the coast artillery units were lined up and 25 men were taken from each artillery unit to go to France. In the count, he was 26. During the unloading and loading of supplies on ships, one of the first 25 in his unit was killed when a load on a crane broke and crushed him. This happened at Fort Getty, on the west side of the island. He became number 25. The horses had to go over two weeks before the unit did, so they could recover from the shipping. My grandfather was a muleskinner on the island, and was then assigned as a wag-oner when he became number 25. The officers were in need of a French-speaking interpreter, and he was the only one in his unit who could speak French. Therefore, he went over with the officers and the horses two weeks before the rest of the unit came over. He acted as interpreter when needed.[6]

President Wilson had been calling up units of the National Guard as early as March, but on July 25 he summoned the entire Guard into service. On that day Rhode Island's three batteries reported at Cranston Street Armory "in prescribed uniform for an indefinite period of field service."[7]

Shortly before the men left for the new war, they gathered with a contingent of Civil and Spanish-American War veterans to dedicate an elegant bronze plaque on the front wall of the Benefit Street Arsenal to remember those who had before gone from the building to fight the enemies of the United States. The young men of 1917 were very different in appearance from the aged men there to greet them. But they still served the same purpose as defenders of the old flag. Seventy-year-old Dr. George B. Peck, a former PMCA major and now a retired med-ical doctor, stepped forward to address the mixed grouping of veterans before him, but he specifically looked into all of the eyes of the young soldiers before him, who were anxiously awaiting their turn to perform their duty. After telling them of their heritage as Rhode Island artillerymen, Maj. Peck continued:

> Comrades of the Olive Drab! I have outlined as briefly as possible the record of your comrades of the red cord of the elder days, comrades *all* in that we have sworn to obey the orders of our

superiors, *irrespective.* Some of the survivors I see before me. Doubt not that they will follow in your footsteps with the closest attention. *Beat* their record if you *can!* Personally I congratulate you on the branch of the service you have selected. Preferable as was the light artillery half a century ago far more to be desired is the field artillery of today. I congratulate you upon the perfection of the armaments with which you have been and will be supplied. I congratulate you upon your officers who have already proven themselves men you may trust. I congratulate you in that you will presumably defend on foreign soil your mothers and your children, your wives and your sweethearts, your homes, your all, therby preserving them from the horrors of Belgium, and France, or Poland, and of Serbia, and of Romania. Especially do I congratulate in that you will take part in overthrowing a slavery as debasing and as cruel as any that ever existed; as debasing in that it enchained not only body but mind and soul; as cruel that it is more reigned. I affirm in this presence I *know* you will do *your best!* Whatsoever your footsteps are directed some will succumb to disease. *More* sure it is a number of *us* will be missing on your return, for many are living on borrowed time. It, therefore, remaineth for me but to salute you each as an individual– Comrade, Hail! Farewell! and if forever, still *forever,* fare thee well![8]

Pvt. Almase Forgue was one of many European immigrants in the 103d (RG).

In April of 1861 Lieutenant Governor Samuel Arnold had reminded the men from the PMCA to do their duty to the utmost in the Civil War. Now, over fifty-five years later, George Peck had done the same to yet another generation of young men to leave the Benefit Street Arsenal. The torch had been passed from the generation of men who had saved the United States; now the young men in olive drab had to uphold the sacrifice again "to make the world safe for democracy."

Church bells rang throughout the city as the green-clad men, staggering under the weight of their barrack bags, climbed up Providence's steep Waterman Street to the arsenal. After a short drill, the men returned downtown to join all of the state's National Guard troops in a farewell parade. "Rhode Island had turned out en masse to say farewell to its boys," recalled one of the new soldiers. "And the boys did well, at least everyone said so, and we were conceited enough to believe that we marched as well any veterans could."[9]

The following day, the batteries left for Quonset Point, their departure station on Narragansett Bay, an agreeable spot, most of the men decided, to spend the summer. "The Bay was close at hand, Providence was only a few miles away, and as yet neither discipline nor work had become irksome enough to interfere with the men's spirit." The men thought they were going to spend a peaceful summer training there. Others were naïve enough to think that the three batteries would not be called for as the war would be over before they could deploy.[10]

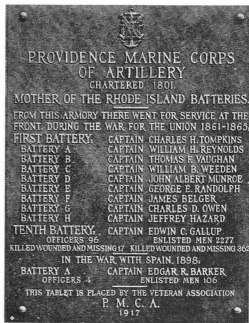

Left: *The World War I helmet insignia of the 103d Field Artillery Regiment, part of the Yankee Division (RG).* **Right:** *This plaque was dedicated by a congregation of Civil and Spanish-American War veterans in 1917 shortly before the young men of Rhode Island again went to war (RG).*

By the end of August the three Rhode Island batteries joined the rest of the 103d Field Artillery in Boxford, Massachusetts, for more training and drill. Without the artillery material that would be used in France, the men spent most of their time mastering close order drill, learning the routines of service life, and pitching pup tents. Still, the stay in Boxford was not without value, according to the regiment's historians: "Little, if any, of the knowledge thus acquired was to be used on the Western Front, but the period at Boxford brought officers and men in contact with each other. Already the regiment was beginning to develop that intangible quality which the French call 'esprit de corps.'" The cannoneers had to learn to work together; if they did not the cannon would not be fired. They had to learn how to grease shells, clean the cannon, and properly sight the weapon. A member of Battery A recalled that "teamwork [was] the essential success of the gun crew." Many of the Rhode Islanders came from Providence, some from the upper crust of society who had never known how to ride a horse. Under the watchful eyes of the veterans, all soon became adept at this and the difficult process of becoming a soldier by learning to take orders. One of the main attributes instilled was discipline. Henry Samson related, "At Boxford we began for the first time to realize that we were part of the United States Army — something more than just a body of guardsmen from the State of Rhode Island."[11]

On September 20, the Second Battalion, which included Batteries C and D and which was commanded by Maj. Everitte St. John Chaffee, left Boxford for a critical assignment; transporting some 5,000 horses and mules across the Atlantic, from Newport News, Virginia, to St. Nazaire, France. Not until January would this battalion join the rest of its regiment. The First and Third battalions, which included the remaining batteries of the 103d, embarked on the S.S. *Baltic* at Hoboken, New Jersey, on October 9. Two days later, the *Baltic* arrived in Halifax, Nova Scotia, where it became the flagship of a nine-ship convoy. "All precautions

The 103d Field Artillery and the Yankee Division came together at the Boxford Camp (RG).

were taken against submarines, the ships proceeding in a zigzag course," recalled the Battery A historian. "The men were forced to wear lifebelts at all times, and frequent lifeboat drills were held."[12]

Long periods below deck offered the men ample time for reflection as they headed to battlefields on foreign shores. "Stretched out in our bunks because of the orders to stay below," recalled one, "we thought of many things, of our homes, of our new lives as soldiers, of our quiet, almost stealthy departure for foreign shores. And then we fell to wondering what the future held in store for us."[13]

The ships were nearly twenty days in crossing the Atlantic; some of the Rhode Islanders thought they would never see dry land again. After all, it was the Providence *Marine* Corps of Artillery from whom these men were descended. Despite the weary hours below deck, the men knew that action was sure to come once they landed in Europe. As the convoy neared the Irish coast, three English destroyers met the ships to provide added protection in the submarine-infested waters off Ireland. On October 23, the convoy finally dropped anchor in the Mersey River at Liverpool, England. Less than a week later, after traveling by train to Southampton, the men were once again plying rough and dangerous waters, the English Channel, en route to France.[14]

After two days and nights in a cramped cattle car, the men arrived at Camp de Coëtquidan, an artillery camp in Brittany built by Napoleon in 1804. Indeed the great tactician had once said, "God fights on the side with the best artillery." The camp, with its stone barracks and extensive artillery range, would be the home of the 103d for the next three months. The First and Third battalions were already well tuned in the tactics by the time the Second arrived six weeks later. Amusements were few, the nearest village was several miles away, and drills were intense. But many believe the later success of the 103d was due in large part to the training at Coëtquidan, or "Coqui," as it was called by the men. "What the artillery manuals call 'fire-discipline,' that peculiar efficiency of a gun section that determines its value in active operations, can only be acquired by weeks of grueling, monotonous effort in park or on the drill field, " wrote one historian. "That the batteries of the 103d were able to give such a good account of themselves in the famous offensives of Aisne-Marne, St. Milhiel and Meuse-Argonne was due in large part to the tireless energy and able leadership of veteran French commissioned and noncommissioned officers who spent day after day at Coëtquidan instructing the gun crews in the mysteries of the 'service of the piece.'" Despite the efficient training received from the French, the Rhode Islanders had to be watchful. Throughout the conflict both the French and the English tried to assume command of the American Expeditionary Force. Gen. John "Blackjack" Pershing was adamant that Americans would serve only under American officers in an American army.[15]

Since their days at Quonset, the men and officers had heard rumors that they were to become a heavy artillery regiment in France and would not be using the three-inch guns that had distinguished them in the light artillery category. Sure enough, several weeks after arriving at Coëtquidan the regiment was issued 155mm Schneider-Cruesot howitzers, considered the most sophisticated artillery piece of its time. Each of the six batteries received four 1917 models of these howitzers, which had been designed two years earlier by the famous French firm of Schneider et Cie. "[These were] guns that packed a mighty wallop, whose range was nearly seven miles and for which, when properly elevated, 'dead space' practically ceased to exist," noted Capt. William F. Kernan in his history of the 103d. "They looked heavy and they were heavy, these snub-nosed, bell-mouthed hussies; they made horses and men lather, but once in position, they spoke with an authority not to be denied." Upon receiving the howitzers, members of Battery C considered them "the best in the world."[16]

Conditions at Coëtquidan through that long, cold and rainy winter were primitive. Food and fuel were scarce, the barracks were poorly heated and ventilated, and candles provided the only light. "The men kept at their training, conquering their first enemy in France, the

An early World War II photograph of the 155mm Schneider howitzer which was effectively used by the 103d in France (RG).

mud," wrote one of the regiment's historians. Among the most useful tactics and skills learned were mock battles where the cannoneers would fire blanks to simulate being under fire. In addition, command posts and firing positions were cut out to simulate firing by battery, battalion, and regiment. Here the officers put the practical side of their training to use by being able to learn how to control their batteries in a simulated scenario. Despite these activities, however, the soldiers of the 103d were growing restless. They knew how to use their howitzers but wanted to put the knowledge and skills to practical use at the front. On February 2, when new English gas masks were issued, there was the sense among the more astute that "something was bound to happen" soon.[17]

Two days later the regiment was on its way to the Western Front. The 103d, still considered green, was sent first to Chemin-des-Dames, a relatively quiet sector at this time. It was here that the men mastered the "techniques and tactics" of the Western Front, learned largely from the veteran French soldiers who were now well into their third year of war. The Americans admired the French meticulousness and attention to detail, while the French expressed delight over the American's good humor and energy, qualities that would serve the war-weary Allies well in those final crucial encounters with the Germans.[18]

A product of the French artillery training was Chester Files, here a newly minted second lieutenant. Only two years earlier, Pfc. Files had chased his mules around Texas (PMCA).

At the end of March, the 103d was sent to defend the Toul sector, a move that involved an exhausting fifteen-day hike through mud and rain. It was here that most people agree the 26th Division, known as the "Yankee Division," began to prove its mettle. Battery A's historian wrote of it:

> In looking back, it becomes more and more clear that in every respect, save that of time, the Toul front was for the Battery its initial fighting front. True, at Soissons [Chemin-des-Dames] the men performed all their duties with a zeal, a precision and an excellence that was highly lauded by the French commanders. Those duties, nevertheless, were pleasant and free from danger, for there chanced to be during this period but little artillery activity. However, in the Toul Sector, seldom a day passed but that some gas, fatally sweet, painfully injurious, and with a name of about thirty-five letters, contaminated the air. And times without number the dugouts trembled beneath the loud crash of large caliber shells. At Soissons, the men were receiving the finishing touches to their military education; at Toul they were veteran fighters. At Soissons, the Yankee Division was brigaded with the experienced French Army; at Toul, without aid, it held a front of 22 kilometers.

The test was not what many had desired, thinking the life of a soldier to be grand. One Battery A soldier wrote, "There is but little romance in the life of an artillerymen; little of the element of the general helishness [*sic*] of life that appeals to the artists, correspondents, and fiction writers. But there are exciting moments, and moments of great danger, around the big guns." This first taste of combat was something that none of the men who had enlisted in the three Rhode Island batteries of the 103d could ever have imagined. After the war, one soldier from Providence recalled it: "I would not have believed we could have endured it, but it was the knowledge that we were driving the Huns before us which kept us going."[19]

But life would get harder for the Yankees long before it got better. On July 15 the Germans launched a general attack along the line. From Toul the division was hurled into "the fire and fury of the Champagne-Marne defensive,"[20] and from there it would move directly into the brutal Aisne-Marne campaign. Here, the 103d Field Artillery Regiment was under the command of Col. Pelham D. Glassford, the officer who had been assigned to Battery A as an inspector instructor during its difficult years just a decade earlier. Now he was doing it again with an entire regiment of New England artillerymen. The guns of the regiment kept well to the front, "always on the heels of the infantry." The Second Battalion was sent into the rat infested trenches for the first time and earned the colorful title of "Glassford's Trench Mortars," for the pin-point precision firepower they delivered for the infantry of the Yankee Division.[21]

Assisting Col. Glassford in his operations was none other than Lt. Col. Everitte St. John Chaffee. "These two men made up a working-fighting team that was hard to beat in such a rapidly changing and highly complicated situation," noted Capt. Kernan. "They never demanded more of their men than they were willing to undergo themselves and their energy and aggressive spirit, never shown to better advantage than in the Second Battle of the Marne."

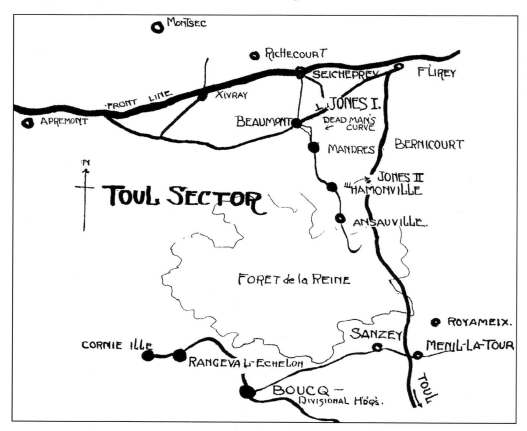

The Toul sector was the Yankee Division's first test of combat (RG).

Desirous of seeing things for themselves, they were continually in the forefront of action and many stories of their utter disregard of danger are still recounted in the Regiment." The relationship between Glassford and Chaffee was remarkably similar to that between Col. Charles Tompkins and Lt. Col. J. Albert Monroe in the Civil War. Both men had worked in tandem to insure the Rhode Island Light Artillery was a potent force; now that effort was played out again on the Western Front.[22]

The Second Battle of the Marne in August marked the start of the German retreat and a decisive turn of the tide. Gen. Ferdinand Foch, supreme commander of the Allies, began to believe victory was possible by the fall, but only by striking the Germans a succession of well-timed blows. The nearly two million men in the American Expeditionary Force greatly bolstered the strength of the Allies, who now turned to the Americans to plug the huge gaps in their lines. "The 103d Field Artillery, blissfully ignorant of the works and ways of the high command, spent the latter part of August in a 'rest area' on the Haute Marne," recalled Kernan. "Here in the little towns of Latrect and Leugley, amidst the hedgerows and orchards of the Cote d'Or, the war seemed far away and well forgot. The men read and wrote letters, brushed up their French, ate enormous meals washed down with vin ordinaire, took leaves to Paris and returned to boast of their adventures along the boulevards." The losses in the 103d had been light to date, with only a few combat casualties. Despite this, the rest was needed and helped to build unit cohesiveness that was invaluable the next time they took the field.[23]

This idyllic and much-needed respite would come to an abrupt end on August 27 at a party given by Glassford for the men. During a performance of the division minstrel show, Glassford suddenly took the stage holding an ominous telegram. 'Men,' he said, 'we're off for another fight.' Two hours later the First Battalion was pulling out of Leugley and the populace, stunned and anxious at the sudden departure, turned out with cheers and tears to see us march away," wrote the Battery B historian.[24]

Gen. Foch had assigned the newly formed American field army the mission of defending the Paris-Avricourt railway and the reduction of the St. Mihiel salient. The 26th Division was to be one of fourteen divisions employed in the operation. The assault on the St. Mihiel salient was scheduled to begin at 5:00 A.M. on September 12, but preparation fires were to be put down four hours earlier in torrential rain. Kernan described it:

> With all watches synchronized, a thunderous crash broke through the storm on the stroke of one and a cyclone of bursting shell struck the enemy positions—shrieking, rumbling, screaming, whining, away they went destroying machine gun emplacements, trenches, C.P.'s, barbed wire, as the corporals of the 103d pulled the lanyards and twirled breech blocks to the tune of the fiercest bombardment the Regiment had as yet put down. This was a Corp's battle and no mistake about it. Down in the pits the men, full of enthusiasm and too excited to mind fatigue or discomfort, worked with machine-like precision, calling from time to time between explosions the old war cry of the artillery, "Give 'em hell."

All along the line, the 103d artillery fired, supporting the attack of the Yankee Division. The soldiers from New England were more than making a name for themselves. One French officer said, "Your Gallant American Division has set us free against the Barbarians." One of the main reasons for the successful assault was the combined firepower of the three battalions of the 103d Field Artillery.[25]

Within two days, the objectives of this campaign were nearly achieved and by September 16 the whole of the Bois-des-Rappes had been captured. "The entire success of this first offensive by the American Army greatly stimulated the morale of the Allies and depressed that of the Germans," noted Capt. Kernan. "Nearly 16,000 prisoners and 443 cannon had been captured, and over 200 square miles of territory, with its remaining French population, had been restored to France. The railroads in the vicinity of St. Mihiel had been freed for the use of the

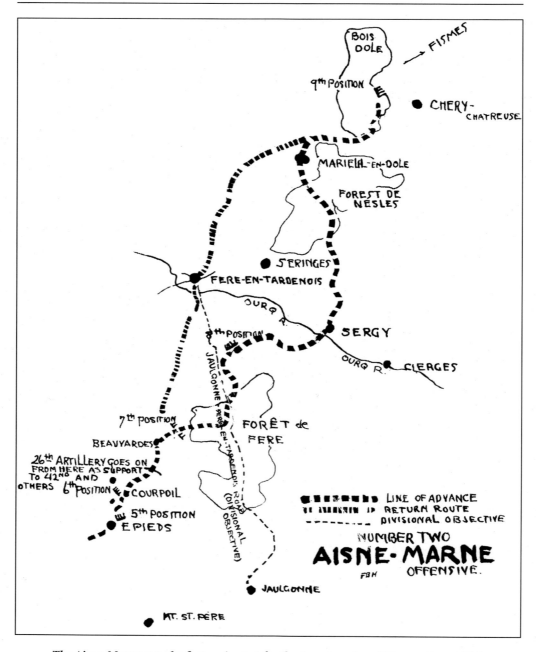

The Ainse-Marne was the first major test for the American Expeditionary Force (RG).

Allies, and the threat of the salient against surrounding territory had been removed." Only a few months earlier it had been the Germans who had been continuing their relentless push west towards Paris. Now the American Expeditionary Force was beating them back at every turn.[26]

Life on the Western Front was pure misery for the men from Rhode Island. They faced constant dangers each day and night, as the Germans kept up a ruthless bombardment. The soldiers had to live underground to escape the fire above. Trenchfoot was a constant problem caused by the poorly fitted wool and leather uniforms that had not changed much since the Civil War; they disintegrated in the harsh conditions and were not easily replaced. Soldiers were covered with "cooties," or body lice, while rats ran through the trenches nibbling on everything in sight. Horrible food, such as crackers and "bully beef," and tainted water added to the misery through disease. Gas was a constant threat as well; no soldier went anywhere without his gas mask always being available. In addition to these threats, aircraft would occasionally bomb and strafe the positions. Camouflage was essential, and much time was spent digging in, while the drivers cared for the horses, many of whom simply weakened and died. It was almost a return to the long days on the siege line at Petersburg, some fifty years earlier. The soldiers of the 103d had to be on their toes all hours of the day, ready to respond to any threat. Life in France was hell on earth, but the tough men of the Yankee Division were making the difference.[27]

Although its mission was accomplished, Foch kept the 26th Division in place to deflect German attention from the Allies' next and final great offensive,

Pvt. Anthony Sylvia of Providence fell at the Second Battle of the Marne (RG).

between the Meuse River and the Argonne Forest. Until October 17, when the 103d became actively engaged in the Meuse-Argonne campaign, the artillery batteries did their best to harass the Germans with raids and counterattacks. It was during this time that Maj. Harold R. Barker, now commander of the Second Battalion, invented a game that came to be called "snipe hunting with a 155 howitzer," which involved relentless harassing and retaliation fire.[28]

With the offensive on the Meuse under way, Foch was increasingly concerned by the slow progress of the right flank of the American First Army, which was hampered by the superior position of the enemy. He turned to the New Englanders for help. The 103d was placed north of Verdun, terrain the Germans had fought over in 1916 and which they knew well. "A battery, carelessly emplaced or insufficiently camouflaged was a battery lost," noted Kernan. Gen. Foch credited the resourcefulness and tactical knowledge of Col. J. Alden Twachtman, now regimental commander, with keeping the batteries from being spotted and enabling them to put down their most effective fire.[29]

As the 103d found itself on a Western Front, which was anything but quiet, several events occurred that normally would have distracted the corps. The century's worst epidemic of influenza was filling the hospitals with patients, killing many of its victims. Indeed as Peck had announced before the Rhode Islanders sailed for France, more of their number would die

Top: *The men of Battery A enjoy a brief respite while reading the* Providence Journal *(RG).* Bottom: *Battery A of the 103d fought bravely on the Western Front as seen in this wartime sketch (RG).*

because of disease than because of combat injuries. Besides the disease that so often plagued the unit yet another disaster occurred. On October 22, in the midst of the Meuse-Argonne campaign, Gen. Pershing relieved the popular commander of the 26th Division, Maj. Gen. Clarence E. Edwards.

Although Edwards was of the Regular Army, he was widely respected by his Guard subordinates. The reason for the removal was because Edwards was very much like the Yankees

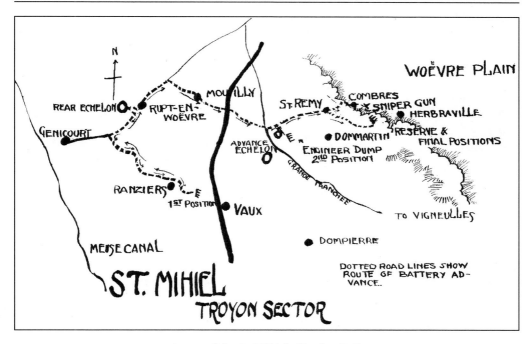

A map of the St. Mihiel offensive (RG).

Battery B moves up to the front on September 14, 1918, during the Meuse-Argonne Offensive (RG).

under his command — sharp tongued, tough, and self-reliant. He did not obey orders to the point other American officers did and worked as he saw fit. In the end he burned too many bridges for Blackjack to cross and was relieved of his command. Unlike other army officers, Edwards had retained most of the Guard colonels and one brigadier when he took over the division from its National Guard general. He won the confidence of the division by sending its units to ports of embarkation as soon as they were formed, with the division arriving in Europe well ahead of most regular units. In fact, the 26th Division — the Yankee Division — compiled the longest combat record of any of the Guard divisions. Furthermore, Gen. Edwards had put confidence into his men, he was a strict disciplinarian and the combat record of the New Englanders was second to none. The 26th was known for its good behavior and pushing forward when all others fell back.[30]

Replacing Gen. Edwards was Brig. Gen. Frank E. Bamford, who immediately removed two of the Guard colonels and the commander of the 52nd Infantry Brigade, three well-liked men who had started as privates in their original Guard units and had worked their way up through the ranks. "Once more one witnessed the apparent blindness of those who, conducting

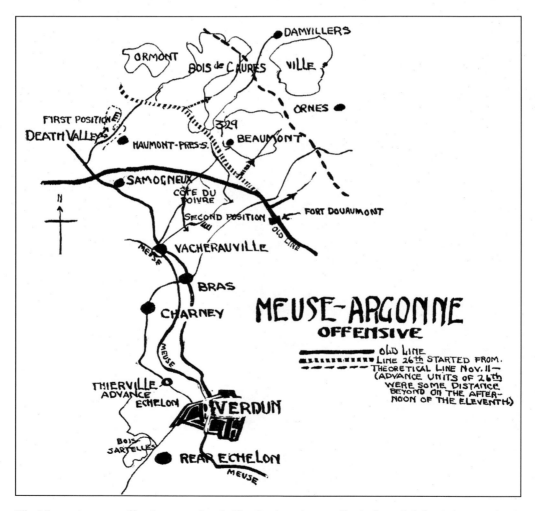

The Meuse-Argonne offensive, spearheaded by the Americans, effectively ended the Great War (RG).

Captain Gordon Colley of Battery A receives the French Croix de Guerre from Yankee Division commander General Clarence Edwards (PMCA).

the game of war, neglect to consider the psychology of the pawns on the chessboard," wrote the division historian.[31]

With the final campaign heating up around them, the men at the front gave little thought to these distractions. "They had long ago committed to memory the immortal line of Kipling: 'If you want to win your battles—take and work your blooming guns.'"[32] And that they did. The regiment began an ordeal that would last right up until the Armistice, one that "made the old days on the Toul front and even St. Mihiel seem mild by comparison." Indeed it was October 24, 1918, that would be the worst day of the war for the 103d Field Artillery. That night the Germans opened a terrific bombardment on Rhode Island's Battery C. Several direct hits were scored, and six men were killed. Despite the carnage, the men stood by their cannon and their brothers. Three men of Battery C were among the eight members of the regiment to earn the Distinguished Service Cross, the United States' second highest military decoration.[33]

The Meuse-Argonne offensive was taking its toll on the 103d Field Artillery Regiment, much as it had been with the First Rhode Island Light Artillery during the brutal Overland Campaign of 1864. Despite this toll, the campaign was bringing the Germans to their knees. As was the case in earlier struggles, the artillery in particular was playing a vital role in destroying the enemy positions. One historian wrote, "In the course of the campaign Pershing's artillerymen fired a tonnage of munitions that exceeded the totals fired by the entire Union Army during the course of the Civil War." After forty-seven days of nonstop combat, the Rhode Islanders had finally accomplished their mission.[34]

November 11, 1918, found the batteries of the 103d in position near Beaumont, ready to continue their fire into enemy emplacements. The Battery B historian recorded the event:

> Then at 9:45 that morning we received news that seemed too good to be true. An armistice had been agreed upon, and we were to stop firing at 11:00. The men went wild. Up until 11:00 we gave Heinie everything we had. On the last shot every member of the firing battery, all the cooks included, as well as a number of officers from G.H.Q. [Gen. Headquarters], helped to pull the long lanyard which had been brought out for the purpose. For a moment there was silence, not a gun to be heard anywhere. Then the men gave vent to their feelings. We joined the French in celebrating. It was a wonderful sight.

In Battery C, the men were doing much the same as those in Battery B. Henry Samson recalled when it was all over: "An awesome silence settled over the sector."[35]

The initial euphoria of seeing the war finally end quickly dissipated, however, as the men began to suspect they would not be going home anytime soon. Furloughs broke up the monotony of daily drills, but even a weekend in Paris was no match for the warmth of home, hearth and family. After ten grueling months of war, coping with mud, rain, rats, and body lice, and fighting a relentless foe, the men eagerly awaited orders to embark. They would wait more than four months for those orders to come, but on March 31 "packs were made up for the last time on French soil and the men were ferried out to the S.S. *Mongolia* [which] pointed her nose toward the rosy sunset and the good old United States."[36]

The Yankee Division received an enormous welcome upon its arrival in Boston and Batteries A, B and C enjoyed an equally enthusiastic greeting on their return to Providence in April 1919. As had happened fifty-five years earlier, thousands of Rhode Islanders were there, along with the governor and the old veterans of the PMCA. The cannoneers were showered in gifts of chocolate, candies, and sandwiches. Despite this, many just wanted to get back home and on with their lives. Unlike many National Guard divisions, the 26th had preserved much of its regional character, symbolized by the blue and green "YD," the Yankee Division, patch worn on the left arm, and it was one of the rare cases in which the artillery had remained with its parent division. Some in the Regular Army continued to dismiss the skill and discipline of the guardsman, but those who had witnessed his work and courage in Europe were truly impressed. After the 102nd Infantry Regiment of the 26th Division advanced into forty German batteries and captured them on February 28, 1918, the colonel commanding the regiment insisted that the American militia had reestablished its reputation: "The American militiaman, when he is properly led, is the finest soldier who ever wore shoe leather."[37]

The fighting on the Western Front was the most horrific up to that time in world history. Not even the terrible carnage and slaughter of the moonscape of Spotsylvania in 1864 could compare. The

Maj. Gen. Clarence Edwards was the beloved commander of the Yankee Division (RG).

Battery C effectively used the 155mm Schneider howitzer (PMCA).

Left: *Corp. Walter F. Lyons of Battery C was one of eight 103d soldiers awarded the Distinguished Service Cross for heroism under fire in World War I (RG).* Right: *Thomas Hickey was one of the most highly decorated members of the 103d. He stood by his gun in the midst of a furious bombardment.*

The parade of the Yankee Division in April of 1919 marked the return of the battle-hardened troops (PMCA).

officers and men of the 103d fought with extreme gallantry, but as always, that bravery came at a great cost. The following members of the Rhode Island batteries of the 103d gave their lives in World War I: *Battery A*: Capt. Joseph C. Davis, Sgt. Joshua K. Broadhead, Corp. Ernest H. Munroe, Pfc. John E. Benson, Pvt. Fred A. Almquist, Pvt. Dona J. Dugal, Pvt. Carl F. Green, Pvt. Charles E. Jenkins, Pvt. Beverly S. Lake, Pvt. William D. Packer, Pvt. George A. Rieo, and Pvt. Eugene J. St. Amour. *Battery B*: Lt. Archibald Coats, SSgt. Edgar P. Black, Corp. Ray C. Betherman, Pfc. William J. Brailsford, Pvt. Albert C. Butts, Pvt. Frederick A. Harmon, Pvt. Willie J. Bacon, Pvt. William H. Francis, and Pvt. Harry C. Leeman. *Battery C*: Sgt. Lawrence E. Redmond, Corp. James Hemphill, Pfc. Lawrence S. Ayer, Pfc. Gaskin P. Williams, Pfc. Boleslaw Osmolski, Pfc. David Paineau, Pfc. Anthony F. Sylvia, Pvt. Edgar H. Green-haulgh, Pvt. Richard J. Dennis, Pvt. Russell K. Bournce, Pvt. Charles Bacon, Pvt. Wilmer H. Eicke, Pvt. Fred L. Humphreys, Pvt. Henry Becker, Pvt. Jewel B. Rumsey, and Pvt. Albert Payette. "Dulce et Decorum est Pro Patria Morte."[38]

The men from Rhode Island who had gone to war wearing olive drab rather than the traditional blue again elicited praise from their commanders and comrades. The soldiers from the three Rhode Island batteries of the 103d were always at the front, working the Schneiders under any weather conditions and battlefield situations. As George Peck had promised before they went "over there," the men had indeed selected the right branch of the service and had carried on the traditions laid down by their remarkable forefathers. In a testament to the regiment, Gen. Clarence Edwards, the original Yankee Division commander, wrote after the war: "I will recall the fine work of the 103d Field Artillery with their heavy guns. They were under desperate shelling and almost constant gas, but they kept their nerve and continued their fire, and only stopped at eleven o'clock on the morning of November 11, Armistice Day."[39]

Several years after the war, the veterans of the 26th Yankee Division raised funds for the memorial chapel to the division built at the Ainse-Marne American Cemetery. The original chapel had been destroyed by the fierce fighting in nearby Belleau Wood. During the peace it was rebuilt by the division and dedicated as a monument to the fallen American soldiers and

SOUVENEZ-VOUS DANS VOS PRIÈRES
DE

DAVID PAPINEAU

DU 103ÈME RÉGIMENT. BATTERIE C

MORT AU FRONT. EN FRANCE

LE 19 JUILLET 1918

A L'ÂGE DE 30 ANS

R. I. P.

Cœur sacré de Jésus, j'ai confiance en vous!   (*300 jrs chaque fois.*)

Left: **A member of the 103d wore this uniform on the Western Front. On the front is the crest of the 103d; the gas mask is ever present (PMCA).** *Right:* **The French-Canadians of the Pawtuxet Valley remembered David Papineau, of Battery C, who fell on the Western Front (RG).**

their French comrades. Of particular note are the names of those 103d soldiers who lost their lives, which are carved in stone as a lasting memorial of their sacrifice. As the cannoneers of the Civil War had done, the men who fought on the Western Front again banded together after the war to form their veteran's organization. They had to readjust to civilian life and learn to come and go as they pleased. It was again a trying experience — trying to forget the horrors of trench warfare. On May 30, 1919, Decoration Day, the PMCA held a memorial service at the Benefit Street Arsenal in honor of those who died in the war.[40]

For the first time the gallant artillerymen from Rhode Island had flexed their muscles overseas and had proved to their French and British allies, in addition to their German foe, their fighting prowess. They had been the first New England and National Guard unit to fire in anger in France. Furthermore, the 103d had spent 284 days on the line. Their epitaph was written by Gen. John H. Sherburne: "Often weary, sleepless, and exhausted, officers and men showed unfailingly a spirit of courage, determination, and cheerfulness typifying the very highest standard of American ideals." The Rhode Islanders had performed their duty, carried on the tradition of artillery greatness, and performed superbly under fire. Fortunately for the 103d Field Artillery Regiment, it would be nearly twenty years before they were called again, this time in a changed world.[41]

12

Between the Wars

A time of great distress...

— Brig. Gen. Harold R. Barker,
68th Field Artillery Brigade

With their return from the Western Front, the 103d Field Artillery was all but disbanded and mustered out of the service on April 29, 1919, at Camp Devens, Massachusetts. The men were given their honorable discharges, personally signed by Col. J. Alden Twachtman, and then they returned to their homes. As their grandfathers had done some fifty years before, the new veterans tried to move on with their lives, while their relics would soon adorn the Benefit Street Arsenal. Now the men who had survived the Western Front silently marched beside aging men in blue uniforms each May 30 to honor their own comrades who had died. The American Legion came to represent these men. In World War I, the three battalions of the 103d Field Artillery Regiment had comprised men from three New England states. Now, in a changing world, the name of the 103d would soon come to represent just one: Rhode Island.

Battery D of New Hampshire returned to form the nucleus of the 197th Field Artillery, while the two batteries from Connecticut, E and F, returned to their state as well to become the 192nd Field Artillery. The Headquarters Battery and Batteries B and C were also mustered out of the service for the time being, and there were barely enough men to keep Battery A alive. These veterans from the harsh combat in France, men such as Harold Barker, Chester Files, and others, kept Battery A active after the war. By 1921 the War Department saw the need for a battalion of field artillery in Rhode Island and reauthorized the raising of the First Battalion of the 103d Field Artillery Regiment. The new battalion was recruited in the summer of 1921 and on November 25, the 103d Field Artillery was once again resurrected as a member unit of the Rhode Island National Guard. Headquarters and Headquarters Battery, along with the venerable Battery A and a new Batteries B and C, moved into the new Armory of Mounted Commands in Providence. The overall battalion command would fly the colors of the regiment, with the battle honors extending back to the Civil War, as would the guidon of Battery A. The soldiers of Batteries B and C of the 103d trace their lineage directly back to the units activated for service during World War I, not the units by the same name of the First Rhode Island Light Artillery Regiment in the Civil War.[1]

The number of enlisted men and officers in the Rhode Island National Guard fell off dramatically in 1919. Most veterans returning home from the Great War had lost enthusiasm for military affairs and were eager now to pursue other interests. The country was at peace and Americans were ready to enjoy a dizzying decade of prosperity. Concerned about the country's lack of preparedness in 1916, Washington legislators and high-ranking military officers talked about resurrecting the universal military training that had been a cornerstone of the militia system in Colonial America. Now, however, this training was viewed as a way to boost Federal forces and many in the Guard saw it as a threat to the state systems. Heavy lobbying from the National Guard Association, coupled with support from those who defended states' rights, defeated the proposals. Without the draft, the army general staff felt it necessary to reshuffle the Guard's divisions in case of a national emergency, grouping smaller states together in single divisions. Under the new organization, the Rhode Island Guardsmen joined those of Maine, Vermont and Connecticut to form the 43rd Infantry Division. Within this division, the 103d Field Artillery Regiment was part of the 68th Field Artillery Brigade, headquartered in Providence. Rhode Island would be home to an artillery headquarters for over the next eighty years.[2]

Many at the state level, concerned that the federal government was encroaching on their authority, stressed that the hierarchy of the state systems must remain unchanged, except in a national emergency. In his 1925 report, Rhode Island's adjutant general, Maj. Gen. John J. Richards, wrote: "The National Guard is that portion of the R.I. Militia that has accepted the provisions of the National Defense Act. It should be kept in mind, however, that the Federal government recognizes the fact that the Guard is primarily a state force and still a part of the R.I. Militia and the governor is commander-in-chief until such time as the troops enter Federal service."[3]

Col. J. Alden Twachtman was the last commander of the 103d in World War I (RG).

The independent chartered companies that had declined to accept the provisions of the State Militia Act in 1876 and were, therefore, not part of the state's National Guard, still existed, some in name only. Among those to go was the venerable First Light Infantry. During World War I they provided the nucleus of a Home Guard, but their military value to the state had diminished considerably. Still, Adjutant General Richards always spoke respectfully of their origins and lineage, recognizing the role all the independents had played in the early years of the state military system: "The chartered organizations with their quaint, high-sounding names, their gaudy uniforms and their parades and field days attracted to their ranks men of prominence and standing. They became and continued to be for many years the state's nursery for military officers." Replacing these organizations would be the Reserve Officer Training Corps, chartered in 1916 to provide initial military training to college students. The University of Rhode Island was quick to add a program that has turned out many 103d officers over the years.[4]

In the early twenties, the 103d Field Artillery and the state's cavalry moved into the

Armory of Mounted Commands on North Main Street. The large structure provided the necessary drill space, equipment storage, social hall, and stables for the mounted force. By 1930, the field artillery became fully motorized and the cavalry was disbanded, but the building continued to be called by that name and still is today. The loss of the horses and the switch to trucks to pull the cannon represented a complete change in the history of the 103d. The PMCA had pioneered the development of the hard-hitting, mobile tactics used by the light batteries during the Civil War. These standard practices were taught again and again to each new generation of artillerymen. Now the horses, long considered part of the battery itself, were sold off into retirement. The men had shown countless hours of devotion to these animals, going so far as to give them an annual Christmas party. At this party the horses were turned loose in the riding rink and fed at plank tables in the center with feed and apples. The last actions of the horses on the border and in France had brought amusement and hours of nonstop attention to the command. Now the former drivers, farriers, and veterinarians would have to be retrained as truck drivers, mechanics, and other functions needed to support an ever-changing army. The change from horses to trucks severely upset one new recruit whose sole reason for joining the 103d had been for the famed polo team the regiment sponsored when the horses were not being used for their assigned duties.[5]

While the field artillery lost its horses, so too did Rhode Island's remaining battalion of mounted cavalry. This ancient arm had lost all effectiveness on the modern battlefield. After much debate on what to do with the soldiers, the War Department decided to take the three remaining troops and form a second battalion of the 103d Field Artillery Regiment: Batteries D, E, and F. As they had done in the past, the units remained quartered at the Armory of Mounted Commands. The regiment welcomed the reinforcements as it made the 103d a complete, two-battalion, regiment of artillery. In addition, during this period Rhode Island added units of quartermaster, military police, ordnance, and repair companies. The mission of the 68th Field Artillery Brigade became support for the infantry of the 43rd Division, troops from Maine, Vermont, and Connecticut.[6]

The Armory of Mounted Commands in Providence has been home to the 103d Field Artillery since the 1920s (PMCA).

While the 103d Field Artillery and the Rhode Island National Guard changed after the Great War, so too did a venerable organization, the Providence Marine Corps of Artillery. Since its redesignation as Battery A in 1874, the unit had served a secondary function as a veterans association, with membership open to any member of a Rhode Island battery in the Civil War or former PMCA member, before the unit became Battery A. With membership waning due to the loss of so many of the veterans in the first years of the twentieth century, the PMCA again changed with the times.

While prior to 1874 it had been a combat oriented group, the new unit but still the same PMCA, sought to remember the service of its members as a veterans association for the soldiers of the 103d Field Artillery Regiment who had seen service in France and those who would serve in Amer-

Sgt. John (Spud) Murphy was a living legend in the 103d, as his numerous service stripes attest (PMCA).

ica's future wars. Membership became automatic for any serving member of the 103d, while the Benefit Street Arsenal changed its role as well. Still the home of a Guard unit, the small building took on a cherished meaning to the veterans as they decorated its upper floors with memorabilia and images of the great soldiers who had left the structure for war. The large drill hall became a function room, while the upstairs offices became places where the veterans of the various wars could talk and remember the old days. This mission of the PMCA became to provide support to the 103d and its veterans and continues to do so to this day.[7]

It was during these years, before the artillery was motorized, that the PMCA found a unique way to fuel its endowment fund. Members sold the manure from the regiment's horses to local nurseries and greenhouses. Enlistment for the Rhode Island Guard gradually increased through the 1920s, but the Great Depression in the 1930s boosted numbers much higher as men sought additional sources of income. Through those difficult years, guardsmen often transported food and clothing to the needy and drove the state's unemployed to federal work projects.

Despite the aid they gave, the Rhode Island National Guard was not a reflection of modern times. With so little money available in the depression years, the Regular Army was barely getting state-of-the-art technology and weapons; the National Guard was receiving the leftovers. Despite the reforms of the Dick Act, it appeared again that they were reverting to their Revolutionary status of farmers with pitchforks. In the 103d, officers and men wore the same style of uniforms that had been worn on the Western Front. Bolt action rifles remained, while the old three-inch cannon which had been used for training before deploying to World War I were again pulled out of storage and put back into service. Drill pay remained at one dollar per drill for privates. These were dark days for the soldiers from Rhode Island.[8]

In 1931, each regiment and battalion in the United States Army adopted a Distinguishing Unit Insignia, or "DUI," which all members wore on their uniform to indicate they were members of a specific unit. The crest of the 103d Field Artillery, according to the U.S. Army Institute of Heraldry, was designed and approved March 28, 1931, and represents the following: "The field piece and cannonballs on a mound are taken from the old Providence Marine Corps of Artillery coat buttons. The cannon refers to the Civil War service at Bunker Hill, Virginia. The gold chevron indicated the cavalry origin of the Second Battalion, while the six fleurs-de-lis represent service during World War I." In addition, the 103d had adopted the motto "Play the Game." This small enameled crest, cherished by every soldier in the regiment, is a day-to-day reminder of the origin and service of the 103d Field Artillery.[9]

In those days, Brown University regarded military service as a "maturing experience for students." During the Civil War, many of the finest of the First Rhode Island Light Artillery, such as J. Albert Monroe, T. Fred Brown, and G. Lyman Dwight, had left the school to go to war. Even after the conflict, many Brown students remained members of the PMCA or later joined Battery A as enlisted men, thus meeting fellow soldiers who might come from lower social standings than the Providence elite. Young men whose grades left something to be desired were gently but firmly pushed towards the First Battalion of the 103d Field Artillery of the Rhode Island National Guard as a means of learning self-discipline and life skills not taught at any university. The training was an invaluable part of the education experience, so much so that in the 1920s Battery A later received the title of the "Brown Battery," as it contained many Brown graduates and students who would fire salutes at home games and on other occasions. An early form of ROTC, the Brown Battery gave graduates a practical course in leadership and mathematical skills that could be found nowhere else; indeed, some Brown students became "lifers" and made the National Guard a career. Among them was Robert Kenny Sr., who joined the Brown Battery as a student in the 1920s and by the time the United States entered World War II had risen to the rank of captain. In January 1945, as a battalion commander, he led his troops in an amphibious invasion of the Philippines. After the war he

Sgt. Maj. Frank Neri was known as the soldier's soldier and risked his life to save an important piece of paper during World War II (PMCA).

remained in the Guard and retired as a brigadier general, in addition to serving as a dean at Brown University.[10]

As the depression dragged on, guardsmen across the country were called to perform another duty that some found onerous. With labor disputes erupting across the nation, the guardsmen, many of them blue-collar workers themselves, were often called upon to intervene. Although the National Guard generally tried to take a neutral position in these disputes, viewing its job as keeping the peace and preventing violence, its role angered many laborers. In September of 1934 a series of strikes in Rhode Island culminated in September with what the adjutant general described as "one of the most serious riots that the state has ever experienced."[11]

On September 4, the United Textile Workers called a strike in all textile mills in Rhode Island. Many of the mills closed as a result of the strike, but those that continued

The 103d Field Artillery adopted this distinguishing crest in the 1930s; the colors are gold and red (PMCA).

to operate attracted angry picketers. In the early morning hours of September 11, the crowds of strikers around the Saylesville Finishing Plant, which stretches along Lonsdale Avenue in Saylesville and Central Falls, grew so large that state and local police feared they were losing control. Governor Theodore Francis Green ordered the mobilization of the Guard and by 6:00 A.M. the units were held in their armories in a state of readiness.[12]

The next day, with the violence increasing, Green ordered the troops to relieve the state police and put down the rioting. The 103d Field Artillery, under the command of Col. Harold R. Barker, were sent to Central Falls. His two small battalions were dispatched against 5,000 angry Rhode Islanders. The men were instantly met by a barrage of sling shot and rocks from the rioters. Under tight orders the cannoneers did not return fire but deployed around the city to prevent looting. When a large force approached one battery position, the men threw tear gas to drive back the rioters. A large detachment of rioters deployed into Mosshachuck Cemetery, threatening the flank and safety of the entire position of the 103d.

Faced with no other option, Col. Harold Barker gave the order to fire over the heads of the strikers to push them back. The message had its effect and the strikers were pushed back. A few cemetery headstones were accidentally damaged by the fire. In addition one fifteen-year-old who had skipped school to observe the riot was on a nearby rooftop when he was struck by a ricochet round and instantly killed. The guardsmen also suffered a few nasty concussions and other minor violence. The men of the 103d did their duty and the strikers peaceably went back to work after seeing the firepower and resolve of the redlegs. Many of the soldiers did not want to perform this duty; they were workers themselves and shared sympathy with their fellow Rhode Islanders trying to get a better way of life. But orders were orders.[13]

On September 21, 1938, the 103d Field Artillery and indeed the entire Rhode Island National Guard mobilized to help fight the worst natural disaster in the history of the state, the 1938 hurricane. Within hours the members of the Guard had assembled at their armories and had begun to spread out throughout Rhode Island. The soldiers protected property against

Left: *Brig. Gen. Harold Barker rose from private to general to command the 43rd Division Artillery in World War II (RG).* Right: *Lt. Col. William McCormick commanded the 103d during the strikes and the initial stages of World War II (RG).*

This tombstone in Central Falls is a grim reminder of the textile strikes (RG).

looters, assisted in cleanup duties, and found those who needed attention. A sobering task was searching for the many people from the state who lost their lives in the catastrophe. Despite it all the cannoneers carried out the tasks and helped to relieve their state.[14]

Among the many young men who joined the 103d Field Artillery during the Great Depression was Howard F. Brown of Warwick. Brown was a 1936 graduate of La Salle Academy and began working for the manufacturing firm of Brown and Sharpe after high school. The young man took a deep interest in military matters and had it not been for the objections of his mother he would have joined the Regular Army. Instead he decided to join the Rhode Island National Guard. A coworker at Brown and Sharpe was a captain in the 118th Combat Engineers and told Brown to join the 103d, based on their reputation as a fine combat outfit, but, more important for the ambitious soldier, an in-house version of Officer Candidate School that allowed men with a high school diploma to become commissioned officers. Howard Brown enlisted as a private in 1937 in the Second Battalion of the 103d and three years later was 2nd Lt. Brown. The 103d

Col. Howard Brown enlisted as a private during the Great Depression and retired as a Regular Army colonel in 1968 (PMCA).

would hear many things from this man in the years to come. In 1937 he put on the stripes of a private and thirty years later took off the eagles of a colonel when he retired.[15]

One of the major changes for the 103d Field Artillery came in 1938 when Brig. Gen. Herbert R. Dean, who had been commanding the 68th Field Artillery Brigade, resigned his commission to become Rhode Island's adjutant general. This opened the door for yet another man to serve as the commander of the New England artillery, following in a tradition that had begun at the Battle of Dorchester Heights in 1776 with Henry Knox, who literally blew the British out of Boston. Men such as Charles Tompkins and John G. Hazard served in the same position in the Civil War and Pelham Glassford in the Great War. New Englanders had always known how to properly use their cannon on the battlefield. Now another great soldier rose to this prominent post. Dean was replaced by Col. Barker of the 103d. Barker had done something truly amazing in rising from private to the stars of a brigadier general.[16]

The twenties and thirties were a changing time for the 103d and the PMCA. Men who had served in the Great War as battery and section commanders now took on greater roles as battalion and regimental leaders. A fresh crop of enlisted men, some of them brand new Americans, raised the fighting strength of the corps, while constant training, a benchmark of the command since the Civil War, continued in full force. When the call to arms came again, the Rhode Islanders would be ready with their usual ardor. This time they would fight one of the worst enemies ever seen in warfare, in a land half a planet away.

13

WORLD WAR II

Munda was a tough nut.
— Col. Howard F. Brown, 169th Field Artillery

Throughout the Great Depression, tensions had been heating up in Europe with the rise of Hitler and in the Pacific as the Japanese expanded their empire. The army staff and President Roosevelt knew that if the United States was called to fight, the National Guard would play a vital role to boost the ranks of the United States Army. Now it was not a question of whether the country would go to war, but only a matter of time before it occurred. Even the most pacifist isolationist could not deny that the United States was about to embark on another global crusade. In Rhode Island, recruitment efforts were expanded in an attempt to raise the ranks of the six batteries of the 103d to full war strength. In addition, the other Rhode Island National Guard units such as the 118th Engineers and the 243rd Coastal Artillery also began recruiting at a feverish rate. Among those to join the 243rd would be a young Thomas Caruolo. While most of the soldiers from the 243rd spent the war guarding Narragansett Bay from U-boat attack, Sgt. Caruolo transferred to the infantry. From here he would be sent to France, where he would fight, from Normandy through the Battle of the Bulge, to the final victory against the Nazis. After the war, Caruolo would rejoin the Guard as a member of the 103d and serve until he reached the rank of command sergeant major, one of just many men to rise to prominence in the years of war ahead.

On February 24, 1941, a total of 12,000 National Guardsmen from Vermont, Maine, Connecticut, and Rhode Island raised their right hands and were mustered into federal service for a period of one year's intensive training. The men from Rhode Island spent two weeks in Providence organizing equipment and uniforms, undergoing physicals, and learning more about the task before them. On March 4, 1941, the vehicle convoy left the Armory of Mounted Commands. A few days later the bulk of the regiment traveled by train for Camp Blanding, Florida, some 850 miles away. For some men who had never left their state, it was the journey of a lifetime. They would not return for over four years.[1]

The 43rd spent the next few months training at Camp Blanding before taking part in the Louisiana Maneuvers during August and September. In November, the 43rd Division also took part in the Carolina maneuvers, one of only three army divisions to take part in both. The Rhode Islanders had left Providence with the famous French 75mm gun of World War I vintage, but when they relocated to Camp Shelby, Mississippi, these were exchanged for the new, powerful 105mm howitzer. The two battalions of the 103d, along with the rest of the 43rd Division, drilled relentlessly. The open expanses of the Mississippi pines and Carolina flatlands finally afforded the necessary maneuver space that was not available in Rhode Island. Camp Shelby in Mississippi was especially useful as a site to test the soldiers under a variety of field conditions. As William Sprague and Charles Tompkins had done a century earlier, Gen. Harold Barker was the reason the men succeeded at the rigorous regimen.

With the Japanese bombing of Pearl Harbor on December 7, 1941, the one-year training period was terminated and the soldiers from the 103d Field Artillery were now in for the duration of the war plus six months at the discretion of the army. Sgt. Bill Fusco remembered that the men were "ready to go and uttered no complaints." Patriotism ran high, and many of the Rhode Islanders wanted revenge. Indeed, one soldier was in the process of having his discharge typed up for disability. When the clerk heard the news, it was torn up and the soldier went in for four years of war. The training had proved very successful and helped to forge a powerful instrument of war, the 43rd Infantry Division.[2]

When mobilized for federal service, the 43rd Division included two infantry brigades: the 85th from Connecticut and the 86th from Maine and Vermont, each with two infantry regiments. The firepower came from the 68th Field Artillery

Corporal Thomas W. Caruolo, 243d Coast Artillery 1940 (PMCA).

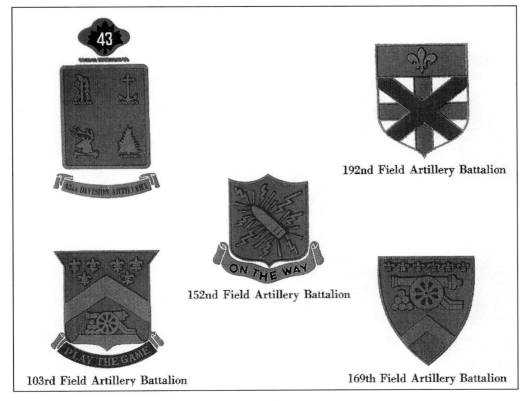

192nd Field Artillery Battalion

152nd Field Artillery Battalion

103rd Field Artillery Battalion

169th Field Artillery Battalion

The 43d Division Artillery adopted the following Distinguishing Unit Insignia (DUI) during World War II (RG).

Brigade, which included the 103d Field Artillery Regiment from Rhode Island, the 152nd Field Artillery Regiment hailing from Maine, and the 192nd Field Artillery Regiment of the Connecticut National Guard.[3]

Being organized with four regiments of infantry resulted in the nickname "square" division. However, this was recognized to be a very large and ungainly structure; and in March 1941, the secretary of war ordered all army divisions to reorganize into a smaller, more manageable "triangular" structure. The "triangularization" of the 43rd Infantry Division did not occur until early 1942, when the division was training at Camp Shelby, Mississippi. The new structure now included three infantry regiments, while the artillery was reorganized into a Division Artillery, commanded by Brig. Gen. Barker. Because of the downsizing of the division, the 43rd Infantry Division found itself losing some of its most experienced officers and men to other organizations. This was a severe blow to the morale of the division, as many friends and neighbors left to serve in other units. The 43rd Division Artillery now included four artillery battalions, the 103d, the 152nd, and the 192nd. New to the divisional artillery was the 169th Field Artillery Battalion. With the reduction of field artillery units from regiments to battalions, the Second Battalion of the 103d was simply redesignated as the 169th.[4]

Each battalion included a headquarters and headquarters battery. The Battalion Headquarters Battery provided all command and fire control elements, while the remainder of the battery provided administrative support to the entire unit. The battery also included three firing batteries and a service battery, which was responsible for providing all logistical support for the battalion, including ammunition, fuel, food and water. By doctrine, the three infantry regiments of the "triangular" division were habitually supported by the same artillery battalion from the division artillery in order to facilitate coordination and efficiency. The new force was given the colorful acronym of DIVARTY.

The artillery mission of "direct support" means that the fires of a direct support battalion were dedicated to a specific infantry regiment. Consequently, within the 43rd Infantry Division, the 103d Infantry Regiment from Maine was supported by the 152nd Field Artillery Battalion. The 169th Infantry from Connecticut was supported by the 169th Field Artillery, and the 172nd Infantry, the "Green Mountain Boys" of the Vermont National Guard, was supported by the 103d Field Artillery. This pairing of Rhode Island artillery and Ver-

Sgt. Bill Fusco was a truck driver as well as a cannoneer. In this photograph taken in 1941, he trains with his rifle (PMCA).

Battery D of the 103d on its way to Ft. Blanding, Florida, in 1941 (PMCA).

mont infantry was a continuation of a historical association. During the Civil War, the batteries of the First Rhode Island Light Artillery had supported the First Vermont Brigade on many bloody fields. The next level of artillery support is the "general support" mission, normally assigned to the artillery battalion with 155mm howitzers, which in the 43rd was the 192nd. This battalion was used to support or reinforce any other unit in the division.[5]

The organization of the 43rd Division Artillery was quite different from the smaller units that had fought in the Civil War. In total, Gen. Barker, when the division was at full strength, commanded 2,111 men divided among the four battalions, much greater than Col. Tompkins' famed Sixth Corps Artillery Brigade. Of these, 114 officers and men comprised the Division Artillery Headquarters, responsible for communicating with each battalion and providing firing data. A medical unit and an observation section were also included. At full strength, each 105mm battalion consisted of 497 soldiers, 126 in the headquarters battery and seventy-four in the service battery. The main fighting strength of each battalion was in its three firing batteries. Each contained four howitzers and ninety-nine men at full strength. It was commanded by a captain, aided by a first lieutenant and two second lieutenants, along with a first sergeant. There were also eight sergeants and eight corporals. In addition, twenty drivers took over the role of the mounted men of the previous century. As support, there were four mechanics to take care of the vehicles, three cooks to feed the hungry cannoneers, and three radiomen to communicate with headquarters. The most important soldiers, as they had been in the past, were the forty-eight who joined the elite brotherhood of the cannoneers. The batteries equipped with the 155mm howitzer were only slightly larger because of the size and weight of the howitzers. The 103d would maintain this structure through much of World War II.[6]

For nearly a year while the American forces battled, and lost heavily in their initial engagements with the enemy, the men of the 43rd Division continued to train at Camp Shelby,

This small collection of officers and radios shows the fire control center of Headquarters Battery, 169th Field Artillery, during the Munda Campaign (RG).

Mississippi, and await further developments. As his officers and men completed their training, Brig. Gen. Harold Barker prepared to carry on an old tradition. In 1861, Samuel Arnold had notified the members of the First Rhode Island Battery of the duty before them. In 1917, George Peck had done the same to the soldiers deploying to France. Now Gen. Barker, who had listened to the speech by an aged Civil War veteran twenty-five years earlier, issued the following rousing general order to his soldiers:

> Headquarters
> 43rd Division Artillery
> Camp Shelby, Mississippi
>
> To the Officers and Men of the 43rd Division Artillery
>
> Once again, the men of our nation have been called to defend our country and the ideals of our nation from the attacks of the forces of aggression. The development of a force of men capable of carrying the battle to the foe and stamping out the enemy is no easy task. Yet it is a task to which we as a nation have pledged ourselves. To accomplish this end will require the utmost effort. To turn a nation of peaceful citizens into an army of trained, efficient fighters is a job to test the mettle of every officer and every enlisted man. This job, however, we have set ourselves to do. During the arduous days that we spend training and in the time when we shall be a part of the striking force on whatever battlefront, it shall fall to our lot to engage the enemy. I am sure that the officers and men of the 43rd Division Artillery will acquit themselves with honor.
>
> H.R. Barker

Gen. Barker had made his point very clear. His artillery battalions existed for one reason — to support the infantry. Wherever the infantry went, the artillerymen from New England would not be far behind. Yet another generation of Rhode Islanders trained in the traditions of the Providence Marine Corps of Artillery was off to war, this time to make the world free.[7]

Finally, in September of 1942 the orders came for the New Englanders to prepare for their

At Camp Shelby, the men learned how to become field soldiers (PMCA).

overseas deployment. A cross-country train ride took them to Fort Ord near Salinas, California. Here they practiced two months of amphibious training. The United States was not going to risk sending untrained soldiers into combat. In World War I, the 103d had been part of the famed Yankee Division, fighting on the Western Front in Europe. This time the men of the 103d Field Artillery and the 43rd Division were going to sail from San Francisco and would fight in the Pacific.[8]

As the Rhode Islanders prepared to again enter a war zone, the 103d Field Artillery was an odd mixture of remaining combat veterans from the Great War and the strike riots, hurricane duty, and those newer soldiers who are the continued life blood of any unit. All those who had attended the prior year's "summer camp" had fired the 75mm howitzer. At the head of the command, however, were two of the finest cannoneers the smallest state ever produced, and who would serve as inspirational leaders to their men in the battles to come.[9]

The *Providence Journal* called Harold R. Barker the epitome of the citizen-soldier, "a businessman who during years of peace devotes part of his time and energy to preparing himself for the defense of his country when that demand is made on him." Nearly seventy years after Pearl Harbor, a sergeant under his command remarked, "What a soldier." Indeed, from the Mexican border to the fields of France and, finally, to the Solomon Islands and the Philippines, Gen. Barker distinguished himself not only as a soldier but also as a leader of men. Barker was a second-generation artilleryman. His father, Edgar R. Barker, had served as captain of Battery A and commander of the PMCA from 1892 to 1899.[10]

Harold Barker joined Battery A as a private in 1913, and in 1916 he went with the battery to the Mexican border as a second lieutenant. When the United States entered World War I a year later, Captain Barker was the commander of Battery A, 103d Field Artillery, a component of the famed 26th Yankee Division. After a string of assignments that took him away from his beloved battery, he eventually rejoined the unit at the Soissons (Chemin des Dames) sector on the Western Front in France. By the end of the war he held the rank of major and was given command of the Second Battalion. A member of Battery C called him, "A fearless fighter, devoted to his men and loved by them."[11]

Between wars, Barker trained scores of younger men in the 103d Field Artillery Regiment who would later distinguish themselves in World War II, though few were as widely recognized as Barker himself. The Guard took up much of Barker's time, but he still devoted himself to other career pursuits. A graduate of Bryant College, the general worked in the Industrial Bank in Providence and would eventually become its vice president. He also devoted a great deal of time to becoming an amateur historian. In the Pacific, where he commanded the 43rd Division Artillery, and at times, the XIV Corps Artillery, Barker was known at the highest levels of command as an artilleryman of exceptional ability and resourcefulness. In the Solomons, he was awarded the Legion of Merit, and it was there that he and his artillery established their reputation with the infantry. That reputation would continue to grow as Barker led his troops to New Guinea and then on to the sandy beaches of Linguyen Gulf in the Philippines. Gen. Barker's men never failed to impress the infantrymen with their uncanny accuracy and relentless firing. What Col. Charles H. Tompkins was to the First Rhode Island Light Artillery Regiment in the Civil War, Gen. Barker was to the 43rd Division Artillery in World War II.

In 1944 the DIVARTY began using light planes to adjust artillery fire. If aviation was to be part of artillery, Barker was determined to master it; at the age of fifty-three, he learned to fly. After arriving in Japan, Barker piloted a plane over the Imperial palace in Tokyo, something, he said, he had been longing to do for some time. His aviation accomplishments were later recognized with the awarding of the Air Medal. Gen. Barker's decorations included two Silver Stars, one for World War I and the other for World War II, two Legions of Merit, and the Bronze Star for "courageous and brilliant leadership" in the Philippines.[12]

Once a private citizen again, Barker became a vice president of the Industrial National Bank. Between wars, he had been treasurer and general manager of the Fulford Manufacturing Company and the Fulford Realty Company. After retiring, Gen. Barker left the busy streets of Providence for a more tranquil life in Pascoag. Here the general wrote a book on his experiences with the 43rd Division Artillery in World War II, which was soon followed by his epitome, *History of the Rhode Island Combat Units in the Civil War*, which remains a standard reference to this day. Both were dedicated to the troops who served so bravely.

Beginning in 1959, Barker served as the military advisor to the Rhode Island Civil War Centennial Commission and was instrumental in advising the state on remembering this critical period. Indeed, the general's grandfather had served in the First Rhode Island Detached Militia. When a bronze plaque in his honor was dedicated at the state house, Barker replied in characteristic fashion: "Without the men whose names do not appear on this plaque, there would have been no history or record of achievement." Brig. Gen. Harold R. Barker died on Memorial Day, May 30, 1968, at the age of seventy-three. He was laid to rest in Providence's Swan Point Cemetery. Ironically, buried next to him was another Rhode Island artillery hero, George W. Potter, who was awarded the Medal of Honor for heroism in the Civil War.[13]

Throughout World War II, Gen. Barker was fortunate to have a brave, brilliant, and important right-hand man. In the course of his remarkable life, Chester A. Files was mobilized for federal duty four times: first the Mexican border, then World War I, two decades later to World War II, and finally, just before he was forced to retire because of age, the Korean War. He ended his illustrious military career as a brigadier general wearing a Legion of Merit as well as the Bronze Star Medal. Gen. Files joined Battery A in 1914, shortly after graduating from Brown University. Two years later, while still a private, Files was part of the "Border

Gen. Barker (right) learned to fly and was instrumental in the development of aircraft to observe the effects of artillery fire. He is shown here with his pilot Lt. Duncan Doolittle (PMCA).

Battery" stationed in El Paso, Texas, and was assigned as a mule skinner. By 1917, when the United States entered World War I, Files was wearing sergeant's stripes and was part of Battery B in the 103d Field Artillery Regiment.

After attending both the Saumur Artillery and the Tractor Artillery School in France, Files was assigned to the 144th Field Artillery of the 40th Division as a second lieutenant. Soon after the war ended, Lt. Files was promoted to first lieutenant in the Officers Reserve Corps. Postwar promotions came irregularly: captain in 1921, major in 1937 and lieutenant colonel in 1940, all in the National Guard. Called to service again in February 1941, Lt. Col. Files was named the first commander of the 169th Field Artillery Battalion and later executive officer of the 43rd Division Artillery, serving as Brig. Gen. Harold Barker's right-hand man in the Pacific. In 1943, Col. Files was awarded the Legion of Merit for his role in the New Georgia Campaign, and two years later he was recognized with the Bronze Star Medal for his participation in the fighting in the Philippines. Nine months after returning home in 1946, Files assumed command of the 43rd Division Artillery as a brigadier general. In September 1950, when the 43rd was once again mustered into federal service, he went with his command to Camp Pickett for training. In March of the following year, much to his regret, General Files was mandatorily retired when he reached age sixty.[14]

He often told colleagues that being unable to travel with his batteries to Germany was a source of great disappointment. As a soldier Gen. Files was both loved and feared. He reminded one of his subordinates of Gen. Douglas MacArthur: stern, but at the same time caring for the men under his command. As a civilian, He was a partner in the former investment firm of Sturges, Chaffee and Hazard, founded by two long-time friends from the PMCA.

He served as commander of the PMCA from 1966 to 1972. His son, Maj. Chester A. Files Jr., carries on his legacy as a current member of the organization. General Files died November 9, 1987, at the age of ninety-six. His funeral cortege at Swan Point Cemetery included three general officers and three colonels, as honorary pallbearers, and the traditional riderless horse.[15]

During the Civil War, the units of the federal army had each adopted a "corps badge" to represent their specific corps on the battlefield. It was a cherished symbol, very important to the veterans, who proudly wore it into old age and decorated their monuments with the design. The U.S. Army had officially adopted division patches in World War I. When the 43rd Division was activated on March 21, 1925, the design approved by the United States Army Institute of Heraldry was described as follows: "A grape leaf on a red quatre foil. The red color signified that the home of the 43rd's units, New England, was once a British territory. The four branches of the quatre foil represented the states of Maine, Vermont, Connecticut, and Rhode Island. The grape leaf in the center recalled the original name given to the New England area by the early explorer Lief Ericsson, 'Vinland,' because of all the wild grapes he discovered there." During the war, the 43rd became known as the "Winged Victory Division," a tribute to the beloved commander of the division, Maj. Gen. Leonard F. Wing of Vermont. It was in fact only one of three World War II units named after their commander, the other two being the famed Edson's Raiders, a Marine Corps special forces battalion, and Merrill's Marauders, which took part in the fighting in Burma.[16]

Brig. Gen. Harold Barker (left) awards the Legion of Merit to Col. Chester Files for gallant leadership during the Solomon's Campaign (RG).

By October 1942, the Japanese had completed their conquest of the Philippines in the southwest Pacific. In the South Pacific Theater, they were continuing to threaten American lines of communication to Australia, despite the recent loss of Guadalcanal. Helping to secure the long chain of islands northeast of Australia was to be the 43rd's first assignment. The 172nd Infantry and 103d Field Artillery would be sent to Guadalcanal to help relieve battered United States Marines who had been fighting bitterly for control of the embattled island.[17]

On October 6, 1942, the 172nd Regimental Combat Team, including the 103d Field Artillery Battalion, boarded the *President Coolidge* in San Francisco and headed for Espiritu Santo in the New Hebrides Islands. Entering Espiritu Santo's Pallikula Bay, the ship accidentally struck two allied mines. To save as many lives as possible, the captain tried to beach his vessel on a reef as close to shore as possible. Among the 4,000 men aboard, mostly Vermonters and Rhode Islanders, was

Sgt. Bill Fusco, a truck driver and cannoneer. The sergeant was eating breakfast when he heard a "crash." He was ordered to report to his duty station, but he soon noticed that the vessel was listing and sinking. Using instinct rather than orders, he joined the other soldiers who were abandoning ship. Sgt. Fusco commented, "It was an awful sight to see."

As the *Coolidge* sank some men turned to other thoughts. First Sgt. Frank Neri of the 103d knew his battery roster was on his bunk, and true to the creed of the NCO, he raced back below decks to find it so he could hold a roll call to account for all of his men when ashore. When the ship finally slid off the reef where it was grounded, and sank; only two lives were lost, including one soldier, the 103d's Capt. Elwood J. Euart of Pawtucket, Rhode Island. The captain was well respected by his men. During the training at Camp Shelby, he would frequently give soldiers who did not have any money for weekend passes a few dollars to enjoy themselves. He would do anything for his artillerymen.[18]

Capt. Euart happened to be mess officer of the day and was supervising the enlisted men at lunch when the explosion went off. Because the public address system had failed, one of the batteries in the 103d had not heard the order to abandon ship. When Euart learned the men were trapped in the hold, he immediately went to their aid. By lashing himself to the lower end of a rope, he was able to hold it tight enough for men to climb to safety, even though the ship was listing badly. When Euart attempted to ascend, after all others were safe, the ship keeled over on its port side and trapped him below. As the vessel began to list he remained at his post, helping his soldiers to escape. Once everyone was cleared, the captain tried to escape out a hatch by a rope, but the *Coolidge* was sinking rapidly. His best friend, Capt. Warren K. Covill of East Providence, attempted to save his Euart's life but was unable to reach his brother officer. Capt. Euart became trapped belowdecks, the first soldier from the 103d Field Artillery to perish in World War II. A comrade wrote, "Elwood died a hero's death."[19]

Brig. Gen. Chester Files was activated to federal service four times in a career that spanned thirty-seven years (RG).

43d Division Patch.

Capt. Euart was posthumously awarded the Distinguished Service Cross, the nation's second highest award for valor, in 1943. He was the most highly decorated 103d soldier in

The sinking of the Coolidge *almost spelled disaster for the 103d and brought the command its first World War II hero (RG).*

World War II, and a VFW post in Pawtucket is named in his honor. Capt. Covill received the Soldier's Medal for his heroism. Nearly all of the Green Mountain Boys and the 103d's equipment and supplies went down with the ship. "They were left with nothing but the shirts on the men's backs," recalled Col. Howard F. Brown, who was with the 169th Field Artillery Battalion and not aboard the *Coolidge*. The Army had planned to send the 172nd Regimental Combat Team directly to Guadalcanal to help the Marines defend the area, but with the loss of all supplies and equipment, those plans were scratched. The Rhode Islanders stayed in Espiritu Santo and did not join the rest of the division until just before the Munda Campaign in New Georgia. The New Englanders missed the chance to be the first American army division to enter combat in the Pacific. The rest of the 43rd spent its first month in the Pacific in New Zealand.[20]

After a month of training there, the division, minus the 172nd Regimental Combat Team, was sent to defend New Caledonia, an island directly in the path of air and sea lines between Australia and the United States. Its rich mineral resources made it especially attractive to the Japanese, although the division experienced no combat while there. The artillery used its time at New Caledonia to study the special methods, techniques and tactics that would be needed later in the jungles of the South Pacific. A reconnaissance party of artillery officers visited Guadalcanal, in January of 1943, where fighting was still in progress. "Their report greatly added to the study of this subject," noted Gen. Barker in his history of the 43rd Division Artillery.[21]

New Caledonia was relatively safe and well out of reach of Japanese bombers, but the

Left: *Capt. Elwood J. Euart gave his life trying to save his fellow soldiers off Vanuatu and was posthumously awarded the Distinguished Service Cross (PMCA).* Right: *Warren Colvill, a captain from East Providence, risked his life to save his best friend on the* Coolidge *and was rewarded with the Soldier's Medal (PMCA).*

men still recall a constant battle with the mosquitoes there. At times they were of more pressing concern than their real enemy. "Fortunately they weren't the kind that carry malaria," Col. Brown said. The real killers would come later. The training in the jungle environment, totally different from Camp Shelby, strengthened the men for the rigors of jungle warfare.[22]

By the time the division arrived at Guadalcanal in February 1943, most of the fighting had ended, although air bombings by the Japanese were a regular occurrence. The Allied command in the South Pacific now planned to attack New Georgia to halt Japanese infiltration down the Solomon Islands, but such a large undertaking was still seen as unrealistic. The occupation of the Russell Islands, however, seemed feasible. The Russells, which lie about 125 miles southeast of New Georgia, had been used by the Japanese as a staging area for shipping troops to Guadalcanal and would serve as a useful base for the Allied forces in an invasion of New Georgia. Unopposed, the first echelon went ashore at Pavuvu, the largest of the Russell Islands, on February 21, 1943.[23]

By the following day the 43rd Division and attached units took over the entire archipelago. The Japanese bombed the 43rd frequently but were usually driven off by American fighters from Guadalcanal. During the campaign in the Pacific Theater the Allied High Command selected certain strategic islands to be seized, while leaving others to be neutralized by being bypassed and literally dying on the vine. Any island with an airfield was prime real estate and worth taking. New Georgia's Munda Airfield was within grasp by early that summer, but first the Allied forces had to seize the beachheads at Rendova, Wickham Anchorage, and New

Georgia's harbor areas. The 43rd Division took its time to carefully prepare itself for the harsh fighting to come. New camouflage uniforms, M-1 Garand rifles, and equipment were issued to help the soldiers better prepare for the task ahead. The men also removed their beloved division patches from their uniforms, lest the patches be seen in the jungle; officers concealed their rank under their collars to prevent them from being fired upon by snipers.[24]

Early in the morning of June 30, the first wave of troops landed on Rendova and secured it. By that evening, the 103d and 169th Field Artillery battalions was lobbing shells across the Blanche Channel at Japanese outposts on New Georgia. On July 9, the entire DIVARTY joined in firing one of the heaviest artillery preparations thus far in the Pacific. In one hour's time, almost 6,000 rounds had been thrown at Munda by the four battalions of the 43rd Division as the 172nd and 169th Infantry regiments prepared to assault the airfield. The Vermonters and Nutmeggers did not get very far before being beaten back by determined Japanese who met them in small patrols in the jungle and overwhelmed the Americans, who were unused to the horrors of jungle warfare. The combat was often short, sharp, and brutal. Flamethrowers and automatic weapons were freely used to drive the Japanese from their positions.[25]

On July 12, 1943, a second beachhead was established at Laianna near Illangan Point, which considerably shortened the supply line from Rendova. Through the entire period, the artillery fire was merciless in its killing power. "It is really more than I can bear," wrote a Japanese soldier in his diary, after forcing his men to hold their dugout positions during a bombardment. A captured Japanese battalion commander later told a Rhode Islander that had it not been for the artillery firing constantly at Munda, his 13th Regiment could have defeated

It was the firepower of the 43rd DIVARTY *that opened the way for the Americans to capture the strategic Munda airfield (PMCA).*

the demoralized 43rd Division infantrymen. The 105mm howitzers were firing hundreds of rounds as the New England soldiers advanced to strike the enemy.

Despite the constant support, the soldiers from New England were starting to feel the effects of combat, as nearly a fourth of the 169th Infantry went down with combat fatigue. Because they were stationed far from the front lines and did not engage in the harshness of close-quarters battles, combat fatigue did not affect the cannoneers. It took the 172nd three days to advance 1,500 yards into the hellish jungle. Eventually it was realized that the New England Division alone could not take the heavily fortified Munda field. Maj. Gen. Oscar W. Griswold, the XIV Corps commander, cabled to Adm. Bull Halsey, the supreme commander: "The 43rd Division will never take Munda, about to fold up." Acting with his steady nerve, Halsey instantly dispatched the 25th and 37th divisions to support the men who wore the grape leaf. Despite the additional support, acts of unbelievable heroism still occurred in the 43rd DIVARTY.[26]

The night of July 13 was one of heavy combat as the Japanese probed and tried to push back the new landings. Gen. Barker and a small party of his staff were out reconnoitering ahead of the division command post. In the darkness, the American soldiers made contact with a large force of Japanese infantrymen who were going to attack and overwhelm the post. Immediately Gen. Barker knew what to do. With only carbines and pistols, the party of officers would be helpless to stop the attack. Fortunately for the Americans, the Japanese had missed cutting one wire line to the 43rd DIVARTY Fire Direction Center.

Gen. Barker got on this line and began calling in requests for fire support to his fire control officer, Lt. Col. Edward Berry. Berry then relayed target data to the batteries of the 136th Field Artillery (155mm) which was attached to the 43rd DIVARTY from the 37th Division. The guns began firing immediately; the 136th was equipped with the powerful 155mm Schneider howitzer of World War I vintage. It was these large shells that now flew towards Gen. Barker's position. One American officer remembered the actions of Gen. Barker and his staff: "It was a gunner's masterpiece. One trivial error of calculation and the guns would have done the job the Japs so far had failed to do — blown the whole camp area to glory. For six hours the guns dropped a curtain of high explosive about us. Never once was a burst farther than 200 yards from the perimeter and only twice was one closer than 20 yards."

In the darkness, Gen. Barker stood erect, cursing the enemy in a thick New England accent while making minute corrections to the fire and constantly calling in to the fire control center. At one point the rounds were dropping in only fifty yards from his position. The 192nd kept up the bombardment until dawn, when the Japanese were repulsed. Remarkably, only one member of the 43rd Division staff, Lt. Col. Elmer Watson, the G-3, was hit. Gen. Barker's feat was a superb testament to his skill and gunnery. One Rhode Islander wrote to the *Providence Journal*: "The General is all nerves and energy." For his heroism that night at Munda, Gen. Harold Barker was awarded his second Silver Star[27] (see Appendix VII for 24 July 43 General Barker letter).

The Allied forces now saw they had underestimated Japanese strength on New Georgia and the adjacent islands, and that Munda had been reinforced. The Rhode Islanders recognized that the enemy soldiers were well trained and well equipped but they had no respect for human life and were quite arrogant towards Americans. This overconfidence would be their downfall. After receiving, and recovering from, their baptism by fire, the soldiers of the 103d, 169th, and 179th infantries were ready for the second round. With the two new American divisions ashore, Gen. Barker was put in command of the XIV Corps Artillery. As the Americans pushed out of the jungle and began to actually see the objective of the airfield, it was clear that the firepower alone of 105mm and 155mm howitzers would not be enough. Over 200 aircraft and several naval destroyers pummeled the target. The airfield at Munda was heavily protected by reinforced concrete pillboxes that had to be neutralized before the infantry could advance and take the position.[28]

The tremendous bombardment was destroying the murderous fire from the pillboxes, allowing the infantry to advance ever closer to the vital airfield. Finally, after six weeks of terrible carnage and at a cost of 1,500 American lives, it was over. One soldier, Lt. Robert Scott of the 172nd Infantry, was awarded the Medal of Honor for holding his position alone while critically wounding, constantly emptying his carbine and throwing grenades at the enemy. Quite literally, a patrol stumbled onto the airfield and realized that the Japanese had all either been killed or escaped. The Munda Offensive continued until August 5, when the airfield was finally in Allied hands. It was a grueling campaign.

From June 30 to August 6, 1943, the 43rd DIVARTY fired an incredible total of 118,529 rounds of ammunition, mostly from adjacent islands directly on target, causing massive destruction, mirroring the role Battery A, First Rhode Island Light, had played at Antietam. The *Providence Journal* recorded this: "The ferocity of the American artillery was noteworthy, but its accuracy was a constant marvel to those who witnessed it. This was largely due to General Barker, rated as one of the nation's finest artillerymen. General Barker's artillery is referred to in these parts as the hottest damn guns in the whole United States."[29]

"The incessant firing of our artillery during the six-week period produced two contrasting effects on the nerves of both sides," noted Gen. Barker in his study of the war. "Our own infantry often stated that these rounds continually landing in front of their lines and on [enemy] positions was one of their best morale builders, especially at night. The effect on the

Camouflage was an important part of the Munda Operation (RG).

A "Long Tom" of the USMC artillery stands ready to fire (PMCA).

Jap[anese soldier] was to produce severe cases of war neurosis." The firepower of Barker's guns shellshocked, starved, and overwhelmed the enemy, most of whom were killed in their concrete bunkers by the brilliant employment of artillery by the general with graying hair and thick glasses who hailed from Providence.[30]

While the artillery had more than proved its worth, there were some limiting factors because of the jungle terrain. Often, Gen. Barker was forced to risk his life and those of his fellow officers by advancing dangerously close to enemy lines in order to accurately observe where the rounds were landing. The 43rd Division Staff managed to acquire the use of an Army Air Force bomber, but accurately observing and correcting fire from the large, lumbering aircraft was difficult as it flew too fast over the target area. What was needed was a slow, low-flying aircraft, piloted by officers also trained as artillery observers. Gen. Barker was desperate for a better solution and soon the answer came to him.[31]

"The Munda Campaign in New Georgia was our first real combat experience," reported Col. Brown, "and it was probably the toughest campaign the 43rd participated in. We still lacked experience in this kind of warfare and the fighting was a lot like the Marines faced in Guadalcanal. We landed in the wrong place and it was terrible." Even the usually upbeat artillery commander had concerns about the operations on New Georgia. "Munda was a tough nut," acknowledged Gen. Barker. "Much tougher in terrain, organization of the ground and determination of the Jap than we had thought." Indeed it had nearly destroyed the 43rd's infantry, but not the spirit of the artillerymen.[32]

Indeed, the campaign took a tremendous toll on the 43rd Division, which was now down to just over half its original strength. In addition to the casualties suffered in combat, tropical

Top: *The 43rd Division Artillery fired relentlessly during the Munda Campaign (RG).* Bottom: *Two soldiers from the 172nd Infantry wait for the artillery to stop before advancing into the jungle at Munda. The strain of the campaign can be seen on their faces (PMCA).*

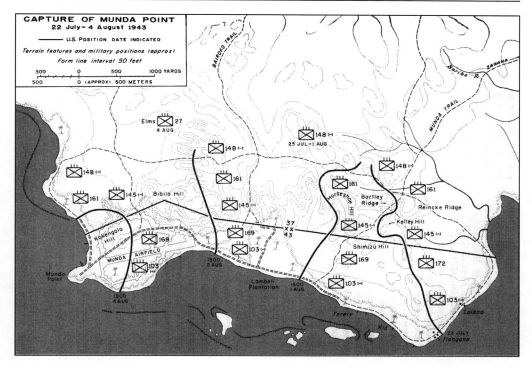

The 43rd Division battled hard for possession of the Munda airfield (RG).

diseases such as malaria, dengue fever, typhus and various jungle sores had greatly weakened the division. Although most of the fighting was over by September, the 43rd stayed in New Georgia until early the following year to defend the area. By February 1944 its work in the Solomon Islands was finished. Eager for some rest and desperately in need of reinforcement and reconstitution, the division returned to New Zealand.

New Zealanders, eternally grateful to the Americans for their military help, treated the soldiers well. The men enjoyed liberal pass privileges and the abundant food available helped the men regain much of the weight they had lost in the jungles of the Solomons. After a month of rest and relaxation, however, training intensified and replacements were integrated into the existing units. By June, the division was fully reconstituted. It was then that the 43rd learned it would leave the South Pacific Command and join the forces of Gen. MacArthur in the Southwest Pacific. MacArthur remained determined to reoccupy his beloved Philippines and to liberate the men he had been forced to abandon more than two years earlier. The forces of the Southwest Pacific Command were to move northwest along the coast of New Guinea and via the islands northwest of the Vogelkop Peninsula, Halmahera and Morotai into the Philippines. The first step in this drive was the seizure of the Hollandia-Aitape region in Australian New Guinea.[33]

While the 43rd was in New Zealand, they finally received proper forward observation support. The twin seat Piper Cub was known as being a small and nimble aircraft, capable of flying low and slow — exactly what Gen. Barker needed to observe the effects of his unit's fire. Ten aircraft and pilots arrived in March 1944. Two aircraft were assigned to each battalion and two to division headquarters. The new lieutenants in command were not just army pilots, but also trained artillery officers, fully capable of leading a battery in combat or adjusting artillery fire. The pilots could see above the jungle cover and would use their new tools with effect. Barker was skeptical at first that the small wooden aircraft would perform the task, but after watching them in training exercises, he was convinced they would work.[34]

One interesting anecdote related by Lt. Duncan Doolitle involved 1st Sgt. Frank Neri:

> One day while on maneuvers in Rotorua, New Zealand, a young private came up to me and said, "Lieutenant, you and Lt. Braucci don't want to take up 1st Sgt. Neri anymore in that plane of yours." When I asked why not, he replied, "Well, you see Lieutenant Braucci had the Sergeant up, and they flew over the battery street, and Sgt. Neri saw us all goofing off. Then Lt. Braucci flew lower, and Sgt. Neri leaned out the plane window and gave us hell. And he did it again when he came back to the Battery. No sir, Lieutenant you don't want to take up Sgt. Neri anymore in your plane!"

Although the soldiers had been heckled by their first sergeant from the air, as well as the ground, Sgt. Neri was acting in their best interest; the strict discipline and grueling training the Rhode Islanders undertook in New Zealand would soon be put to use, as General MacArthur had promised to return.[35]

While the soldiers of the 103d and 169th trained and fought relentlessly in the South Pacific, back home in Providence the Providence Marine Corps of Artillery was still a very active organization. Under the command of Lt. Col. Rush Sturges, the unit was carrying on an equally important task in providing for soldiers' families in the tough times, encouraging recruitment, and assisting in war drives. In addition they sent supplies to the men at the front. The presence of the PMCA on the home front was a much needed relief during the tough times of war.[36]

The 41st Infantry Division initiated the Aitape campaign in April of 1944. When the first elements of the 43rd arrived on July 15, 1944, they went immediately to help hold the main line of resistance at the Driniumor River. On August 7, 1944, the 43rd relieved the 32nd Division, which had borne the brunt of artillery support in the campaign, and took over all of the Aitape defensive installations. From August 16 to 25, the principal combat missions in the Aitape area were carried out by the 43rd as they blasted into the rain forest to support the infantry. It was here that Gen. Barker began using small Piper Cub aircraft to observe the effects of the artillery fire. The pilots were worried about the risk of being shot down, but no enemy aircraft were in sight. The general had initially been skeptical of their use but soon came to appreciate the small aircraft. In time, the general himself took the backseat of the aircraft to personally observe the effects of the terrible bombardments which were pushing the enemy ever north towards Japan itself.[37]

The 43rd, having become acclimated to the rigors of jungle combat, managed to beat back the Japanese forces on New Guinea with only minimal loss. Again the firepower of the 43rd Division Artillery won the day. The campaign was a significant success for the Allied forces; Japan's 18th Army had suffered a decisive and costly defeat. By October 1944, the 43rd knew it would be participating in the landing operation in the Linguyen Gulf area of Luzon in the Philippine Islands. On December 28, 1944, having turned the Aitape area over to the Sixth Australian Division, the 43rd left New Guinea to join other troop convoys for the Luzon attack. On January 9, 1945, troops totaling 68,000, including those in the 43rd, hit the beaches in Linguyen Gulf and by nightfall they were in control of a fifteen-mile beachhead. Of all the amphibious assaults made by the 43rd Division Artillery during the war, Gen. Barker considered the landing at Lingayan Gulf the best planned and most efficiently executed.[38]

Brig. Gen. Harold Barker would not ask his men to go anywhere he was not willing to go himself first. In the Philippines Campaign, he was sure that the aircraft sections would be needed more than ever. At over fifty years old, and an original horse artilleryman, General Barker was determined to learn to fly. He had a few lessons with a seasoned pilot, but soon was taking early morning flights by himself to master the craft, much to the surprise and

Gen. Barker addresses his officers in New Guinea (PMCA).

amazement of his air section pilots. A master at everything he did in life, the general soon mastered flying. One of the pilots wrote, "He was such an active man who would go anywhere to get a better view of the enemy." Many were surprised that Barker could fly, because of his thick glasses, but the short, slim Rhode Islander disproved all doubters. In the campaign to come, Gen. Barker would display his new-found aviation skills and was awarded the Air Medal.[39]

The bravery and skill of Gen. Barker and his men were recognized in a citation from Gen. Headquarters: "[Gen. Barker] led his reinforced units ashore to face enemy artillery of vastly superior strength. He swiftly and skillfully thrust his battalions into daring forward positions, always preceding his elements to seek the most advantageous and protected positions for his troops." Often overlooked due to other major amphibious operations such as Normandy and Iwo Jima, was the fact that the Rhode Islanders of the 43rd conducted numerous amphibious assaults throughout the Pacific campaign.

On D-day in the Philippines, the 43rd landed in the first wave. The DIVARTY soldiers were there to support the infantry as usual. With the American forces taking fire on the beach, Capt. John Congdon of the 103d landed a gun there. The captain had his men push the 105mm howitzer right out of the Higgins boat and through the surf as the Rhode Islanders prepared to engage in the sand. The howitzer went into direct fire against an enemy battery. The Japanese artillery fire was silenced as Capt. Congdon pushed inland with his battery. Guns, ammunition, and other equipment were soon landed as the 103d prepared itself for the final push. By participating in the landings, the unit earned another coveted arrowhead award, representing an amphibious assault.[40]

Although the men of the 103d and 169th landed in the first wave on the Philippines, the cannoneers were not the first Rhode Island soldiers to arrive on the islands. This honor went to Capt. William Farrell of Providence. Three months before the landing, the captain had been "volunteered" for a top secret mission. He was inserted by submarine on Luzon two months before the main American landing to rally Filipino guerrillas in the area to begin sabotage operations to disrupt Japanese command and communications systems. Capt. Farrell was successfully dropped off on the beach and made contact with his party, which included several escaped American officers from Bataan, which had fallen nearly three years earlier. Farrell and his party performed their mission with ardor and contributed to the success of the initial landings through the use of radio communications to indicate where enemy patrols were. The guerrilla force took part in many small hit and run raids, which confused the enemy, until the main assault took place. After the 43rd Division landed, the captain returned to the 169th. For his heroism in taking part in this daring mission, Capt. Farrell was awarded the Silver Star and the Legion of Merit.[41]

For the next 173 days, the 43rd Division saw nearly continuous combat in the Luzon Campaign, a campaign that included the seizure of the initial beachhead and the capture of the hills north of the Linguyen Plain. The cannoneers from Rhode Island participated in the destruction of enemy defenders at Stotsenburg, the crushing of the left wing of the Shimbu Line, and finally, the seizure of Ipo Dam. The latter was a very viable target, as it provided the people of Manilla with the bulk of their water supply and had to be captured before the Japanese contaminated the supply. Ipo Dam was a tough final battle, but the Green Mountain Boys of the 172nd Infantry, supported by the 103d Field Artillery, finally captured the strongpoint, thus ending major combat on the island. Like Munda, the Japanese had built up their defenses, which required high explosive rounds to break up.

Throughout the campaign the 43rd Division Artillery remained at the front, firing at all hours around the clock and constantly moving forward with the infantry. In the air Gen. Barker's Piper Cubs were constantly airborne searching out Japanese targets and calling in not only artillery but air strikes as well. One aircraft was shot down. The pilots faced constant danger from sharpshooter fire, as well as an occasional Japanese fighter plane. On those fortunately rare encounters, they had only their wits and the maneuverability of their small planes to help them. The officers themselves became exhausted as they flew five hours per day; still, the missions were carried on with vigor and several pilots were decorated for their actions. The fighting again became stalled by a desperate enemy resistance to prevent the Americans from taking Manilla, the capital. At sea the United States Navy faced waves of kamikaze assaults. In the mountainous regions of the Philippines, the artillery became bogged down as the Rhode Islanders struggled to push on with the advancing infantry.[42]

The firepower provided by the battalions under Gen. Barker's command were having their effect; indeed, the captured Japanese soldiers confessed it was the American artillery that drove them out of their defenses. In light of his actions on the Philippines, Harold Barker was awarded his second Legion of Merit. In awarding it, Gen. Douglas MacArthur, Supreme Allied Commander, issued the following citation recognizing Rhode Island's Gen. Barker:

> In the initial landings on Luzon he led his reinforced units ashore to face enemy artillery of vastly superior strength. He swiftly and skillfully thrust his battalions into daring forward positions always preceeding his elements to seek the most advantageous and protected positions, and throughout 173 days of continuous combat relentlessly carried the fight to the enemy. He is cited also for outstanding tactical skill, brilliant leadership, and superior resourcefulness.

Also decorated for heroism under fire was Barker's friend and executive officer, Col. Chester Files, who was the recipient of the Bronze Star Medal. The cannoneers from Rhode Island fired relentlessly in the campaign and their actions were recognized with many awards for individual acts of heroism.[43]

After taking the Ipo Dam in June, all missions in the division's zone of action had been accomplished. The 43rd Division's *Providence Journal* correspondent wrote, "The 43rd Division did one spectacular, difficult job of destroying methodically the chief force of the Japanese." Despite the support, the division's infantry took heavy casualties in the fighting. Throughout the latter part of the fighting Gen. Barker was the temporary commander of several more artillery battalions and assigned Col. Chester Files to command the heavy artillery batteries. They were constantly on the heels of the infantry as they made the final push towards Manilla.

Gen. Barker developed tactics to concentrate the fire from his batteries on a single target, such as a grouping of pillboxes, to destroy them so the infantry could punch through and attack. One of his favorite skills, carried over from World War I, was the old game of "snipe hunting," or using the howitzers in counter-battery fire to destroy enemy gun positions. At one point the Rhode Island general was sure his men had destroyed all the Japanese gun positions. On July 4 MacArthur declared Luzon secure, and on July 11, 1945, the 43rd was relieved from all combat responsibility there. The Japanese had grown to respect and fear the artilleryman from Rhode Island who wore glasses, knew how to fly, and control his guns in combat. The 43rd Division had earned the sobriquet of the "Munda Butchers" from the Japanese. Indeed, it was Gen. Barker, Col. Files and the four battalions of the 43rd Division Artillery who had been responsible for much of the butchering. With the Philippines now secure, Gen. MacArthur and the Americans had finally returned as promised four years earlier.[44]

Allied commanders were now busy preparing plans for the final assault of the war: the invasion of Japan. Had the Japanese not surrendered the following month, the 43rd would certainly have been part of this assault. The division was now widely recognized as one of the three great divisions in the South Pacific, as remembered by Col. Howard Brown. The other two were the 32nd, another National Guard Division from the upper Midwest and the 1st Cavalry Division. The 1st Cavalry had the distinction of being under the command of Major General William C. Chase of Providence. Chase had been a member of the 103d's Battery A on the Mexican border and personally knew the senior leadership of the 43rd DIVARTY from the "old days." As a testament to the quality of those Battery A soldiers who had gone to war against Pancho Villa, five became general officers in World War II, while 100 men from that historic unit became commissioned officers in the two world wars.[45]

Harold Barker was both a soldier and a historian. He often looked into the past to find answers for the present. In his book on the 43rd Division Artillery, the general concluded that the heroic actions of his artillerymen on the bloody fields of Munda, New Guinea and Luzon were born on the

Lt. Col. Walter Lampton commanded the 103d in the latter stages of World War II (RG).

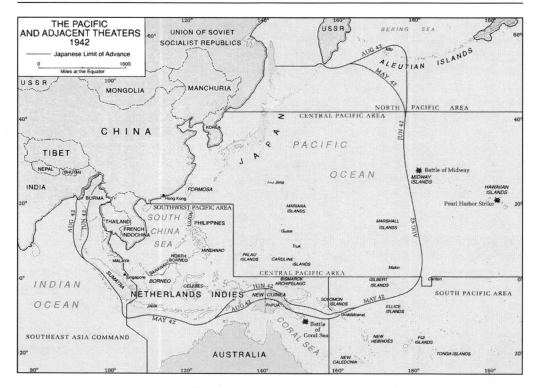

A map of the Pacific Theater of Operation (RG).

fields of Antietam, Gettysburg, Cedar Creek, and the Muese-Argonne. The cannoneers of the 43rd who had undergone so much fighting in the malaria-filled jungles and hellish valleys of the South Pacific continued the tradition of excellence started by the PMCA so many years earlier. The direct support provided by their cannon gave the 43rd Division's infantry the critical support they needed to fulfill their missions. Barker wrote:

> At no time during World War II did the Artillery of the 43rd Infantry Division lose sight of its Mission, i.e, *the support of its Infantry in Combat.* Instead of paying verbal tribute to its Infantry the Division Artillery seized every opportunity to give its total support to the Infantry to which it was assigned. By the use of liaison detachments, forward observers, communication, and survey details, continual contact was maintained at all times with front line Infantry units. The development of the *Infantry-Artillery Team* was paramount and the records attest to the success of this organization.

In his conclusion, Gen. Barker noted, "The genuine achievement and heroic traditions established by Rhode Island Artillery in our previous Wars resulted in setting a standard that was second to none."[46]

The cost of the fighting in the Pacific had been heavy for the 103d Field Artillery. The close-in fighting in the jungle terrain, often carried out with the fieldpieces in close proximity to the enemy, resulted in many casualties. Fifty soldiers were wounded in action, and the following eleven Rhode Islanders made the supreme sacrifice: Capt. Elwood J. Euart, 1st Lt. Dominic J. Braucci, Corp. James J. Carlone, Corp. Matthew A. Melone, Corp. Daniel L. Roberts, Tec. 4 Charles L. Urban, Tec. 5 Wilbert E. Goldsby, Pfc. Jerry Di Girolamo, Pfc. William A. Dulong, Pfc. Walter Gula, and Pfc. Albert Silva. These men, as well as those wounded, were awarded the Purple Heart for their sacrifice. In addition, the rest of the

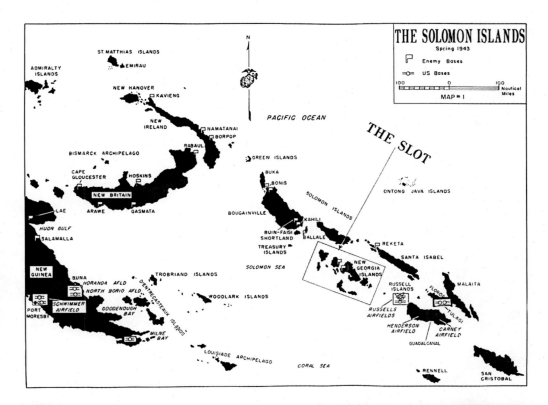

Top: *A map of the Solomons Campaign (RG).* Bottom: *A group of 103d World War II veterans at the dedication of the National World War II Memorial (PMCA).*

Despite giving up their horses years earlier, the soldiers of the 103d and 169th still became stuck in the mud during the New Guinea Campaign (PMCA).

battalion compiled quite the record in terms of decorations, comparable to the First Rhode Island Light Artillery in the Civil War. One soldier was awarded the Distinguished Service Cross, three Silver Stars, one Legion of Merit, thirty Bronze Star Medals, four Soldier's Medals, and three Air Medals.[47]

Although the 103d Field Artillery Regiment served in World War II as a single battalion unit, the Second Battalion of the 103d formed the 169th Field Artillery, which fought throughout the war as part of the 43rd DIVARTY. Whatever the men of the 103d saw at Munda, New Guinea, and Luzon, the soldiers in the 169th saw as well. Among the many soldiers of this battalion to rise to prominence was Capt. Howard F. Brown, who retired after a remarkable thirty-year career as a Regular Army colonel and then pursued a teaching career.

The men of the 169th Field Artillery who gave the last full measure were as follows: 1st Lt. Nathaniel J. Heidelberger, 1st Lt. Hugh B. Miller, 1st Lt. Earl M. Payne, 2nd Lt. Arthur F. Malone, 2nd Lt. Warren Mansfield, SSgt. Richard Gray, Sgt. John Cordeiro, Corp. Norbert F. McElroy, Pfc. Sylvester M. Beckman, Pfc. Warren A. Harvey, Pvt. La Verne M. Anderson, and Pvt. Willard Chandler. The officers and men of the 169th were recognized for their heroism under fire as much as those of the 103d were. The soldiers of the 169th received four Distinguished Service Crosses, nineteen Silver Stars, six Legions of Merit, and two Soldier's Medals. Thirty-two men received the Bronze Star Medal and three received Air Medals, while an incredible 118 soldiers received the medal no one wanted to receive, the Purple Heart for combat wounds.[48]

On September 7, 1945, the 43rd Division left Manila, arriving at Yokohama six days later. It was among the first American divisions to land in the Tokyo area. Upon release from combat team conditions, the 43rd Division Artillery took over guard of the main camp and the town of Kumagaya. The 43rd Infantry Division fully expected to spend the winter in Japan, but on September 18 it received orders to return to the United States where it would be demobilized. On September 29, the first of a convoy of troop ships left Yokohama for California, the state from which the 43rd had embarked for the Pacific Theater more than three years before. "There is an Army saying that 'an old soldier never dies, but simply fades away,'" wrote Gen. Barker. "The 43rd Division Artillery did not die at Camp Stoneman, California, but simply faded away, to be ready when the next national emergency requires its services."[49]

The 43rd Infantry Division was released from active federal service and again reconstituted as a National Guard division in 1946. In the firestorm of the Pacific, the men of Rhode Island who served in the batteries of the 103d and 169th Field Artillery had added to the almost mythical reputation of the cannoneers from the smallest state. At Munda and in the Philippines they had more than proved their worth, supporting the 43rd

Lt. Col. Wilbur E. Brandt commanded the 169th Field Artillery. He was known as a tough commander who pushed his men and their guns to the limit in the pursuit of glory (PMCA).

Division with pinpoint firepower. The men who had led the 103d and 169th in World War II again carried on the tradition and had trained a new crop of battery and battalion commanders for the next round of warfare sure to come. The motto of the 103d is "Play the Game." The game these soldiers play is waged on the battlefield, with serious consequences for all participants. Indeed, it has been played many times before. Little did its members realize that they would have to play the game again less than five years later.

14

KOREA AND THE COLD WAR ERA, 1946–1989

We trained constantly to maintain the peace.
— Brig. Gen. Richard Valente, 103d Field Artillery Brigade

With World War II behind them, most veterans eagerly returned to civilian life. College, now available because of the G.I. Bill, was increasingly attractive, as was marriage and raising a family. A strong economy and plenty of jobs awaited the returning men. The horrors that had been seen in the South Pacific were gradually suppressed; but the veterans honored their fallen comrades every Veterans Day and looked forward to the annual reunions of the 43rd Infantry Division Veteran's Association each summer, much as their ancestors had done after the Civil War.

Still, the National Guard attracted veterans, particularly officers, who wished to continue their military life part time. Maj. Gen. Harold Read, for example, who was the longest serving commander of the PMCA, from 1973 to 2006, joined the 103d Field Artillery after returning home in 1946. In Europe, he had served first as an NCO in the Troop Carrier Command, then as a military police lieutenant in charge of security at LUCKY FORWARD, General Patton's headquarters. Brig. Gen. Harold R. Barker, who had commanded the 43rd Division Artillery in the Pacific, retired shortly after the war and returned to life as a banker in Providence. He would frequently go out of his way to see his old soldiers, while his Yankee foul-mouth language often made women gasp on the streets. Many of the officers and men who had served under him rejoined the Guard and their former regiment and rose to great prominence.[1]

With the retirement of Gen. Barker in 1946, Col. Chester A. Files assumed command of the 43rd Division Artillery and was promoted to brigadier general. Files, always an active and popular member of the 103d, had launched his military career in 1914 with Battery A. He was a tough fighter who had gone from a single chevron to a star. World War II was the third time he was mobilized into federal service, but it would not be the last.

Gen. Files' division artillery would contain some of the same outfits that had served under him when he was the executive officer of the 43rd Division Artillery. Rhode Islanders comprised the DIVARTY headquarters battery and the 103d Field Artillery Battalion; the 169th Field Artillery assumed the role as an antiaircraft artillery (AAA) battalion to shoot down enemy aircraft. The 152nd Field Artillery was redeployed and in its place came the 206th Field Artillery of the Vermont National Guard and the 963rd Field Artillery of the Connecticut National Guard. In July of 1950, with the outbreak of the Korean War, the 43rd Infantry Division, including Gen. Files and his New England artillerymen, were mobilized once again.

In September 1950, the 43rd Division made a motorized march to Camp Pickett in Virginia, where it trained for a full year in preparation for being sent overseas. After twelve months of training at Camp Pickett, the men were sent to Augsburg, Germany, where their mission was to provide a deterrent to a new enemy, the Soviet Union. Because of the need to pull Regular Army forces out of Europe and send them to Korea, the men of the "Winged Victory Division" would now have the primary responsibility of reinforcing NATO forces and protecting American interests in Western Europe.

The 103d Field Artillery was again part of the 43rd DIVARTY and would provide the necessary firepower to support the 43rd's infantry in the event that the Soviets attacked Western Europe. For a time the New Englanders were the only National Guard division in Europe, until they were joined by the 28th Division from Pennsylvania. Unfortunately for the 103d, it would be the first time in nearly four decades that they would be without a beloved comrade. Forced into mandatory retirement at age sixty, Brig. Gen. Chester Files was not able to follow his command to Germany. It was, he often said, a source of great regret. "This after 37 years in the Army," wrote PMCA historian Everett S. Hartwell. "What a man!"[2]

The 43rd remained in Germany until 1953, when the colors were returned to the United States and the division was reflagged as the Fifth Infantry Division. The 103d Field Artillery was redesignated the 21st Field Artillery. Many of the soldiers had served in World War II less than a decade earlier, and after their two-year tour of duty in Germany the bulk of the officers and men of the 43rd Infantry Division were anxious to return home to the United States. A few soldiers, such as Col. Howard Brown, who had their civilian careers interrupted once too often, opted to stay on active duty and served until retirement from the United States Army many years later. Many of the men who had served in World War II had now started new jobs and families, but as good soldiers they accepted their two-year tours of duty with few complaints. Although the threat of attack from the Soviets was real, much of the time was spent touring the countryside and waiting.[3]

Even in the middle of winter, the soldiers of the 103d had to remain on diligent watch in Germany during the Cold War. A young Capt. Harold Reed is in the center (PMCA).

Top: *A 155mm howitzer stands ready to fight against the Warsaw Pact in 1952 (PMCA).* Bottom: *The headquarters of the 43rd* DIVARTY *in Germany, 1951–1953 (PMCA).*

In October 1951, the men held a small celebration at their base at Sheridan Kasserne in Augsburg, marking the 150th anniversary of the Providence Marine Corps of Artillery, a milestone that was also being celebrated back home in Rhode Island at the Benefit Street Arsenal, where, as George B. Peck had done in 1917, Everett S. Hartwell gave an important historical address. Because the men in Germany would not be able to take part in the festivities back home in Providence, the PMCA donated 300 dollars for a special artillery feast, including cake. The soldiers of the 103d and 169th considered the PMCA their "fairy godmother" and greatly enjoyed the event. Among those present was Capt. Thomas Barker, the DIVARTY operations officer. His father was none other than Gen. Barker, thus making him the third generation of Rhode Island artillerymen to serve with distinction. Capt. Barker read the same address in Germany that was given at the Benefit Street Arsenal.[4]

The 43rd Division Artillery would not be mobilized for federal duty again in the twentieth century, though its services were sometimes needed by the state. In 1954, for example, the men were sent to Oakland Beach after Hurricane Carol plowed across the state on August 31 and left shoreline communities in ruin. It was the worst disaster in Rhode Island since the 1938 hurricane, which the 103d was called out for as well. Guardsmen aided in the evacuation of residents, prevented looting and provided supplies.[5]

The face of the National Guard has changed over the last fifty years. In 1948, shortly after World War II, Americans of every race were integrated in the units; by 1970, women, other than nurses, were invited to accept noncombat positions. Certainly the membership list of today's PMCA reads quite differently from that of two hundred years ago, when nearly every name was of Anglo-Saxon origin. What the boys from Rhode Island had set forth to accomplish

During the Korean War, the soldiers of the 103d trained frequently in response to the constant threat of Soviet attack (PMCA).

A 155mm howitzer is pulled by an M-5 artillery tractor in Germany during the Korean War (PMCA).

in 1861 was finally realized; they had broken down barriers and abolished the old system. Finally all were accepted for who they were: Americans.

There remain some recent members who can trace their lineage back to the early days of the PMCA and whose families have been represented in the organization for most of its 200 years. Lt. Col. Frederick Lippitt, for example, a descendent of charter member Moses Lippitt, commanded the First Battalion of the 103d during the 1950s. Col. Duncan Mauran commanded the 103d Field Artillery Brigade from 1972 to 1975. Mauran, Files, Barker and Kenny are other surnames that have appeared on the membership roster over the course of several generations.[6]

Following release from active federal service on June 15, 1954, and the return from Europe, the 43rd Infantry Division and all organic units were again reconstituted as a National Guard Division, and continued the never-ending cycle of training and reorganization. However, for the next three decades, National Guard units that had served second to none on the battlefields of the world gradually fell into a "second class" citizen category. The proximate cause was the tight defense budgets, which placed the National Guard into competition with the active army for the limited funds available.

However, this was also a world of changing threats and possible response scenarios. National defense strategy in the 1950s was predicated on the preeminence of United States nuclear weapons, delivered by the new United States Air Force. In such a setting, ground forces were seen as almost irrelevant, and defense funding reflected this philosophy. However, since then, American national defense policy has evolved greatly to reflect the need for a balanced defense force able to respond across the entire spectrum of warfare, from nuclear deterrence to ground combat against nonnuclear powers anywhere in the world.[7]

The impact on the 43rd Infantry Division and the 103d Field Artillery reflected the changing world climate. After twenty-four years of exemplary service to the state and nation, the 43rd Infantry Division was deactivated in 1964. Its heritage lives on today in organizations such as the 43rd Infantry Division Veterans Association and successor units such as the 43rd Infantry Brigade of the Connecticut National Guard. Other current units in the Rhode Island National Guard still reflect the linkage to the numeral "43," such as the 43rd Military Police Brigade, the 1043rd Medical Detachment, the 1043rd Maintenance Company, in fact even the 143rd Tactical Airlift Wing of the Rhode Island Air National Guard.[8]

The 103d Field Artillery has also undergone several transitions. In the late 1950s, the army experimented with an ill-fated concept, the Pentomic Division, which changed the triangular division to a five-sided structure. This structure upped the major maneuver commands from three to five. At this time, the 43rd Division Artillery was restructured to three 105mm howitzer battalions, the Second, Third, and Fourth battalions of the 103d and the First Battalion, which was the general support battalion. The First Battalion was organized as a rocket/howitzer battalion, equipped with one eight-inch howitzer battery and one Honest John rocket battery. The Honest John was an early type of battlefield tactical nuclear rocket, developed when it was thought that the only way to defeat the Warsaw Pact nations was through this extreme form of warfare. Due to monetary constraints, the unit never received or fired the Honest John.[9]

On March 18, 1963, the 43rd Division Artillery was reorganized and redesignated as the XVIII Corps Artillery, to which the four battalions of the 103d Field Artillery were assigned. On May 1, 1968, the Corps Artillery Headquarters and Headquarters Battery was reorganized and redesignated as the Headquarters Battery of the 103d Artillery Group. Again the First, Second, Third, and Fourth battalions of the 103d Field Artillery were incorporated into this nondivisional structure. The 103d Artillery Group was redesignated the 103d Field Artillery Group on March 1, 1972.[10]

On October 1, 1979, the 103d Field Artillery Group was again reorganized as the 103d Field Artillery Brigade and existed in this structure until September 6, 2008, when the 103d Field Artillery Brigade was inactivated. At that time, the lineage and tradition of the 103d passed to the First Battalion of the 103d Field Artillery Regiment. It was the first time in modern memory that the state of Rhode Island had not had a higher field artillery organization headquartered in the state. The descendent of the DIVARTY so masterfully handled by Gen. Barker in the South Pacific was no more.[11]

Due to a presidential decision not to conduct a large activation of the National Guard during the Vietnam War, very few units were called to active duty. However, continuing its tradition of excellence, the 103d was rated as six out of twelve weeks ready for mobilization in early 1968. At approximately this time the 103d was upgraded from 105mm howitzers, to 155mm howitzers; and in recognition of the change of weapon system the mobilization readiness rating was dropped back by one week. Consequently, when there was a need to mobilize additional artillery units from the area, the 211th Field Artillery from nearby Massachusetts, which was already equipped with the 155mm, was mobilized rather than the 103d.

Following the Vietnam War, morale in the army as well as defense funding reached new lows. During this period the men and officers of the 103d soldiered on, attending regular drills, special schools, and conducting the fifteen-day annual training period at Fort Drum, New York. During this period, authorized equipment was always in short supply. Invariably old Korean War vintage, and in many cases inadequate substitutes for the authorized vehicles and equipment — which somehow never seemed to materialize — were in use. During the 1960s, the 105mm howitzer artillery ammunition fired was often reloaded World War II–era ammunition. However, rather than allowing this obvious second-class equipment status to result in second-class performance, the officers and men of the 103d continued their predecessors' efforts of always striving for excellence.[12]

In the 1970s, the army chief of staff, Gen. Creighton Abrams, issued planning guidance to correct the major national policy error of not mobilizing the National Guard for Vietnam when he stated that never again would the Regular Army go to war without the National Guard and the Reserve at its side. This policy set in motion significant changes in the training philosophy for the National Guard. Almost to underscore the lessons learned in the Pacific by General Barker, from 1972 to 1976, the 103d Field Artillery Group was assigned its own aviation section consisting of four OH-6 Recon helicopters and pilots.

Training became more aggressive, and in 1980 and again in 1982, the 103d made a motor march to Fort Bragg, North Carolina, for their annual training. In 1983, Charlie Battery, Second Battalion of the 103d Field Artillery, took part in REFORGER (Return of Forces to Germany), the annual exercise held in West Germany designed to demonstrate to the Soviets the commitment and the ability of the United States to reinforce its troops in West Germany. While this very challenging exercise was completed satisfactorily, it showed the huge differences in equipment between the active army and the National Guard. Charlie Battery was still equipped with the towed 155mm M114A1 howitzers of World War II vintage. Vehicles were still the older 1950s vintage gas-powered models rather than the more powerful diesels.[13]

The years between the late 1970s and into the mid 1980s saw a quantum leap in training, equipment and war planning. In keeping with Gen. Abrams' guidance, National Guard units were fully integrated into major war contingency plans. Under the CAPSTONE program, the Department of the Army directed the alignment of major commands for wartime missions. This first-time-ever program fully integrated the Regular Army, the National Guard and the Army Reserve, without regard to component, under the "One Army Concept." Consequently, the 103d Field Artillery Brigade assumed a directed training and war planning association with several artillery battalions. These were the Regular Army's Second Battalion, 34th Artillery, stationed at Fort Sill, the Third Battalion of the 75th Artillery, an Army Reserve unit from Missouri, the Fourth Battalion of the 92nd Artillery, another Army Reserve battalion from Pennsylvania, and the First and Second battalions of the 103d Field Artillery Regiment from Rhode Island.[14]

The soldiers of the 103d Field Artillery Brigade wore this patch, based on a PMCA design, until their consolidation with a New Hampshire Guard unit in 2008.

Another leader of the 103d during the Cold War was Richard J. Valente. Born in Fall River, this officer graduated from LaSalle Academy in Providence. He continued his education at Rensselaer Polytechnic Institute, receiving a B.S. in electrical engineering. At the same time, he was commissioned a second lieutenant through ROTC. He then attended the field artillery basic officer course and was stationed at Fort Sill before joining the 103d. Over the next twenty-six years Gen. Valente held every officer position in the 103d, from section, battery, battalion, to the brigade level. During this period he also transitioned into the Army Reserve for a period of eleven years, serving as an instructor in the branch officer advanced course, instructor at the Army Command and General Staff College, and as the executive officer of the Fourth Brigade of the 76th Division, as well as completing a one-year tour to the Rhode Island National Guard's Plans and Operations Officers for the Logistics Section.

As the 103d Field Artillery Brigade commander, then Col. Valente was responsible for two National Guard and two Army Reserve battalions, plus a battalion at Fort Sill. He was appointed a brigadier general in August of 1988 and given command of the 43rd Military Police Brigade. Gen. Valente served at this posting for six years and developed aggressive overseas training for units of the brigade. The brigade was activated for the First Gulf War, but the headquarters was not activated. In August of 1994, Gen. Valente was assigned to the position of Assistant Adjutant General, Deputy Commanding General of the Rhode Island Army National Guard until his retirement in September 1995.

Though the Guard and Reserves took up much of Gen. Valente's time, he devoted himself to other career pursuits. As a registered professional engineer in electrical engineering, he was employed by Engelhard Corporation, Engineered Products Division, as the manager of plant engineering. He was also a registered professional engineer in Massachusetts and California. The general served as an EMT and captain of the Warren Fire Department Rescue Squad and as an officer of the PMCA. After his retirement, Gen. Valente continued to support the military through his tireless efforts associated with veteran's affairs, including serving as the chairman of the Rhode Island Gulf War Veterans Commission. Since 2006, the general has served as the Commander and Lieutenant Colonel of the Providence Marine Corps of Artillery.

As part of the long overdue modernization of the United States Army, starting in 1984, the 103d Field Artillery Brigade units began receiving the newest equipment in the army inventory. In May of 1984, the Second Battalion of the 103d became one of the first units in the country to receive the new 155mm M198 howitzers. Brig. Gen. Richard J. Valente, then commander of the Second Battalion, recalled "they were so new, that the Rock Island Arsenal data plates indicated they had just come off the production line!" At annual training at Fort Drum that year, the battalion made the transition to the new weapons. In preparation, the battalion had put together a training team to work with the training team from Fort Sill. However, when delays caused the Fort Sill team to miss the training window with the battalion, the 103d in-house training team headed by SGM Paul Lambert carried out the transition training without a hitch. When the first round was fired from the new weapons, there was a brief break to take a photograph of those involved.

Each howitzer in the six firing batteries was named after a battle honor for the 103d, from the Civil War, World War I and World War II. Each chief of section had to learn of the details of the battle his howitzer was named for and then impart this lesson in unit history to his gun crew. The gun crews always had a visual reminder of their history from names such as Gettysburg, Ainse Marne and Luzon. The receipt of the new howitzers was followed almost immediately by the receipt of new M925 five-ton turbo diesel prime movers, as well as the new CUCV's, a military version of the GMC Blazer, for command and control uses.[15]

Almost immediately the nuclear capable First and Second battalions had to undergo a new "Nuclear Army Training and Evaluation Program" (ARTEP). This grueling three-day continuously running tactical exercise evaluated all aspects of the unit to prove its competence

Top: *The first shot fired by the 103d's new M198 howitzers. The lanyard was pulled by Gen. Valente (PMCA).* Bottom: *After the first mission on the M198 howitzers at Fort Drum was fired this photograph was taken to record the moment. LTC Valente, 2d Bn commander, is on the left, Col. Cyril Frost, 103d FA BDE commander, is on the right.*

and readiness to perform its wartime mission by their delivery of accurate fire around the clock in all weather and terrain conditions. Both Rhode Island units scored extremely well, as did the assigned CAPSTONE units. While it was labeled a training program by the army, failure to demonstrate competence was reason enough for many battalion commanders to see their careers terminated.

The new equipment and organizational structures, as well as newly honed skills, were soon put to the test. Planning for Annual Training 1986 was well underway in 1985. In fact it was such a major exercise that it received an official army operation name, "Caber Valiant." This exercise encompassed the movement of all five CAPSTONE battalions— approximately 2,000 soldiers— to Fort Sill via rail, road convoy, and Boeing 747 military charter aircraft. In fact, at that time, it was the largest deployment of Rhode Island Guardsmen outside the state since the Korean War. In scope, this was the logistical equivalent of a REFORGER, without crossing the Atlantic. After specialized training in loading military equipment on a train, the 103d became adept at both loading and unloading the mile-long train, cutting the final unloading time to sixteen hours.[16]

Upon arrival at Fort Sill the CAPSTONE brigade commanded by Col. Richard J. Valente, who was then also serving as the senior major of the PMCA, along with his staff and soldiers, who were also PMCA members, conducted a continuous ten-day tactical field exercise. During that exercise, the brigade fired around 5,000 rounds of 155mm and 8-inch ammunition, conducted a "time on target" (TOT), and massed fires of the entire brigade, some eighty howitzers. A TOT is a type of fire exercise requiring very detailed fire direction calculations and control, as all rounds must land in the target area simultaneously no matter where they are fired. It was perhaps the culmination of the process begun in the Civil War of massing all available cannon to enemy positions to clear a path for the infantry to advance. It is for good reason that the field artillery has earned the title "King of Battle."

Following the field exercise, a formal five-battalion Brigade Pass in Review was conducted, with then Brig. Gen. Dennis J. Reimer, III Corps Artillery commander, serving as the reviewing

The 103d prepares to deploy by train to Fort Sill, Oklahoma, in 1986 (PMCA).

Top: *Veterans of the 103d gather at their traditional meeting grounds at the Squantum Club for the bicentennial of the PMCA. Left to right are Col. Ray Gallucci, Col. Charles Walsh, Maj. Gen. Reginald A. Centracchio, Gen. Dennis J. Reimer, Brig. Gen. Richard J. Valente, Col. Howard F. Brown, CSM Thomas Caruolo, Maj. Gen. Harold N. Read, CSM John McDonough (PMCA). Bottom: Brig. Gen. Richard J. Valente, the current PMCA commander, in 1986 in civilian clothes on the East German border (PMCA).*

Providence Marine Corps of Artillery

Founded 1801   Benefit Street Arsenal · Providence, Rhode Island 02903

Calendar of events celebrating the 200th Anniversary of the Providence Marine Corps of Artillery

The bicentennial year begins October 2001 and ends September 2002.

Events commemorating the Providence Marine Corps of Artillery are as follows:

9 November 2001 - Rhode Island National Guard Military Ball

The 26th annual RING ball will be held at Rhodes on the Pawtuxet. During the evening, the history of the PMCA will be featured. PMCA Commander, MG Harold N. Read, will introduce the bicentennial year celebration. Immediately following his remarks, the battlestreamer pageant of the PMCA/103d FA Bde will be presented. (Note: The wearing of St. Barbara and Molly Pitcher medals is appropriate.)

1 December 2001 - The 103d Field Artillery Brigade Review

The PMCA is the parent organization of all current Rhode Island Artillery units. During the review at the Armory of Mounted Commands, a Rhode Island Senatorial proclamation, recognizing the PMCA contributions to Rhode Island history, will be read. The review will be followed by a reception at the Squantum Association where traditional St. Barbara's day activities will take place.

4 May 2002 - Rhode Island Independence Day

This event is to formally recognize the contributions of the PMCA to the history of the State of Rhode Island. A Gubernatorial Proclamation and Field Artillery Cannon Salute will be held at the statehouse followed by a reception for members of the PMCA and invited guests.

6 June 2002 - PMCA Annual Membership Meeting/Dinner

The Annual Membership Meeting/Dinner will mark the culmination of the bicentennial year events. This years meeting will be held at the Squantum Association. The featured speaker will be General Dennis J. Reimer, former Chief of Staff - United States Army. Gen. Reimer worked with the 103d Brigade during various training exercises.

A schedule of events from the bicentennial year in 2001 and 2002 (PMCA).

officer. This notable ceremony ended on a historical note, as the horse-drawn field artillery half section from Fort Sill was the last unit marching off the field. Truly a glimpse of the 103d of some seventy years earlier.[17]

In 2002 retired Army Chief of Staff Gen. Dennis J. Reimer honored the 103d by traveling

Top: *Ghost from the past: The 103d of 1916 meets the modern day unit at Fort Sill in 1986 (PMCA).* Bottom: *The colors of the 103d on parade at Fort Sill (PMCA).* Opposite page: *The State of Rhode Island commemorated the bicentennial of the PMCA by issuing this rousing circular (PMCA).*

State of Rhode Island and Providence Plantations
OFFICE of the GOVERNOR

The Governor

of the

State of Rhode Island

Extends His

Greetings and Congratulations to

The Providence Marine Corps of Artillery

In Recognition of

**Two Hundred Years of Artillery
Service to Our State and Nation
Since Its Organization in 1801**

and

*Today, the Citizen Soldiers of the 103d Field Artillery
Brigade continue to carry on the proud traditions of their
forefathers and stand ready to answer the call to
defend and serve their State and Nation.*

*In recognition whereof, I have hereby set my hand and caused the Executive
Seal of the State of Rhode Island and Providence Plantations to be
hereunto affixed this 4th day of May 2002.*

Lincoln Almond

**Lincoln Almond
Governor**

Col. Valente (right) and LTC Dowling confer in the field at Fort Sill.

to Rhode Island to take part in the ceremonies and being the guest speaker at the bicentennial anniversary dinner of the PMCA /103d Field Artillery held at the Squantum Association in East Providence. Rhode Island. Under the CAPSTONE mission, the 103d, with all assigned battalions, was responsible for reinforcing V Corps Artillery in West Germany. Consequently, most senior officers and sergeants spent an additional two to three weeks each year training with V Corps in Germany for various exercises and war games.

These new training opportunities saw soldiers from the 103d on the East German border, then the limit of the western free world, carrying on the same mission as the 43rd Division in 1951. However, as part of the security for such border tours, the soldiers were required to use civilian clothes, as the East German soldiers in the guard towers would photograph units to identify shoulder patches for their order of battle analysis. During one exercise, a Regular Army soldier approached the Rhode Islanders, and upon noticing the patch with an anchor on their shoulders asked if they were United States Marines. The reply was "you're half right," and he was given a thumbnail sketch of the origins of the 103d as seafaring cannoneers under the Providence Marine Corps of Artillery banner.[18]

During Operation Desert Shield/Desert Storm in 1990 and 1991, very few National Guard combat forces were mobilized, although many military police and combat service support units were. A few soldiers from the 103d did volunteer and deploy with units of the 43rd Military Police Brigade from Rhode Island. As part of a continued military drawdown prompted by the ill-fated concept of a "peace dividend," the 103d's Second Battalion was inactivated in 1992, its members being transferred to the other batteries. The 103d Field Artillery Brigade and the First Battalion of the 103d Field Artillery Battalion continued to aggressively train, with horizons expanded to the Pacific again after the fall of the Soviet empire. The 103d trained with I Corps Artillery of Utah and again deployed to Japan for the first time in fifty years.[19]

Also in the 1990s, the battalion underwent significant changes as the older Cold War veterans retired and were again replaced by new recruits. The soldiers carried on the routine of monthly drills, additional training opportunities in the United States and overseas, and — for senior leaders and staff — the weekly Tuesday night assemblies in an unpaid status, or "for the flag." It was just something that had to be done to assure a smoothly functioning organization. Each spring the battalion would deploy to Fort A.P. Hill, Virginia, to put the art of gunnery into practice and fire their primary weapon system, the M198 howitzers. Time permitting, there might even be a "staff ride" to a Civil War battlefield where the First Rhode Island Light Artillery had distinguished itself over a century before. The Rhode Islanders' rigorous training remained a set standard and helped to keep them the best among their peers. The 103d Field Artillery continued this regimen until September 11, 2001. With the terrorist attack on the United States, these Rhode Island artillerymen knew, as had their forebears on December 7, 1941, that their world was about to change dramatically.[20]

15

THE WAR ON TERROR

We get hit with rockets and mortars here almost everyday or night.
— SSgt. Christopher Potts, Battery A, 103d Field Artillery

The morning of September 11, 2001, dawned much as it had the previous day. Americans greeted the day by proceeding with their usual routines. However, unfathomable events would unfold that day which would shake the American people from these routines as the war on terror came to America. The 103d Field Artillery again responded to the nation's call and over a five-year period added to the already gallant history through meritorious service on the home front and in the Iraqi Theater of Operations. It would see Battery A fire the first hostile round of any 103d unit since World War II and other batteries of the 103d Field Artillery deploy to Iraq and Afghanistan to accomplish a variety of nonstandard missions. The first of these missions began with homeland security.

In response to the attacks on September 11, the Department of Defense reinforced security at key defense installations across the United States. To conserve strength the air force and army agreed to deploy 8,000 Army National Guard soldiers to bolster security at Air Force National Guard installations across the continental United States. In late November 2002, the First Battalion of the 103d Field Artillery received mobilization orders to support Operation Noble Eagle II, Homeland Security Operations, becoming the first 103d unit to mobilize since the Korean War. The unit was tasked to augment security operations at Quonset Point Air National Guard Base in North Kingstown, Rhode Island.[1]

On January 30, 2003, thirty-two soldiers mobilized and traveled to Fort Drum, New York, for training in military police procedures. Following two weeks of training, Headquarters Battery of the First Battalion was placed under the command of the 108th Infantry of the New York Army National Guard and deployed to Quonset, the historic training ground of the Rhode Island National Guard, on February 12, 2003, for an additional week of Air Force security operations training and the start of the unit's mission to augment the security of the 143rd Airlift Wing at the Air National Guard Base.[2]

Throughout the deployment, Air Force security training continued with National Guard personal working together to plan, test, and review the readiness of all base security forces. This provided the artillerymen and airmen with an excellent experience in joint operations. The 143rd Security Forces team was very insightful in ensuring National Guard soldiers received proper weapons training throughout the deployment to stay current with Air Force and Army weapons qualifications. On December 10, 2004, the 103d Detachment at Quonset completed a very successful mission and after four days of demobilization at Fort Drum, New York, the unit returned to Rhode Island and was released from federal service.[3]

With the War on Terror declared, the United States liberated Afghanistan against a fanatical Taliban government in the fall of 2001. These operations, mostly involving air support

193

and special forces, did not require a full-scale mobilization of the National Guard. In March 2003, fearing that Saddam Hussein was harboring weapons of mass destruction, a coalition force invaded Iraq in Operation Iraqi Freedom. This was the first large-scale deployment of American forces since the First Gulf War in 1991. With the operations still underway in the fall of 2003, National Guard units began to be called up to fight in the Iraq Theater of Operations. On November 21, 2003, Rhode Island National Guard received orders from the Department of Defense activating elements of the First Battalion of the 103d Field Artillery Regiment for federal service. The cannoneers from Rhode Island were being called to fight for the first time in sixty years.[4]

The first battery of the First Battalion of the 103d to receive a call-up notice was Battery A, the direct descendent of the PMCA. Capt. Christian Neary, PMCA member and commander of Battery A, was mustered in on December 3, 2003, along with 10 percent of the command to prepare for the activation. From the start it was not clear what Battery A would do. Many artillery units deployed without their artillery pieces and were sent to Iraq to function in a military police or infantry role. However, in spite of the unknowns, Neary and his men trained hard. On January 6, 2004, Battery A left Rhode Island for a month of training at Fort Hood, Texas. The famed redlegs of the smallest state would be serving as cannoneers, exactly what they had been trained to do.[5]

Because the rest of the battalion had not been activated, Battery A was attached to the First Battalion of the 206th Field Artillery, Arkansas Army National Guard. The men of Battery A quickly earned the nickname of "Those Dam Rhodies" from their southern counterparts. Training in Louisiana followed as the unit underwent maneuvers similar to those that had prepared the 103d for combat in World War II. Finally, after weeks of training under simulated combat conditions, including living at a forward base and performing security operations, Battery A deployed to Kuwait on March 7 and on March 16 finally arrived in Iraq. In the long history of firsts for Battery A, they were the first unit of the 103d to deploy into a hostile country since 1951.[6]

Battery A was assigned to the First Cavalry Division, which had been commanded in World War II by a former Mexican border Battery A soldier, Maj. Gen. William C. Chase. The area of operations assigned was Taji, a dangerous area north of Baghdad. The cannoneers had been trained at Fort Hood in military police procedures. When they arrived in theatre, they were initially assigned the duty of security operations at "Gunner Gate," the main entry control point to Camp Cooke, a division headquarters and home to 10,000 coalition forces. Alpha Battery was responsible for processing and searching more than 1,500 Iraqi laborers and professionals and 150 vehicles arriving at Camp Cooke for the daily support security operations. They were also responsible for defensive operations at the southwest corner of the camp where the entry point was located. In order to deter potential sabotage at the entry point, the battalion commander decided to implement a defense-in-depth policy of trying to neutralize the threat before it penetrated the main line of the base. He solicited recommendations from Battery A soldiers and the initial recommendations from these soldiers were adopted, implemented, and continually improved operations in country. Eventually the model recommended by the Battery A soldiers became the standard for any entry control point.

However, according to Capt. Neary, "The battery never lost sight of our artillery mission; that is to destroy, neutralize, or suppress the enemy by cannon, rocket, and missile fires, and to assist in integrating fire support into combined arms operations." They soon received the opportunity to function as artillerymen, using a battery of Marine Corps 105mm M102 howitzers, which were of Vietnam War vintage. These howitzers differed from Battery A's more modern 155mm M198 howitzers in that they were an easier piece to service. The M102 used thirty-five pound, semi-fixed ammunition rather than the 100-pound, separate-loading pro-

The headquarters of the 103d Field Artillery in Baghdad (PMCA).

jectile and powder bag of the M198. In addition, an M109-A6 Paladin 155mm self-propelled howitzer was available for use when greater ranges were required.

The Battery A soldiers were required to become familiar with the Advanced Fire Control System on the Paladin as well as the Advanced Field Artillery Targeting and Direction System (AFATADS) of the M102 howitzers. However, as Capt. Neary pointed out, he also maintained a manual fire direction capability as a backup to the electronic fire direction equipment. In addition to performing these duties, some officers and sergeants also assisted in training the new Iraqi National Guard and police as part of the transfer of combat operations to Iraqi forces. Later, the battery transferred into a light infantry role, as they boarded armored vehicles to conduct convoy security missions.[7]

On the night of June 1, a detachment of Battery A under SSgt. Luis Ortiz was waiting in their battery area as usual, near the howitzers, when a message came in alerting the battery of a potential fire mission. A flight of AH-64 Apache helicopters was sent in to monitor and call in the target information, much as Barker's Cubs had done in the South Pacific. Within minutes, the soldiers from Rhode Island had correctly computed fire commands and fired twelve rounds with pinpoint accuracy, neutralizing the target. These were the first artillery rounds fired in anger by the 103d since the Philippines in 1945. The shell casing of the first round fired was recovered and autographed by all members of the gun crew before being sent back to Providence for display at the Armory of Mounted Commands, a testament to the ongoing tradition of Rhode Island artillerymen. The guns would be called into action many times, with Battery A firing 6,000 rounds during their tour of duty.[8]

The soldiers of the 103d had been very fortunate in their first six months in Iraq. Besides dodging the regular mortar or rocket attacks, the occasional sniper, and insurgents, the role

Soldiers from Battery A fire the first artillery round fired in combat by the 103d since World War II (PMCA).

of the unit had been largely one of security operational control of the main entry control point to the First Cavalry Division camp at Taji and providing supporting fire from the howitzers. In August, however, that role drastically changed when the battery was assigned the task of patrolling the thirty-kilometer stretch of Route 1, conducting convoy security and convoy escort duties. Mounted on the same vehicles the unit drove in from Kuwait, the gun sections became infantry squads. Duties included patrolling mounted and dismounted as well as building relationships with the local Iraqi community. The battery's mission was specific: protect the community and coalition forces while identifying and capturing insurgents. During this mission Battery A instituted night observation points consisting of a single squad along Route 1 at selected times. The "be seen out there and watch rather than blend into the environment" philosophy initiated by Maj. Neary caused confusion among insurgents, which resulted in a reduction of IED detonations on that stretch of highway by 50 percent during Alpha's watch.[9]

The cannoneers of Battery A were often sought out for additional missions. The battery sent two gun sections, led by 1st Lt. Mark Bourgery, mounted on M1025 Humvees to escort First Cavalry assets to the holy city of Najaf. Coalition forces were then fighting to recapture the city, which was under siege by insurgents. Subsequent to the battle for Najaf, the First Cavalry Division's attention turned to Tamaria as an insurgent hotbed. Battery A again deployed two gun sections, led by Capt. Daniel Smith, to secure the First Division radio RETRANS station at Forward Operating Base (FOB) Animal, an Iraqi army camp. The camp known to be zeroed in on by insurgent mortars, the detachment came under mortar fire several times during the three-day mission. The battery also distributed school supplies mailed

Top: *The 103d prepares for another convoy mission (PMCA)*. Bottom: *A howitzer stands ready to be used by Battery A (PMCA)*.

The 103d spent much of its time training Iraqi police (PMCA).

from Rhode Island for Iraqi children, and on October 2, 2004, the public schools in Iraq finally opened.[10]

Many of the soldiers from Battery A had "adopted" Rhode Islanders back home and wrote to them frequently about their missions. Among them was Sgt. Christopher S. Potts of Tiverton. Potts was thirty-eight years old and had served for fourteen years in the Guard. He had left behind a job as a Marine mechanic, as well as his wife, Terri, and sons Christopher and Jackson to go to Iraq. In a letter home to a teenaged pen pal, Sgt. Potts wrote, "We have lost too many people since I've been here — none in my battery, thank God. We get hit with rockets and mortars here almost everyday or night. The bad guys like putting bombs on the sides of the roads, also."[11]

On October 3, Sgt. Potts was leading a nine-man patrol from the 103d in the city of Taji, some twelve miles north of Baghdad. The day had been slow for the Americans. They, with some Iraqi troops, had been on a search and destroy mission, trying to route out suspected insurgents. The "Rhodies" target was a car shop that had been suspected of selling weapons to insurgents. When Sgt. Potts' squad arrived, they found the weaponry and captured several insurgents, placing them in the Humvees. At 5:00 in the afternoon local time, gunshots rang out as the squad of Rhode Islanders were detaining the terrorists. Immediately Sgt. Potts ordered his men into action and into a crowded neighborhood to apprehend the insurgents. They maneuvered for several hundred yards, engaging the enemy all the way. As soon as the squad entered the neighborhood, they came under heavy enemy fire. Sgt. Potts yelled to his men, "Stay back!" as he rounded a berm to get a better shot at the terrorists. Recently promoted Maj. Christian Neary recalled, "He knew it was hot as soon as he stepped out and ordered the guys to stay back. It was a massive hail of fire." Less than one minute later, Sgt. Christopher

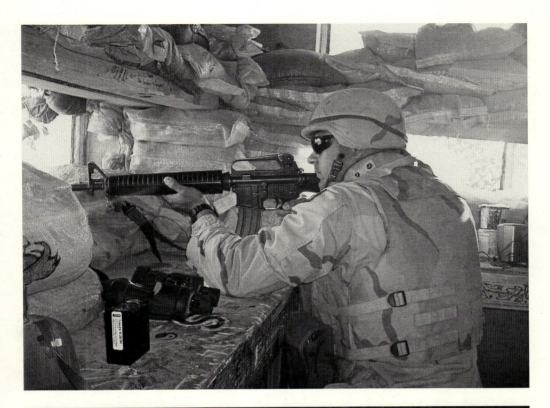

Top: *A Rhode Islander staffs his post (PMCA).* Bottom: *The view from inside a Humvee during operations (PMCA).*

Potts, devoted husband, father, and soldier, fell at the head of his squad while engaging the enemy. He was the first member of the 103d to die in combat since World War II.[12]

The next soldier in line was Sgt. Russell Collier of Arkansas. At forty-eight, Sgt. Collier was a bit older than the rest of the men and not even a Rhode Islander. He had spent time in both the Regular Army and the navy before joining the Guard as a medic. "Doc," as he was called, was attached to Battery A as their medic. As Sgt. Collier saw Sgt. Potts fall, he dropped his rifle and grabbed his medical bag. Collier ran to his fallen comrade's side but was shot down before he could administer aid. The seven remaining soldiers engaged the enemy with vigor before the enemy broke off contact. In the lull of battle, the bodies of Sergeants Potts and Collier were recovered. They would be returned with honor to their home country. Two days later, back in camp, the soldiers from Arkansas and Rhode Island, once bitter enemies in the Civil War but now united by brotherhood, held a joint memorial service for the fallen brave. The two sergeants were remembered for their unflinching devotion to their men.[13]

Even though the soldiers of Battery A had lost two of their comrades, combat operations still had to go on. The following day, Maj. Neary of Cumberland led another mission into Taji. There they rounded up fifty-two insurgents and an amazing assortment of weapons. The soldiers of the 103d were confident they had captured the terrorists responsible for the deaths of their brothers. Throughout the rest of their tour in Iraq, the battle cry of Battery A was "We are doing this for Pottsy and Doc." For that mission every member of Battery A was decorated with the Army Commendation Medal and the Combat Action Badge.[14]

A sad, solemn occasion, played out many times before, came to Rhode Island on October 9, 2004. Sgt. Potts had finally returned from Iraq. His flag-draped casket was brought to Warwick's Green Airport where it was met by a procession of soldiers from the 103d who had come to welcome their brother home. Thirty-eight years old, Sgt. Potts exemplified the citizen-soldier; he had left everything dear in life to go perform his mission. Potts felt that he was

Sgt. Christopher Potts stops to stretch and smile during a lunch on one of the many firing ranges Battery A qualified on for post-mobilization training at Ft. Hood, Texas (PMCA).

Members of the 103d frequently communicated with schoolchildren back home in Rhode Island (PMCA).

helping the people of Iraq and confided in his commanding officer that he was there so his sons would not have to perform the same mission in the future. Sgt. Potts' bravery had not gone unnoticed. He was posthumously awarded the Bronze Star Medal with V for valor, the Purple Heart, and the Rhode Island Cross for his courage under fire. In addition, he was posthumously promoted to staff sergeant. According to Maj. Neary, Sgt. Potts was the "best of the eight" in relation to his squad leaders.[15]

In November, the soldiers celebrated Thanksgiving away from home, and in December they held their traditional St. Barbara Day festivities by inducting ten members into the ancient order. After the festivities, Battery A returned to conducting security and providing defense of support and operations at the entry control point to Camp Cooke. On December 13, the anniversary of the bloodiest day in Rhode Island history at Fredericksburg, the command had yet another brutal firefight. A platoon from the First Cavalry Division came under fire at a crossroads known as the "T Bone." The soldiers instantly returned fire, but the vehicles were being badly shot up. The men continued to fight even as their ammunition was beginning to run dangerously low. The sole operating Humvee towed the other three to base. Orders were issued to load as much ammunition as possible into every available vehicle, which included that of a brigadier general. Soldiers of Battery A responded quickly, loading the ammunition assisted by the general himself, and the convoy returned to the battleground with the much-needed ammunition. In this action, the Rhode Islanders helped successfully neutralize the enemy without incurring any loss of life.[16]

A cold Christmas was spent on point, with the soldiers receiving a hot meal in celebration of the day wherever possible. On January 30, Battery A again provided security during the

Top: *Soldiers from the 103d mourn the loss of Sergeants Collier and Potts in Iraq (PMCA).* Bottom: *Sgt. Russell "Doc" Collier rests between missions outside his trailer at Taji, Iraq, during Operation Iraqi Freedom II–III (PMCA).*

A group of officers enjoys a brief moment of rest during an Iraqi snowstorm (PMCA).

historic first Iraqi free elections. Coming under fire again that day the soldiers of Battery A maintained their ground and no successful attack or casualties were experienced at the voting site the battery secured. After this, the year of service in Iraq was over.

On March 15, 2005, the soldiers of Battery A departed Kuwait for a brief stopover in Germany, where the local beer was freely sampled. The battery spent a week at Fort Sill preparing for their muster out. Finally, on March 22, two C-130J's of the Rhode Island Air National Guard's 143rd Airlift Wing were sent to retrieve the Rhode Islanders. On March 23, the aircraft arrived at Quonset Point Rhode Island Air National Guard Base where they were met by hundreds of cheering family members, friends and civic officials. Among those present was Terri Potts, who came to see her husband's comrades return. Battery A, First Battalion, 103d Field Artillery, was officially released from federal active duty on April 24, 2005, after spending 479 days on active duty.[17]

While Battery A was serving in Iraq, the rest of the battalion was not idle. Immediately after the first call, the "Killer B's" of Battery B were called up in February of 2004. The primary mission of this battery in Iraq would be a military police role and providing convoy protection. The battery was mustered together with the 1043rd Maintenance Company, which was attached to the 103d Field Artillery Brigade. Battery B left Rhode Island on February 27. At the deployment ceremony, the soldiers were the recipients of a reproduction Civil War artillery guidon. It was presented to them by a Civil War reenacting unit, representing the legendary Battery B, First Rhode Island Light Artillery, which had fought through the hell of Fredericksburg, Gettysburg, and Ream's Station. The guidon was presented without battle honors, allowing the soldiers to earn their own on the fields to come.[18]

A two-week premobilization training phase was held by moving the unit's annual train-ings from their scheduled dates to February 2004. With little idea of what the unit's specific mission would be once deployed, premobilization training concentrated on the basics: move — shoot —communicate. The unit trained at Camp Fogarty, Rhode Island, and used the weapons trainer and ranges available there. As it was not a requirement for artillerymen, few of the soldiers had previous experience with the 9mm pistol or the M249 light machine gun. How-ever, both of these weapons became the focal point for the weapons training being conducted. Extensive driver training was conducted utilizing military police Humvees. Most soldiers in the unit were already qualified to drive the larger M925 five-ton prime movers for the M198 howitzers. While the "turtle back," M1025-model Humvee was a new experience for most of them, the training was not difficult. Advanced radio training was also conducted. The soldiers had to become very proficient in not only using the radio but also in loading it, performing maintenance, and troubleshooting the entire system.[19]

Leaving Rhode Island, the soldiers deployed to Fort Dix, New Jersey, for their training. Military police training was very different from that of artillery, but by the time Battery B entered the theatre on May 5, 2004, they were as trained for the unknown mission as could be expected. Arriving in Iraq, the soldiers of Battery B lost their artillery designation and were redesignated as Hotel Company, 89th Military Police Brigade. The first task of the outfit was to teach, train, assist, and coach (TTAC) Iraqi police (IP) in five Iraqi police stations (IPS) and the detainee facility in the 31st Combat Support Hospital. Bravo Battery had the secondary mission of providing force protection at the police stations.[20]

After a month in the police stations, the mission was changed to provide a personal secu-rity detail for a tier one member of the interim Iraqi government. The unit was assigned to protect the only existing member of the government at that time, Prime Minister Alawi. The unit provided all security requirements, both static (his home and office) and escort (anytime

Members of Battery B and the Iraqi National Guard clear a house near Baghdad (PMCA).

Top: *A lone sentry from the 103d stands on guard in Taji (PMCA).* Bottom: *A soldier from Battery B discovers an IED alongside an Iraqi highway; it was safely destroyed (PMCA).*

Members of Battery B, a Civil War reenacting unit, give a reproduction Civil War guidon to Battery B of the 103d at a deployment ceremony in February 2004 (RG).

he moved). After a month, following the transfer of sovereignty for the Iraqi government, the unit became the second Rhode Island National Guard and army unit in forty years to protect an American embassy, a duty usually handled by the United States Marine Corps. (In 1991, Rhode Island's 115th Military Police Company had protected the American embassy in Kuwait before the arrival of the traditional Marine Corps detail.) Providing security in Baghdad's "Green Zone," the Rhode Islanders remained on duty for two months, until the Marines came to relieve them. After the deployment to the American embassy, Battery B's mission changed again. The new mission was to provide security for the United Nations complex located in the "International Zone" (formerly known as the "Green Zone"). This required around-the-clock manning of traffic control points and the complex entrance.[21]

In addition to this critical mission, the soldiers from Rhode Island, in coordination with navy SEALS, protected members of Iraq's government, providing both escort and security details for the top five interim Iraqi government personnel, including the prime minister, the president, two vice presidents, and the deputy prime minister. This was a very rare position for a National Guard unit but one for which the Rhode Islanders were well trained. Battery B left Iraq on April 3, 2005, for their return to Rhode Island. As always, they were returned to Rhode Island aboard Rhode Island Air National Guard C-130 J Hercules aircraft to their loved ones at Quonset. Their commander wrote, "B Battery stood strong, and ready to accomplish any mission assigned them." As the unit motto proclaimed, "ALWAYS FORWARD."[22]

Another force that deployed to Iraq in 2004 was the headquarters of the 103d Field Artillery Brigade, based at the Armory of Mounted Commands in Providence and commanded by Col. Joseph Rooney. While the soldiers of Batteries A and B were concentrated on providing

103d soldiers trained at Fort Dix, New Jersey, before deploying to Iraq (PMCA).

security, firepower, and training support, Col. Rooney and his forty-eight solders were to assume command and control of three National Guard battalions: the Second Battalion of the 130th Field Artillery from Kansas, the First Battalion of the 141st from Louisiana, and the First Battalion of the 303rd Field Artillery Regiment from Washington State. The units were responsible for providing base security at Camp Victory near Baghdad. Col. Rooney oversaw the implementation of new technologies into the command by using advanced electronics and surveillance equipment to perform the mission. Most important, the new equipment made the life of the American soldier more livable in the compounds, as they could see the threat and neutralize them before they posed a danger.[23]

In March of 2005, the headquarters was transferred to the northern city of Mosul, where Col. Rooney with his battalions began the dangerous mission of training and equipping the Iraqi army, the Iraqi police and the Iraqi border forces to undertake security in their own country. The headquarters of the 103d extended its role in providing leadership and training in current tactics, techniques, and new technologies and teaching the Iraqis in their use through a partnership program. This program allowed the Iraqis to have the latest tactics and technology to combat the insurgents and the al-Qaeda threat to their country and a stronger working relationship with the Americans. The soldiers faced a tough summer in Iraq, with high temperatures and broken down vehicles. Still, the mission to win the hearts and minds of the Iraqi people and defeat the insurgency through command and control continued until August 16, when the unit departed Iraq. On August 24, Col. Rooney and his detachment arrived back in Rhode Island and were demobilized.[24]

While Batteries A and B, along with the Headquarters and Service Battery of the 103d, deployed to Iraq, they left one unit at home, Battery C. The battery, based in Bristol, had been

Col. Joseph Rooney (right) commanded the 103d in Iraq. Here he is with Maj. Gen. Peter W. Chiarelli (PMCA).

a community staple for many years even before being assigned to the 103d. It was a close-knit unit, with brothers and cousins serving together from the eastern part of the state; indeed, some members rejected promotion if it would take them away from the unit they loved so well. While their comrades fought and were securing victory, the soldiers of Charlie waited, still performing their usual cycle of training. In August 2006, Battery C, along with the some recently returned soldiers of the 103d, deployed to the Mexican border, much as Battery A had done in 1916, only this time there were no mules. Their task was to conduct patrols and man observation points to identify potential illegal border crossings. During this mission, Charlie Battery assisted in the capture of over 100 illegal aliens attempting to enter the United States. They were on duty for three weeks before coming home. When the unit was alerted for deployment in December 2006, Capt. Mark Bourgery and 1st Sgt. Jeffrey Andrade began to build the team that would deploy as Battery C.

Activated in September of 2007, the unit departed on September 27 for Fort Dix, New Jersey, for training and arrived in Iraq on December 25. Battery C was fairly large, with 171 officers, men and women deploying under the command of Capt. Bourgery. However, the soldiers of Charlie were not all combat novices, as over forty soldiers, including both the battery commander and the first sergeant, who had previously seen combat with the rest of the 103d, voluntarily deployed on a second tour with Battery C. Many felt that they could help steady the unit and soften its transition into the war zone, as they had been there before.

Battery C was assigned to Camp Victory at Baghdad International Airport. The unit was assigned to Task Force 134, MP North, under the 177th Military Police Brigade, and was later commanded by the 300th Military Police Brigade in a transfer of authority on April 15, 2008. Fortunately for the band of comrades, a surge in American troop strength had reduced the terrorist threat. Nevertheless, danger presented itself daily. In their operations, Battery C had a unique and challenging assignment. They were to protect and operate their own forward operating base, FOB Future, which housed the only juvenile detention education facility in Iraq.[25]

The school serviced all juveniles detained by Coalition Forces "outside the wire" (a term used by soldiers to describe the area outside the secured perimeter), on suspicion of participation in insurgent activities. The program was designed to provide an educational service and to minimize the insurgent recruitment potential for these individuals while detained and when released. At the time Charlie Battery accepted control, there were four units operating the facility. As the other units redeployed, Battery C remained as the single unit tasked with improving security and operations, directly reporting to the Task Force 134, MP North Command.

The school, named Dar al Hikmah ("House of Wisdom"), was accredited by the Iraq Ministry of Education, allowing the students to transfer their credits to other schools throughout Iraq upon release from detention. The curriculum was composed of general studies, civics and religious studies, taught by 200 Iraqi civilian teachers, clerics and social workers who lived on FOB Future. While Charlie Battery ran operations for the school, the attendance rate increased to 90 percent. The students were transported to and from the Theatre Interment Facility on Victory Base Complex by Battery C soldiers and attended school for five hours a day.

The battery soldiers serving as guards in the classrooms or on transportation were also charged with intelligence gathering while securing and observing the juveniles. The soldiers were to ensure rules were followed and discipline maintained; however, they were also expected to read the subtleties of Iraqi juvenile behavior to identify any ongoing insurgent activity occurring at Dar Al Hikmah within this population. Charlie Battery soldiers directly contributed to the identification of the most dangerous juveniles, a contribution which assisted the professional intelligence organizations in further mitigating insurgent behavior "inside the wire." Many of the Iraqi juveniles also learned new skills that could be put to use in a new Iraq.[26]

The battery performed many other duties in the area of force protection and was responsible for housing, sustaining and protecting the Iraqi civilian teachers in FOB Future. This included intelligence gathering through observation, biometrics, and screening review to ensure the best of the Iraqi population was interacting with the juvenile detainees and mitigating any infiltration of insurgents into this sensitive population.

The battery also helped to improve the quality of life for the Iraqis living on FOB Future while ensuring their protection by working alongside them, understanding their needs and merging that knowledge with the resources available on Victory Base Complex. This relationship between Battery C soldiers and the Iraqi population was critical and important to the success of Dar Al Hikmah; it was exactly the type of cooperation essential to the successful future of Iraq. The battery also had a major role in special events, including public affairs related to Dar Al Hikmah, protecting VIPs, and participating in "Lion's Dawn" ceremonies where up to 300 detainees would be released each month.

The soldiers from Charlie Battery never fired a shot in anger but were constantly engaged in a "war of the mind," participating in nonlethal combat intelligence gathering. Furthermore, the unit provided services to the detainees, each one of which was a suspected insurgent, by influencing them with good treatment in the hopes of a better integration into Iraqi society. The soldiers were very fortunate in their time on the front; 171 members went and 171 soldiers returned home safely. Redeploying from Iraq on September 11, 2008, Battery C, First Battalion of the 103d Field Artillery Regiment, finally arrived at home on September 20, 2008.[27]

While the soldiers of the 103d served in the deserts of Iraq, their spouses served as well on the home front. Life had to go on as their loved ones carried out the dangerous mission. E-mail and the occasional telephone call provided the only solace to the war-weary. Rhode Island National Guard family support units were available to assist when needed and greatly comforted those who received assistance. Much as their soldiers banded together, the families did as well, supporting each other through the tough times. The local Rhode Island community assisted as well, donating turkeys for Thanksgiving on one occasion. For many of the families there was a drastic difference between the pay received in the private sector and active duty. Much as the more experienced sergeants watched over their men, the spouses of those on their second or third deployment provided knowledgeable assistance to those dealing with their first deployment. The year-long deployments took their toll. Indeed, the best sight that many ever saw in their lives was when the large, lumbering C-130J's of the 143rd Airlift Wing buzzed over Narragansett Bay before landing at Quonset with their loved one aboard.[28]

Since the time Charlie Battery returned from Iraq, the 103d has been involved in the retraining and recertifying of its field artillery soldiers in their core cannoneer and gunnery tasks of preparing the data for, and actually firing, the howitzers. As 2009 arrived, the battalion received word they had been selected over numerous other Army National Guard field artillery units and would be only the second National Guard battalion to receive the newest artillery weapon system in the inventory, the M777A1 howitzer. This cannon is 7,000 pounds lighter than the old M198 guns and they have a greater range capability. The selection of the First Battalion of the 103d to receive this weapon system in late 2009 once again demonstrates the United States Army's confidence and trust in Rhode Island redlegs to effectively deliver its mission as part of the 197th Fires Brigade and the United States Army.[29]

In the years since September 11, nearly every soldier of the First Battalion of the 103d Field Artillery Regiment has seen active duty in Iraq, rightfully earning the Iraq Campaign Medal. Some have earned other awards, including the Bronze Star, Purple Heart, Army Commendation, and the Combat Action Badge. Above the ribbons and medals, however, there has remained the same distinguishing feature since 1801—a Rhode Island cannoneer. Hailed throughout the world as the best in what they do, the soldiers from Rhode Island have carried on the proud tradition of excellence in their trade. No one can ever know what tomorrow will bring, but one thing is sure—that the cannoneers of the Rhode Island National Guard, as always, will be ready to meet any challenges in the future. All of this was started by those intrepid sea captain founders of the Providence Marine Corps of Artillery in 1801.

As the Department of the Army's recognized founder of today's 103d Field Artillery, membership in the PMCA today is automatic for all those who have served or who are currently serving in the 103d. In 1995 an associate organization, the Providence Marine Corps of Artillery Museum, was established by Maj. Gen. Read, then commander of the PMCA, to highlight examples of the unit's rich history and to preserve them for future generations. While most of the dues-paying members of the Providence Marine Corps of Artillery Museum are members of by virtue of their service in the 103d, memberships are available to military personnel who have not served in the 103d during their career, as well as selected civilians who have a deep interest in the history of the PMCA or the 103d, which continues to be commanded by an elected lieutenant colonel and has a board that meets quarterly.

In early June each year there is an annual PMCA/103d Field Artillery banquet held at the regimental home, the Benefit Street Arsenal. Dining tables in the drill shed are covered in red tablecloths, the branch color of the artillery, and each year sees a convivial group of old 103d veterans along with the youngest-serving members of the 103d. As recently as 1985, this banquet was attended by three World War I veterans of the 103d, the last of the old guard. The PMCA continues to show its support for the 103d Field Artillery by funding the annual

Battery C of the 103d returns home after a year in Iraq. Hundreds were on hand to celebrate their return (PMCA).

103d Family Day. In early December, there is the annual Artillery Review, and the annual Saint Barbara awards ceremony, as well as the Gen. Barker luncheon. Later in March, there is the Generals Files and Read luncheon. Both these luncheons continue to be held in order to remember and honor the past great leaders of the PMCA and the 103d. As a further illustration of the brotherhood of arms and old artillery friendships, each month a small group of former 103d artillerymen gather for lunch on the third Friday, a tradition well over sixty years old.[30]

At each reunion and gathering, the regimental colors of the 103d Field Artillery Regiment, Rhode Island National Guard, is proudly displayed. Hanging from the staff are the official battle streamers awarded by the United States Army which testify to the service the Rhode Islanders have participated in: Bull Run, Peninsula, Antietam, Fredericksburg, Chancellorsville, Gettysburg, Wilderness, Spotsylvania, Cold Harbor, Petersburg, Appomattox, Virginia 1861–1865, Mexican Border Champagne-Marne, Ainse-Marne, St. Mihiel, Meuse-Argonne, Ile de France, Guadalcanal, Northern Solomons, New Guinea, Luzon, Noble Eagle, and Iraq. These simple strips of cloth bear mute testament to the service, traditions, and sacrifice of the PMCA and the 103d Field Artillery.[31]

Maintenance of the historic arsenal and the many artifacts collected over the years is the sole responsibility of the PMCA. Military memorabilia displayed within the arsenal include weapons, uniforms and other souvenirs from the Dorr War, the Civil War, the Spanish American War, the Mexican border, World War I and World War II, and now artifacts from Operation Iraqi Freedom. The building, a landmark in the city, continues to serve as a powerful monument to the soldiers who once trained there and the sacrifices they made.[32]

Through the massive doors of the Benefit Street Arsenal have marched some of the finest soldiers ever to serve in the United States Army (Library of Congress).

Although the Providence Marine Corps of Artillery serves primarily a social function today, it plays a critical role in the State of Rhode Island. The PMCA provides support for the state's artillery, but, more important, it places Rhode Island's citizen-soldiers within the context of a truly legendary institution. They are, after all, directly descended from the men who helped quell the Dorr Rebellion, who pioneered the development of horse-drawn artillery, who brought honor to their state on southern battlefields, who won national recognition on the Mexican border, who fired relentlessly on the Western Front, who untiringly pushed back the enemy in the Pacific, and who today fight an enemy bent on destroying the American way of life. From the ranks of the PMCA rose governors, senators, generals, police chiefs and others of local and national prominence. Most important were the common soldiers of every time and age who have answered the call time and again when their country asked them to go and do the right thing. The continued presence of the Providence Marine Corps Artillery ensures that the achievements, courage and sacrifices of its remarkable ancestors live on.

Postscript: On October 1, 2009, Major General Robert Bray, the Adjutant General of Rhode Island, received orders to activate the First Battalion of the 103d Field Artillery to support combat operations as part of Operation New Dawn. Soldiers of the First Battalion 103d FA returned from this deployment in August 2010. As of September 2011, historic A Battery has been alerted for deployment as a firing battery to Afghanistan. Historians cannot know what the future holds, but it is known that the soldiers of the 103d will carry on with their usual ardor, as they always have. Whatever lies ahead, one thing for sure is that the assault will always be supported by those redlegs from Rhode Island.

APPENDICES

I: Commanders of the Providence Marine Corps of Artillery

Unless indicated otherwise, all the following took the rank of lieutenant colonel in the Rhode Island Militia. This information is drawn from the PMCA records at the Benefit Street Arsenal.

1801–1803: Seth Wheaton
1804–1809: Amos M. Atwell
1810–1813: Charles Sheldon
1814–1817: Cornelius G. Bowler
1818–1819: Joshua Mauran
1820–1823: Eleazer Elderkin
1824: Charles Stewart
1825: Charles B. Parker
1826–1827: Peter Carpenter
1828: William Tibbitts Pearce
1829: No returns were made to the general assembly and there is no record of an election.
1830: William Tibbitts Pearce
1831–1832: William Rea
1833: Thomas Pearce
1834: William P. Bullock
1835: Albert G. Greene
1836: Tully Bowen
1837: Randall Holden
1838: George Earle 2nd
1839: Randall H. Greene
1840: Cyrus Taft
1841–1844: George C. Nightingale (Col. in 1844)
1845–1846: Augustus M. Tower (Col.)
1847–1848: Walter E. Simmons (Col.)
1849–1852: Joseph P. Balch (Col. 1850–1852)
1835–1855: George L. Andrews (Col.)
1856–1859: William Sprague (Col.)
1860–1861: Charles H. Tompkins (Col.), replaced by Governor Sprague's appointee, Benjamin F. Remington, when Tompkins became colonel of the First Rhode Island Light Artillery Regiment
1862: Henry B. Barstow (Col.)
1863: Edwin C. Gallup
1864: Samuel A Pearce, Jr. After his resignation Frank G. Allen was appointed by Governor James Y. Smith.
1865–1866: George H. Smith
1867: Joseph P. Balch
1868–1869: J. Albert Monroe
1870: Elisha Dyer, Jr.
1871: David Duncan
1872–1873: Elisha Dyer, Jr.
1874: Robert Grosvenor
1875–1876: Frank G. Allen
1877: Robert Grosvenor
1878–1879: John D. Lewis
1880: Elisha Dyer, Jr.
1881–1882: Horace G. Peck
1883–1888: John A. Russell
1889–1891: Andrew Gray
1892–1899: Edgar R. Barker
1900–1909: Charles H. Weaver
1910: John A. Corey
1911–1918: Ralph S. Hamilton, Jr.
1919–1924: Everitte St. John Chaffee
1925–1945: Rush Sturges
1945–1965: Harold R. Barker
1966–1972: Chester A. Files
1973–2006: Harold N. Read
2006– : Richard J. Valente

II: The Original Members of the PMCA

This is a listing of the original members of the Providence Marine Corps of Artillery, with their dates of birth and death (where known), the date they joined, their ages at the time, and whether they were charter members or members of the Providence Marine Society (PMS). Some of the information is missing from the PMCA records, making a complete listing impossible.

Date Joined	Name	Birth and Death Dates	Age	Charter	PMS
April 10, 1802	Seth Wheaton	1759–1827	42	Yes	Yes
Same	Amos M. Atwell	1765–1815	37	Yes	Yes
Same	Charles Sheldon	1769–1850	33	Yes	Yes
Same	Benjamin Gorton	1765–1822	37	Yes	Yes
Same	Samuel Allen	1760–1814	42	Yes	Yes
Same	Cornelius Bowler	1767–1843	34	Yes	Yes
Same	Zephaniah Graves	1775–1851	26	Yes	Yes
Same	William Tillinghast		28	Yes	Yes
Sept. 13, 1802	Stephen A. Aplin	1762–1836	39	Yes	Yes
Same	James Hall			Yes	Yes
Same	Frederic Bowler	1763–1804	39	Yes	Yes
Same	John Dunwell	1774–1835	28	Yes	Yes
Same	Daniel Olney	1757–1811	45	Yes	Yes
Same	David Hicks			Yes	Yes
Mar. 9, 1803	Joseph B. Cook	1765–1850	38	Yes	Yes
Same	John Updike	1760–1804	43	Yes	Yes
Same	John Warner			Yes	Yes
Same	Moses Lippitt			No	No
Same	Benjamin Dexter	1760–1829	43	Yes	Yes
Same	William F. Magee			Yes	Yes
Same	Jonathan Aborn			Yes	No
Same	William Rodman	1759–1809	43	Yes	No
Same	Robert Davis	1750–1817	50	Yes	Yes
Same	William S. Brown	1778–1844	25	Yes	Yes
Same	Samuel P. Allen	1760–1814	43	No	No
Same	Charles Spooner	1772–1809	31	Yes	Yes
Same	Zebadiah Farnum			Yes	Yes
Same	Pearce Coggeshall	1785–1831	18	Yes	Yes
Same	Wanton Steere	1769–1819	34	Yes	No
Same	Samuel Wheaton	1769–1838	34	Yes	Yes
Same	Jonathan Dennison	1752–1809	51	Yes	Yes
Same	Nathaniel Bailey	1759–1810	44	Yes	Yes
Same	Thomas Laing	1759–1821	44	Yes	Yes
Same	Samuel Packard	1761–1820	42	Yes	Yes
Same	Samuel McClellan	1760–1850	43	Yes	No
Same	Scott Jenckes			Yes	No
Same	Henry Mathewson	1777–1851	26	Yes	No
Same	Peter S. Mawney				
Same	John F. Greene	1773–1852	30	Yes	No
Same	Stephen Jackson	1764–1826	39	Yes	Yes
Same	Oliver Earle	1770–1824	33	Yes	No
Same	Christopher Godfrey			No	No
Same	Henry Olney			No	No
same	Joseph Whitney	1772–1816	31	Yes	No

Date Joined	Name	Birth and Death Dates	Age	Charter	PMS
Same	Burroughs Aborn	1772–1835	31	Yes	Yes
Same	Samuel Young	1745–1817	58	Yes	Yes
Same	John Cook			No	No
Same	Nathaniel Pearce	1770–1851	33	Yes	Yes
Same	Thomas Dring	1757–1825	46	Yes	Yes
April 12, 1803	John F. Fry	1770–1809	33	No	No
Same	Richard Fenner	1753–1842	50	No	No
Same	Zephaniah Graves	1785–1825	18	No	No
Same	Sylvester Simmons			No	No
Same	Benjamin Taylor			No	No
Same	Sheldon Hawkins			No	No
Same	Thomas Holden	1784–1849	19	No	No
Same	Charles Spooner			No	Yes
Same	Thomas Foster			No	No
Same	Joseph Harris			No	No
Same	James Hall			No	No
Same	Robert Lillibridge			No	No
Same	George M. Allen			No	No
Same	John Earle	1750–1810	53	No	No
Same	James Rhodes			No	No
April 25, 1803	Joseph B. Stephens			No	No
Same	James Foot			No	No
Same	Charles Stewart	1778–1860	25	No	No
Same	Benjamin S. Dexter			No	No
Same	Israel Bullock	1781–1814	22	Yes	No
Same	James Anthony	1770–1836	33	No	No
Same	John Alverson	1757–1856	46	No	No
Same	Henry P. Franklin	1777–1849	26	No	No
Same	Joseph Foot	1773–1843	30	No	No
Same	Thomas Clark	1775–1837	28	No	No
April 26, 1803	Richmond Bullock	1760–1822	43	Yes	Yes
Same	Moses Adams	1769–1812	34	No	No
Same	James Bird	1772–1808	31	No	No

III: The Bicentennial of 2001

As of 2001, the bylaws of the Providence Marine Corps of Artillery provided for four categories of membership.

An ACTIVE member is an officer or enlisted person who is currently serving in the Rhode Island National Guard Field Artillery. Such membership continues until the resignation of the officer, or the discharge of the enlisted person.

A LIFE member is any officer or enlisted person who served as an officer of the Corps, as well as all who served in the 103d Field Artillery in World War I, or the 68th Field Artillery Brigade, or the 43rd Division Artillery in World War II, or the Korean War. It now includes those members who have served on active duty overseas during the War on Terror

An ASSOCIATE membership may be granted to any officer or enlisted person not eligible for active or life membership who has served in the Rhode Island National Guard Field Artillery, upon application to and approval by the Standing Committee.

An HONORARY membership may be granted to a person distinguished in the military or civilian sector, who is deserving of such recognition for their support of the Providence Marine Corps of Artillery by a vote of the Standing Committee.

Our original intent was to list all members of the PMCA during the bicentennial year which would have included *all* members of the 103d Field Artillery Brigade at that time. However, with the impossibility of getting this listing correct a decade later, it is felt more appropriate to paraphrase General Barker. Without the dedicated service of the 103d soldiers throughout the years, there would be no history to write. It is the tradition of their service and sacrifice that has established the honor of being a Rhody Redleg.

Thank you all.

Brig. Gen. Richard J. Valente, USA (Ret)
Lt. Col. Commanding
Providence Marine Corps of Artillery
Former Commander 103d Field Artillery Brigade

IV: Rhode Island Batteries in the Civil War

This listing of the Rhode Island batteries is drawn from the 1893 *Revised Register of Rhode Island Volunteers.* This important book details the battles, commanders, and dates of service of the Rhode Island batteries that went forth from the Benefit Street Arsenal.

First Regiment, Rhode Island Light Artillery

Field and Staff Officers:
Colonels: Charles H. Tompkins, John G. Hazard.
Lieutenant Colonels: William Reynolds, J. Albert Monroe, John A. Tompkins.
Majors: Alexander S. Webb, Samuel P. Sanford, J. Albert Monroe, John G. Hazard, T. Fred Brown, George W. Adams.
Adjutants: Jeffrey Hazard, Crawford Allen, Jr., T. Fred Brown, G. Lyman Dwight.
Surgeons: William T. Thurston, John H. Merrill
Assistant Surgeons: Francis S. Bradford, John H. Merrill.
Chaplain: John A. Perry.
Hospital Steward: Eli Messinger.
Note: Regiment never served together as a cohesive unit, but rather batteries were deployed as needed. Regimental headquarters existed in name only; in effect each battery was a separate entity with its own history.

Battery A "Arnold's Battery" —
June 6, 1861 to August 12, 1864

Veterans and recruits consolidated with Battery B September 23, 1864.

Commanders: Capt. William H. Reynolds, Capt. John A. Tompkins, Capt. William A. Arnold, 1st Lt. Gamaliel Lyman Dwight, 1st Lt. William S. Perrin.

Battle Honors: First Bull Run, Bolivar Heights, Edward's Ferry, Yorktown, Fair Oaks, Savage Station, Glendale, White Oak Swamp, Glendale, Malvern Hill, Chantilly, South Mountain, Antietam, Fredericksburg, Chancellorsville, Gettysburg, Bristoe Station, Mine Run, Morton's Ford, Wilderness, Todd's Tavern, Po River, Spotsylvania, North Anna, Totopotomoy, Swift's Creek, Cold Harbor, Petersburg, Deep Bottom.

Armament: Originally armed with 12 pdr. James rifles. Original battery lost at Bull Run and guns transferred from First Rhode Island Battery. Equipped with four 10 pdr. Parrott rifles and two 12 pdr. field howitzers in November 1861. Howitzers turned in on the Peninsula and another Parrott section added. Parrotts used until Antietam when replaced by 3-inch ordnance rifles, which were used till muster out.

Battery B "Brown's Battery" — August 13, 1861 to June 12, 1865

Commanders: Capt. Thomas F. Vaughn, Capt. Walter O. Bartlett, Capt. John G. Hazard, 1st Lt. Raymond H. Perry, Capt. T. Fred Brown, 1st Lt. William S. Perrin, 1st Sgt. Willam Child, 1st Lt. William B. Westcott, Capt. James Chase.

Battle Honors: Ball's Bluff, Edward's Ferry, Yorktown, Fair Oaks, Glendale, White Oak Swamp, Malvern Hill, Antietam, Fredericksburg, Marye's Heights, Thoroughfare Gap, Gettysburg, Bristoe Station, Mine Run, Wilderness, Po River, Spotsylvania, North Anna, Totopotomoy, Cold Harbor, Petersburg, Deep Bottom, Ream's Station, Hatcher's Run, Fall of Petersburg, Farmville, Appomattox.

Armament: Originally armed with 12 pdr. James rifle. In November 1861 assigned four 10 pdr. Parrott rifles and two 12 pdr. field howitzers. In July 1862 issued 12 pdr. Napoleons used till muster out.

Battery C "Weeden's Battery" — August 25, 1861 to November 1, 1864

Veterans and recruits consolidated with Battery G December 29, 1864.

Commanders: Capt. William B. Weeden, 1st Lt. Frederick M. Sackett, Capt. Richard Waterman, 1st Lt. Jacob Lamb.

Battle Honors: Yorktown, Williamsburg, Hanover Court House, Mechanicsville, Gaines Mills, Malvern Hill, Second Bull Run, Antietam, Shepherdstown, Fredericksburg, Chancellorsville, Gettysburg, Rappahannock Station, Mine Run, Wilderness, Spotsylvania, North Anna, Cold Harbor, Petersburg, Snicker's Gap, Opequon, Fisher's Hill, Cedar Creek, Defenses of Washington, D.C.

Armament: Originally armed with 12 pdr. James rifle. Equipped with 10 pdr. Parrott rifles in November 1861 used till muster out.

Battery D "Monroe's Battery" — September 4, 1861 to July 17, 1865

Commanders: Capt. J. Albert Monroe, Capt. William W. Buckley, Capt. Elmer Corthell.

Battle Honors: Massaponnax Church, Brawner's Farm, Second Bull Run, Antietam, Fredericksburg, Morgan's Raid, Campaign of East Tennessee, Siege of Knoxville, Campbell's Station, Wilderness, Spotsylvania, Defenses of Washington, D.C., Opequon, Fisher's Hill, Cedar Creek, Charles Town.

Armament: Originally armed with 12 pdr. James rifle. Equipped with 12 pdr. Napoleon in November 1861 and used till muster out.

Battery E "Bucklyn's Battery" — October 5, 1861 to June 11, 1865

Commanders: Capt. George E. Randolph, 1st Lt. Pardon S. Jastram, 1st Lt. Ezra K. Parker, Capt. John Knight Bucklyn, Capt. William B. Rhodes, Capt. Jacob H. Lamb.

Battle Honors: Yorktown, Williamsburg, Fair Oaks, Oak Grove, Glendale, Charles City Crossroads, Malvern Hill, Second Bull Run, Chantilly, Fredericksburg, Chancellorsville, Gettysburg, Kelly's Ford, Mine Run, Payne's Farm, Wilderness, Spotsylvania, North Anna, Cold Harbor, Petersburg, Defenses of Washington, D.C., Hatcher's Run, Fall of Petersburg.

Armament: Originally armed with four 10 pdr. Parrott rifles and two 12 pdr. field howitzers. Assigned 12 pdr. Napoleon on the Peninsula used till muster out.

Battery F "Belger's Battery"— October 29, 1861 to June 27, 1865

Commanders: Capt. Miles G. Moises, Capt. James Belger, 1st Lt. Phillip S. Chase, Capt. Thomas Simpson.

Battle Honors: Roanoke Island, New Berne, Little Creek, Kinston, Whitehall, Rawle's Mill, Washington, NC, Blount's Creek, Bermuda Hundred, Drewry's Bluff, Proctor's Creek, Petersburg, Fort Harrison, Chaffin's Farm, Fall of Richmond.

Armament: Originally armed with four 10 pdr. Parrott rifles and two 12 pdr. field howitzers. In 1864 the howitzer section was dropped and two additional Parrotts were added and used till muster out.

Battery G "Adams' Battery"— December 2, 1861 to June 24, 1865

Commanders: Capt. Charles D. Owen, Capt. Horace S. Bloodgood, Capt. George W. Adams, 1st Lt. Benjamin E. Freeborn.

Battle Honors: Yorktown, Edward's Ferry, Fair Oaks, Malvern Hill, Antietam, Fredericksburg, Marye's Heights, Gettysburg, Mine Run, Wilderness, Spotsylvania, North Anna, Cold Harbor, Petersburg, Snicker's Gap, Opequon, Fisher's Hill, Cedar Creek, Defenses of Washington, D.C., Fall of Petersburg, Sailor's Creek, Appomattox.

Armament: Originally armed with four 20 pdr. Parrott rifles and two 12 pdr. field howitzers. In March 1862 received six 3-inch ordnance rifles used till muster out.

Battery H "Allen's Battery"— October 23, 1862 to June 28, 1865

Commanders: Capt. Charles H.J. Hamlin, Capt. Jeffrey Hazard, Capt. Crawford Allen, Jr.

Battle Honors: Defenses of Washington, D.C., Spotsylvania, Petersburg, Fall of Petersburg, Sailor's Creek, Farmsville, Appomattox.

Armament: 12 pdr. Napoleon.

Independent Batteries

First Rhode Island Battery "Tompkins' Battery"— April 18, 1861 to August 6, 1861

Commander: Capt. Charles H. Tompkins
Battle Honors: Defenses of Washington, D.C., Harpers Ferry, Bunker Hill.
Armament: 12 pdr. James rifle.

**Tenth Rhode Island Battery "Marine Battery"—
May 24, 1862 to August 30, 1862**

Commander: Capt. Edwin C. Gallup

Battle Honors: Defense of Washington, D.C. (reorganized in 1863 to defend Narragansett Bay).

Armament: 12 pdr. Napoleon.

V: The Forlorn Hope

The Medal of Honor holds a special place in American History. Authorized in 1862 by President Lincoln, it is awarded to members of the military for deeds of valor "above and beyond the call of duty." During the last assault of the Civil War, seven men from a Rhode Island artillery battery were awarded the Medal for "one of the most perilous exploits of the war."

Battery G, First Rhode Island Light Artillery, was raised in the fall of 1861, comprising soldiers from the capital of Providence and the rural communities from the southwestern corner of the state. Originally assigned to duty on the upper Potomac River, they were assigned to the Second Corps and fought through the Peninsula Campaign and were heavily engaged at Antietam and Fredericksburg. The following May they fought at Marye's Heights where they lost a quarter of their strength and were transferred to the Sixth Corps. Two months later, they fought at Granite Hill during the retreat from Gettysburg. The Overland Campaign challenged Battery G, but they won glory in the 1864 Valley Campaign, where at Cedar Creek one-third of the command went down trying to save the guns. After this battle, Battery G was reconstituted by consolidating with their brothers from Battery C. The new Battery G was commanded by Capt. George W. Adams. A sometime alcoholic and severe disciplinarian, Adams was beloved by his men. Furthermore, he had been a private in the PMCA in the 1850s while attending Brown University. Originally enlisting as a private, he had risen through the ranks and led the unit through the quiet winter of 1865. All this was about to change.[1]

Lt. Gen. Ulysses S. Grant pondered the situation in late March 1865. For nine months the Army of the Potomac had been besieging Richmond and Petersburg. Lee's lines were stretched to the breaking point, his 40,000 men stationed along a forty-mile front. With deserters pouring in each day, Grant knew it was time to move. He now planned to launch the campaign to finally capture Richmond and end the Civil War. The massive attack was set for 4:00 on the morning of April 2, 1865.[2]

After receiving notice of the attack, Capt. Adams went to Maj. Gen. Horatio Wright with a mission he had been considering since his arrival at Petersburg. When the infantry charged, they would capture the enemy's cannon. These guns could be used to support the infantry charge and if need be repel any Confederate counterattack. Capt. Adams proposed to take a section of his battery on foot and charge the lines with the infantry. Once inside the fortifications they would capture the cannons and use them on their former owners. If this failed, the detachment would "spike and render them useless, as circumstances might warrant." Corp. Edward P. Adams called it "a movement so full of hazard." Before granting permission, Gen. Wright "warned him of its extreme danger." Adams would not back down. Finally Wright gave his consent and the captain hurried back to the battery to prepare the men for the mission.[3]

Capt. George W. Adams laid his plan before the cannoneers of Battery G. He would only take volunteers with him, knowing full well that this charge could be a costly one. Adams stressed the extreme importance and danger of the mission; no one would be looked down upon who did not volunteer. The captain explained this to the cannoneers and then called for the men. As one cannoneer recalled, "It was a dangerous enterprise, but the men were eager for a trial." Every member of the command stepped forward to volunteer. Finally, the captain selected twenty men for the storming party, two detachments of soldiers he knew would carry out the mission. Unlike the infantry, who were armed with musket and bayonet, the cannoneers would only be carrying their sponge-rammers and lanyards. With his detachment ready, Adams left camp and moved up to the front to find a position to charge from, while the section commanders took command of the remaining men as they prepared the guns for action once more.[4]

At midnight, the Rhode Islanders reported for duty. The infantry were formed in echelon; the first line would smash through the defenses as the lines to the rear followed through. The Sixth Corps were formed up in the shape of a spear, with the cannoneers positioned in the front line. The volunteers of Battery G were part of the "forlorn hope"—the first to enter the works but also very likely the first to be shot. The position of the detachment was to be in the rear of the first line of infantry; as soon as the parapet was clear, the cannoneers would work the guns.[5]

It was a moonless, misty, cold night as the men clutched the ground, their thick overcoats protecting them from the morning cold. A heavy ground fog filled the trenches; and was so thick the soldiers could not see twenty yards in front of them. Furthermore, the Confederates thought something was occurring and kept up a sporadic fire all night long. The twenty artillerymen in Capt. Adams' detachment went over the plan again and again with their commander: take the guns, swing them around, and begin using them against the enemy. Four o'clock came and there was no firing, as Grant waited for the fog to lift somewhat so that the Union fire would not endanger the advancing columns. It was the moment of truth for the cannoneers. Capt. Adams asked the men for the final time if any wanted to depart and return to Battery G. Three men did and left seventeen to go forward. After four hours of waiting, it was time to go.[6]

Capt. George W. Adams was promoted from private to colonel during the course of the Civil War and planned the successful mission to capture the cannon at Petersburg (RG).

The first shot was fired at 4:40 in the morning by Battery E, First Rhode Island Artillery, on the extreme left of the Sixth Corps line at Fort Rice. Immediately every gun in the Army of the Potomac began shelling the city. Because of the immense noise from all of the cannon going off at the same time, there was a ten-minute delay before the men knew that it was actually the signal to go in. A regiment of Vermonters took the lead, then the rest of the Sixth Corps followed after them and soon 14,000 men were advancing towards the enemy lines. Dr. George Stevens of New York recorded, "Without wavering, through the darkness, the wedge which was to the split the confederacy was driven home."[7]

As the Sixth Corps deployed, Capt. Adams and his men suddenly realized they had lost contact with the New Yorkers to their right. Instead, the detachment angled to the left and followed the Green Mountain Boys as they pressed on. Gen. Lewis Grant had selected a six-hundred-yard-long ravine that led directly to the weak point in the Confederate line. It was in this ravine that nearly 2,000 Vermonters now charged. Capt. Adams saw them and ordered his seventeen men to follow the Fifth Vermont; they would be the first to strike the Confederate line. Battery G and the Vermont Brigade were intimately familiar with each other, the two having supported each other on numerous occasions.

The very guns that Battery G had been sent to capture were firing salvos of canister, knocking down many of the Vermonters. Although the Confederates were poorly equipped, they still had plenty of fight left. Charles Anson of the Eleventh Vermont remembered: "Rushing to their guns a terrible fire of shot and shell, grape and canister pouring into the advancing columns. Thick and fast came the cannon shot, thicker and faster came the bullets." In fifteen minutes, 1,100 members of the corps went down. Despite this, the seventeen Rhode Islanders kept pushing onward. Rushing forward into the smoke-filled entrenchments, the artillerists saw a prime target before them: an earthen gun emplacement. The position was located near a swamp in a woodlot. The Vermonters shouted out, "Capture that battery!" as the eager soldiers promptly obeyed. This is what George Adams' Rhode Islanders had been sent to accomplish.[8]

Around the fortification was a line of earthworks being held by a brigade of North Carolinians commanded by Gen. James Lane, but most important was what the works contained. The Confederates earthworks presented a deadly position for the Vermonters to charge, as it contained two twenty-four pound howitzers in the left side of the salient; another howitzer, two other cannon, and an eight-inch mortar were positioned on the right of the ravine. These guns were from the Rockbridge Artillery of Virginia. The howitzers were formerly Union pieces, captured in battle by the Confederates; now they would be reclaimed by their former operators.[9]

Battery G sets out on the morning of April 2, 1865, to strike the Confederate line (RG).

A party of men from Company G of the Fifth Vermont had lost their way in the initial bombardment as they crossed no-man's-land; now Capt. Charles Gould led thirty men to the left as they went for the cannon. The Virginians did not abandon the guns without a fight. Lt. Robert Pratt of the Fifth remembered the sanguinary fight for the guns as a Virginian stood by, lanyard in hand, ready to fire in the faces of the Vermonters: "We soon got possession of the fort taking a good many prisoners. I struck a man with my saber that was just going to fire the cannon bearing on our troops. Knocked him under the gun but did not kill him. I sent him to the front as a prisoner." Four more Confederate cannoneers were killed, while

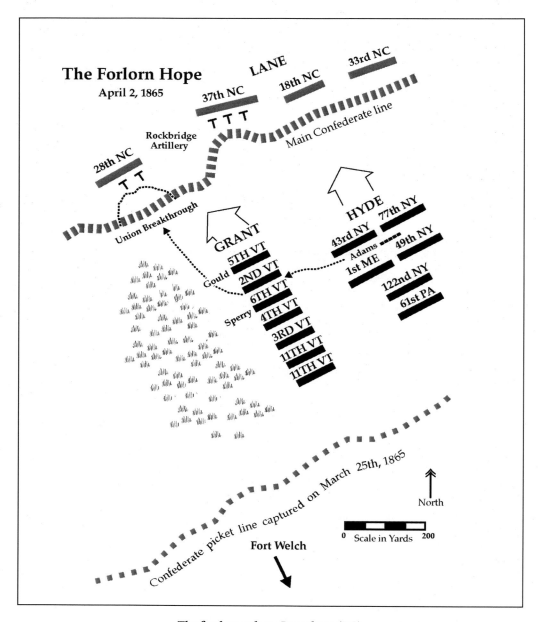

The final assault on Petersburg (RG).

six were wounded, three of them being captured. Lt. Pratt left the guns and prisoners as the rest of Company G re-formed and pushed further into the Confederate works.[10]

Directly in back of Gould's men was Maj. William Sperry of the Sixth Vermont. Sperry saw the two abandoned howitzers and knew exactly what needed to be done. He took charge of the operation, rallied a dozen men from the Vermont Brigade, and ordered the two guns turned around on the fleeing mass of North Carolinians and Georgians. Maj. Sperry then directed some of his men from the Sixth and a few wayward members of the 11th Vermont to load the two pieces. Unable to find any primers amongst the debris of the battlefield, Sperry directed his men to fire blanks from their muskets into the vents of the cannon. Twelve rounds were fired in this manner. Maj. Sperry would later earn the Medal of Honor for his actions in taking the guns and ordering them turned on the enemy.[11]

Battery G, in the confusion of the battlefield, finally found their target and went in as the Vermonters fired the howitzers. The men scrambled up the steep fortification and found the Vermonters fast at work. Maj. Sperry instantly realized what Adams and his men were there to accomplish and surrendered the position to the artillerymen. His party from the Sixth and 11th Vermont re-formed their ranks and joined in the pursuit of the Confederates.[12]

While they were waiting to charge, some of the Rhode Islanders had worried that many of their number would be lost in the charge, but fortunately it was almost bloodless. As the Carolinians ran away, they fired one last ragged volley. Two Coventry men from Battery G were wounded in the exchange. Pvt. Luther Cornell received a paralyzing injury from a minie ball to the right shoulder from which he would never recover. George W. Potter was hit in the left eye, which instantly blinded him. The men had done their duty by volunteering to go. Knowing what was ahead of him, Capt. Adams ordered both severely wounded cannoneers to the rear and the waiting surgeons. Cornell made it back on his own, while Potter required two men to help carry him. This left only Adams and thirteen men to work the guns.[13]

Nearly fifty Rebel guns were taken, including a dozen in Battery G's sector of the line, but the fourteen Rhode Islanders could only man two of them — the captured howitzers. The infantry then angled to the right and began to march towards Petersburg itself. The sun was starting to rise as the Confederates made a determined stand to hold their line, directing their fire against Battery G's position. Despite a hurricane of lead, the boys from Hope stood firm. A historian recorded how the Rhode Islanders used the howitzer: "When they began to work them it was necessary to fire along the line of works in order to drive the enemy out of the embrasures at the end of the pits."[14]

As Capt. Adams looked through the smoke of the battlefield, he witnessed "one of the most perilous exploits of the war." In the early morning light, with the unnerving noise of shouting and minie balls giving the perfect backdrop, the artillerists remained by their captured twenty-four pound howitzers, continuing to load and fire. These fourteen men, two gun detachments, were working exactly as they had been trained for over three years. The howitzers was turned to the right and left as shot after shot was fired into the Confederate ranks. "The gun was kept hot by the rapid fire with which the little band poured into the enemy," Adams said. This sustained fire and additional Union reinforcements finally pushed back the last remaining Confederate defenders.

All resistance collapsed as the Confederates ran for their lives towards Petersburg itself. The Rhode Islanders continued to work the pieces until the ammunition was expended. Nearly one hundred rounds were fired from the cannon in the brief engagement. It was a "deed of valor." These cannoneers remained by their gun in the midst of a furious assault and continued with the mission they were sent to accomplish. This artillery fire was responsible for holding the Confederates back as the remaining troops came up. As the rest of the battery found it impossible to stand and fight, these men remained. "The seven who served this gun so nobly, standing up unflinchingly before the terrific fire of the enemy were rewarded for their bravery and daring," recorded a postwar publication about Civil War heroes.[15]

Among the cannoneers who fought so valiantly were seven who ultimately received the Medal of Honor, and who gave a representative cross section of the men who composed Battery G. Sgt. Archibald Malbourne was a recent Battery C transfer who was a mill worker from West Greenwich. Sgt. John H. Havron was an Irish immigrant living in Providence. Corp. James A. Barber was a fisherman from Westerly who joined in 1861. Pvt. John Corcoran was a machinist from Pawtucket. Pvt. Charles D. Ennis came from a farm in Charlestown, and Corp. Samuel E. Lewis and Pvt. George W. Potter resided in Coventry. One historian referred to them as "Adams' intrepid band of cannoneers."[16]

The action of these seventeen men who volunteered to follow their captain into the jaws of hell led Adams to nominate them all for the Medal of Honor. Established in 1862, it was the only award medal for military bravery in the United States at the time. During the Civil War, it was sometimes given to men for superfluous actions, but most of these were later rescinded, in the early 1900s. In his letter, the captain wrote his men as being "worthy of medals, such as other brave men have received." On April 23, Adams sent in his nomination to Maj. Andrew Cowan, who endorsed it and sent it to his superior, Gen. Wright, who, adding his own endorsement, forwarded it to the War Department. Finally, in April of 1866, only one year later, it became official and the seventeen Rhode Islanders were awarded the medal. The official citation of each soldier stated, "For gallant conduct at Petersburg, VA., April 2, 1865. Being one of a detachment of twenty picked artillerymen who voluntarily accompanied an infantry assaulting column and who turned upon the enemy the guns captured in the assault."

From the beginning, a major problem arose. Adams brought seventeen men into the assault; two were wounded and two helped their comrades to the rear. This left thirteen, plus Adams, to work the cannons. All had been equally brave, but the War Department did not take note of the difference among the names of who went to the rear and who went into the fort. The seventeen medals were struck and engraved with the names and units of each man. On June 1866, four were sent to Rhode Island to award to Sergeants Malbourne and Havron, along with Corporals Barber and Lewis as the noncommissioned officers who had led the detachments in the action. There was no formal presentation; they simply arrived at the men's homes in simple boxes with a certificate announcing the award. This also entitled them to a small monthly increase in their meager pensions. Unfortunately, however, the officer in charge of sending out the awards had failed to mail them to the privates.

In the decade and a half immediately after the war, many of the veterans simply wanted to put the past behind them and move on with their lives. However, by the 1880s, with the resurgence in interest in the Civil War, some Battery G members began to wonder where their medals were. They knew Adams had nominated them, but none of the fourteen privates had ever received their award. George Potter never made it to the fort. However, by 1885 he

Corp. Samuel E. Lewis of Coventry was one of seven men in Battery G awarded the Medal of Honor (RG).

had become aware that four members of the command had been awarded to date and that Adams had nominated seventeen and all seventeen had been awarded the Medal of Honor on paper, but only four had actually received it. He brought this to the attention of Henry J. Spooner, his congressmen and himself a veteran. In a letter of inquiry to the secretary of war as to why Potter and the other men had not received the award yet, Spooner wrote. "He believes himself entitled to such medal. His participation in the assault can be proven by his comrades."

The War Department clerks returned to the records and noticed the mistake from 1866. They argued that only the four noncommissioned officers had been nominated, not the fourteen privates, despite the fact that Adams was clear that all were to be awarded. Potter was already a Medal of Honor recipient but was being denied his award because of government bureaucracy. Henry Spooner, however, was a powerful House Republican and the War Department backed off and finally mailed Potter's medal in 1886. The following year John Corcoran applied through Congressman Spooner for his award.

Corp. James A. Barber proudly wears his Medal of Honor (RG).

At the time, with veterans' rights at the forefront of politics, it was not frowned upon for a soldier to seek his own glory and what he thought was rightfully his. Unlike Potter, Corcoran had remained by the cannon. He claimed, "I was one of the selected men from that battery who scaled the enemys works, capturing their guns, turning them upon the enemy, and rendering such other service that bronze medals were ordered for presentation to us from the government in recognition of such service." Corcoran followed the same route as Potter, through Spooner, this time including affidavits from Samuel E. Lewis and George W. Potter. Corcoran received his award in 1887.

The last cannoneer to receive the Medal of Honor was Pvt. Charles D. Ennis. The medal came nearly thirty years after the war. Both Potter's and Corcoran's awards had come through a combination of their own requests and that of Henry Spooner. In 1892, Rhode Island's quartermaster general, Charles R. Dennis, stepped up "on behalf" of Ennis in writing to the War Department requesting his award. Dennis had personally traveled through Rhode Island, meeting with Barber, Malbourne, Lewis, Potter, and Corcoran to interview them and insure that Ennis was truly a worthy recipient. He was. The award arrived a few months later. This was the last Medal of Honor awarded to a member of Battery G. Even though seventeen men had been nominated and awarded the medal, only seven would actually receive it and the final outcome would take nearly thirty years.

When he was investigating Potter's case, Spooner actually went to the War Office and, upon inquiring, was shown a drawer containing all of the Medals of Honor, inscribed with the names of each member of Battery G. The medals were there, but "laid away & quite corroded in the case." After Ennis was sent his medal, the War Department issued special orders allowing any Battery G veteran who had been named by Adams to write in and receive the award. The problem was that most of the recipients were either dead or had left the conflict behind in their youth and simply did not care anymore. Capt. George W. Adams himself wrote as to why the Medal of Honor had not been awarded to all earlier: "It is possible that these soldiers have been overlooked, this particular service having been performed so near the close of the war."[17]

The ten men of Battery G who were nominated and received the Medal of Honor but never had the award mailed to them were Corporals Henry Griffith and Henry Randall, along with Privates Luther Cornell, Warren P. Franklin, Karl Guhl, John P. Kronke, Henry Krull, William F. Short, James A. Taft, and Horace Tanner. Even though their deed was performed 150 years ago, these brave men earned the Medal of Honor and deserve to be recognized. Instead of receiving a medal, Adams was promoted to full major and brevet colonel. The seven Medals of Honor awarded to Battery G represent the most issued to a single command for one engagement in the Civil War and the most to any one artillery battery in the history of the United States Army.

After the charge was over, Adams' detachment returned to their own guns and pushed forward towards Petersburg. Here they helped to repulse an enemy battery before turning west to join in the pursuit towards Appomattox. On April 9, they were among the first to fire a salute in honor of Lee's surrender. Battery G was mustered out on June 24, 1865, after serving in every battle with the Army of the Potomac from Yorktown to Appomattox. The command had suffered a 50 percent casualty rate.[18]

Capt. Adams became a merchant after the war and lived until 1883. All of the recipients returned to their former occupations, reliving the war through Grand Army of the Republic meetings. In the 1870s Sgt. John Havron moved to New Orleans, where he spent the rest of his life. James Barber returned to being a fisherman, while Lewis, Potter, Malbourne, and Corcoran all became involved in manufacturing and later farming in their native state.

In time, the seven Medals of Honor would, as would the story of how they were earned, be lost to the ravages of time. Not one survives in a museum or collection for the public to gaze upon in amazement, thinking of the deed done in the trenches of Petersburg. The seven men faded into obscurity, the only acknowledgement of their feat being a special grave marker showing they were each an American hero.

VI: Memorial Roster of the First Rhode Island Light Artillery

This is a roster of all the known dead of the First Rhode Island Light Artillery Regiment in the Civil War. This is the first such listing of all of the men in the regiment. Some of the following deceased may have joined the PMCA before or during the war, but the records from the period are very scanty. Therefore they are listed as members of the First Rhode Island Light Artillery. It should be noted that some soldiers died in the period 1866–1868, after the Civil War. Their names are not on the Soldiers and Sailors Monument in Providence, but the direct, attributable cause of their death was the disease that they contracted in the service of their country, brought home and died of at a date outside of 1861–1865. This roster is drawn from the individual battery histories, *Revised Register of Rhode Island Volunteers,* Ken Carlson's "Rhode Island Civil War Dead," and cemetery visits by the editor. "It is altogether fitting and proper that we should do this," that these men, those well trained by the PMCA who fought and died on many bloody fields, finally be given their full credit in writing.

For the sake of brevity, the following abbreviations are given to denote rank here and in the text:

Pvt: Private
Corp: Corporal
Sgt: Sergeant
1Sgt: First Sergeant
Mus: Musician
Art: Artificer
Bvt: Brevet
2 Lt: Second Lieutenant
1 Lt: First Lieutenant
Capt: Captain

Battery A

Name	Rank	Residence	Date of Death	Battle/Illness	Place
Bosworth, Joseph T.	Pvt.	Providence	Sept. 17, 1862	Antietam	
Bourne, William E.	Pvt.	Providence	July 9, 1861	Accident	Washington
Bupp, Frederic	Pvt.	Providence	July 21, 1861	Bull Run	
Chaffee, George W.	Pvt.	Providence	Jan. 13, 1863	Dysentery	Providence, RI
Church, Norris L.	Pvt.	Hopkinton	May 31, 1864	Swift's Creek	
Creamer, Simon W.	Pvt.	New Jersey	July 3, 1863	Gettysburg	
Creighton, Phillip	Pvt	Massachusetts	Oct. 14, 1863	Bristoe Station	
Dickerson, Joseph C.	Art.	North Kingstown	Sept. 13, 1865	Cholera	Syracuse, NY
Farrell, James F.	Pvt.	Providence	Aug. 2, 1864	Dysentery	Andersonville, GA
Gladding, Olney D.	Pvt.	Providence	July 21, 1861	Bull Run	
Grady, John.	Pvt.	Massachusetts	July 13, 1863	Gettysburg	
Higgins, John	Pvt.	Warwick	July 8, 1863	Gettysburg	Gettysburg, PA
Hunt, Peter	1 Lt.	East Providence	June 14, 1864	Swift's Creek	Washington
Lannegan, Patrick	Pvt.	Providence	July 3, 1863	Gettysburg	
Lawrence, Charles A.	Pvt.	Providence	May 6, 1864	Wilderness	
Lawrence, John H.	Pvt.	Providence	Sept. 17, 1862	Antietam	
Marcy, Albourne W.	Pvt.	Providence	July 21, 1862	Drowned	Hampton, VA
Moran, John	Pvt.	Providence	Oct. 14, 1863	Bristoe Station	
Morse, Nathan T.	Corp.	Providence	July 9, 1861	Accident	Washington
Read, Charles M.	Sgt.	Providence	Sept. 17, 1862	Antietam	
Salisbury, William	Pvt.	Johnston	Oct. 14, 1863	Disease	Washington
Slocum, Moses F.	Pvt.	Warwick	April 17, 1863	Typhoid	Warwick, RI
Stalard, George	Pvt.	Providence	Aug. 7, 1864	Scurvy	Andersonville, GA
Stone, Edwin W.	Pvt.	Johnston	Sept. 17, 1862	Antietam	
Vose, Warren L.	Pvt.	Providence	July 21, 1861	Bull Run	
Walker, Arnold A.	Corp.	Coventry	Feb. 19, 1863	Dysentery	Coventry, RI
Wiley, Loring W.	Pvt.	Maine	May 10, 1864	Po River	
Worsely, Hiram B.	Pvt.	Providence	Aug. 8, 1862	Disease	Providence, RI
Zimala, John	Pvt.	Providence	July 3, 1863	Gettysburg	

Battery B

Name	Rank	Residence	Date	Battle/Illness	Place
Adams, Charles H.	1 Sgt.	Providence	Aug. 25, 1864	Ream's Station	
Austin, George R.	Pvt.	West Greenwich	Aug. 31, 1862	Typhoid	Hampton, VA
Ballou, Henry H.	Corp.	Cumberland	July 4, 1863	Gettysburg	
Barber, Henry J.	Pvt.	Exeter	Dec. 2, 1862	Disease	Washington
Bennett, Ira Z.	Pvt.	Maine	July 2, 1863	Gettysburg	
Blanchard, Thomas	Pvt.	New York	Aug. 25, 1864	Ream's Station	
Breene, John	Pvt.	Cumberland	July 16, 1863	Gettysburg	Gettysburg, PA
Brown, Christopher	Pvt.	Cumberland	Jan. 9, 1865	Disease	Cumberland, RI
Brown, Fenner A.	Pvt.	Scituate	Aug. 6, 1864	Disease	New York, NY

Name	Rank	Residence	Date	Battle/Illness	Place
Burton, Hazard W.	Pvt.	Hopkinton	Oct. 15, 1862	Disease	Washington
Burton, Joseph C.	Pvt.	Hopkinton	Dec. 16, 1862	Disease	Falmouth, VA
Clark, Charles	Pvt.	Barre, MA	Oct. 21, 1863	Bristoe Station	Washington
Dennis, William	Pvt.	Providence	May 9, 1864	Po River	
Dickerson, William A.	Corp.	North Kingstown	Oct. 31, 1862	Disease	Harpers Ferry, WV
Fowles, Ezra L.	Pvt.	Maine	May 9, 1864	Po River	
Flynn, Michael	Pvt.	Massachusetts	July 2, 1863	Gettysburg	
Gardner, Alfred G.	Pvt.	Swansea, MA	July 3, 1863	Gettysburg	
Glynn, John	Pvt.	Providence	Aug. 25, 1864	Ream's Station	
Greene, Caleb H.H.	Pvt.	West Greenwich	Dec. 25, 1864	Fredericksburg	West Greenwich, RI
Hamilton, William	Corp.	Pawtucket	Dec. 4, 1862	Disease	Frederick, MD
Hendrick, Albert E.	Pvt.	Exeter	Dec. 23, 1862	Fredericksburg	Falmouth, VA
Herman, Frederick G.	Pvt.	Boston, MA	Nov. 4, 1864	Disease	Salisbury, NC
Hunt, Chester F.	Pvt.	Warwick	Oct. 14, 1863	Bristoe Station	
Jones, William	Pvt.	Providence	July 3, 1863	Gettysburg	
King, David B.	Pvt.	Scituate	July 2, 1863	Gettysburg	
Luther, Joseph	Pvt.	North Providence	Feb. 24, 1863	Fredericksburg	Washington
Milne, Joseph S.	2 Lt.	East Providence	July 8, 1863	Gettysburg	Gettysburg, PA
Moffett, Thomas	Pvt.	Providence	Nov. 8, 1864	Disease	Washington
Olney, Luther C.	Corp.	Providence	Oct. 22, 1862	Balls Bluff	Providence, RI
Pearce, Harvey	Pvt.	Richmond	April 28, 1864	Disease	Richmond, RI
Pearce, William H.	Pvt.	Richmond	Nov. 13, 1863	Disease	Richmond, RI
Phillips, Albert A.	Pvt.	Foster	Dec. 15, 1862	Disease	Falmouth, VA
Pierce, John G.	Pvt.	New York	May 12, 1864	Spotsylvania	
Sanford, Herbert D.	Pvt.	Providence	July 18, 1863	Gettysburg	New York, NY
Seamans, Ezekiel W.	Pvt.	North Providence	Dec. 16, 1862	Typhoid	Falmouth, VA
Sisson, John J.	Pvt.	Exeter	Dec. 15, 1864	Disease	Exeter, RI
Smith, Francis A.	2 Lt.	Providence	Feb. 9, 1862	Bronchitis	Providence, RI
Smith, James	Pvt.	New York	Aug. 25, 1864	Ream's Station	
Straight, Albert	Sgt.	Exeter	Nov. 16, 1863	Dysentery	Fairfax, VA
Tanner, William B.	Corp.	West Greenwich	Oct. 21, 1861	Balls Bluff	
Trescott, John F.	Pvt.	Providence	Mar. 29, 1862	Tuberculosis	Providence, RI
Tucker, Olney	Sgt.	Providence	Oct. 22, 1862	Disease	
Winsor, William W.	Pvt.	Scituate	Feb. 22, 1865	Disease	Salisbury, NC

Battery C

Name	Rank	Residence	Date of Death	Battle/Illness	Place
Baker, Henry M.	Pvt.	Providence	Jan. 13, 1863	Typhoid	Falmouth, VA
Blanchard, Sheldon L.	Pvt.	Foster	April 30, 1863	Disease	Washington
Brown, Charles E.	Pvt.	Pawtucket	July 29, 1863	Dysentery	Warrenton, VA
Donohoe, Hugh	Pvt.	New York, NY	Mar. 1, 1862	Accident	Washington
Downing, Henry	Pvt.	Providence	Sept. 15, 1862	Malvern Hill	Philadelphia, PA
Ham, George W.	Pvt.	Little Compton	July 1, 1862	Malvern Hill	
Hanna, Augustus S.	Sgt.	Pawtucket	May 3, 1863	Chancellorsville	
Hewitt, Henry	Pvt.	Providence	July 20, 1862	Dysentery	Harrison, VA
Holden, George W.	Pvt.	Foster	Sept. 17, 1862	Disease	Washington
Irving, William	Pvt.	Providence	June 27, 1862	Gaines Mill	
Lampheir, Thomas F.	Pvt.	Providence	June 4, 1864	Cold Harbor	
Lovely, Judson A.	Pvt.	Providence	Aug. 4, 1862	Epilepsy	Washington
McVeigh, Hugh	Pvt.	Warwick	Oct. 7, 1861	Accident	Washington
Moises, Frederic S.	Sgt.	Pawtucket	May 3, 1863	Chancellorsville	
Montgomery, Frank E.	Pvt.	Moosup, CT	Dec. 13, 1862	Fredericksburg	
Nason, Henry	Pvt.	Maine	Jan. 13, 1864	Mine Run	Washington
O'Brien, Patrick	Pvt.	Warwick	Aug. 13, 1863	Dysentery	Warwick, RI

Name	Rank	Residence	Date of Death	Battle/Illness	Place
Parker, Gideon B.	Pvt.	Coventry	June 27, 1862	Gaines Mill	
Perry, George A.	Sgt.	Smithfield	Nov. 1, 1864	Cedar Creek	Baltimore, MD
Randall, Thomas	Pvt.	Killingly, CT	Jan. 22, 1863	Disease	Killingly, CT
Reynolds, John T.	Pvt.	Richmond	April 5,1862	Yorktown	
Ryan, Daniel	Pvt.	Providence	Oct. 20, 1864	Cedar Creek	
Swan, John E.	Pvt.	Milford, MA	June 27, 1862	Gaines Mill	
Terry, David	Pvt.	Providence	June 27, 1862	Gaines Mill	
Testen, Henry E.	Pvt.	Blackstone, MA	June 27, 1862	Gaines Mill	
Thayer, Elisha D.	Pvt.	Smithfield	July 1, 1862	Malvern Hill	
Thursby, Samuel	Pvt.	New York	July 1, 1862	Malvern Hill	
Thompson, William B.	Corp.	Pawtucket	July 1, 1862	Malvern Hill	
Town, Samuel	Pvt.	Providence	Feb. 13, 1863	Typhoid	Providence, RI
Watson, Charles H.	Corp.	South Kingstown	July 1, 1862	Malvern Hill	

Battery D

Name	Rank	Residence	Date of Death	Battle/Illness	Place
Burt, Everitt B.	Pvt.	Providence	Sept. 17, 1862	Antietam	
Caesar, Daniel	Pvt.	Smithfield	Mar. 26, 1863	Disease	Hampton, VA
Carroll, Edward	Pvt.	Warwick	Sept. 17, 1862	Antietam	
Collins, William	Pvt.	Bristol	May 1, 1864	Disease	Knoxville, TN
Doran, Hugh	Pvt.	Warwick	Aug. 30, 1862	Second Bull Run	
Dorsay, John	Pvt.	Providence	June 6, 1863	Murdered	Lexington, KY
Eldred, George A.	Corp.	Coventry	Aug. 30, 1862	Second Bull Run	
Fox, Samuel	Pvt.	New York	Nov. 22, 1864	Disease	Winchester, VA
French, Joseph S.	Pvt.	Providence	Oct. 22, 1862	Antietam	Sharpsburg, MD
Galloughly, John	Pvt.	Providence	Sept. 17, 1862	Antietam	
Gilmore, Solomon	Pvt.	Providence	April 11, 1867	Disease	Providence, RI
Graves, Leander W.	Pvt.	New York	Dec. 21, 1864	Cedar Creek	Washington
Greene, John T.	Pvt.	Coventry	Mar. 6, 1863	Typhoid	Newport News, VA
Hawkins, Richard S.	Pvt.	Coventry	Mar. 27, 1863	Disease	Coventry, RI
Hicks, Otis F.	Corp.	Providence	Aug. 30, 1862	Second Bull Run	
Hopkins, Daniel	Pvt.	Foster	Nov. 10, 1862	Disease	Annapolis, MD
Kenison, Charles H.	Sgt.	Providence	June 27, 1864	Disease	Providence, RI
Kilburn, Bernard	Pvt.	North Providence	Sept. 17, 1862	Antietam	
Kimball, Charles H.	Sgt.	Scituate	Dec. 14, 1863	Disease	Knoxville, TN
Lafont, Louis	Pvt.	Wisconsin	June 8, 1863	Accident	Lexington, KY
McGovern, John	Pvt.	Providence	Sept. 17, 1862	Antietam	
Norris, Bradley J.	Pvt.	Walden, VT	Jan. 3, 1864	Disease	Knoxville, TN
Oakes, William A.	Pvt.	Providence	Dec. 28, 1868	Disease	Providence, RI
Peckham, William S.	Pvt.	South Kingstown	April 13, 1863	Typhoid	South Kingstown, RI
Pickett, Erastus	Pvt.	New York	Nov. 23, 1864	Disease	Winchester, VA
Robbins, Duty	Pvt.	Warwick	Sept. 17, 1862	Antietam	
Taylor, Charles	Pvt.	New York	Nov. 11, 1864	Disease	Harrisburg, PA
Watson, Charles H.	Pvt.	Coventry	Feb. 19, 1863	Disease	Hampton, VA
Webb, Edward J.	Art.	North Providence	June 2, 1863	Disease	Somerset, KY
Worden, Charles H.	Pvt	South Kingstown	Mar. 14, 1863	Disease	Hampton, VA

Battery E

Name	Rank	Residence	Date of Death	Battle/Illness	Place
Bailey, William H.	Pvt.	Warwick	Oct. 10, 1864	Dysentery	New York, NY
Beadle, John	Pvt.	Pennsylvania	July 2, 1863	Gettysburg	
Bennett, Jeremiah	Pvt.	Providence	April 2, 1864	Disease	Providence, RI
Beard, William	Pvt.	Johnston	July 2, 1863	Gettysburg	

Name	Rank	Residence	Date of Death	Battle/Illness	Place
Brannan, John	Pvt.	East Providence	Aug. 27, 1862	Second Bull Run	
Burgess, Samson	Pvt.	Foster	April 16, 1866	Disease	Foster, RI
Colvin, John	Pvt.	Scituate	June 30, 1862	Typhoid	Malvern Hill, VA
Colwell, Albert N.	Pvt.	Scituate	Nov. 7, 1863	Kelly's Ford	
Corp, Stephen M.	Pvt.	Foster	Dec. 24, 1866	Disease	Foster, RI
Fiske, George W.	Pvt.	Coventry	June 27, 1862	Typhoid	Fair Oaks, VA
Galvin, Edward	Pvt.	Providence	Aug. 28, 1862	Second Bull Run	
Greene, Lemuel A.	Corp.	Coventry	Aug. 27, 1862	Second Bull Run	
Harrop, Joseph.	Pvt.	Warwick	July 1, 1862	Malvern Hill	
Higgins, George	Pvt.	Canterbury, CT	Nov. 21, 1862	Accident	Falmouth, VA
Hilton, Alvin.	Pvt.	Maine	July 2, 1863	Gettysburg	
King, William H.	Pvt.	North Providence	Sept. 5, 1862	Typhoid	Washington
Leavins, Marvin M.	Pvt.	Providence	Mar. 3, 1863	Typhoid	Falmouth, VA
Martin, Francis H.	Pvt.	Pennsylvania	July 22, 1862	Gettysburg	Gettysburg, PA
Mason, William	Pvt.	Warwick	Dec. 13, 1862	Fredericksburg	
Matteson, Edwin	Pvt.	West Greenwich	Dec. 13, 1862	Typhoid	Falmouth, VA
Matthewson, John B.	Pvt.	Barrington	Jan. 1, 1862	Typhoid	Washington
Matthewson, John E.	Corp.	Scituate	Dec. 5, 1862	Typhoid	Falmouth, VA
Medbury, Lewis A.	Pvt.	Scituate	Mar. 30, 1864	Disease	Washington
McCaffery, Edward	Pvt.	Moosup, CT	Oct. 28, 1864	Dysentery	City Point, VA
Moore, Charles	Pvt.	Pawtucket	July 2, 1863	Chancellorsville	Washington
Morris, Malon	Pvt.	Providence	Oct. 8, 1862	Disease	Washington
Mullen, Francis	Pvt.	Cumberland	July 1, 1862	Malvern Hill	
Potter, Elisha E.	Pvt.	Scituate	May 3, 1863	Chancellorsville	
Potter, Thomas H.	Pvt.	Scituate	May 11, 1863	Tuberculosis	Foster, RI
Pratt, James F.	Pvt.	Providence	Dec. 2, 1862	Accident	Washington
Rose, Richard	Pvt.	Bristol	Dec. 13, 1862	Disease	Washington
Sayles, Crawford A.	Pvt	Glocester	Aug. 27, 1863	Gettysburg	Washington
Shaw, Thomas	Pvt.	Providence	Aug. 29, 1863	Disease	Washington
Simpson, Ernest	Pvt.	Providence	July 2, 1863	Gettysburg	
Sisson, Pardon	Pvt.	Scituate	Aug. 27, 1862	Second Bull Run	
Slavin, John	Pvt.	Providence	Aug. 23, 1862	Disease	Washington
Sullivan, Cornelius	Pvt.	Providence	Dec. 13, 1862	Fredericksburg	
Sutcliffe, Robert	Pvt.	Warwick	June 27, 1862	Typhoid	Hampton, VA
Trescott, Albert E.	Corp.	Providence	July 28, 1862	Typhoid	Harrison, VA
Williams, Henry B.	Pvt.	Warwick	Aug. 22, 1863	Disease	Warwick, RI
Zinn, John	Pvt.	Maine	May 3, 1863	Chancellorsville	

Battery F

Name	Rank	Residence	Date of Death	Battle/Illness	Place
Bartlett, John E.	Pvt.	New Bedford, MA	June 28, 1862	Typhoid	New Berne, NC
Baten, Nathan J.	Pvt.	Coventry	Feb. 10, 1865	Disease	Coventry, RI
Baxter, Henry H.	Pvt.	Pawtucket	Feb. 2, 1862	Pneumonia	Annapolis, MD
Benway, Thomas	Pvt.	Grafton, MA	Oct. 7, 1864	Disease	Hampton, VA
Conner, James	Pvt.	Providence	Oct. 30, 1863	Lung Disease	New Berne, NC
Dailey, David	Pvt.	Coventry	May 12, 1864	Drewry's Bluff	
Davis, James C.	Pvt.	Rehoboth, MA	May 30, 1864	Proctor's Creek	Richmond, VA
Davis, William M.	Pvt.	Providence	Aug. 27, 1862	Typhoid	New Berne, NC
Draper, Benjamin H.	Sgt.	Providence	May 27, 1862	Horse Accident	New Berne, NC
Easterbrooks, Sylvester	Pvt.	Warren	May 24, 1864	Proctor's Creek	Hampton, VA
Gavitt, James L.	Pvt.	Westerly	Dec. 16, 1862	Whitehall	
Goff, Amasa	Mus.	Coventry	June 28, 1865	Disease	Richmond, VA
Hall, Henry	Pvt.	Thompson, CT	Sept. 28, 1864	Proctor's Creek	Brattleboro, VT
Hazard Job E.	Pvt.	South Kingstown	Dec. 17, 1862	Diphtheria	New Berne, NC

Name	Rank	Residence	Date of Death	Battle/Illness	Place
Healey, William B.	Pvt.	Providence	Mar. 19, 1862	Typhoid	New Berne, NC
Horton, Alonzo C.	Pvt.	Providence	Feb. 18, 1862	Typhoid	Annapolis, MD
Horton, Henry R.	Pvt.	Westerly	July 4, 1864	Drewry's Bluff	Petersburg, VA
Kenyon, Welcome H.	Pvt.	Charlestown	Sept. 12, 1864	Typhoid	Baltimore, MD
Larkin, Reuben T.	Pvt.	Richmond	June 11, 1862	Typhoid	New Berne, NC
Martindale, Benjamin F.	Corp.	East Greenwich	May 2, 1862	New Berne	New Berne, NC
McCabe, Patrick	Pvt.	Providence	May 16, 1862	Drewry's Bluff	
McComb, John	Pvt.	Providence	Aug. 31, 1862	Typhoid	New Berne, NC
Nesbit, William	Pvt.	Westerly	Dec. 16, 1862	White Hall	
Nye, Jonathan R.	Pvt.	South Kingstown	Aug. 3, 1862	Diphtheria	New Berne, NC
Schmidt, Casper I.	Sgt.	Providence	Oct. 7, 1864	Petersburg	
Sheldon, Nehemiah K.	Pvt.	Smithfield	Mar. 24, 1866	Disease	Smithfield, RI
Stanley, Milton	Pvt.	Providence	Dec. 6, 1864	Tuberculosis	Providence, RI
Whitman, Benjamin	Corp.	Providence	Sept. 18, 1864	Disease	Andersonville, GA
Wood, John	Pvt.	New Bedford, MA	Nov. 18, 1863	Disease	New Berne, NC
Young, Edward S.	Pvt.	Scituate	July 9, 1864	Disease	Petersburg, VA

Battery G

Name	Rank	Residence	Date of Death	Battle/Illness	Place
Barker, William A.	Pvt.	Providence	July 21, 1865	Disease	Providence, RI
Bowen, George W.	Pvt.	Providence	Dec. 3, 1864	Cedar Creek	Baltimore, MD
Braman, Joseph H.	Pvt.	South Kingstown	Sept. 11, 1862	Typhoid	Philadelphia, PA.
Brennan, Patrick	Pvt.	North Providence	April 28, 1864	Marye's Heights	North Providence
Briggs, Edward C.	Pvt.	Coventry	Sept. 28, 1862	Disease	Washington
Brown, Elizer H.	Pvt.	Providence	Mar. 22, 1862	Pneumonia	Washington
Callahan, James	Pvt.	Pawtucket	July 23, 1864	Disease	Andersonville, GA
Canning, John	Pvt.	Providence	Dec. 23, 1862	Disease	Washington
Carrigan, Patrick	Pvt.	Providence	Dec. 16, 1862	Horse Accident	Falmouth, VA
Chace, Henry E.	Corp.	Westerly	Oct. 19, 1864	Cedar Creek	
Coffery, Michael	Pvt.	Providence	Oct. 18, 1862	Disease	Harpers Ferry, WV
Cole, James A.	Corp.	Scituate	Sept. 18, 1862	Disease	Hampton, VA
Conley, William	Pvt.	Providence	Oct. 3, 1863	Disease	Washington
Connery, John	Pvt.	Providence	Dec. 23, 1862	Disease	Washington
Douglass, William C.	Pvt.	Westerly	Oct. 19, 1864	Cedar Creek	
Farnsworth, Henry	Pvt.	East Providence	Sept. 20, 1862	Disease	Hampton, VA
Fenner, George D.	Pvt.	Johnston	May 13, 1864	Spotsylvania	
Gardner, Charles G.	Pvt.	Barrington	Oct. 19, 1864	Cedar Creek	
Hudson, George W.	Pvt.	Smithfield	Aug. 24, 1862	Typhoid	Philadelphia, PA
Johnson, John K.	Pvt.	Westerly	May 3, 1863	Marye's Heights	
Kelley, Benjamin E.	2 Lt.	Providence	May 3, 1863	Marye's Heights	
Kent, Jacob F.	Sgt.	Warwick	Dec. 5, 1862	Tuberculosis	Warwick, RI
Lawrence, Charles H.	Pvt.	New York	May 3, 1863	Marye's Heights	
Lewis, William H.	Mus.	Providence	Oct. 21, 1864	Cedar Creek	Middletown, VA
Mars, Thomas F.	Mus.	East Providence	May 9, 1863	Marye's Heights	Washington
McDonald, James	Pvt	Providence	Nov. 1, 1864	Cedar Creek	Winchester, VA
McManus, Charles	Art.	New York, NY	Sept. 21, 1863	Disease	Washington
Mulligan, William F.	Pvt	New Jersey	May 3, 1863	Marye's Heights	
Norton, George R.	Pvt.	Providence	Feb. 22, 1869	Disease	Providence, RI
Pomeroy, Elijah	Pvt.	Providence	Sept. 12, 1862	Disease	Portsmouth, RI
Rathbun, John L.	Pvt.	Exeter	Oct. 18, 1862	Disease	Baltimore, MD
Rice, Charles H.	Pvt.	Coventry	Jan. 20, 1868	Disease	Coventry, RI
Salpaugh, Jacob H.	Pvt.	New York, NY	Dec. 11, 1862	Typhoid	Falmouth, VA
Scott, Charles V.	Bvt. Capt.	Providence	Jan. 21, 1865	Cedar Creek	Winchester, VA

Name	Rank	Residence	Date of Death	Battle/Illness	Place
Starboard, Simeon	Pvt.	Davisville, ME	Jan. 1, 1865	Cedar Creek	Winchester, VA
Stephens, George W.	Pvt.	Charlestown	Sept. 9, 1862	Typhoid	Washington
Sullivan, Edward G.	Sgt.	Coventry	Mar. 22, 1865	Disease	Petersburg, VA
Sunderland, Joseph W.	Pvt.	South Kingstown	April 20, 1864	Marye's Heights	Washington
Tabor, William O.	Pvt.	Richmond	Jan. 27, 1863	Typhoid	Washington
Taft, John	Pvt.	Providence	Jan. 24, 1862	Disease	Washington
Tanner, Charles	Pvt.	Providence	Sept. 25, 1862	Disease	Washington
Travers, Augustus F.	Pvt.	Providence	Oct. 19, 1864	Cedar Creek	
Williams, Jason L.	Pvt.	Coventry	July 21, 1862	Disease	Portsmouth, RI
Wilbur, William B.	Art.	Providence	Aug. 10, 1863	Disease	Warrenton, VA

Battery H

Name	Rank	Residence	Date of Death	Battle/Illness	Place
Arnold, Henry N.	Pvt.	Coventry	Feb. 12, 1864	Poisoned	Washington
Bennett, Samuel	Pvt.	Richmond	Oct. 29, 1863	Tuberculosis	Richmond, RI
Booth, James	Pvt.	Burrillville	Oct. 11, 1864	Disease	Petersburg, VA
Carpenter, George P.	Sgt.	Springfield, MA	Mar. 1, 1863	Disease	Washington
Carter, Benjamin	Sgt.	Providence	Dec. 9, 1868	Disease	Providence, RI
Carter, Thomas	Art.	Providence	April 2, 1865	Petersburg	
Derby, Edwin B.	Pvt.	Providence	May 6, 1865	Disease	City Point, VA
Goff, Thomas	Mus.	Warren	Oct. 1, 1863	Disease	Washington
Hill, Gerritt S.	Pvt.	New York	April 2, 1865	Petersburg	
Manter, William G.	Pvt.	Providence	Feb. 13, 1863	Disease	Washington
Phillips, John	Pvt.	Providence	Mar. 1, 1863	Disease	Washington
Phimney, Henry	Pvt.	Warwick	April 24, 1864	Disease	Washington
Slocum, Northrop	Pvt.	New York	June 1, 1864	Disease	Washington
Springer, William H.	Corp.	Providence	July 24, 1864	Disease	Washington
Tongue, Eben	Pvt.	Providence	April 2, 1865	Petersburg	
Tracey, George E.	Art.	Providence	Sept. 1, 1863	Disease	Washington
Turner, Andrew	Pvt.	Scituate	Oct. 14, 1863	Disease	Scituate, RI
Vaslette, Charles	Pvt.	Cumberland	April 2, 1865	Petersburg	
Webster, Clement L.	1 Lt.	Providence	Oct. 16, 1864	Disease	Providence, RI
Williams, George A.	Pvt.	Providence	May 30, 1864	Disease	Providence, RI

Independent Rhode Island Batteries

First Rhode Island Battery

Name	Rank	Residence	Date	Battle/Illness	Place
Horton, James	Pvt.	Providence	Aug. 24, 1862	Disease	Glocester, RI

Tenth Rhode Island Battery

Name	Rank	Residence	Date	Battle/Illness	Place
Flate, James	Corp.	New York, NY	Aug. 6, 1862	Accident	Washington

VII: 24 July 1943 General Barker Letter

General Barker wrote the following to his son (Thomas), a recruit in training:

HEADQUARTERS
43rd DIVISION ARTILLERY
A.P.O. 43, c/o Postmaster
San Francisco, Calif.

24 July, 1943

Pvt. T. R. Barker,
E - 10 - 4, FARC
Ft. Bragg, North Carolina.

Dear Richards,

To say the least, the last 24 days have been most hectic. Sgt.
Whitaker said he dropped you a few lines the other day which was most
thoughtful of him as I have not had a minute to myself, nite or day.
The following will give you some idea of the experiences I have gone
through. This is not for publication or distribution to any one except close friends. Each of the following paragraphs will cover an
incident.

Taking of Rendova: Climbed aboard our transport at Guadalcanal
at 1500, 29 June, 1943. Sailed at 1600 minus some signal equipment
which we did not have time to load. Had supper with the Captain of
the ship, a more or less unpleasant character. All lights went out
in the ship at dark and portholes closed. Ventilation poor. Breakfast at 0300 AM in large dining room with light furnished by one
candle. Put on equipment, went out on deck. Raining and dark. Plan
called for two infantry companies (Barracudas) to land one hour ahead
and secure beachhead. I went off in the first boat with the battalion
commander just as dawn was breaking and made a dash for the beach.
Then discovered that the Barracudas had been stranded on a reef and
had been unable to secure the beachhead. The Japs were waiting for
us on land and opened fire with rifles and machine guns. The battalion
commander (Major Devine) and myself and party jumped out the front
of the Higgins boat in water up to our waists and rushed ashore. All
I could think of was my good watch which I didn't want to get wet and
the braces in my shoes which also annoys me when wet. The men followed
and we drove the Japs off the beach and back into the cocoanut grove.
About 25 or 30 Japs were killed here and no prisoners were taken. One
youngster got 5 Japs before a 25 Cal. bullet went through his leg. He
was so elated that he walked back to the beach in spite of his wound.
One Jap came forward with his hands raised, saying that he was a friend
of the Americans. He should have been more careful in the selection of
his friends as one of the infantry boys emptied his clip into him. I
had the same feeling that one has in a football game. Excitement but
no fear. About this time the Barracudas arrived and we pushed forward.
In trying to contact the 103rd FA which had landed at another beach I
had the doubtful pleasure of being sniped at several times while covering the trails. The day ended by driving the Japs into the jungle and
establishing our lines. The 103rd FA came in on "D" day and the 192nd
FA followed on "D" plus one.

-1-

Jap Bombing Strikes: On "D" plus two we started to register the
battalions. We had a good OP and things were going along smoothly
when someone said, "General, how about using your glasses on this
flight of planes coming over? I can't make out the insignia". By
that time it wasn't necessary. 18 Jap bombers were overhead and
were unloading their bomb racks. For the first time since the last
war I really hit the dirt. The Japs had caught us with our pants
down, skimming in over the mountains under our Radar protection and
our casualties were heavy. Air activity was terrific for several
days. We, of course, obtained air supremacy but we did get a good
pasting on this one.

Artillery Plan: This called for grouping together several
batteries under a Fire Direction Center on separate islands. Strange
as it may seem, we had to make very few changes from the original
plans and the effect of our fires was far beyond our expectation.
We were able to register all batteries from OP's and tie in all group-
ments by survey and were able to mass our fires almost anywhere in the
enemy territory. Forward observers from the batteries were with every
Infantry company in the front line, as well as our Liaison detachments
with the Infantry Battalion Headquarters. We also used planes for
observation. The work of our forward observers has been outstanding.
Time and again the infantry withdrew behind them and they conducted
fire on targets within 100 yards of themselves. This under continuous
sniper and mortar fire. I personally had the pleasure of registering
a battery on a Jap machine gun nest 100 yards from where I lay, and was
able to see a shell hit a tree 50 yards from me and knock a sniper out
of the tree. God knows this was close enough and old man dispersion
might have done me a bad turn but didn't. When we went forward we
found that 3 machine guns had been knocked out and 10 Japs killed.
Lt. Wild, while acting as forward observer one day surprised 5 Japs
around a machine gun. He killed four with his .45. The other one
got away. It happened that that morning he had lost his pistol and
I took the pistol away from my aide and gave it to him. Will see that
he gets a citation for this. Every day I have visited the forward
observers and have had several close ones. One incident I will relate
later. At night the forward observers bring in the protective fires
close to our lines, and these concentrations are used for interdiction
the entire night. It has saved their necks several times and the infantry's praise for the artillery is outstanding. You can appreciate
the importance and difficulty of maintaining communications from
islands where the artillery is operating to the mainland where the
infantry is operating. We use cable underwater, and even W-110 wire
all of which is supplemented by radio.

Everyone has been most complimentary about our work. The Corps
Commander, General Griswold, called me back to compliment me and tell
me how pleased he was with our work. He said, "I now place you in
command of all artillery in this sector and in addition to your duties
as the Division Artillery Officer you will act as Corps Artillery
Officer. This includes the handling of 10 battalions of Field Artillery,
Antiaircraft and Coast defense guns in addition to this. For the
moment I'm the fair-haired boy. One mistake and I'll be back in the
dog house . The drive is not over and other details I cannot give
you at the moment.

-2-

Ambushed: In one of our attacks I went forward to see how close
the infantry followed our concentrations. I was again with Major Devine.
After the preparation I started down the trail. Devine said, "Wait a
minute. There's nobody in front of you. At least we ought to have a
platoon of infantry. About a dozen men got in ahead of us and we
started down the trail. We came to a Jap strongpoint which had been
heavily shelled. A dozen-odd men in front of us fanned out and I
started to look over the installation. I wanted to get an idea as to
what type fuses we should use on the installation. There were several
kegs which the Japs used to bring fish in laying around on the ground.
I turned one over and sat down to rest and remarked to a Marine Officer
who had joined us that I could use those kegs back on my farm in Pascoag
to advantage. He said he had a farm down south too and was interested in
antiques. At about that time the Japs opened up on us with machine
guns. The first burst went about 10 yards to my right. We dove behind
a large tree, trying to see through the jungle which was only about
15 yards away, but could see nothing. By that time machine gun fire
opened up on our right and left and a Jap knee mortar started firing
from our left rear. The next burst of machine gun fire went to the
left of the tree and a youngster five feet away was hit in the arm. He
crawled over beside our tree. We sprinkled sulfanalimide powder on the
wound and gave him first aid. He wanted to know if he should try to
get back and we told him to sit tight until things quieted down. Another
burst of machine gun fire and he was punctured through the lungs and
killed. An infantry runner came in from our right and a burst of
machine gun fire got him in both legs. Devine whispered,"We sure are
in a tight spot", which I certainly agreed. As these bastards were
closing in on us our only chance seemed to be to crawl back to our
right rear and we signalled those behind us to start the movement.
When my turn came I moved back on my belly, following an infantry man
Another burst of machine gun fire as we moved and the infantryman, five
feet behind me was shot through the back and killed. We continued
crawling and listening to the machine gun fire. Several of us were
able to make our way out. To cap the climax we took the wrong trail
and almost walked into the knee mortar which had been firing. I
figured I had stretched my luck far enough that day and I went back
to the Command Post. My aide, a young lieutenant whom you do not
know, by name of Peterson, was slightly knicked and Chamberlain who
had been with me got the thrill of his life. Since this incident I
have been forced to the ground several times by machine gun fire but
have been able to work back as I was not surrounded. Hester finally
issued me orders that I was to keep out of the front lines. Haven't
been up more than once a day since. I feel it is my duty to go where-
ever I send my own officers and observers and the way these bastard
Japs fight the war there are no safe spots.

Attack on the Division Command Post: Each night I have slept
at the Division Command Post and one evening at about six, in coming
back down the trail I was greeted with the news that 200 Japs were
1000 yards down the trail, making for the Division Command Post. We
immediately threw out a perimeter defense with the men around Headquarters which may have numbered 100 to 150. There was no infantry
within supporting distance. I had a line back to Col. Berry on the
island that the 103rd FA Bn was on, asked him for God's sake to get
some boats and men over to us as quickly as possibly . By that time
the Jap snipers had started to work. We had just about an hour before

-3-

darkness set in. I^N three quarters of an hour Berry was able to get
100 Artillerymen with rifles to us and we had to make the best of it
with what we had. Everybody was in a hole and any movement whatever
called for fire from friend or foe. It is a standing order that any
move outside a trench at night calls for fire. The Japs who are
night fighters waited till dark and then rushed our position. With
rifles and two machine guns we drove them off. They withdrew about
100 yards to a hill and we could hear them digging in there their
trench mortars and clearing fields of fire. Someone in a whisper
called to me out of the dark. As the Japs speak English and know
the names of all the officers I did not dare to answer. Finally,
it was repeated together with the pass word and I stuck my head out.
It was the Assistant G-3 of the Division who wanted to know if there
was any way the artillery could help by artillery fire on the trench
mortars. He assured me we were gone if we couldn't. We were several
thousand yards back of our own front lines with no registration. All
lines were out with the exception of one artillery line to Berry. I
told him it simply couldn't be done and I was willing to attempt it
only as a last resort. As the Jap machine gun got heavier and then
the chopping got louder, I finally gave permission to Ruhlin who had
the one telephone which was working in his trench with him to contact
Berry and see what he could do. He started his registration and after
what seemed to be an interminable time. God knows how Berry figured
it out but the first round landed almost on top of us. Being in the
trench unquestionably saved many casualties. I realized the importance
of getting over into the trench with Ruhlin, also realizing the danger
of being shot up by my own people in doing so. Finally took a chance
and crawling on my belly, calling out my name and the countersign as I
went I finally reached the trench with Ruhlin and the telephone. By
whispering commands which strange as it may seem Berry was able to hear
we adjusted 4 guns of a battery by sound on the high ground held by the
Japs with their mortars. God was leading us by the hand and this
certainly saved our goose. After adjusting the four guns which happened
to be a 155 howitzer battery, the only one available at the time we
gave Berry a schedule, calling for fire every 2 or 3 minutes all night
long. The Japs rushed us from time to time during the night and each
time we called on Berry for fire. We also had Berry radio to the
mainland for a battalion of infantry to land at daybreak and relieve us.
I have never spent such a long night. The ground was raked by machine
gun and the next morning I found that my tent, flight bag and equipment
had been riddled. This was incidental. At day break we could hear the
infantry landing from their boats and then patrols came forward. The
Japs withdrew. Within 15 yards of my hole 4 Japs had been killed and
I cut the insignia from the squad leader who had been riddled and will
turn it over to you. About 25 Japs were found in the morning and many
more were unquestionably killed which we did not find as the Japs take
his dead and wounded back with him. We of course had casualties too
which I cannot for obvious reasons advise. What a night and did I
pray! It does look as if old Annette was right when she said I was
born to be hung.

As I read over some of these experiences I am sure that Mother
and Frannie should not hear about them as they are bound to worry.
Frankly, I believe things are under control now. We have all gained
lots of experience in the past 3 weeks. I am satisfied nothing will
happen to me so don't give it a second thought. I went through the
same thing 25 years ago and said little or nothing about it. I hope I

am not making a mistake by putting this in writing this time, as the last thing in the world I want to have is anyone worrying about me. I have a feeling and know nothing will happen to me and I repeat that at the time the excitement is about the same as a football game so <u>don't worry</u>.

In your last letter you were still waiting word for you to go to Sill to OCS. Of course this is straightened out by now. Physically I am in fine condition and have never felt better. Have even been eating onions lately. Due to the heat I have lost weight but so has everybody else.

Be a good boy and take things in your stride.

Love,

Dave

CHAPTER NOTES

The following are the sources used to compile *"Rhody Redlegs": A History of the Providence Marine Corps of Artillery, Rhode Island Army National Guard, 1801–2010*. This editor has decided to draw a line in the sand, quoting only from, and selecting, those primary and secondary sources directly relating to this story. With a two-century-old unit, the reader would be dragged into useless addenda — about events and people that do matter to the story — that are trivial in the larger context of the PMCA. Needless to say, a volume such as this is worthy of receiving this extra material, but it is doubtful the reader would take note of it or remember it. There are scores of books that fill in the necessary social, military, and political background on these secondary subjects, from the Revolutionary period to the present. Therefore, the following notes reference only the sources consulted directly in the writing of this project.

Chapter 1

1. *Providence Gazette*, May 12, 1798.
2. Ibid., July 4, 1801.
3. Ibid.
4. Tristam Burges, *An Oration Delivered in the Meeting House in Providence, on the Fourth of July 1801* (Providence: John Carter, 1801), 3.
5. *Providence Gazette*, May 12, 1798.
6. Russell F. Weigley, *The American Way of War: A History of United States Military Strategy and Policy* (New York: Macmillan, 1973), 42–44.
7. Joy Hakim, *Freedom: A History of US* (New York: Oxford University Press, 2003), 44–47.
8. *Charter, Laws, &c of the Providence Marine Society* (Providence: Barnum, Field, 1824), 10–12.
9. Burges, *Oration*, 22.
10. *Providence Gazette*, July 11, 1801.
11. Robert L. Sherman, "The Providence Washington Insurance Company: Two Hundred Years," *Rhode Island* 57, no. 1 (February 1999), 3–27.
12. Providence Marine Corps of Artillery Records, "Charter Incorporating the Providence Marine Corps of Artillery," October 1801, Rhode Island Historical Society (henceforward PMCA), Scrapbook A, 1801–1861.
13. Marcus Cunliffe, *Soldiers and Civilians: The Martial Spirit in America, 1775–1865* (Boston: Little, Brown, 1968), 217–218; Richard M. Bayles, ed., *History of Providence County, Rhode Island* (New York: W.W. Preston, 1891), 368–375.
14. John J. Richards, *Rhode Island's Early Defenders and Their Successors* (East Greenwich: Rhode Island Pendulum, 1937), 14–15; Anthony Walker, *So Few the Brave* (Newport: Seafield Press, 1981), 109–110; Thomas J. Abernethy, "Crane's Rhode Island Company of Artillery," *Rhode Island History* (Winter 1970), 46–51. One of the distinct helmets is now housed at the Varnum Museum in East Greenwich. The Artillery Company of Newport served in the Civil War as an infantry company.
15. PMCA Scrapbook A, Minutes of Meeting of PMCA, April 26, 1802.

16. Most of this information was gleaned from PMCA, Box 2, Register 1802–1870, from the Rhode Island Cemetery Transcription Project database at the Rhode Island Historical Society and from genealogical records held at the RIHS. Andrew Boisvert of the Old Colony Historical Society in Taunton, Massachusetts, was invaluable in helping trace these people. See Appendix II for a full list of the men who joined during the first two years of the PMCA's existence.
17. PMCA Scrapbook A.
18. John C. Stockbridge, *Memorials of the Mauran Family* (Providence 1893).
19. PMCA Scrapbook A, undated receipt.
20. Ibid., Election Returns.

Chapter 2

1. A.J. Langguth, *Union 1812: The Americans Who Fought the Second War of Independence* (New York: Simon & Schuster, 2006), 129–156.
2. Warren Lippitt, "Memoirs" (1847), Typescript in Rhode Island Historical Society Vertical File VF Biog. L765W.
3. Lippitt, "Memoirs," PMCA Necrology.
4. Langguth, *Union 1812*, 129–156.
5. PMCA Scrapbook A, Receipts from May 3, 1808, and April 2, 1809.
6. PMCA Scrapbook A, Report of Committee on Uniform and Equipment, May 8, 1808.
7. PMCA Scrapbook A, undated anonymous letter.
8. Langguth, *Union 1812*, 129–156.
9. PMCA Scrapbook A, report dated August 6, 1812.
10. PMCA Scrapbook A.
11. Edward Field, *Revolutionary Defenses in Rhode Island* (Providence: Preston and Rounds, 1896), 45–46: 56; William A. Spicer, *History of the Ninth and Tenth Regiments Rhode Island Volunteers and the Tenth Rhode Island Battery in the Union Army in 1862* (Providence: Snow and Farnum, 1892), 326. The only military engagement during the War of 1812 to occur in Rhode Island was a British

frigate that became stuck on a sandbar off Newport in 1813. A party of local militia attempted to burn it but were fired upon and the frigate was freed. Despite this there was fear, as the British had held Newport during the Revolution and had blockaded Narragansett Bay. In 1814, a British squadron struck at nearby Stonington, Connecticut.

12. PMCA Scrapbook A, 1813 Receipts.

13. PMCA Scrapbook A.

Chapter 3

1. Robert G. Emlen, "The Great Gale of 1815: Artifactual Evidence of Rhode Island's First Hurricane," *Rhode Island History* (May 1990), 51–61.

2. J. Stanley Lemons and George Kelner, *Rhode Island: The Ocean State* (Sun Valley, CA: American Historical Press, 2004), 43–61.

3. Joyce M. Bothello, *Right and Might: The Dorr Rebellion and the Struggle for Equal Rights*, vol. 1, *Road to Rebellion* (Providence: Rhode Island Historical Society, 1992), 13–22. The PMCA records were donated to the Rhode Island Historical Society by General Chester Files in 1948. Despite much searching, this editor cannot locate the missing records anywhere in Providence.

4. PMCA Box 1, Book 1, Minutes (April 11 1840), 27.

5. PMCA Box 4, Annual Reports (mostly necrology), 1887–1908, 97–101.

6. Details from PMCA Box 4, Book 4, "Necrology," 86–93.

7. Bothello, *Road to Rebellion*, 16–25; PMCA Box 1, Book 1, Charter, 1842.

8. Arthur M. Mowry, *The Dorr War, or the Constitutional Struggle in Rhode Island* (Providence: Preston & Rounds, 1901), 1–222.

9. Spicer, *Ninth and Tenth Rhode Island*, 326; "Accounts of Last Week," undated cutting from *Providence Journal* pasted into PMCA Box 1, Book 1, 45–47.

10. Obituary of Sullivan Dorr, Jr., in RIHS Scrapbook Vol. VIII, 57, quoted in Marvin Gettleman, *The Dorr Rebellion: A Study in American Radicalism, 1833–1849* (New York: Random House, 1973), 121–122.

11. *Providence Journal*, May 19–20, 1842 and May 29, 2005. After the Dorr Rebellion, Tantae and Pallas were turned over to the Warren Artillery Company. Put on display for the next century and a half, they were stolen by scrap dealers in 1981. Unable to sell them, the thieves cut the magnificent pieces, cast in 1760, into several large chunks and threw them into a pond in Roger Williams Park in Providence. They were recovered in 1994 and now a small group of historians is trying to raise funds to repair the cannons (*Providence Journal*, May 12, 1994).

12. Joyce M. Bothello, *Right and Might: The Dorr Rebellion and the Struggle for Equal Rights*, vol. 3, *Rebellion, Reform, and Repression* (Providence: Rhode Island Historical Society, 1992), 45–53. Russell J. DeSimone, *The Dorr Rebellion Chronicled in Ballads and Poems* (Middletown, RI: Bartlett, 1993), 8.

13. PMCA, Necrology.

14. PMCA Box 1, Book 1 (June 17, 1842), 58. Later target practices took place at Field's Point and were usually accompanied by a traditional New England clambake.

15. William Rodman's full account of what transpired in Chepachet, which has never before been published, is printed as Appendix III.

16. DeSimone, "Ballads and Poems," in *The Broadsides of the Dorr Rebellion*, ed. Russell J. DeSimone and Daniel C. Schofield (Providence: Rhode Island Supreme Court

Historical Society, 1992), 54–55; Spicer, *Ninth and Tenth Rhode Island*, 326. The muskets issued were Model 1816 flintlocks, made at the United States Arsenal at Springfield, Massachusetts. Today the Waterman Tavern stands at the corner of Route 116 and Route 44 in Greenville, Rhode Island. It is now owned by the Smithfield Historical Society and was recently restored. A proposed Dorr Rebellion museum is to be erected at Acote's Hill.

17. DeSimone, "Ballads and Poems," 8; Rodman, "Account."

18. PMCA Box 1, Book 1 (June 27, 1842), 64; Richards, *Early Defenders*, 51–53.

19. Rodman, "Account"; Bothello, *Rebellion, Reform, and Repression*, 45–53; *Providence Journal*, June 3, 2007. The other fatality was Alexander Kelley of Woonsocket, who was accidentally shot while walking home one night from work when a militiaman fired and Kelley had the misfortune of being in the wrong place at the wrong time.

20. Rodman, "Account"; Frances Harriet McDougall, *Might and Right* (Providence: Stillwell, 1844), 280–281.

21. Rodman, "Account."

22. The PMCA was fortunate to have a uniform during the period. Most of the men who fought in the Dorr War were quite literally farmers who wore their regular clothing and carried squirrel guns.

23. PMCA Box 1, Book 1 (July 5, 1842), 68.

24. *Providence Journal*, May 2, 1902.

25. Joyce M. Bothello, *Right and Might: The Dorr Rebellion and the Struggle for Equal Rights*, vol. 4, *Politics, Power and the Law: The Legacy* (Providence: Rhode Island Historical Society, 1992), 64–72.

Chapter 4

1. Providence Deeds, Book 85, 243.

2. PMCA Box 1, Book 1 (April 16, 1852), 217.

3. The deed is now displayed at the Benefit Street Arsenal.

4. PMCA Box 1, Book 1 (March 11, 14, 1843), 92–93.

5. Ibid. (March 22, 1843), 93–94.

6. PMCA Box 1, Book 2 (April 4, 1859), 177–178.

7. PMCA Box I, Book 1 (Wednesday August (nd) 1842), 76–79. The "poem" commemorating this occasion was thereafter sung at convivial gatherings, for example on the PMCA's outing to Lonsdale in May 1849, when the clerk recorded this: "After enjoying our dinner and singing the old song descriptive of the Mariners' excursion to Newport & Stonington in 1842, we harnessed up our horses" (see PMCA Box 1, Book 1 (Monday May 28, 1849), 185).

8. PMCA Box 1, Book 1 (August 11 1843), 112.

9. Rhode Island General Assembly, *Acts and Resolutions*, Section 30 (June 1843), 11.

10. PMCA Box 1, Book 1 (Saturday October 16, 1847), 167.

11. *Providence Journal*, May 12, 1848. Vinton's papers are housed at the Providence Public Library.

12. George B. Peck, *John Albert Monroe: A Sketch* (Providence: The Society, 1892), 11–12. By the time of the Civil War, there would be many other militia batteries that would adopt the ways and means of the PMCA as their standard. During the Civil War, the Boston Battery became the First Massachusetts Battery and served alongside several Rhode Island units and was, ironically, part of a brigade commanded by Col. Charles Tompkins.

13. Ibid. (Thursday September 28, 1848), 176–178.

14. Ibid. (Saturday October 7, 1848), 178.

15. Ibid. (October 8, 1857), 214.

16. John R. Bartlett, ed., *Memoirs of Rhode Island Officers Who Were Engaged in the Service of Their Country During the Great Rebellion with the South* (Providence: Sydney S. Rider & Brothers, 1867), 387–390; PMCA "Necrology," 154–159.

17. Spicer, *Ninth and Tenth Rhode Island*, 325.

18. This "poetic effusion" was placed in Book 1 (227–228) of the PMCA minutes on December 16, 1864.

19. Spicer, *Ninth and Tenth Rhode Island,* 325.

Chapter 5

1. Spicer, *Ninth and Tenth Rhode Island*, 324.

2. *Memoirs of R.I.,* 105–114. For a good brief study on the life of Sprague, refer to Henry Wharton Shoemaker, *The Last War Governor: A Biographical Appreciation of Colonel William Sprague* (Altoona, PA: Altoona Tribune, 1916).

3. PMCA Box 1, Book 2 (June 10, 1856), 37.

4. Ibid. (April 4, 1859), 180; Frederic P. Todd, *American Military Equipage, 1851–1872,* vol. 2, *State Forces* (New York: Chatham Square, 1983), 1,158.

5. PMCA Scrapbook A.

6. PMCA Box 1, Book 2 (July 4, 1856), 42.

7. Ibid. (June 17, 1857), 91–94.

8. Ibid. (October 12, 14, 1857), 107–108; Rhode Island Death Records, vol. 10.

9. PMCA Box 1, Book 2 (November 16, 1857), 113–114; Emmons Clark, *History of the Seventh Regiment of New York, 1806–1889* (New York: Seventh Regiment, 1890), 416.

10. PMCA Box 1, Book 2, undated press cutting from *Providence Journal,* 219.

11. PMCA Box 1, Book 3 (April 25, May 2, 1864), 208–209.

12. PMCA Box 1, Book 2 (May 29, 1858), 126.

13. Ibid. (July 21 1858), 133–137.

14. Ibid. (July 28, 1858 and August 9, 1858), 140–141.

15. Ibid., Sprague address, 1859.

16. *Providence Journal,* December 15, 1889. All of this information was deduced from the PMCA records at the Rhode Island Historical Society.

17. *Inauguration of the Perry Statue at Cleveland on the Tenth of September 1860* (Cleveland: Fairbanks, Benedict, 1860), 27–28: 63: 71.

18. *Memoirs of R.I.,* 374–382.

Chapter 6

1. J. Albert Monroe, *Battery D, First Rhode Island Light Artillery at the Second Battle of Bull Run* (Providence: Providence Press, 1886), 6–7.

2. Battery G, First Rhode Island Light Artillery, Monthly Returns, May–August 1863, Rhode Island State Archives.

3. William F. Barry, William H. French, and Henry J. Hunt, *Instructions for Field Artillery* (New York: NP, 1860), 46–47.

4. Monroe, *Second Bull Run,* 6–7; Augustus V. Kautz, *The 1865 Customs of Service for Officers of the Army* (Philadelphia: J.B. Lippincott, 1865), 223–260.

5. Kautz, *Customs of Officers,* 17–195; Monroe, *Second Bull Run,* 8.

6. John D. Billings, *Hardtack and Coffee: The Unwritten Story of Army Life* (Lincoln: Nebraska University Press, 1993), 169; August V. Kautz, *The 1865 Customs of Service for Enlisted Men of the Army* (Philadelphia: J.B. Lippincott, 1865), 131–149.

7. Kautz, *Customs of Enlisted Men,* 165–171.

8. Monroe, *Second Bull Run,* 8–9; Kautz, *Customs of Enlisted Men,* 116–131.

9. Kautz, *Customs of Enlisted Men,* 103–115; William Marvel, *The First New Hampshire Battery: 1861–1865* (South Conway, NH: Lost Cemetery, 1985), 11–12.

10. *Providence Journal,* August 10, 1861; Barry, Hunt, French, *Field Artillery,* 363–371.

11. Kautz, *Customs of Enlisted Men,* 68–91.

12. Billings, *Hardtack and Coffee,* 171; Monroe, *Second Bull Run,* 7–8; John H. Rhodes, *History of Battery B, First Rhode Island Light Artillery* (Providence: Snow and Farnum, 1894), 2–3.

13. J. Rhodes, *Battery B,* 180–181; Billings, *Hardtack and Coffee,* 182–183.

14. Barry, Hunt, French, *Field Artillery,* 74–78.

15. Barry, Hunt, French, *Field Artillery,* 74–78; Augustus Buell, *The Cannoneer: Recollections of Service in the Army of the Potomac* (Washington, DC: National Tribune, 1897), 215–216.

16. J. Rhodes, *Battery B,* 3; Barry, Hunt, French, *Field Artillery,* 127–135, 294–295.

17. Barry, Hunt, French, *Field Artillery,* 74–78.

18. Ibid., 273–279.

19. J. Albert Monroe, *Battery D, First Rhode Island Light Artillery at the Battle of Antietam* (Providence: Providence Press, 1886), 17–21; Kautz, *Customs of Officers,* 343; J. Howard Wert, "Brown's Battery B." The latter is a poem that tells of a Rhode Island battery in action at Gettysburg and fully captures the essence of the artillery in combat.

20. Barry, Hunt, French, *Field Artillery*; *Providence Journal,* November 9, 1861.

21. J. Rhodes, *Battery B,* 171.

22. Barry, Hunt, French, *Field Artillery,* 6–14; Hazlett, Olmstead, and Parks, *Field Artillery Weapons,* 23–24; Buell, *The Cannoneer,* 20–22, 57–58.

23. Barry, Hunt, French, *Field Artillery,* 6–14; Hazlett, Olmstead, and Parks, *Field Artillery Weapons,* 109–125; Buell, *The Cannoneer,* 20–22, 146–147.

24. John D. Imboden, "Incidents of the First Bull Run," in *Battles and Leaders,* vol. 1, 229–239; William Reynolds to William F. Barry, November 7, 1861, Rhode Island State Archives. In 1984, during an archaeological dig in Manassas, Virginia, James projectiles were found three miles from where the Rhode Islanders had fired the guns. They came from only one source: Battery A, First Rhode Island Light Artillery.

25. Barry, Hunt, French, *Field Artillery,* 6–14; Hazlett, Olmstead, and Parks, *Field Artillery Weapons,* 88–93; Buell, *The Cannoneer,* 20–22.

26. Melton and Pawl, *Artillery Projectiles,* 29–35.

27. Ibid., 20–40.

Chapter 7

1. Edwin W. Stone, *Rhode Island in the Rebellion* (Providence: Knowles, Anthony, 1864), xvi–xix.

2. Welcome Arnold Greene, *The Providence Plantations for Two Hundred and Fifty Years* (Providence: J.A. & R.A. Reid, 1886), 91. Among the contributing writers of this massive history was Dr. George Peck, who joined the PMCA in 1863 while still a student at Brown University. He later became the historian for the PMCA and its Veteran Association.

3. Greene, *The Providence Plantations,* 92.

4. Records of the PMCA, 1861–1868, Box 1, Book 3.

5. William Sprague to Abraham Lincoln, April 11,

1861, Abraham Lincoln Papers (Library of Congress); Stone, *Rebellion*, xvi–xix.

6. The First Rhode Island Detached Militia was composed of ten militia companies, including those from Newport, Pawtucket, Bristol, and Westerly, and six from Providence. Bishop Clark also accompanied the regiment (see *Providence Journal*, April 19, 1861).

7. PMCA Box 1, Minutes: 1861–1868, 7.

8. *Providence Journal*, April 19, 1861. Raising and equipping the First Regiment and Battery required money that needed to be authorized by the general assembly, which could not be called into special session in time to send the troops off by April 18. Governor Sprague and his family business, A & W Sprague, offered a guaranty that all accounts would be paid, preventing any delay (Greene, *The Providence Plantations*, 92). Lieutenant governor-elect Samuel G. Arnold accompanied Tompkins' First Battery. From 1843 to 1863, the PMCA elected both a colonel and a lieutenant colonel as a result of a change in the Militia Law. In 1863, the law was repealed and the PMCA reverted to its original charter, with the commander holding the rank of lieutenant colonel.

9. The 6th Massachusetts Volunteers (infantry) left later that day but not as fully equipped for combat as the First Battery.

10. Just two days after the departure of the artillery battery, the First Regiment, Rhode Island Volunteers (infantry), under the command of Col. Ambrose E. Burnside, left the city in two detachments. Regiment and battery were temporarily quartered at the Patent Office in Washington until Camp Sprague, a mile north of the capital, was opened to the Rhode Islanders on May 18.

11. PMCA Box 1, Minutes: 1861–1868, 17.

12. Roy P. Bastler, ed., *The Collected Works of Abraham Lincoln*, vol. 4 (New Brunswick: Rutgers University Press, 1953), 352–353. Although the First Battery was the first artillery battery in Washington, it was not the first state militia to arrive there. Who left first and who arrived in the nation's capital first was long a matter of dispute between the PMCA and the 6th Massachusetts Volunteers. Most historians of the two organizations eventually agreed on the following account: The 6th Massachusetts Volunteers left their state late in the day on April 18, several hours after Rhode Island's 1st Battery. The battery's stay in Pennsylvania, however, allowed the Massachusetts infantry to march into Washington first (see *Providence Journal*, December 15, 1889).

13. By the fourth year of the war, when labor was low and enthusiasm waning, Lincoln and his generals would regret that the enlisted term had not read "whichever is longest."

14. Battery A was the first of eight batteries comprising the Rhode Island Regiment of Light Artillery. Reynolds, who held the title lieutenant colonel within the PMCA, was second in command to Charles Tompkins, the PMCA's colonel. Tompkins and Reynolds were reelected to their positions by the PMCA later that year; but because both were serving on the front in the same positions in the First Rhode Island Light Artillery Regiment Governor Sprague appointed Benjamin F. Remington the PMCA's colonel and Henry B. Barstow its lieutenant colonel.

15. *Providence Journal*, June 7, 1861.

16. PMCA Records, 24.

17. PMCA Box 1, Minutes: 1861–1868, 55.

18. Augustus Woodbury, "First Light Battery Rhode Island Volunteers," *Revised Register of Rhode Island* (Providence: E.L. Freeman, 1893), 708–710.

19. Augustus Woodbury, *A Narrative of the Campaign*

of the First Rhode Island Regiment in the Spring and Summer of 1861 (Providence: Sydney S. Rider, 1862), 224–225.

20. Elisha Hunt Rhodes, *All for the Union: The Civil War Diary and Letters of Elisha Hunt Rhodes*, ed. Robert Hunt Rhodes (Woonsocket: Andrew Mobray, 1985), 16–18; *Memorial of Colonel John S. Slocum* (Providence: R.A. and J.A. Reid, 1886), 66.

21. Although its three-month obligation had expired, the First Regiment volunteered to remain in service to participate in the engagement at Bull Run.

22. *Memorial of Slocum*, 66–70.

23. One of the difficulties at Bull Run was that many of the volunteer militia still wore their own, often elaborate, uniforms, making it difficult to distinguish friend from foe. The Rhode Islanders wore a unique uniform of a high black hat, blue pullover blouse, gray trousers, and a red poncho-blanket.

24. Harold R. Barker, *History of the Rhode Island Combat Units in the Civil War* (Providence: 1964), 15; *Providence Press*, July 31, 1861.

25. Barker, *Rhode Island Combat Units in the Civil War*, 19; *Providence Press*, July 31, 1861.

26. Thomas Aldrich, *The History of Battery A, First Regiment Rhode Island Light Artillery, in the War for the Preservation of the Union* (Providence: Snow and Farnum, 1904), 4; J. Albert Monroe, *The Rhode Island Artillery at the First Battle of Bull Run* (Providence: Sydney S. Rider, 1878), 2–3; J. Rhodes, *History of Battery B*, 17–18.

27. Stone, *Rebellion*, 374; Theodore Reichardt, *Diary of Battery A, First Regiment Rhode Island Light Artillery* (Providence: N. Bang Williams, 1865), 14–15.

28. Monroe, *First Battle of Bull Run*, 28–31.

29. Aldrich, *History of Battery A*, 23–25.

30. *Providence Journal*, July 15, 1909; William Marvel, *Burnside* (Chapel Hill: University of North Carolina Press, 1989), 420–421.

31. *Providence Journal*, July 15, 1909.

32. J. Rhodes, *History of Battery B*, 11–13.

33. *Memoirs of R.I.*, 105–114; Stone, *Rebellion*, 55–63.

34. Spicer, *Ninth and Tenth Rhode Island*, 324.

35. Ibid., 317–324.

36. First Rhode Island Light Artillery, Records, Benefit Street Arsenal; PMCA Box 1, Minutes: 1861–1868, 158. The enlistment book for each battery indicates that the soldiers of 1861 were enlisting as members of the "*number* battery of Marine Artillery." When activated, they lost the state designation and took their letter as a company of the First Rhode Island Light Artillery.

37. The First and Tenth batteries. The Tenth Battery was organized twice, first in 1862 for the defense of Washington, D.C., and then again in 1863 for the defense of Narragansett Bay's West Passage.

38. PMCA Box 1, Minutes: 1861–1868, 111–112.

39. Ibid., 94.

40. Battery A Papers, Antietam National Battlefield; Rhodes, *All for the Union*, 72–73.

41. John Tompkins succeeded William Reynolds as the commander of Battery A when Reynolds was promoted to lieutenant colonel of the First Rhode Island Light Artillery Regiment in 1861. Tompkins ended the war as a lieutenant colonel. This is the jacket on display, not the coat he wore at the battle.

42. *Providence Journal*, September 19, 1862; *Narragansett Weekly*, October 9, 1862. These were all Regular Army batteries in the Mexican War. Magruder and Bragg became Confederate generals. Sherman is Thomas West Sherman of Newport, Rhode Island, who commanded

troops in South Carolina and Louisiana during the Civil War.

43. *Narragansett Weekly*, October 9, 1862.

44. Geoffrey Ward, *The Civil War* (New York: Random House, 1991), 170.

45. J. Rhodes, *Battery B*, 139–145.

46. Ibid.

47. Barker, *History of R.I. Combat Units in the Civil War*, 131; Rhodes, *All for the Union*, 84; *Narragansett Weekly*, December 25, 1862. The casualty figures for Rhode Island at Fredericksburg were appalling. The Second Rhode Island lost eight wounded, the Fourth one killed and nine wounded, the Seventh Regiment forty-four dead, 136 wounded, forty missing in action, the Twelfth Rhode Island twenty-four killed, ninety-four wounded, Battery A five wounded, Battery B three dead and thirteen wounded, Battery C one dead, Battery D one wounded, Battery E two killed and two wounded, and Battery G one wounded. The total loss was 384, not counting men in the Regulars or other state units.

48. Phillip S. Chase, *Battery F, First Rhode Island Light Artillery in the Civil War, 1861–1865* (Providence: Snow and Farnum, 1892).

49. *Providence Journal*, May 8 and 11, 1863.

50. George E. Lewis, *History of Battery E, First Rhode Island Light Artillery* (Providence: Snow and Farnum, 1892), 193–216; James A. Barber, Diary, July 2, 1863, Hay Library, Brown University, Providence, Rhode Island.

51. J. Rhodes, *Battery B*, 201–210. For more information on the Gettysburg Gun, refer to the Charles Tillinghast Straight papers at the Rhode Island Historical Society. In 1988, the reactivated Battery B, with the help of the Rhode Island National Guard, brought the gun to the spot where it had been silenced 125 years earlier. The gun was returned to the state house in November of that year and remains there today. For its modern journey, see the *Providence Journal*, November 17, 1987. Contrary to popular belief, the round in the cannon was not shot there, but placed by Sgt. Straight at Gettysburg.

52. *Providence Journal*, July 5, 1962.

53. Ibid., December 15, 1889. A "copperhead" was a Northerner who supported the South during the Civil War.

54. PMCA Box 1, Minutes: 1861–1868, 170.

55. J. Rhodes, *History of Battery B*, 145–202.

56. *Memoirs of R.I.*, 381–382, 394, 416–417.

57. Ibid., 381–386.

58. PMCA Box 1, *Minutes: 1861–1868*, 271.

59. Ibid., 272–273.

60. For the best and total view of Rhode Island in the Civil War, refer to the two-volume *Revised Register of Rhode Island Volunteers* (Providence: E.L. Freeman, 1893).

61. George B. Peck, *Historical Address: Rhode Island Light Artillery in the Civil and Spanish Wars* (Providence: Rhode Island Printing, 1917), 2–10; William Fox, *Regimental Losses in the American Civil War* (Albany: Brandow, 1898), 412–413.

62. Benjamin H. Child and John Knight Bucklyn, Medal of Honor Files, NA.

63. Fox, *Regimental Losses*, 412–413.

64. *History of the State of Rhode Island, 1636–1878* (Boston: A.J. Wright, 1878), 47.

65. Thomas Williams Bicknell, *The History of the State of Rhode Island and Providence Plantations*, vol. 2 (New York: American Historical Society, 1920), 819–820.

66. Spicer, *Ninth and Tenth Rhode Island*, 324–325.

67. Edwin Bearss to this author, January 7, 2008.

68. Peck, Historical Address, 15–18.

Chapter 8

1. From a biographical sketch of John Albert Monroe, written by George B. Peck in 1891 for the Veteran Association of the PMCA; Box 4, Annual Reports, 1887–1908, 79.

2. Richard Herndon, *Men of Progress: Biographical Sketches and Portraits of Leaders in Business and Professional Life in the State of Rhode Island and Providence Plantations* (Boston: New England Magazine, 1896), 249–250. Peck wrote three pamphlets for the Soldier's Society, edited the history of the Seventh Rhode Island Infantry, and left behind a vast written record, which is maintained at the Rhode Island Historical Society.

3. PMCA Box 4, Adjutant's Records, Veteran Association, 79.

4. The *Veteran's Advocate* was a weekly newspaper published in Concord, N.H., by Ira C. Evans, who owned and operated a small print shop in that city. The publication, Evans noted in the editorial box on page two, was "devoted to the interests of the G.A.R. and all veterans of the War of the Rebellion."

5. *Veteran's Advocate* 6, no. 42, Concord, NH (Oct. 16, 1889), 2 (PMCA Box 3).

6. PMCA Box 4, Adjutant's Records, 79.

7. Ibid., 80.

8. Peck, *Monroe*, 11–13.

9. Ibid. Next to more than eighty names in the roll book kept at the time is the notation "dropped in June 1867." No explanation is given in the minutes of the meetings. Next to the names of several dozen others is the word "expelled." For those expelled, charges included insubordination, behavior unbecoming to a soldier, poor attendance at weekly drills, and failure to pay one's dues.

10. State of Rhode Island, *The Monument in Memory of the Rhode Island Soldiers and Sailors Who Fell Victims to the Rebellion* (Providence: Providence Press, 1869). The monument still stands in Exchange Place, but today is quite an eyesore as vagrants and vandals have continued to desecrate this sacred site.

11. *Veteran's Advocate* 6, no. 42 (Concord, NH, Oct. 16, 1889), 2 (PMCA Box 3).

12. Todd, *American Military Equipage*, 1,156–1,158.

13. *Annual Report of the Adjutant General of the State of Rhode Island for the Year 1874* (Providence Press, 1875), 9. All Rhode Island Adjutant General's Reports are found at the Rhode Island State Archives in Providence. Rather than giving full bibliographic citations for each, this editor has shortened it to the year and page number of the report being mentioned so as not to be redundant.

14. Under the law of 1875, the state militia was divided into two brigades, each headed by a brigadier general. The First Battalion was part of the Second Brigade.

15. PMCA Box 1, Minutes: 1868–1876, 490–491, 514.

16. PMCA Box 4, Adjutant's Records, 91–92.

17. Ibid.

18. Greene, *Providence Plantations*, 181.

19. PMCA Box 4, Veteran Association, Clerk's Records, 1874–1915, 3.

20. George Peck's official title in the organization was "adjutant." Peck delivered a well-received historical address at the dedication of the tablet on July 19, 1917.

21. PMCA Box 4, Veteran Association, Clerk's Records, 1874–1915.

22. The Gatling gun was an early type of machine gun consisting of a cluster of barrels around an axis rotated by a hand crank, with each barrel fired once during each rotation.

23. *Providence Journal*, August 13, 1877.

24. *Adjutant General's 1881 Report*, 4. Barney replaced LeFavour, who died unexpectedly in 1878 after just a few years as adjutant general. LeFavour had succeeded Edward Mauran, a former member of the PMCA who served as adjutant general for nearly two decades. In 1882, another former PMCA member held the office: Elisha Dyer, Jr.

25. *Adjutant General's 1878 Report*, 6.

26. *Adjutant General's 1880 Report*, 8.

27. The name adopted for the camp at Quonset Point was the "Camp of Rhode Island Militia." Unlike previous camps, it was not named after a distinguished person.

28. Charles R. Dennis, George H. Kenyon, and Frederic M. Sackett, *Annual Report of the Adjutant General, Quartermaster General, and Surgeon General for the Year 1895* (Providence: E.L. Freeman, 1896), 41–51.

29. Francis E. Kinnicut, *Rhode Island in the War with Spain: 1898–1900* (Providence: Snow and Farnum, 1901), 18–21.

30. http://www.firstworldwar.com/poetsandprose/newbolt.htm.

31. Allan R. Millet and Peter Maslowski, *For the Common Defense: A Military History of the United States of America* (New York: Free Press, 1984), 269–271; Fred A. McKenna, ed. in chief, *Battery A, 103rd Field Artillery, in France* (Providence: Livermore & Knight, 1919), 13.

32. McKenna, *Battery A, 103rd Field Artillery, in France*, 14.

33. Everett S. Hartwell, *An Historical Sketch of the Providence Marine Corps of Artillery, 1801–1951* (Providence: Providence Marine Corps of Artillery, 1952), 9–10. According to *Battery A in France* (14), 25 percent of the men subsequently joined the Regular Army and the navy and went to the Philippines. At least one pushed on to Peking at the time of the Boxer uprising.

34. *Providence Journal*, October 31, 1901.

35. *Providence Journal*, October 31, 1901; Barry J. Stein, *U.S. Army Heraldic Crests: A Complete Illustrated History of Distinctive Unit Insignia* (Columbia: University of South Carolina Press 1993), 50.

36. Jerry Cooper, *The Militia and the National Guard in America since Colonial Times* (Westport, CT: Greenwood, 1993), 88.

37. Known by Rhode Islanders as the Cranston Street Armory, the Providence Armory took almost five years to build and was completed in 1907. The drill shed, which measures 235 feet by 170 feet, provided sufficient space for a full review of a brigade of artillery consisting of two battalions, a band, and one or more separate companies. The building is currently unoccupied (see Howard F. Brown, and Roberta Mudge Humble, *The Historic Armories of Rhode Island* (Pawtucket: Globe, 2000), 113).

38. Millet and Maslowski, *For the Common Defense*, 312–314.

39. Cooper, *The Militia and the National Guard*, 99.

Chapter 9

1. *1906 Adjutant General's Report*, 4.

2. "Removal of Old Armory, Benefit Street," *Board of Trade Journal* 18, no. 9 (September 1906), 452; "Old Armory on Benefit Street," *Providence Evening Bulletin*, September 20 1906.

3. *1906 Adjutant General's Report*, 5.

4. *1907 Adjutant General's Report*, 57–58.

5. *1908 Adjutant General's Report*, 5.

6. *1910 Adjutant General's Report*, 5. Glassford was an officer of the Regular Army assigned to work with Battery A at its summer training camps.

7. Hartwell, *An Historical Sketch of the Providence Marine Corps of Artillery*, 10. (At that time, Sturges lived at 79 Williams Street in Providence. He would later move to 55 Power Street, a house now owned by Brown University and used as living quarters for its presidents. The transfer of ownership to Brown in 1948 involved a large donation by Sturges in memory of his father, who graduated from Brown in 1876.)

8. Hartwell, *Historical Sketch of Providence Marine Corps of Artillery*, 10.

9. *Providence Journal*, March 21, 1967.

10. Charles W. Abbott, *1911 Adjutant General's Report* (Providence: E.L. Freeman, 1912), 15, 32.

11. *Providence Journal*, August 10, 1971.

12. *Providence Journal*, August 10, 1971; Henry T. Samson and George C. Hull, *The War Story of C Battery, One Hundred and Third U.S. Field Artillery, France 1917–1919* (Norwood, MA: Plimpton, 1920), 44.

13. McKenna, *Battery A, 103rd Field Artillery, in France*, 15; *1914 Adjutant General's Report*, 13.

14. Shoemaker, *Last War Governor*, 86–93.

Chapter 10

1. Millet and Maslowski, *For the Common Defense*, 316–317; John K. Mahon, *History of the Militia and the National Guard* (London: Collier, Mifflin, 1983), 151.

2. Henry R. W. Stiness, ed. in chief, *Battery A on the Mexican Border* (Providence: E.S. Jones, 1917), 2. In addition to Battery A, the Rhode Island National Guard sent three cavalry companies and an ambulance company.

3. This ten-day march was to take the place of the battery's usual encampment at Tobyhanna, Pennsylvania, which that year was canceled.

4. Stiness, *Battery A on the Mexican Border*, 3. A few veterans of the First Rhode Island Light Artillery were still alive to see the new batteries off to France.

5. Ibid.

6. Stiness, *Battery A on the Mexican Border*, 3–6; Chester A. Files, "Tales of an Old Soldier," Benefit Street Arsenal.

7. Mahon, *History of the Militia and the National Guard*, 152.

8. McKenna, *Battery A, 103rd Field Artillery, in France*, 17–18; Stiness, *Battery A on the Mexican Border*, 3. The original order, listing all the batteries by rank, is still proudly displayed at the Benefit Street Arsenal.

9. Mahon, *History of the Militia and National Guard*, 52.

10. Stiness, *Battery A on the Mexican Border*, 3–10.

11. Ibid.

12. Stiness, *Battery A on the Mexican Border*, 10; Millet and Maslowski, *For the Common Defense*, 324–326.

13. Cooper, *The Militia and the National Guard*, 107.

14. Mahon, *History of the Militia and the National Guard*, 153.

15. Millet and Maslowski, *For the Common Defense*, 325; Cooper, *The Militia and the National Guard*, 106.

16. Mahon, *History of the Militia and the National Guard*, 152.

17. *Providence Journal*, November 10, 1987.

Chapter 11

1. Millet and Maslowski, *For the Common Defense*, 328–331.

2. *Providence Journal*, May 5, 1917.

3. *The History of Battery B, 103rd Field Artillery* (Providence: E.L. Freeman, 1922), 10. *Providence Journal*, May 7, 1917; Samson and Hull, *War Story of Battery C*, 2–4.

4. *The History of Battery B*, 9–10; Samson and Hull, *War Story of Battery C*, 2–5.

5. Battery E had been mustered out of service from the Mexican border on March 19, 1917, and was called back into federal service less than two weeks later to protect Bridgeport, CT, from possible attack by an enemy submarine.

6. Thomas Frezza to author, September 4, 2008.

7. *The History of Battery B*, 11.

8. Peck, *Historical Address*, 16–18.

9. *The History of Battery B*, 12.

10. McKenna, *Battery A, 103rd Field Artillery, in France*, 23; Samson and Hull, *War Story of Battery C*, 5–7.

11. William F. Kernan and Henry T. Samson, *History of the 103rd Field Artillery, 26th Division, AEF, World War I, 1917–1919* (Providence: Remington), 8–9; McKenna, *Battery A, 103rd Field Artillery, in France*, 105; Samson and Hull, *War Story of Battery C*, 9–16.

12. Samson and Hull, *War Story of Battery C*, 20–22; McKenna, *Battery A, 103rd Field Artillery, in France*, 25.

13. McKenna, *Battery A, 103rd Field Artillery, in France*, 25; *Providence Journal*, November 5, 1933; Millet and Maslowski, *For the Common Defense*, 336–337.

14. *The History of Battery B*, 21; Samson and Hull, *War Story of Battery C*, 30–33.

15. Kernan and Sampson, *History of the 103rd*, 14; Samson and Hull, *War Story of Battery C*, 38–48; Millet and Maslowski, *For the Common Defense*, 346–349.

16. Kernan and Sampson, *History of the 103rd*, 16; Samson and Hull, *War Story of Battery C*, 40–41. It should be noted that Capt. Kernan was not a member of the 103rd in World War I. He was a Regular Army officer instead. Kernan was a noted military historian who was paid by the PMCA to write the history of the 103rd Field Artillery. Henry T. Samson had fought on the Western Front with Battery C (see *Providence Journal*, November 6, 1933).

17. Samson and Hull, *War Story of Battery C*, 45–46; McKenna, *Battery A, 103rd Field Artillery, in France*, 28.

18. Kernan and Sampson, *History of the 103rd*, 18; *Providence Journal*, November 5, 1933.

19. Millet and Maslowski, *For the Common Defense*, 353–354; McKenna, *Battery A, 103rd Field Artillery, in France*, 32–3: 102; *Memorial to the Employees of the Brown & Sharpe MFG. Co. Who Served at Home and Abroad in the Great World War* (Providence: Brown and Sharpe, 1919), 75.

20. Kernan and Sampson, *History of the 103rd*, 53; *Providence Journal*, November 5, 1933.

21. Kernan and Sampson, *History of the 103rd*, 64; Samson and Hull, *War Story of Battery C*, 88–95.

22. Kernan and Sampson, *History of the 103rd*, 74; *Providence Journal*, November 5, 1933. In September of 1917 Col. Glassford was promoted to brigadier general in command of the 51st Field Artillery Brigade. After the war, he became chief of police in Washington, D.C.

23. Millet and Maslowski, *For the Common Defense*, 354; Kernan and Sampson, *History of the 103rd*, 86; Samson and Hull, *War Story of Battery C*, 117–119; Millet and Maslowski, *For the Common Defense*, 354.

24. *The History of Battery B*, 68.

25. Kernan and Sampson, *History of the 103rd*, 91; Samson and Hull, *War Story of Battery C*, 139–141.

26. Millet and Maslowski, *For the Common Defense*, 354–355; Kernan and Sampson, *History of the 103rd*, 94.

27. McKenna, *Battery A, 103rd Field Artillery, in France*, 87–115.

28. Millet and Maslowski, *For the Common Defense*, 354–355; Kernan and Sampson, *History of the 103rd*, 116–118.

29. Kernan and Sampson, *History of the 103rd*, 124; Samson and Hull, *War Story of Battery C*, 160–166; *Providence Journal*, November 5, 1933.

30. Mahon, *History of the Militia and the National Guard*, 162. Samson and Hull, *War Story of Battery C*, 166–167. After the war, Rhode Island would honor the memory of Gen. Edwards by erecting a plaque to his honor in the state house.

31. Emerson Gifford Taylor, *New England in France, 1917–1919* (Boston: Houghton Mifflin, 1920), 251.

32. Kernan and Sampson, *History of 103rd*, 127; *Providence Journal*, November 6, 1933.

33. Kernan and Sampson, *History of 103rd*, 128, 177–180; Samson and Hull, *War Story of Battery C*, 171–178.

34. Millet and Maslowski, *For the Common Defense*, 357–358.

35. *The History of Battery B*, 85; Samson and Hull, *War Story of Battery C*, 189–191; *Providence Journal*, November 11, 1918 and November 6, 1933. The last round was fired by Battery B. The coordinates are noted in a diary written by one of the men; the diary is now housed in the Benefit Street Arsenal.

36. Kernan and Sampson, *History of the 103rd*, 147.

37. *Providence Journal*, May 2, 1919; Samson and Hull, *War Story of Battery C*, 232–234; Mahon, *History of the Militia and the National Guard*, 168.

38. McKenna, *Battery A, 103rd Field Artillery, in France*, 71; *History of Battery B*, 159–163; Samson and Hull, *War Story of Battery C*, frontispiece.

39. *History of Battery B*, frontispiece.

40. Samson and Hull, *War Story of Battery C*, 235–237; McKenna, *Battery A, 103rd Field Artillery, in France*, 249. Most of the fallen from the 103rd are buried in the Ainse-Marne American Cemetery in France (see *Ainse-Marne American Cemetery and Memorial* (Washington, D.C.: American Battle Monuments Commission, 2005)).

41. Kernan and Sampson, *History of the 103rd*.

Chapter 12

1. Army Heritage Command, Lineage of the 103rd Field Artillery Regiment, Benefit Street Arsenal.

2. Millet and Maslowski, *For the Common Defense*, 365–367.

3. *Adjutant General's Report*, 1925, 4. The 68th Field Artillery Brigade was a senior Field Artillery Headquarters unit activated on March 7, 1930. The brigade headquarters was at the Armory of Mounted Commands in Providence and consisted of the 103rd Field Artillery (RI), the 152nd Field Artillery (ME), and the 192nd Field Artillery (CT) (*The 1940 National Guard Yearbook* (Providence, Rhode Island National Guard, 1940), 3).

4. *Adjutant General's Report*, 1925, 20.

5. Millet and Maslowski, *For the Common Defense*, 379–381. There was some discussion about changing the armory's name but as the name is carved in granite above the door the state decided to retain it.

6. *National Guard Yearbook*, xxxi–xxxiii.

7. PMCA Bylaws and Membership Lists, Benefit Street Arsenal.

8. Glenn Laxton, "Gone But Not Forgotten: 1934 Textile Strike," Private Collection.

9. Stein, *U.S. Army Heraldic Crests*, 50. The field service at Bunker Hill, near Harpers Ferry, was the first active service of the PMCA in Virginia.

10. *Brown Yearbook: 1924* (Providence: Brown University, 1924), 279; Interview with Bob Kenny, Jr., June 3, 2001.

11. *Adjutant General's Report*, 1934, 5.

12. *Providence Journal,* September 12, 1934; *1940 National Guard Yearbook,* xxxii–xxxiii. The 103rd Field Artillery Regiment was organized into riot detachments armed with Thompson submachine guns, Browning machine guns, gas guns, clubs and gas (*Adjutant General's Report, 1934,* 8).

13. *Providence Journal,* September 13, 1934; Laxton, "Gone But Not Forgotten." *1940 National Guard Yearbook,* xxxii–xxxiii.

14. *1940 National Guard Yearbook,* xxxiv.

15. Howard F. Brown communication to Robert Grandchamp, March 6, 2009.

16. *1940 National Guard Yearbook,* xxxiii.

Chapter 13

1. *Providence Journal,* February 25, 1941.

2. Bill Fusco, "Remembrances," Benefit Street Arsenal.

3. Fusco, "Remembrances"; *Historical and Pictorial Review,* 8–9.

4. Harold R. Barker, *History of the 43rd Division Artillery, World War II* (Providence: John F. Greene, 1960), 10–27. For images of the DUI of the various units comprising the 43rd Division Artillery, refer to the front matter in the *History of the 43rd Division Artillery.*

5. The 192nd received newer models of the 155mm howitzer just before the New Guinea Campaign in 1944.

6. Kent Robert Greenfield, Robert R. Palmer, and Bell I. Wiley, *The Army Ground Forces: The Organization of Ground Combat Troops* (Washington, DC: Government Printing Office, 1947), 304–307, 478–479; *1940 National Guard Yearbook,* 82–119.

7. *Historical and Picture Review,* 34.

8. Fusco, "Remembrances."

9. Millet and Maslowski, *For the Common Defense,* 397–401.

10. *Providence Journal,* May 31, 1968; Fusco, "Remembrances." Sgt. Fusco served under Gen. Barker as a truck driver in the 103rd.

11. *Providence Journal,* May 31, 1968; Samson and Hull, *War Story of Battery C,* 126.

12. Gen. Barker's wartime service, awards, and ranks are taken from a brief biography of him that serves as back matter for *History of the Rhode Island Combat Units in the Civil War.*

13. *Providence Journal,* May 31, 1968.

14. Hartwell, *An Historical Sketch of the Providence Marine Corps of Artillery,* 14.

15. Glenn Laxton to author, September 22, 2008; *Providence Journal,* November 10, 1987.

16. *Historical and Picture Review,* 7; Fusco, "Remembrances."

17. Millet and Maslowski, *For the Common Defense,* 420–422.

18. *Providence Journal,* December 22, 1942; Fusco, "Remembrances"; Sgt. Maj. Tom Caruolo to author, September 9, 2008; Howard F. Brown, "Remembrances," Benefit Street Arsenal. The best description of the loss of the *Coolidge,* which is now a major tourist site in Vanuatu, is in Peter Stone, *The Lady and the President: The Life and Loss of the S.S.* President Coolidge (Yarram, Australia: Ocean, 2007).

19. *Providence Journal,* December 22, 1942.

20. Brown, "Remembrances"; Fusco, "Remembrances." Col. Brown was captain of the Headquarters Battery in the 169th Battalion. The 169th went directly to New Zealand from the United States.

21. Barker, *43rd Division Artillery,* 28.

22. Brown, "Remembrances."

23. Millet and Maslowski, *For the Common Defense,* 420–422; Rafael Steinberg, *Island Fighting* (Richmond: Time Life Books, 1979), 75–86.

24. Brown, "Remembrances."

25. Steinberg, *Island Fighting,* 75–86; Brown, "Remembrances"; Fusco, "Remembrances."

26. Barker, *43rd Division Artillery,* 50; *Providence Journal,* September 3, 1943; Steinberg, *Island Fighting,* 75–86.

27. *Providence Journal,* September 3, 1943; Steinberg, *Island Fighting,* 84.

28. Steinberg, *Island Fighting,* 84–86; Barker, *43rd Division Artillery,* 63,73; Fusco, "Remembrances."

29. *Providence Journal,* August 26 and September 3, 1943; Steinberg, *Island Fighting,* 84–86.

30. Barker, *43rd Division Artillery,* 65.

31. Doolittle, *Barker's Cubs,* 5.

32. Barker, *43rd Division Artillery,* 109; Brown, "Remembrances."

33. Rafael Steinberg, *Return to the Philippines* (Richmond: Time Life Books, 1979), 48–49; Millet and Maslowski, *For the Common Defense,* 433; Barker, *43rd Division Artillery,* 125.

34. Duncan H. Doolittle, *Barker's Cubs: Piper Cub Planes and Their Pilots in the 43rd Division Artillery, 1944–1945* (Narragansett: Anawan, 1991), 1–7.

35. Ibid., 1–6.

36. *Providence Journal,* March 7, 1952.

37. Barker, *43rd Division Artillery,* 130–145; Doolittle, *Barker's Cubs,* 7–8; Steinberg, *Return to the Philippines,* 48–50.

38. Millet and Maslowski, *For the Common Defense,* 460–461; Steinberg, *Return to the Philippines,* 108–109; Barker, *43rd Division Artillery,* 152; "Hundreds of R.I. men in Luzon go ashore with First Assault Wave," *Providence Journal,* January 11, 1945.

39. Doolittle, *Barker's Cubs,* 11–13, 22.

40. Barker, *43rd Division Artillery,* 200; *Providence Journal,* January 11, 1945.

41. Col. Howard F. Brown communication to author, December 6, 2008.

42. Barker, *43rd Division Artillery,* 228; Doolittle, *Barker's Cubs,* 14–20; *Providence Journal,* January 27, 1945; Steinberg, *Return to the Philippines,* 110–115.

43. Linguyen Gulf and Luzon Plaque, Gun Room, Rhode Island State House, Providence, Rhode Island.

44. *Providence Journal,* June 16, 1945; Millet and Maslowski, *For the Common Defense,* 461.

45. Brown, "Remembrances"; *Providence Journal,* January 29, 1945.

46. Barker, *43rd Division Artillery,* xvii.

47. Barker, *43rd Division Artillery,* 239–241; *Providence Journal,* December 22, 1942.

48. Barker, *43rd Division Artillery,* 235–247.

49. Ibid., 233. After the war, the 169th Field Artillery, this had been originally the Second Battalion of the 103rd reverted back to its original status as the Second Battalion.

Chapter 14

1. Millet and Maslowski, *For the Common Defense,* 490–493; *Providence Journal,* April 25, 2006.

2. Hartwell, *An Historical Sketch of the Providence Marine Corps of Artillery,* 14. For the best view of the Army National Guard in the Korean Conflict, refer to William Berebitsky, *A Very Long Weekend: The Army National*

Guard in Korea, 1950–1953 (Shippensburg, PA: White Mane, 1996).

3. Brown, "Remembrances."

4. Brown, "Remembrances"; *Providence Journal*, March 7, 1952. Thomas Barker retired as a major and a staff officer from the 103rd and is still active in the PMCA, carrying on the traditions of his father.

5. *Providence Journal*, September 1, 1954.

6. PMCA Membership Lists, Benefit Street Arsenal.

7. Millet and Maslowski, *For the Common Defense*, 478–490.

8. 43rd Infantry Division Veterans Association, Papers, Benefit Street Arsenal; Rhode Island National Guard Order of Battle, courtesy of the Rhode Island National Guard.

9. Millet and Maslowski, *For the Common Defense*, 491, 458–459.

10. Army Heritage Command, 103rd Field Artillery Lineage, typescript at Benefit Street Arsenal.

11. Ibid.

12. Brig. Gen. Richard J. Valente, "Remembrances."

13. Millet and Maslowski, *For the Common Defense*, 562–563; Valente, "Remembrances."

14. Valente, "Remembrances."

15. Ibid.

16. Ibid.

17. Ibid.

18. Ibid.

19. Ibid.

20. Ibid.

Chapter 15

1. 103rd Field Artillery, Report for Operation Noble Eagle, Benefit Street Arsenal.

2. Ibid.

3. Ibid.

4. Christian M. Neary, "Report of Battery A, First Battalion, 103rd Field Artillery Regiment, Iraqi Freedom," Benefit Street Arsenal.

5. *Providence Journal*, December 4, 2004 and January 6 and 7, 2004.

6. Neary, "Battery A."

7. Ibid.

8. Ibid.

9. Ibid.

10. Ibid.

11. *Providence Journal*, October 5 and 13, 2004.

12. *Providence Journal*, October 5, 7, and 10, 2004.

13. *Providence Journal*, October 7, 2004. Sgt. Collier was awarded the Silver Star for his actions in trying to save Sgt. Potts.

14. *Providence Journal*, October 7, 2004.

15. Ibid., October 10, 2004.

16. Neary, "Battery A."

17. Neary, "Battery A"; *Providence Journal*, March 24, 2005. Eight members of Battery A were awarded the Bronze Star Medal for Operation Iraqi Freedom.

18. *Providence Journal*, February 27, 2004.

19. Patrick Curran, "Report of Battery B, First Battalion, 103rd Field Artillery Regiment, Iraqi Freedom," Benefit Street Arsenal. The author was the first sergeant of Battery B during the deployment.

20. Ibid.

21. Ibid.

22. Ibid.

23. *Providence Journal*, August 14, 2004; Joseph Rooney, "Report of Headquarters Battery, 103rd Field Artillery Brigade, Iraqi Freedom," Benefit Street Arsenal.

24. Rooney, "Headquarters 103rd Brigade"; *Providence Journal*, August 28, 2005.

25. Mark Bourgery, "Report of Battery C, First Battalion, 103rd Field Artillery Regiment, Iraqi Freedom," Benefit Street Arsenal.

26. Bourgery, "Battery C."

27. Bourgery, "Battery C"; *Providence Journal*, September 27, 2007, December 16, 2007, and September 21, 2008.

28. *Providence Journal*, December 16, 2007.

29. Christian M. Neary communication to Robert Grandchamp, March 24, 2009.

30. Valente, "Remembrances."

31. Stein, *U.S. Army Heraldic Crests*, 50.

32. Up through 1950, a battery was stationed at the arsenal, Battery B of the Rhode Island Guard, commanded by Capt. Duncan Doolittle. After this, Bravo Battery moved to its present home in Smithfield, Rhode Island.

Appendix V

1. Edward P. Adams, "Battery G, First Rhode Island Light Artillery"; *Revised Register of Rhode Island Volunteers* (Providence: E.L. Freeman, 1893), 900–906.

2. Hazard Stevens, *The Storming of the Lines of Petersburg by the Sixth Corps: April 2, 1865* (Providence: Snow and Farnum, 1904), 12–18.

3. *O.R. 46*, 901–905; *Memoirs of R.I.*, 417; *History of Providence County, Rhode Island*, vol. 1, ed. Richard M. Bayles (New York: W.W. Preston, 1891), 243–246.

4. *War of the Rebellion: A Compilation of the Official Records of the Union and Confederate Armies* (Washington, D.C.: Government Printing Office, 1880–1901), 46, 1009–1011[O.R.]; State of Rhode Island, *Annual Report of the Adjutant General of the State of Rhode Island for the year 1865* (Providence: Providence Press, 1866), 776; Thomas W. Hyde, *Following the Greek Cross, or Memories of the Sixth Army Corps* (Boston: Houghton Mifflin, 1894), 249–252.

5. Hyde, *Greek Cross*, 249–252; *The Sixth Corps*, May 11, 1865; Hazard Stevens, "Storming of the Lines at Petersburg," in *The Shenandoah Campaigns of 1862 and 1864 and the Appomattox Campaign 1865* (Boston: Military Historical Society of Massachusetts, 1907), 421–422.

6. O.R. 46, 901–905; Hyde, *Greek Cross*, 249–252; H. Stevens, *Storming the Lines*, 19–21; E. Rhodes, *All for the Union*, 216–218; Walter F. Beyer and Oscar F. Keydel, eds., *Deeds of Valor: How America's Heroes won the Medal of Honor* (Detroit: Perrien-Keydel, 1901), 515–516.

7. Kris VanDenBossche, ed., *Pleas Excuse All Bad Writing: A Documentary History of Rhode Island During the Civil War Era, 1861–1865* (Peace Dale: Rhode Island Historical Document Transcription Project, 1993), 197–99; George Stevens, *Three Years in the Sixth Corps* (Albany: S.R. Gray, 1866), 434–436.

8. A. Wilson Greene, *Breaking the Backbone of the Rebellion: The Final Battles of the Petersburg Campaign* (Mason City, IA: Savas, 2000), 258–260.

9. Robert Driver, *The First and Second Rockbridge Artillery* (Lynchburg, VA: H.E. Howard, 1987), 120–123.

10. Greene, *Breaking the Backbone*, 300–301; Driver, *Rockbridge Artillery*, 120–123; Robert Pratt to Sydney Pratt, April 9, 1865, and Robert Pratt, Diary, April 2, 1865, both courtesy of Tom Ledoux.

11. O.R. 46, 969–970: 973; Beyer and Keydel, *Deeds of Valor*, 518–519.

12. Jean Barber communication to author, September

2, 2007; Greene, *Breaking the Backbone*, 284; O.R. 46, 1,010.

13. Luther Cornell, Pension File, NA; George W. Potter, Medal of Honor File, NA.

14. Hyde, *Greek Cross*, 252–255; Beyer and Keydel, *Deeds of Valor*, 515–516.

15. *Memoirs of R.I.*, 417; Beyer and Keydel, *Deeds of Valor*, 515–516.

16. James A. Barber, John Corcoran, Charles D. Ennis, John H. Havron, Samuel E. Lewis, Archibald Malbourne, George W. Potter, Service Files, NA; Henry S. Burrage, *Civil War Record of Brown University* (Providence: Brown University, 1920), 47; George W. Potter, Student File, Hay Library, Brown University, Providence, Rhode Island; Greene, *Breaking the Backbone*, 324.

17. James A. Barber, John Corcoran, Charles D. Ennis, John H. Havron, Samuel E. Lewis, Archibald Malbourne, George W. Potter, Medal of Honor Medal of Honor Files, NA; Robert H. George, "Their Caissons Kept Rolling Along," 4, Hay Library, Brown University, Providence, Rhode Island; Beyer and Keydel, *Deeds of Valor*, 515–516; O.R. 46, 257.

18. Adams, "Battery G," 905–906.

BIBLIOGRAPHY

The following bibliography is a compiled listing of those sources used or consulted in this project. They are not inclusive to the Civil War or one specific period of the PMCA's history. Rather, they stand to provide the reader with additional references to locate material relating to the regiment in its many guises over the years. As with the notes, this bibliography concentrates most heavily on those works directly relating to the PMCA rather than general works that even the most casual reader is familiar with. The reader is provided with the most up-to-date register of books and articles relating to the PMCA.

Unpublished Primary Sources

Adams, George W. Service File. National Archives, Washington, D.C.

Barber, James A. Diaries. Hay Library, Brown University, Providence, Rhode Island.

Barber, James A. Medal of Honor and Service Files. National Archives, Washington, D.C.

Barker, Harold R. Papers. Benefit Street Arsenal, Providence, Rhode Island. Also Rhode Island Historical Society, Providence, Rhode Island.

Barker, William C. Papers. Rhode Island Historical Society, Providence, Rhode Island.

Brown, Howard. "Remembrances." Benefit Street Arsenal, Providence, Rhode Island.

Bucklyn, John Knight. Medal of Honor File. National Archives, Washington, D.C.

Chaffee, Everitte St. John. Papers. Benefit Street Arsenal, Providence, Rhode Island.

Child, Benjamin H. Medal of Honor File. National Archives, Washington, D.C.

Corcoran, John. Medal of Honor and Service File. National Archives, Washington, D.C.

Cornell, Luther. Pension File. National Archives, Washington, D.C.

Death Records. Providence City Hall, Providence, Rhode Island.

Deed Books. Providence City Hall, Providence, Rhode Island.

Dorr, Thomas W. Papers. Hay Library, Brown University, Providence, Rhode Island.

Ennis, Charles D. Medal of Honor and Service Files. National Archives, Washington, D.C.

Files, Chester A. Papers. Benefit Street Arsenal, Providence, Rhode Island.

First Rhode Island Light Artillery Papers. Antietam National Battlefield, Sharpsburg, Maryland. Also United States Army Military History Institute, Carlisle, Pennsylvania.

First Rhode Island Light Artillery Records. Rhode Island Historical Society, Providence, Rhode Island. Also Rhode Island State Archives, Providence, Rhode Island.

43rd Division Veterans Association Papers. Benefit Street Arsenal, Providence, Rhode Island.

Fusco, Bill. "Remembrances." Benefit Street Arsenal, Providence, Rhode Island.

George, Robert H. "Their Caissons Kept Rolling Along." Hay Library, Brown University, Providence, Rhode Island.

Grand Army of the Republic Records. Rhode Island Historical Society, Providence, Rhode Island.

Havron, John H. Medal of Honor and Service Files. National Archives, Washington, D.C.

Lawrence, John H. Letters. Antietam National Battlefield, Sharpsburg, Maryland.

Lewis, Samuel E. Medal of Honor and Service Files. National Archives, Washington, D.C.

Lincoln, Abraham. Papers. Library of Congress, Washington, D.C.

Lippitt, Warren. "Memoirs." Rhode Island Historical Society, Providence, Rhode Island.

Malbourne, Archibald. Medal of Honor and Service Files. National Archives, Washington, D.C.

Newton, John H. Letters. Hay Library, Brown University, Providence, Rhode Island.

North Burial Ground Records. Providence City Hall, Providence, Rhode Island.

103rd Field Artillery War on Terror Reports. Benefit Street Arsenal, Providence, Rhode Island.

PMCA Necrology. Rhode Island Historical Society, Providence, Rhode Island.

Potter, George W. Medal of Honor and Service Files. National Archives, Washington, D.C.

Providence Marine Corps of Artillery Records. Benefit Street Arsenal, Providence, Rhode Island. Also Rhode Island Historical Society, Providence, Rhode Island.

Providence Marine Society Records. Rhode Island Historical Society, Providence, Rhode Island.

Read, Harold. Papers. Benefit Street Arsenal, Providence, Rhode Island.

Rhode Island Adjutant General Papers. Rhode Island State Archives, Providence, Rhode Island.

Rhode Island, Births, Marriages, and Deaths, 1700–1950. Rhode Island State Archives, Providence, Rhode Island.

Rhode Island Grand Army of the Republic Records. Benefit Street Arsenal, Providence, Rhode Island.

Rhode Island Historic Cemetery Database.

Rhode Island National Guard Records. Benefit Street Arsenal, Providence, Rhode Island.

Rhode Island Quartermaster General Papers. Rhode Island State Archives, Providence, Rhode Island.

Rider, Sydney. Papers. Hay Library, Brown University, Providence, Rhode Island.

Sackett, Charles. Papers. Rhode Island Historical Society, Providence, Rhode Island.

Soldiers and Sailors Historical Society Papers. Rhode Island Historical Society, Providence, Rhode Island.

Straight, Charles T. Papers. Rhode Island Historical Society, Providence, Rhode Island.

Tompkins, John A. Diary. Antietam National Battlefield, Sharpsburg, Maryland.

United States Army Lineage Reports. United States Army Military History Institute, Carlisle, Pennsylvania.

Printed Primary Sources

Abbott, Charles W. *1911 Adjutant General's Report*. Providence: E.L. Freeman, 1912.

Aldrich, Thomas. *The History of Battery A, First Regiment Rhode Island Light Artillery, in the War to Preserve the Union*. Providence: Snow and Farnum, 1904.

Annual Report of the Adjutant General of the State of Rhode Island for the Year 1874. Providence Press, 1875.

Barker, Harold R. *History of the 43rd Division Artillery, World War II, 1941–1945*. Providence: J.E. Greene, 1961.

Barry, William F., William H. French, and Henry J. Hunt. *Instructions for Field Artillery*. New York: NP, 1860.

Bartlett, John R., ed. *Memoirs of Rhode Island Officers Who Were Engaged in the Service of Their Country During the Great Rebellion with the South*. Providence: Sydney S. Rider & Brothers, 1867.

Bastler, Roy P, ed. *The Collected Works of Abraham Lincoln*. Vol. 4. New Brunswick: Rutgers University Press, 1953.

Beyer, Walter F. and Oscar F. Keydel, eds. *Deeds of Valor: How America's Heroes won the Medal of Honor*. Detroit: Perrien-Keydel, 1901.

Billings, John D. *Hardtack and Coffee: The Unwritten Story of Army Life*. Lincoln: Nebraska University Press, 1993.

Brown Yearbook: 1924. Providence: Brown University, 1924.

Bucklyn, John K. *Battle of Cedar Creek*. Providence: Sydney S. Ryder, 1883.

Buell, Augustus. *The Cannoneer: Recollections of Service in the Army of the Potomac*. Washington, DC: National Tribune, 1897.

Burges, Tristam. *An Oration Delivered in the Meeting House in Providence, on the Fourth of July 1801*. Providence: John Carter, 1801.

Burrage, Henry S. *Civil War Record of Brown University*. Providence: Brown University, 1920.

Centracchio, Reginald A. *Annual Report of the Rhode Island Adjutant General and Emergency Management Agency*. Providence: 1995–2008.

Chaffee, Everitte St. John. *The Egotistical Account of an Enjoyable War*. 1951.

Charter, Laws, &c of the Providence Marine Society. Providence: Barnum, Field, 1824.

Chase, John W. *Yours for the Union: The Civil War Letters of John W. Chase, First Massachusetts Light Artillery*. Edited by John S. Collier and Bonnie B. Collier. New York: Fordham University Press, 2004.

Chase, Phillip S. *Battery F, First Rhode Island Light Artillery, in the Civil War*. Providence: Snow and Farnum, 1892.

Child, Benjamin H. *From Fredericksburg to Gettysburg*. Providence: Snow and Farnum, 1895.

Clark, Emmons. *History of the Seventh Regiment of New York, 1806–1889*. New York: Seventh Regiment, 1890.

Dennis, Charles R., George H. Kenyon, and Frederic M. Sackett. *Annual Report of the Adjutant General, Quartermaster General, and Surgeon General for the Year 1895*. Providence: E.L. Freeman, 1896.

DeSimone, Russell J., and Daniel C. Schofield, eds. *The Broadsides of the Dorr Rebellion*. Providence: Rhode Island Supreme Court Historical Society, 1992.

Doolittle, Duncan H. *Barker's Cubs: Piper Cub Planes and Their Pilots in the 43d Division Artillery, 1944–1945*. Narragansett, RI, Anawan, 1991.

Fenner, Earl J. *The History of Battery H, First Rhode Island Light Artillery*. Providence: Snow and Farnum, 1894.

Fox, William F. *Regimental Losses in the American Civil War*. Albany: Brandow, 1898.

Greenfield, Robert Kent, Robert R. Palmer, and Bell I. Wiley. *The Army Ground Forces: The Organization of Ground Combat Troops*. Washington, D.C.: Government Printing Office, 1947.

Historical and Pictorial Review: 43rd Infantry Division, Camp Shelby, Mississippi, 1942. Baton Rouge: Army and Navy, 1941.

The History of Battery B, 103rd Field Artillery. Providence: E.L. Freeman, 1922.

Hyde, Thomas W. *Following the Greek Cross, or Memories of the Sixth Army Corps*. Boston: Houghton Mifflin, 1894.

Inauguration of the Perry Statue at Cleveland on the Tenth of September 1860. Cleveland: Fairbanks, Benedict, 1860.

Kautz, August V. *The 1865 Customs of Service for Enlisted Men of the Army*. Philadelphia: J.B. Lippincott, 1865.

_____. *The 1865 Customs of Service for Officers of the Army*. Philadelphia: J.B. Lippincott, 1865.

Kernan, William F., and Henry T. Samson. *History of the 103rd Field Artillery, 26th Division, AEF, World War I, 1917–1919*. Providence: Remington, 1922.

Kinnicut, Francis E. *Rhode Island in the War with Spain, 1898–1900*. Providence: Snow and Farnum, 1901.

Lewis, George. *History of Battery E, First Rhode Island Light Artillery*. Providence: Snow and Farnum, 1892.

McDougall, Frances Harriet. *Might and Right*. Providence: Stillwell, 1844.

McKenna, Frederick A. *Battery A, 103rd Field Artillery, in France*. Providence: Livermore & Knight, 1919.

Memorial of Colonel John S. Slocum. Providence: R.A. and J.A. Reid, 1886.

Monroe, J. Albert. *Battery D, First Rhode Island Light Artillery, at the Battle of Antietam*. Providence: Providence Press, 1886.

_____. *Battery D, First Rhode Island Light Artillery, at the Second Battle of Bull Run*. Providence: Providence Press, 1886.

_____. *The Rhode Island Artillery at the First Battle of Bull Run*. Providence: Sydney S. Rider, 1878.

The 1940 National Guard Yearbook. Providence, Rhode Island National Guard, 1940.

Peck, George B. *Camp and Hospital*. Providence: The Society, 1884.

_____. *Historical Address: Rhode Island Light Artillery in the Civil and Spanish Wars.* Providence: Rhode Island, 1917.

_____. *John Albert Monroe: A Sketch.* Providence: The Society, 1892.

_____. *A Recruit Before Petersburg.* Providence: N. Bang Williams, 1880.

Revised Register of Rhode Island Volunteers. Providence: E.L. Freeman, 1893.

Reichardt, Theodore. *Diary of Battery A, First Regiment Rhode Island Light Artillery.* Providence: N. Bang Williams, 1865.

Rhodes, Elisha Hunt. *All for the Union: The Civil War Diary and Letters of Elisha Hunt Rhodes.* Edited by Robert Hunt Rhodes. Woonsocket: Andrew Mobray, 1985.

Rhodes, John H. *The Gettysburg Gun.* Providence: Snow and Farnum, 1892.

_____. *History of Battery B, First Rhode Island Light Artillery.* Providence: Snow and Farnum, 1894.

Samson, Henry T., and George C. Hull. *The War Story of C Battery, One Hundred and Third U.S. Field Artillery, France, 1917–1919.* Norwood, MA: Plimpton, 1920.

Smith, Joseph J. *Civil and Military Lists of Rhode Island: 1800–1850.* Central Falls: E.L. Freeman, 1901.

Spicer, William A. *The History of the Ninth and Tenth Regiments of Rhode Island Volunteers and the Tenth Rhode Island Battery in the Union Army in 1862.* Providence: Snow and Farnum, 1892.

State of Rhode Island. *Acts and Resolutions: Section 30, June 1843.* Providence, 1843.

_____. *Annual Report of the Adjutant General of the State of Rhode Island for the Year 1865.* Providence: Providence, 1866.

_____. *The Monument in Memory of the Rhode Island Soldiers and Sailors Who Fell Victims to the Rebellion.* Providence: Providence, 1869.

Stevens, George. *Three Years in the Sixth Corps.* Albany: S.R. Gray, 1866.

Stiness, Henry R.W. *Battery A on the Mexican Border.* Providence: E.S. Jones, 1917.

Stockbridge, John C. *Memorials of the Mauran Family.* Providence: Snow and Farnum, 1893.

Stone, Edwin W. *Rhode Island in the Rebellion.* Providence: Knowles, Anthony, 1864.

Straight, Charles T. *Battery B, First R.I. Light Artillery, August 13, 1861–June 12, 1865.* Pawtucket: NP, 1907.

The Story of American Heroism: Thrilling Narratives of Personal Adventures During the Great Civil War, as Told by the Medal Winners and Roll of Honor Men. New Haven: Butler & Alger, 1896.

Sumner, George C. *Battery D, First Rhode Island Light Artillery in the Civil War, 1861–1865.* Providence: Rhode Island, 1897.

Taylor, Emerson Gifford. *New England in France, 1917–1919.* Boston: Houghton Mifflin, 1920.

VanDenBossche, Kris, ed. *Pleas Excuse All Bad Writing: A Documentary History of Rhode Island During the Civil War Era, 1861–1865.* Peace Dale: Rhode Island Historical Document Transcription Project, 1993.

_____. *Write Soon and Give Me All the News.* Peace Dale: Rhode Island Historical Document Transcription Project, 1993.

Wainwright, Charles S. *A Diary of Battle: The Personal Journals of Colonel Charles S. Wainwright, 1861–1865.* Edited by Allan Nevins. Gettysburg: Stan Clark, 1992.

Wells, Cyril L.D. *Outline History of the 243rd Coast Artillery (HD).* East Greenwich: Greenwich, 1928.

Woodbury, Augustus. *A Narrative of the Campaign of the First Rhode Island Regiment in the Spring and Summer of 1861.* Providence: Sydney S. Rider, 1862.

Printed Secondary Sources

Ainse-Marne American Cemetery and Memorial. Washington D.C.: American Battle Monuments Commission, 2005.

Barker, Harold R. *History of the Rhode Island Combat Units in the Civil War.* Providence: 1964.

Bayles, Richard M., ed. *History of Providence County, Rhode Island.* New York: W.W. Preston, 1891.

Berebitsky, William. *A Very Long Weekend: The Army National Guard in Korea, 1950–1953.* Shippensburg, PA: White Mane, 1996.

Bicknell, Thomas Williams. *The History of the State of Rhode Island and Providence Plantations.* New York: American Historical Society, 1920.

Bioletti, Harry. *The Yanks Are Coming: The American Invasion of New Zealand, 1942–1944.* Glenfield, Auckland : Century Hutchinson, 1989.

Boot, Max. *The Savage Wars of Peace: Small Wars and the Rise of American Power.* New York: Basic Books, 2002.

Bothelo, Joyce M. *Right and Might: The Dorr Rebellion and the Struggle for Equal Rights.* Vol. 1, *The Road to Rebellion.* Providence: Rhode Island Historical Society, 1992.

_____. *Right and Might: The Dorr Rebellion and the Struggle for Equal Rights.* Vol. 2, *The Power of the People: Constitutions in Conflict.* Providence: Rhode Island Historical Society, 1992.

_____. *Right and Might: The Dorr Rebellion and the Struggle for Equal Rights.* Vol. 3, *Rebellion, Reform, and Repression.* Providence: Rhode Island Historical Society, 1992.

_____. *Right and Might: The Dorr Rebellion and the Struggle for Equal Rights.* Vol. 4, *Politics, Power and the Law: The Legacy.* Providence: Rhode Island Historical Society, 1992.

Brown, Howard F. *43rd Infantry Division.* Paducah, KY: Turner, 1994.

Brown, Howard F., and Roberta Mudge Humble. *The Historic Armories of Rhode Island.* Pawtucket: Globe, 2000.

Cooper, Jerry. *The Militia and the National Guard in America since Colonial Times.* Westport, CT: Greenwood, 1993.

Cosmas, Graham A. *An Army for Empire: The United States Army in the Spanish-American War.* College Station: Texas A&M Press, 1994.

Cullum, George W. *Historical Sketch of the Fortification Defenses of Narragansett Bay since the Founding in 1638 of the Colony of Rhode Island.* Washington, D.C.: NP, 1884.

Cunliffe, Marcus. *Soldiers and Civilians: The Martial Spirit in America, 1775–1865* Boston: Little, Brown, 1968.

Datsrup, Boyd L. *King of Battle: A Branch History of the U.S. Army's Field Artillery.* Fort Monroe, VA: U.S. Army, 1992.

DeConde, Alexander. *The Quasi-War: The Politics and Diplomacy of the Undeclared War with France, 1797–1801.* New York: Charles Scribner's Sons, 1966.

DeSimone, Russell J. *The Dorr Rebellion Chronicled in Ballads and Poems.* Middletown, RI: Bartlett, 1993.

Driver, Robert. *The First and Second Rockbridge Artillery.* Lynchburg, VA: H.E. Howard, 1987.

Falk, Stanley L. *Decision at Leyte*. New York: W.W. Norton, 1966.

Field, Edward. *Revolutionary Defenses in Rhode Island*. Providence: Preston and Rounds, 1896.

Gettleman, Marvin. *The Dorr Rebellion: A Study in American Radicalism, 1833–1849*. New York: Random House, 1973.

Greene, A. Wilson. *Breaking the Backbone of the Rebellion: The Final Battles of the Petersburg Campaign*. Mason City, IA: Savas, 2000.

Greene, Welcome Arnold. *The Providence Plantations for Two Hundred and Fifty Years*. Providence: J.A. & R.A. Reid, 1886.

Griffith, Paddy. *Battle Tactics of the Civil War*. New Haven: Yale University Press, 1989.

Gottfried, Bradley M. *The Artillery of Gettysburg*. Nashville: Cumberland House, 2008.

Hakim, Joy. *Freedom: A History of US*. New York: Oxford University Press, 2003.

Hartwell, Everett S. *An Historical Sketch of the Providence Marine Corps of Artillery, 1801–1951*. Providence: Providence Marine Corps of Artillery, 1952.

Haydon, Stansbury, and Tom D. Crouch. *Military Ballooning in the Early Civil War*. Baltimore: Johns Hopkins University Press, 2000.

Hazlett, James C., Edwin Olmstead, and M. Hume Parks. *Field Artillery Weapons of the Civil War*. Chicago: University of Illinois Press, 2004.

Herndon, Richard. *Men of Progress: Biographical Sketches and Portraits of Leaders in Business and Professional Life in the State of Rhode Island and Providence Plantations*. Boston: New England Magazine, 1896.

History of the State of Rhode Island: 1636–1878. Boston: A.J. Wright, 1878.

Hurst, James W. *Pancho Villa and Black Jack Pershing: The Punitive Expedition in Mexico*. Westport, CT: Praeger, 2008.

Jones, Daniel P. *The Economic and Social Transformation of Rural Rhode Island, 1780–1850*. Boston: Northeastern University Press, 1992.

Langguth, A.J. *Union 1812: The Americans Who Fought the Second War of Independence*. New York: Simon & Schuster, 2006.

Lemons, J. Stanley, and George Kelner. *Rhode Island: The Ocean State*. Sun Valley, CA: American Historical Press, 2004.

Mahon, John K. *History of the Militia and the National Guard*. London: Collier, Mifflin, 1983.

Marvel, William. *Burnside*. Chapel Hill: University of North Carolina Press, 1989.

_____. *The First New Hampshire Battery, 1861–1865*. South Conway, NH: Lost Cemetery Press, 1985.

McLoughlin, William G. *Rhode Island: A History*. New York: W.W. Norton, 1986.

Memorial to the Employees of the Brown & Sharpe MFG. Co. who served at Home and Abroad in the Great World War. Providence: Brown and Sharpe, 1919.

Melton, Jack W., and Lawrence E. Pawl. *Guide to Civil War Artillery Projectiles*. Gettysburg: Thomas, 1996.

Millet, Allan R., and Peter Maslowski. *For the Common Defense: A Military History of the United States of America*. New York: Free Press, 1984.

Mowry, Arthur M. *The Dorr War, or the Constitutional Struggle in Rhode Island*. Providence: Preston & Rounds, 1901.

Naisawald, L. VanLoan. *Grape and Canister: The Story of the Field Artillery of the Army of the Potomac, 1861–1865*. Mechanicsburg, PA: Stackpole, 1999.

Nosworthy, Brent. *The Bloody Crucible of Courage: Fighting Methods and Combat Experience of the Civil War*. New York: Carroll & Graff, 2003.

_____. *Roll Call to Destiny: The Soldier's Eye View of Civil War Battles*. New York: Basic Books, 2008.

Peterson, Harold. *Round Shot and Rammers*. New York: Bonanza, 1940.

Richards, John J. *Rhode Island's Early Defenders and Their Successors*. East Greenwich: Rhode Island Pendulum, 1937.

Schroder, Walter K. *Defenses of Narragansett Bay in World War II*. Providence: Rhode Island Bicentennial Foundation, 1980.

Shoemaker, Henry Wharton. *The Last War Governor: A Biographical Appreciation of Colonel William Sprague*. Altoona, PA: Altoona Tribune, 1916.

Stallings, Laurence. *The Doughboys: The Story of the AEF, 1917–1919*. New York: Harper & Row, 1963.

Stein, Barry J. *U.S. Army Heraldic Crests: A Complete Illustrated History of Distinctive Unit Insignia*. Columbia: University of South Carolina Press, 1993.

Steinberg, Rafael. *Island Fighting*. Richmond: Time Life Books, 1979.

_____. *Return to the Philippines*. Richmond: Time Life Books, 1979.

Stone, Peter. *The Lady and the President: The Life and Loss of the S.S. President Coolidge*. Yarram, Australia: Ocean, 2007.

Sylvia, Stephen W., and Michael J. O'Donnell. *Uniforms, Weapons, and Equipment of the World War II G.I.* Orange, VA: Moss, 1982.

Todd, Frederic P. *American Military Equipage, 1851–1872*. Vol. 2, *State Forces*. New York: Chatham Square, 1983.

Walker Anthony. *So Few the Brave*. Newport: Seafield, 1981.

Ward, Geoffrey C. *The Civil War*. New York: Alfred A. Knopf, 1990.

Weigley, Russell F. *The American Way of War: A History of United States Military Strategy and Policy*. New York: Macmillan, 1973.

Wheeler, Keith. *The Road to Tokyo*. Richmond: Time Life Books, 1979.

Zimmer, Joseph E. *The History of the 43rd Infantry Division, 1941–1945*. Bennington, VT: Merriam, 1998.

Primary Articles

Adams, Edward P. "Battery G, First Rhode Island Light Artillery." In *Revised Register of Rhode Island Volunteers*. Providence: E.L. Freeman, 1893.

Lancaster, Jane. "The Battle of Chepachet: An Eyewitness Account." *Rhode Island History* (Spring 2004).

Stevens, Hazard. "Storming of the Lines at Petersburg." *The Shenandoah Campaigns of 1862 and 1864 and the Appomattox Campaign 1865*. Boston: Military Historical Society of Massachusetts, 1907.

Woodbury, Augustus. "The First Light Battery Rhode Island Volunteers." *Revised Register of Rhode Island Volunteers*. Providence: E.L. Freeman, 1893.

Secondary Articles

Abernathy, Thomas J. "Crane's Rhode Island Company of Artillery." *Rhode Island History* (Winter 1970).

Chiles, Paul. "'Artillery Hell!': The Guns of Antietam." *Blue and Gray* (Winter 1998).

Conley, Patrick T. "No Tempest in the Tea Pot: The Dorr Rebellion in National Perspective." *Rhode Island History* (August 1992).

Emlen, Robert G. "The Great Gale of 1815: Artifactual Evidence of Rhode Island's First Hurricane." *Rhode Island History* (May 1990).

Grandchamp, Robert. "Brown's Battery B, First Rhode Island Light Artillery at the Battle of Gettysburg." *Gettysburg* 36 (January 2007).

_____. "'He Stands on Dangerous Ground': Thomas Aldrich, Battery A, and the Controversy at the Angle." *Gettysburg* 39 (July 2008).

Gronert, Theodore G. "The First National Pastime in the Middle West." *Indiana Magazine of History* 30 (September 1933).

Paulhus, David L. "Rhode Island and the Mexican War." *Rhode Island* (August 1978).

"Removal of Old Armory, Benefit Street." *Board of Trade Journal* 18, no. 9 (September 1906).

Sherman, Robert L. "The Providence Washington Insurance Company: Two Hundred Years." *Rhode Island History* (February 1999).

Strum, Harvey. "Rhode Island in the War of 1812." *Rhode Island History* (February 1992).

Newspapers

Narragansett Weekly
Providence Evening Journal
Providence Gazette
Providence Journal
Providence Press

INDEX

255